Statistics for Business

McGRAW-HILL BUSINESS EDUCATION COURSES

Consulting Editor: **Graham Edwards**
Principal
Kirby College
Cleveland

Statistics for Business

Incorporating the Third Edition of *Statistics for Business Studies*

DEREK GREGORY

HAROLD WARD

McGraw-Hill Book Company (UK) Limited

London · New York · St Louis · San Francisco · Auckland · Bogotá
Guatemala · Hamburg · Johannesburg · Lisbon · Madrid · Mexico
Montreal · New Delhi · Panama · Paris · San Juan · São Paulo
Singapore · Sydney · Tokyo · Toronto

Published by McGRAW-HILL Book Company (UK) Limited
MAIDENHEAD · BERKSHIRE · ENGLAND

British Library Cataloguing in Publication Data

Gregory, Derek
Statistics for business.—[3rd. ed.].—(McGraw-Hill business education series).
1. Mathematical statistics
I. Title II. Ward, Harold, b. 1906
519.5′02′438 QA276 78-40773
ISBN 0–07–084606–5

Copyright © 1974, 1978 McGraw-Hill Book Company (UK) Limited. All rights reserved. No part of this publication may be reproduced, stored in a retrieval system, or transmitted, in any form or by any means, electronic, mechanical, photocopying, recording, or otherwise, without the prior permission of McGraw-Hill Book Company (UK) Limited, or of the original copyright holder.

891011 JWA 8321

PRINTED AND BOUND IN GREAT BRITAIN

To
Jennifer and Joyce

Foreword to the Series

Course structures devised by the Business Education Council present an exciting new challenge to lecturers, students, and authors alike. The Council has considered it no longer appropriate to educate for a career in business by means of academic disciplines which, however appropriate in themselves, were brought into, at best, a loose interrelationship, and which were capable of being taught in a fashion, academically sound, but perhaps insufficiently applied to the situations which students might find in the business world.

The new course structure identifies, at all levels (General, National, Higher National), four important central themes an understanding of which, it is argued, is central to all business education, and which underlie all academic disciplines. These central themes are Money (including the most efficient use of the resources which money can buy); People (and their human relationships as producers and consumers); Communication (embracing a much wider concept than mere 'Business English'); and Numeracy (not just 'Business Mathematics' but a logical and numerate approach to business problems). Additionally, the BEC philosophy is that academic disciplines must be interrelated if they are to be meaningful in the solution of business problems.

An important aim of the BEC course structure at both General and National level is therefore;

> to encourage the development of the understanding and skills implicit in the central themes, with particular emphasis on the improvement of the student's standards of literacy and numeracy.

A further aim at General level is:

> to develop basic work competence through practical assignments which relate the knowledge, skills and understanding derived from various parts of the course to business situations.

This, at National level, becomes:

> to develop the student's ability to interrelate knowledge, skills and understanding from various parts of the course through practical assignments derived from business contexts.

Discrimination between the sexes

In a book on the subject of Statistics, using the terminology and current practice of the business world, it has not been possible to eliminate the use of gender and retain a fluent text. The reader is asked to accept that in the majority of cases a deliberate distinction between the sexes is not implied.

Preface to the 3rd Edition

This latest edition of the textbook, first published in 1967, has been prompted largely by certain new syllabus requirements of the Business Education Council. One of the main amendments is the addition of a new chapter on Financial Mathematics, though the text has been completely revised throughout to accord with the course philosophy of BEC in its Applied Statistics module offered from 1978. We quote:

'to provide a sound statistical groundwork for those continuing to further quantitative studies, and to provide a basic numerical appreciation for those who do not;
to cover ground requisite for exemption from relevant professional bodies, examinations and ground now expected by industry and commerce at this level; and to offer a study of use and value in business, finance, distribution and public administration.'

We hope that the text will meet these positive and ambitious aims and that it will continue to enjoy the success it has found with students on past ONC/D, HNC/D courses in the UK, with students of professional institutes, GCE students, and polytechnic and university students, at home and overseas.

The authors gratefully acknowledge the help given in this new edition by a host of education and training institutions, business firms and government agencies, and by Mr David Newton of the North Regional Management Centre, and by Barclays Bank Ltd.

We continue to hope that the many thousands of students who have been helped by this book will be followed by many more who will find it even more useful in this new edition.

Derek Gregory
Harold Ward

1978

1

Introduction to statistics

Statistics defined

Statistics deals with numbers, but not simply with counting. The science of statistics is concerned with the *comparison* of numbers.

For example, the statement that exports were £9 740m in 1976 means nothing to us if we have no idea of what the figure was in 1974 or in 1975. But the statement that a particular person is 2 m 10 cm tall may provoke a certain surprise because we can mentally compare this figure with the normal heights which we know.

Figures in statistics are not significant unless we can make comparisons. This means that the figures we compare must:

(*a*) refer to the same group of things,
(*b*) be of the same kind,
(*c*) be in the same units,
(*d*) be measured to the same degree of accuracy.
Note. Although accuracy is always desirable, it is often not necessary and, more often, not possible. Here we mean, for example, that the figures we compare should be carried to the same number of decimal places.

An example might be as follows:

'In 1976 total exports had increased by more than six per cent on the 1975 figure, when we exported only £83·2m of electrical machinery to the Common Market countries.'

In this statement the errors which hinder true comparison are:

Error	*1975*	*1976*
Group	Common Market countries	All countries
Kind	Electrical machinery	All goods
Units	£million	Percentages
Accuracy	To 1st decimal place	To whole units

The statement, therefore, is nearly meaningless and probably misleading.

Meaning of statistics

Although the word statistics is used loosely to mean collections of figures on different subjects, e.g., Department of Employment statistics, the word also applies to the statistical methods which we use. We can define the two meanings of the word statistics as:

(*a*) a collection of comparable figures in a subject or in a connected group
(*b*) the methods of treating or processing a series of figures

This book deals with both meanings. The first meaning in Chapter 2, and the second meaning in nearly all the subsequent chapters.

Growth of statistics

Statistical method was first used in the nineteenth century when the first serious attempt to gather figures referring to the population was made in the first census of 1801. These figures, known as *vital statistics*, refer to births, marriages, and deaths. But official collections of figures, dealing with persons, cattle, wealth, land, etc., go back to the beginnings of recorded history.

Nobody collects figures on a large scale just for the fun of it. Therefore, every attempt—from Roman times, to the Domesday Book of 1086, to the first census of 1801, to the latest government report—has been made with a definite purpose in mind. Early kings and rulers usually wanted to know the military strength which could be raised from the population under their control. But a simpler reason than this was that kings, like everyone else, must be fed and housed. Yet kings give services rather than produce goods and, because their services have no market value, they must tax their subjects to raise the necessary finance to provide for the court and to carry on the business of government. Whom should they tax? Obviously, those able to pay. Kings must, therefore, compile figures of the wealth and incomes of their subjects by some method, bearing in mind that one of the first charges on the tax revenue which is raised will be the cost of the survey and the cost of collection.

Because early societies were extremely poor by our standards, and because statistics are extremely expensive to collect, only the absolutely essential figures were collected: for example, figures of wealth, incomes, customs, fighting men, and so on, and these figures were usually sketchy and not very accurate.

In the nineteenth century, in the Western world, industry and commerce grew so rapidly and to such proportions that historians gave the name of 'industrial revolution' to the fantastic increase in output and the new methods of production. As countries became richer, so their governments were able to raise larger tax revenues to pay for the heavier jobs they had to do. It became more urgent for the government to discover the extent of the changes in the pattern of wealth which resulted from the industrial development. Because the tremendous revolution in production and trade brought distress and injustice in its wake, there had to be similar revolutions in the sanitary, welfare, educational, and medical fields. Doctors are at a great disadvantage if they lack records of the causes of death, and of how outbreaks of disease are distributed throughout the country. Educationists cannot plan future school building without a knowledge of how many children exist in a country and what their ages are—and even what the birth-rate might be expected to be in the near future. Statistics are required as a *basis for action* in all fields wherever information can be measured.

A similar expansion occurred in the business field. Another feature of nineteenth-century growth was an increase in the average size of the business unit in most industries. It is possible to run a one-man business (or a 'small master' business) by keeping the figures in one's head. But a large concern, probably operating on mass-production techniques, will certainly be split into different departments, almost like government departments. Some of these departments might deal with labour relations, sales, market research, quality control, stock control, production, design, superannuation—depending on the size and nature of the firm. Large firms, each with their own individual 'Department of Employment' and 'Treasury' exist on the basis of figures. The wealth of such firms often encourages them to make seemingly lavish expenditures on the kinds of figures they collect, although no firm is large enough to undertake surveys on the same scale as the Government. A firm may launch a statistical enquiry costing thousands of pounds to discover how many housewives still boil their sheets. This is of limited national interest and would never be the subject of a government inquiry, yet it may be absolutely vital information to a firm manufacturing detergents.

Present and future statistics

Statistics cannot run a business or a government. Nor can the study of statistics do more than provide a few suggestions or offer a few pointers as to a firm's, or a government's, future behaviour. Although production may in the future be carried on by an automated process, nobody will ever be able to produce the right *decisions* for five years ahead simply from figures fed into a statistical computing machine.

Statistics can be used as a tool of management to tell managers what has happened in the past and (if the figures are collected quickly enough) what is happening now, thus providing a surer basis for decision. Every day, managers are trying to predict consumer demand and the government is seeking to understand the changing pattern of our balance of payments by the use of statistics. But the further ahead 'forecasts' are made, on the basis of past and present statistics, the more completely are our forecasts likely to be turned upside down by the course of events. Basically, people and events are so unpredictable and are subject to so many uncontrollable influences, that forecasting is dangerous unless the period of projection into the future is very short indeed.

Today, the output of statistics is almost an industry in its own right with an output which is an ever-growing, and even menacing, flood. Statistics are hurled at the public by newspapers, periodicals, radio, films, television, handouts, posters on hoardings, and through the post. The public are increasingly asked to complete official returns and questionnaires, and to give opinions in the street. Form-filling has become a national pastime, but, though we may voluntarily labour for hours on a football coupon, or willingly complete the personal questions on the page of a woman's magazine to discover if we are good social mixers, we may, nevertheless, rebel when the income tax return is pushed through our letter-boxes.

The use of statistics to persuade people to certain opinions is a popular practice. The danger lies in the fact that there are good and bad statistics and statisticians, just as there are good and bad doctors. The saying that 'figures cannot lie' contrasts well with the cynical comment by Disraeli that, 'There are lies, damned lies, and statistics'. Neither of these statements is necessarily true. Yet we know that:

(*a*) statistics may be collected carelessly,
(*b*) figures may be gathered for one purpose and used (by someone else) for a different, probably contradictory, purpose,
(*c*) statistics may be processed wrongly,
(*d*) statistics may be interpreted wrongly.

It is necessary, though only remotely possible, in a successful democracy for the man in the street to be able to detect lies in figures as well as in words. To do this, he should know how much notice one should pay to the statisticians' figures. He should also know how to deal with their flattering requests for his opinions and the details of his daily life. It is more necessary for the student to be able to detect such fallacies, because as well as taking an examination in statistics, he might well be joining the growing mass of questioners, enquirers, and interrogators who descend on the public, absorb masses of details, process them, and finally disgorge them on a public which is becoming increasingly suspicious of things presented to it in print, on radio, or on television.

2

Collection of data

Method

Primary and secondary data

Primary data consist of figures collected at first hand (by the methods described later in this chapter) in order to satisfy the purposes of a particular statistical enquiry.

Examples in the government field are the Census of Population and the Index of Retail Prices. In the field of business, market research enquiries are the most obvious example.

Secondary data consist of figures which were collected originally to satisfy a particular enquiry, but have been used now, at second-hand, as the basis for a different enquiry (usually because the cost of collecting his own would have been too great for the second enquirer, and he believes that the original figures will adequately suit his needs).

Examples in the government field are figures which go to make up the Balance of Payments calculation, where existing figures are collected for this purpose from many sources, principally from the declarations to customs officials by exporters and importers. In the field of business, an example would be figures relating to productivity (compiled from cost accountants' records and sales records), but this is only one example of secondary data in a field where many departments rely on each other to supply figures for individual purposes.

Note. Secondary data must not be confused with secondary statistics (see page 61).

Methods of the survey

In this section we are concerned mainly with the methods used to collect primary data. The sources and methods used in dealing with secondary data are dealt with in Chapter 19.

The various stages of a survey may be classified as follows:

(*a*) Purpose of the survey
(*b*) Sampling methods
(*c*) Methods of collection
(*d*) Pilot surveys

Purpose of the survey

At the very outset it is essential to consider the purpose of the survey because this will not only affect the questions we ask, but it will also dictate the methods we will use.

The sections which follow after this stage are mainly mechanical in a sense, but the cost of the whole operation in time and money depends on detailed, careful, and thorough planning at the beginning. Even should we decide on the scope and nature of the survey, it must be realized that, in either business or government circles, it is usual to work to a target date and within a limited budget, and initial planning may suggest a point at which we must call a halt to further enquiries. It is often a great temptation to extend the scope of questioning, for example, and to add subsidiary lines of enquiry to the main line on the assumption that a slightly larger questionnaire will do no great harm. Possibly this might be the case (see the questionnaire, page 11). but it is of great importance that all such problems and possibilities be explored at the beginning. Once decided, the terms of reference must be rigidly followed.

Sampling methods

Surveys may be carried out on people or on things. On the production line we could apply a survey technique to control quality; in society we may wish to survey the expenditure habits of the population.

Statistical techniques have improved so greatly that it is not now necessary to investigate all the items in any group from which we may wish to collect information. Instead, we can carry out a survey of a population by merely investigating a fraction, i.e., a sample, of that population. The whole of the group under investigation is known as the *population*, even though the group may consist of factories in N.W. England, or the people in the nation itself. The small number of items from this population actually examined is called the *sample*.

It is not intended here to describe the mathematical theory of sampling, but simply to say that we can tell, with a high probability of being correct, what the characteristics of a population are by investigating only a sample of that population, provided that we observe certain rules. These are:

(*a*) Our sample must be of *at least a certain size*. Generally, the larger the sample the more reliance we can place on our results as being a true cross-section of the population.

(*b*) We must choose the sample from the population in such a way that *each member of the population has an equal chance of being chosen*; this is known as random sampling.

Provided that our sample is truly random (and, of course, large enough) we shall get a representative cross-section. This is really much harder to achieve than it sounds.

For example, if we were to try to choose a random sample of the people walking down the main street, in order to ask them questions on their leisure habits, we should probably find that after a time we tended to choose the slower walkers, the older people, or the people with time to spare and chat. If we questioned a sufficient number of people and analysed the results, we might conclude that the way most people in the area spent their leisure-time was in playing bingo, walking round the park, and watching television. We would tend to miss the busy adult males and, if we took our sample in mid-morning on a weekday, we would miss all the young people. Thus a great range of leisure activities from ballroom-dancing to pigeon-racing would find little place in our survey. Our results would be biased in favour of certain types of people, i.e., they would not be truly representative of the whole. In other words, it would not be a random sample, because some people (business executives, factory workers, school children, etc.) would have little or no chance of being selected.

Had we conducted our survey on a certain Saturday afternoon, hoping to catch such people as we missed before, we might conclude from our results that people in the area were 'sport mad'. Preliminary planning might have warned us not to stand on the road which led from the bus stop to the football ground on that particular Saturday.

This, of course, would have been a glaring mistake. But the techniques of sampling, which enable us to obtain the maximum of information with the minimum of effort, impose rather stricter rules than this on the investigator. Probably it is impossible to make a perfectly random selection. Yet statisticians are constantly trying to achieve the impossible.

One of the methods they have evolved is that of *lottery sampling*. By this method, if one is selecting a sample of people, one should write down the name of each member of the population on a piece of paper, place the papers in a revolving lottery drum, and then pick as many as the sample requires from the drum. Sometimes the *constant skip* (or *systematic*) *method* of selection may be used. This is the selection of a sample by choosing, say, every tenth name from a voting list, or every seventeenth house from a street plan.

This question of better random selection methods and the avoidance of bias is the subject of extremely careful study among statisticians. One further example of the introduction of bias might be given.

It is intended to investigate local tradesmen in an area to discover whether they were born in the area or whether they moved in from elsewhere. To select the names for a sample of 1 000, we might use a copy of the classified trades telephone directory, simply open it 1 000 times at random, and pick a name each time. This would be our list, and we could probably ring up on the spot to ask our questions.

This method would *not* give us a random sample. Bias might be introduced in the following ways;

(*a*) Tradesmen who were not on the telephone, e.g., small shopkeepers would have no chance of selection.

(*b*) The telephone directory, through constant use, falls open at some pages more readily than at others. Therefore, tradesmen's names on rarely opened pages, e.g., violin-makers, would have a smaller chance of selection.

(*c*) Our eye might be attracted, subconsciously, to the more unusual names, e.g., foreigners, on the pages. Thus, anyone with a common name would stand less chance of selection.

(*d*) Some tradesmen who have a telephone might not be in the directory, e.g., newcomers within the current year.
(*e*) The directory might be out-of-date.
(*f*) Some tradesmen might be entered more than once, e.g., cross-referenced under a split trade.

There might also be other sources of bias besides the ones on the above list.

From most of these comments a certain conclusion can be drawn. That is, that the human being is a very poor instrument for the selection of a random sample. In fact, most errors of bias tend to occur because of the human element.

Different methods of applying random sampling may be used, depending on the kind of population one wishes to survey:

STRATIFIED SAMPLING

People fall naturally into different groups according to their social background, sex, age, etc. It is obvious that a survey, say, on pop music, might well draw different opinions and answers from each different group, i.e., not merely from different individuals. For example, old people may not appreciate pop music as much as the young.

We might conduct a survey in a town where the population was largely composed of old people; e.g., 30 out of every 100 were over 60 years old, and 10 out of every 100 were under 21. To stratify our sample in respect of, say, age (i.e., divide the population into age strata) we should have to apportion our interviews as follows in a sample of 1 000:

300 interviews of people over 60 years.
600 interviews of people between 21 and 60 years.
100 interviews of people under 21 years.

This would give us a stratified sample if we chose 300 people at *random* from that part of the population over 60 years, 600 from that part of the population between 21 and 60 years, etc.

Each group would then be better represented (in the correct proportion in the sample), than if we had merely chosen 1 000 people from the whole population. In addition to this, it might be a subsidiary part of the purpose of our survey to compare the answers of the particular groups.

MULTI-STAGE SAMPLING

This is another way of using random choice to select a sample from a very large or widespread population. It can be illustrated as follows:

From the 50 states of the USA, we might choose a random sample of 5 states. Then from each of these 5 states, we would choose a random sample of 20 towns. Then from each of these 20 towns, we would choose a random sample of 100 people. Thus we should have 10 000 interviews. Provided that we kept the sample large enough to cover the large entire population, we should be able to concentrate our interviews with a minimum expenditure of time and cost. The actual selection of the sample would also be much easier.

This method is almost the only practical one when we wish to make a survey of a large population on a limited budget. There are several variations of the method of multi-stage sampling, the most popular being to relate the number of interviews in particular areas proportionately to the population in those areas. In this way, we can reduce the bias likely to creep in because the many small urban communities have a better chance of being selected than the few large urban communities.

QUOTA SAMPLING

In this case, the interviewer is not given a list of the selected names in the sample, but is asked to interview a number (quota) of people (at his own discretion) who fall into certain categories:

Column 1	*Column 2*	*Column 3*	*Column 4*
Category	*Types to be selected*	*Quota to be interviewed*	*Totals*
Possessing car (value over £3 000) Telephone Deep freeze Detached house (owner)	Directors Managers Professional men	10 10 10	30
Possessing car (value £3 000 or less) Television Semi-detached house (owner)	Teachers Civil Servants Shopkeepers Skilled artisans	60 60 60 60	240
No car Television Rented house	Transport workers Shop assistants Labourers	100 130 500	730
		TOTAL	1 000

In a way, this form is similar to stratified sampling with the main difference being that the interviewer can choose the individuals whom he will interview. Here lies an important source of bias as human random selection is extremely faulty. In particular, the interviewers may interpret the types differently. For example, a turf accountant is not usually regarded as a professional man, but a chartered accountant is. This difficulty may be overcome by providing a list of definitions of each type which interviewers must follow. Another fault is that the interviewer, to save time, might choose a large proportion of any category from one particular area. To overcome this last weakness the quota can be stratified so that the interviewer may pick only certain types in each category (see col. 2).

Methods of collection

There are two basic methods of collecting data—the personal interview and the questionnaire.

THE PERSONAL INTERVIEW

A disadvantage in the method of collecting data by means of the personal interview is the high cost, not merely in the expenses of wages for staff, transport, and allowances, but also in the cost of any staff training which may be given.

Most of the points raised in the next section (the questionnaire) apply equally to the personal interview, but the most important difference lies in the necessary personal qualities an interviewer should possess. The qualities most desired are listed here.

(*a*) *Skill*

The interviewer himself is usually the worst cause of bias in a survey, so it is important to give him an initial short course of training in order to avoid the most serious pitfalls. A modern trend in interviewing which would require longer and more expensive training is 'depth-interviewing'. The tendency here is towards longer and deeper questioning, which probes the hidden factors that lead people to answer questions in a particular way.

(*b*) *Character*

Various qualities of character are desirable in an interviewer, and these may briefly be listed as follows: tact, accuracy, amiability, and neutrality.

(i) *Tact.* It is important neither to antagonize nor to flatter interviewees because they may tend to depart from the truth under emotional influence or stress. Maintaining a calm, unflustered, and enquiring attitude at the end of a long hard day is difficult to do when one is repeating a set of questions for the fiftieth time. Nevertheless, the interview should be restricted to a rational and thoughtful imparting of information, and it is the interviewer's responsibility to maintain this state of affairs.

(ii) *Accuracy.* Once the list of interviewees has been drawn up by the central office, the interviewer should keep rigidly to the list. An interviewer who omits to interview a selected person because he lives at the end of a particularly long garden path, or because a growling mastiff guards the entrance, will undoubtedly introduce bias into the carefully prepared list.

Accuracy also means arithmetical accuracy in any short calculations which the interviewer is asked to make, as well as accuracy in recording the answers given and the checking of lists.

(iii) *Amiability.* Many people do not respond well to proposals to investigate their private lives and habits. This imposes a special task on the interviewer—that of having a pleasing and sociable personality without distorting the interview and the answers by being excessively charming or effusive.

(iv) *Neutrality.* It is obvious, by now, that a very special kind of person is required for this job (some might say a genius or a saint). Needless to say, the demand for such people exceeds the supply (at the wages offered), and so

further disadvantage is that no interviewer is on hand to explain the questionnaire, or to ensure that it is filled in completely or correctly.

Features of a good questionnaire

The popularity of this type of enquiry, which is often included nowadays in cut-out pages of magazines and newspapers, has led to much investigation in the extremely difficult task of achieving better design and question-phrasing. A list of 'do's and don'ts' can be made, as follows:

(*a*) Keep the questions themselves, and their number, short.

(*b*) Phrase the questions and the instructions, if any, as unambiguously as possible. An example of a badly phrased question would be: 'Do you make a habit of drinking?'

(*c*) Do not use unusual, pompous, or technical words.
Wrong: 'Indicate your marital status.'
It is a good plan to aim at the lowest intelligence and educational level of the population which you are investigating, without making this too obvious.

(*d*) Do not use leading questions, or words which are currently used in an emotional or abusive way.
Wrong: 'Are you in favour of even more nationalization?'

(*e*) Include check questions, where you expect some people to give unreliable answers. For example, women often have a habit of rounding off ages to the lowest ten below (see Cumulative errors, page 58). In this case, the age (in years and months) can be asked for near the beginning of the questionnaire, and the check question—'Please give your date of birth'—can be inserted later in the form.

(*f*) Always state the precise units in which you require the answer, otherwise the results, when you come to tabulate them, will be useless. But do not ask irritating questions that involve an unnecessarily high degree of accuracy.
Wrong: 'How much coal did you consume last month?'
Does this mean sacks, kilograms, deliveries? 'Consume' means 'eat' to the average person! Here the compiler of the questionnaire might ask *himself* if he meant burn; have delivered; or keep in stock.

(*g*) Do not ask questions which rely too much on memory. Accurate memory of past events fades much more quickly than people realize or are willing to admit.
Wrong: 'How many days were you absent from work because of sickness in the year ending 31 December last?'

(*h*) Try to ask simple questions which can be answered by a yes, a no, or a figure.

(*i*) Do not ask the average man or woman to write an essay for you. This type of question usually indicates lazy thinking on the part of the compiler.
Wrong: 'Please state, as fully as you can, the reasons why you prefer to use biological soap powder?'

great a degree of bias is believed to be introduced by inadequate interviewing, that several studies have been carried out on errors of bias due to interviewers.

When we think of the possible bias in matters of colour, sex, race, religion, and politics which may be subconsciously introduced by the interviewer into the interview, the dangers here are apparent. Should interviewers have strong convictions? Is the present general policy of employing part-time women interviewers a good one? We might well wonder how impassively neutral persons can be tactful and amiable in all situations. It may be comforting to know that, as in most jobs, the ideal is unattainable.

There are obvious drawbacks to the task of making personal contact. For example, evening callers are likely to find a high proportion of stay-at-homes, Saturday afternoon callers will tend to miss the sports fans, etc. In such cases, bias will result, unless the timing of the calls is carefully recorded, and further calls are made on the absentees. Bank holiday and Christmas interview visits are likely to reap their own peculiar rewards!

While the questionnaire method does not suffer from these disabilities, it is much less likely to produce as high a response as direct personal tracking down, and the confrontation method of the personal interview.

THE QUESTIONNAIRE

Let us consider here the questionnaire delivered by post.

Advantages

This method of enquiry is, of course, much less costly to operate than the personal interview method. This means that we can increase the size of our population (i.e., extend the area of our survey) or we can take a larger sample from a given population. By making our sample larger we stand a chance of making our results more reliable, i.e., more representative.

This method, above all, is free from any personal bias which might be introduced by an interviewer.

Disadvantages

We cannot count on a high proportion of replies, unless there is a legal obligation to reply (as in the Census of Population), or where an inducement, usually goods or cash, is offered (a cash contribution was offered to each spender in households which co-operated in the Family Expenditure Surveys). A response of 20 per cent is considered quite good in the average survey. This lack of response may lead to bias, called 'non-response bias'; i.e., our results may not include a certain type of person with whom we wish to make contact and from whom we want information. He may be the kind of person who usually ignores circulars. Often the kind of people who *do* reply are of certain types, e.g., people who are too timid to resist, people who enjoy filling in forms, people with a strong sense of public duty (often the opening appeal of questionnaires asks for 'your co-operation' etc.). As long as certain types are included in the replies, and certain types are excluded, we will not get a representative sample. A

(*j*) *Cafeteria* questions (questions in which the respondent chooses his reply from a range of alternatives) should be of the right kind.

Right

Place a tick against the kind of home in which you live:

(i) flat (in a block of flats)
(ii) bungalow
(iii) semi-detached house
(iv) terraced house
(v) detached house

Note. It is assumed that the survey includes only these types of dwelling.

Wrong

State whether you think that unemployment will:

(i) rise
(ii) fall
(iii) stay about the same during the next six months

The second cafeteria question is wrong because:

(i) Most people, with little knowledge of what is a rather technical question, will answer (iii). They will take the middle course rather than betray their ignorance. In any case, there is no 'don't know' alternative listed.
(ii) 'Rise' and 'fall', in this context mean virtually nothing. For example, does a rise mean an increase of one per cent or 300 per cent? Any calculations made from the answers to such questions will also mean virtually nothing.

(*k*) Do not ask questions which call for calculations.
Wrong: 'How much per annum do you spend on smoking?'
Even if the person knows roughly how much he spends per week, the result of multiplying this by 52 may be inaccurate. He may also jib at the task.

There are many more points to watch for when compiling and designing a questionnaire. Some are obvious. For example:

Date of birth	....
Give, with dates, names and addresses, all the schools you have attended	....

Others are not so obvious.

Remember that you are asking the public to spend time and effort for no apparent reward. You must, therefore, make the questionnaire attractive, and sensible. Explain the purpose of the questionnaire, arrange the questions in a logical sequence, if possible, promise to keep the results confidential and, either collect it, or pay the postage for its return.

Pilot surveys

Pilot surveys are carried out before the actual survey itself, though sometimes the limited budget and the time available will not be sufficient for the added cost of a pilot survey. Also, if a similar kind of survey has been carried out before, a pilot survey might not show anything useful. If the actual survey is on a big scale, and is likely to be an expensive one, there is much to be said for conducting a pilot survey in the early stages.

The pilot survey is essentially a small-scale replica of the actual survey which, except for its coverage, it should duplicate as nearly as possible. Its use does not lie in the actual replies it brings, but in the lessons it teaches. It may reveal faults and weaknesses in proposed methods, especially as it is usually carried out by a highly trained permanent staff. The pilot survey might amply repay the extra time and money spent on it, because it would be far more expensive to have to abandon the actual survey, once begun, if major faults have gone unnoticed. What may seem perfectly clear to officials in the survey office, may appear vague and ambiguous when presented to the man in the street. The only sure check is to test it under actual conditions.

3

Tabulation

Method

Classification

In the last chapter we saw the various methods of collecting data, but before it can be tabulated, interpreted, and presented in its final form, it must first be classified.

Classification is the process of relating the separate items within the mass of data we have collected. Every piece of data has its *characteristics*. Data collected about people may have, for example, characteristics concerning age, sex, height, weight, occupation, i.e., features which characterize the data and make it possible for us to classify it under particular headings.

Characteristics fall generally into two classes:

Measurable attributes (called variables) and Non-measurable attributes. Non-measurable attributes are those attributes of the data which are not ordinarily measurable in units, e.g., disease, sex, colour, beauty.

Variables are those attributes which are measurable, e.g., height (centimetres), weight (kg), absences from work (days), population (numbers), etc.

Discrete and continuous variables

Variables can be further sub-divided into:

Discrete variables, which are those which can be measured only in single units; e.g., numbers in the population, houses in a town, tractors produced, or size of clothing, etc. With this type there are gaps throughout the whole range of values, which are not occupied by any items at all: e.g., shoe sizes; the values jump from, say, $6\frac{1}{2}$ to 7, and there are no items of, say, 6·73.

Continuous variables are those that are in units of measurement which can be broken down into infinite gradations, e.g., temperature (decimals of a degree), height (decimals of a centimetre), etc. In theory, this is always so, but in practice the gradations may be rounded off. For example, it is possible for two people to differ in age by a second, but their birth certificates will merely indicate that they were born on the same day.

This may seem rather surprising and confusing when we recall seeing, in the press, statements such as:

'The average number of children per class in England and Wales is 35·48.'

One cannot have 0·48 of a child and, for classification purposes at least (!), the number of children is regarded as a discrete variable.

Tabulation

This is the process of condensing classified data in the form of a table so that it may be more easily understood, and so that any comparisons involved may be more readily made.

Simple frequency table

Suppose that a survey is carried out in a firm to investigate the absences, over a period, of 200 workers, male and female, on the production line.

A simple survey of the firm's records could be used to collect the information needed, and this might include the following:

name, sex, absences, cause of absence, and nature of illness.

A summary table of the days of absence through illness for each worker might be compiled as follows:

10	15	2	27	4	2	15	5	3	1	1	3	6	7
9	2	14	6	20	11	8	20	5	3	14	1	4	1
11	16	2	1	1	31	2	17	2	25	3	7	4	15
12	2	13	4	18	1	27	3	10	1	5	1	1	42
5	3	4	20	6	26	3	10	6	3	15	2	11	2
7	5	2	4	22	7	1	5	21	6	1	24	3	10

Table 3.1 Number of absences (because of illness) for individual workers in a firm employing 200 in the production department

In addition to the above records, 116 workers had no absences due to illness.

In order to tabulate this data, we must first classify it by the variable 'number of absences'. This is an example of a *discrete variable*, because, by the method of recording absences used by the firm, any absence involving part of a day counts as a full day, no fractions of a day being recorded.

The classification of this data could be done by arranging the above figures into order, highest to lowest, e.g.,

42, 31, 27, 27, 26, 25, 24, 22, 21, 20, 20, 20, etc.,

This arrangement is known as an *array*.

A less tedious method would be to count how many workers were absent for one day, two days, and so on. This might be done as follows by means of *tally marks*:

Class interval	*Class frequency*	
Days absent	*No. of workers involved*	
1	~~1111~~ ~~1111~~ 11	= 12
2	~~1111~~ ~~1111~~	= 10
3	~~1111~~ 1111	= 9
4	~~1111~~ 1	= 6
etc.,	etc.,	etc.,

Table 3.2

When this tallying has been carried out, we should have a long list showing how often workers are absent, with a range from one absence to 42 absences. Such a table, however, would be too lengthy. It would contain many zero frequency entries (e.g., from 32 to 41 inclusive would all be zero!). The list would be wasteful of paper, unbalanced, and not very easy to read.

Instead of using such an *ungrouped frequency distribution* it is usually more convenient (even if a little less precise) to make a *grouped frequency distribution.* In order to do this it is necessary to arrange the data into groups, or classes, into which the frequency of absence will fall. Such classes are known as *class intervals.* The first step is to find the *range.* This is simply the difference between the highest and the lowest values of the variable (number of days absent).

In our example this would read:

Highest variable value = 42 days
Lowest variable value = 1 day
The range = 41 days

In choosing the size and number of classes in which to split the range we must use our discretion. It is incorrect to make the class intervals too small, because this would result in a lengthy list of intervals and would fall into the same error as the ungrouped frequency distribution. It is also incorrect to make the class intervals too large, because this would result in only a few class intervals, and a good deal of precision would be lost. The assumption is that the frequencies within an interval are distributed equally throughout it.

Wrong	Right	Wrong
1 to 2	1 to 4	1 to 9
2 ,, 3	5 ,, 9	10 ,, 19
3 ,, 4	10 ,, 14	20 ,, 29
etc.,	etc.,	etc.,

The number of class intervals in a usual frequency distribution is hardly less than 5 and usually not more than 15. In the wrong examples above we would have had 41 intervals in the first case, and 5 in the second case. In the right example we shall have a table as follows:

Absences (days)	*No. of workers*
1 to 4	37
5 ,, 9	17
10 ,, 14	11
15 ,, 19	7
20 ,, 24	6
25 and over	6
Total	84

Table 3.3 Absences due to illness in production department, December 1976 to 1977

Each class interval gives the number of days (inclusive) of absence, i.e.,

1 to 4 includes 1, 2, 3, and 4
5 to 9 includes 5, 6, 7, 8, and 9, etc.

The last class interval is an example of what is called an *open-ended class interval.* This is a device often used when the items for inclusion are few and widespread (in our example, 6 items only, covering a range of from 25 to 42). To have continued the list of class intervals to encompass the few items involved would have meant lengthy and unproductive work. Such open-ended class intervals may occur at the beginning or at the end of a frequency distribution. For example,

149 and under
150 to 159
160 „ 169
etc.

Complex frequency table

In the table below, our previous table has been further subdivided, and we have compared *attributes* (male and female), as well as simply tabulating the frequencies of the *variables.*

Absences (days)	*Number of workers*		
	Males	*Females*	*Total*
1 to 4	19	18	37
5 „ 9	9	8	17
10 „ 14	5	6	11
15 „ 19	3	4	7
20 „ 24	2	4	6
25 and over	5	1	6
TOTALS	43	41	84

Table 3.4 Absences due to illness in production department, December 1976 to 1977

In the next example, the number of absences due to illness has been further subdivided into 'Accidents at work' and 'Other causes'.

This is a fuller presentation of the complex frequency distribution. The percentage absences in the last row are written in italics to make them stand out from the absolute figures in the table, and they are placed near the totals to which they relate. Notice the variation of line thickness to make certain columns and rows appear more sharply marked off. The footnote on the meaning of 'days' is included for the reader's information, as are the sources of the information.

Absences (days)*	Number of workers								
	Males			Females			Totals		
	Acc. at work	Other	Total	Acc. at work	Other	Total	Acc. at work	Other	Total
1 to 4	4	15	19	6	12	18	10	27	37
5 ,, 9	3	6	9	3	5	8	6	11	17
10 ,, 14	1	4	5	2	4	6	3	8	11
15 ,, 19	0	3	3	1	3	4	1	6	7
20 ,, 24	1	1	2	2	2	4	3	3	6
25 and over	3	2	5	0	1	1	3	3	6
Totals	12	31	43	14	27	41	26	58	84
Total workers in deot.			80			120			200
% absences			*53·8*			*34·2*			*42·0*

* A fraction of a day is counted as a day.

Table 3.5 Absences due to illness in production department, December 1976 to 1977 (AGP/Wages Dept. and Health/Personnel)

Cumulative frequency table

A slightly different type of table can be constructed as shown in Table 3.6 to give the frequency of absences at the various points of the class intervals.

	Col. 1	*Col. 2*	*Col. 3*
	Absences (days)	*'Cum' less*	*'Cum' more*
Row 1	1 to 4	37	84
Row 2	5 to 9	54	47
Row 3	10 to 14	65	30
Row 4	15 to 19	72	19
Row 5	20 to 24	78	12
Row 6	25 and over	84	6

Table 3.6

It is possible, from col. 2, for example, to find how many workers had less than 10 days' absence through illness. If we look along the second row of class intervals in col. 2, the figure is 54. This cumulative table is calculated simply by adding together the successive totals for each class interval in order, from the lowest to the highest class interval. Similarly, in the 'cum' more, col. 3, table we can find, for example, the number of workers who had 15 or more days' absence by looking at this column along the 4th row where we find the answer: 19. This cumulative column is constructed by adding the successive totals for each class interval from the highest to the lowest, in order. In this case we enter the successive totals from the bottom upwards.

Other forms of tabulation are commonly met with and they are noted below.

Tabulation of time series

The tabulation of a times series is the record, over time, of how a variable has changed in value. For further information on time series, the reader is referred to Chapter 10. The table below gives an example of the tabulation of the growth of bank advances over the period 1966 to 1972:

Year (end December)	*Advances (£m)*	
	London Banks	*Scottish Banks*
1966	4 732	514
1967	4 725	503
1968	5 075	520
1969	5 328	548
1970	5 624	586
1971	5 991	634
1972	9 735	865

Table 3.7 The growth of bank advances (Monthly Digest)

A distinguishing feature of a time series table is that columns are rarely totalled, but row totals are often used when data for each year are broken down into sections.

Tabulation by geographical location

Division	*Fatal accidents*	*Total accidents*
West Riding and N. Lincs.	8	7 771
Northern (Leeds)	12	6 694
Midlands (Birmingham)	7	4 565
Midlands (Nottingham)	13	5 114
London (West)	9	4 274
London (North)	6	3 925
London (East)	7	4 446
South Western	9	3 150
Wales	11	4 506
North Western (Liverpool)	10	5 073
North Western (Manchester)	5	3 871
Scotland	11	5 922
TOTALS	108	59 311

Table 3.8 Fatal and non-fatal accidents, third quarter, 1972, by Divisions of Inspectorate (Department of Employment Gazette)

Location, either in time or space (geographical), is not considered as an attribute of an item. That is why this table, and the time series Table 3.7 are not placed under 'Tabulation by attributes.'

Tabulation by attributes

In these cases the characteristic is not measurable and it may refer to occupation, industry, personal details, etc.

Table 3.9 shows the cause of stoppage, i.e., strikes due to industrial disputes:

Principal cause	*Number of stoppages*	*Number of workers directly involved* (00's)
Wages—claims for increases	1 176	8 395
Wages—other disputes	240	588
Hours of work	40	81
Employment of particular classes of persons	423	2 592
Working rules and discipline	355	912
Trade Union status	75	227
Sympathetic action	36	281
TOTALS	2 345	13 076

Table 3.9 Stoppages of work in 1972 (Department of Employment Gazette)

The table below shows an analysis by *industrial sector*:

	Per cent at August 1972
Agriculture and fishing	4·4
Mining and quarrying	1·4
Manufacturing industries	32·1
Building and contracting	5·7
Finance (incl. H.P. Companies)	20·6
Personal and professional	16·1
Services	19·7
TOTALS	100·0

Table 3.10 Loans and overdrafts in Great Britain*

* Advances by members of British Bankers' Association through offices in Great Britain: classified according to the business of the borrower—not the use to which the credit is put.

A feature of this table is that, for quick reference and to help comparison, the whole of the data has been reduced to percentage form.

Rules of tabulation

By its nature, tabulation is extremely flexible, and after a point, it becomes difficult to lay down hard and fast rules. It is always up to the student to exercise his discretion in order to present tables in a clear, intelligible, and attractive form. Nevertheless, there are certain basic rules and hints which should be noted in any tabulation, even of the more complex types:

(*a*) All rows and columns should be headed with clear, explanatory, titles and a note of the units used.

(*b*) Tables should bear suitable titles, and these should combine brevity with as full a description as possible.
(*c*) Margins should be left round the edges of the table and, for neatness, the whole table should preferably be contained in a frame.
(*d*) Double, bold, and feint lines should be used to divide and sectionalize the data, especially where the table is complex.
(*e*) Footnotes explaining points of classification, and any special notes, should be included with the table, as should a note of the source of the data.
(*f*) Provision should be made for totals at the end of columns and rows, if this is necessary.
(*g*) Comparative percentages, ratios, averages, etc., may be included, and should be placed close to the absolute figures to which they refer. (Such derived figures are usually printed in italics.)
(*h*) Tables should not be overloaded and, if this is a danger, it is often better to separate the data into two or more tables.

Use and interpretation

Classification and tabulation

It is a good method to draft out the classification scheme and the actual tables to be used, before the actual survey is undertaken or the recorded data is collected. This is another example of planning the end before beginning with the details. If one proceeds this way, many problems in the drafting of the questionnaire, e.g., deciding what units to use, may be avoided.

In the actual processing of the results, a check for 'errors of transference' between stages should be included, e.g., from questionnaire to classification, from classification to tabulation, etc. Unavoidable errors which may already be present in results, e.g., bias, should not be added to by errors within the statistician's control.

The actual analysis and tabulation of the results is, nowadays, often done by a computer if there are many items involved.

Drafting blank tables

From the methods described previously in this chapter, the student should be able to attempt the tabulation of a simple set of attributes. An illustration is given below of the possible steps in the drafting of a blank table.

Example:

A firm wishes to classify its employees according to type of employment, distinguishing between males and females, and showing trade union membership, if any. Rule up a blank table, with suitable headings, and showing all necessary sub-totals. (*Note*. The vertical divisions of a table are called columns, and the horizontal ones are called rows.)

(*a*) Make a list of the attributes and variables which you are asked to tabulate, with a note of the groups within each attribute.

For example, Type of employment —4 groups + totals and sub-totals
Sex —2 groups
Trade union membership—2 groups

(*b*) Divide the attributes between the columns and the rows, so as to give a well proportioned table.
For example, sex and trade union membership in columns;
type of employment in rows.

Although a table is rectangular, we can only use two sides. The base and the right-hand side of the rectangle are normally used for totals, across and down.

(*c*) Now rule up a rough table. This will probably need amending later, so allow plenty of space, and don't worry about details at this stage. This might look as follows:

Employment	*Males*		*Females*	
	Union	*Non-union*	*Union*	*Non-union*
Skilled Unskilled Sales Admin.				

Table 3.11

(*d*) Totals and sub-totals, at the ends of columns and rows may now be inserted.
(*e*) We now draft the final table, adding any refinements.

Type of employment	*Males*			*Females*			*Totals*		
	Union	*Non-union*	*Total*	*Union*	*Non-union*	*Total*	*Union*	*Non-union*	*Total*
Skilled factory Unskilled factory Sales force Administration									
TOTALS									

Table 3.12 Distribution of employees of Jones Co. Ltd by sex, trade union membership, and type of employment, December 1977

Points to watch:

(i) Note the title, statement of units, and date.
(ii) Note the provision made for check totals at the bottom right-hand corner.
(iii) Note particularly that any sub-total can be easily extracted. This is the final test of a draft tabulation.
(iv) The commonest fault is the omission of some sub-total. The rule is that, once a sequence of headings is established, (e.g., union, non-union,

total) this sequence must be repeated in the final totals column. A similar rule applies to rows, if there is any sub-division of these.

Class intervals

In the Method section we dealt with class intervals when the variable was a discrete series. When the variable is a *continuous* series certain problems arise. These concern the meaning and the limits of the class interval.

For example, if we were presented with class intervals of the age of the population, these might appear as follows:

Ages (years)
0-4
5–9
10–14, etc.,

The limits of the intervals given are:

Lowest: the first value in each interval

Highest: the highest possible value before the lower limit of the next class interval.

Strictly speaking, 0–4 means '0 years to 4·99 (recurring)' years.

The explanation is necessary in the process of tabulation because we may be undecided, when presented with a class interval of 0–4, in which class frequency to place an item value 4 years, 11 months, 27 days. As this is just under 5, the item goes into the first class frequency.

It is also necessary to warn the student that he may expect to meet any of the following descriptions of class interval:

0 but under 5	0 to 4	0–	0–4	0–5
5 but under 10	5 to 9	5–	5–9	5–10

All these are variations on the above example, and are often the source of much confusion. The last example is particularly misleading and should never be used. For example, in which class frequency—1st or 2nd—should an item value 5 be placed?

One should classify according to the limits given (except of course in the single case mentioned above), and if the intervals are written:

–5
–10, etc.,

then, unless the student has evidence to suggest that this is merely another variation of 0–4, he should classify as:

0·01–5
5·01–10
10·01–15, etc.

Similar problems do not, of course, arise in the case of a discrete series, where items should be placed in the class frequency, the interval of which is bounded by the simple inclusive whole units.

4

Charts, diagrams, and symbols

Method

Bar charts

These are usually drawn to represent the total number of items in a group, at any point in time (as in Fig. 4.1).

Note the guide lines, which help the eye to judge the relative heights of the bars, and the vertical scale.

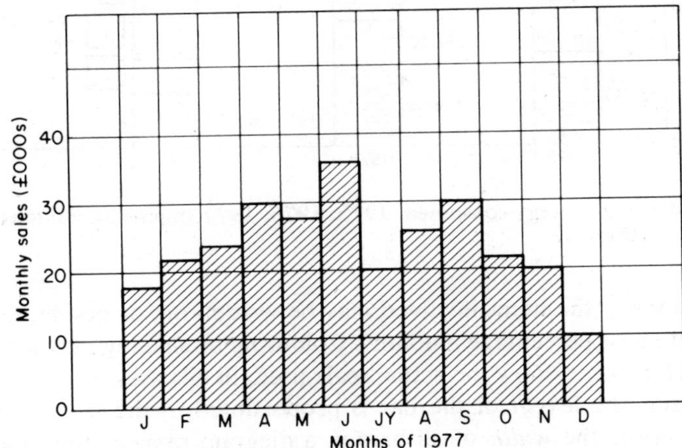

Fig. 4.1 Monthly sales of XY Ltd, 1977

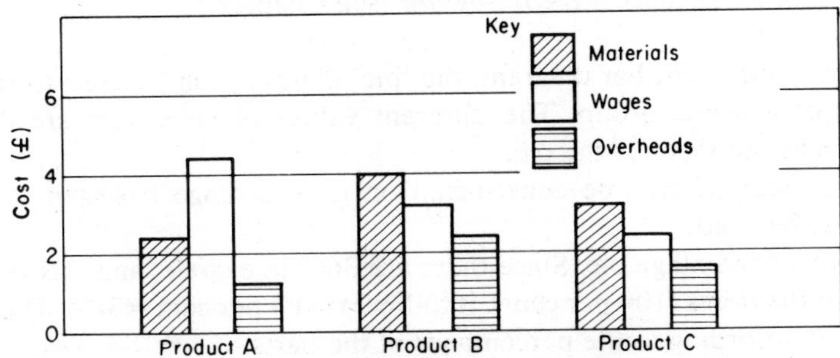

Fig. 4.2 Allocation of unit costs for three products, 1977

Sometimes two or more bars are drawn for each item (see Fig. 4.2). This is a *compound* (or *multiple*) bar chart. If the comparison is in percentages, the diagram is known as a *percentage bar chart. Note* that the bars are drawn vertically. There is no definite rule about this, but in the absence of any specific instruction by an examiner, the student should draw the bars vertically.

Finally, there are *Component bar charts.* These are used to show the breakdown of a total into its component parts, and here again, we may show the actual figures (see Fig. 4.3), in which case the bars will be of varying heights, or we may show a percentage breakdown, in which case the bars will be of equal height, representing 100 per cent in each case.

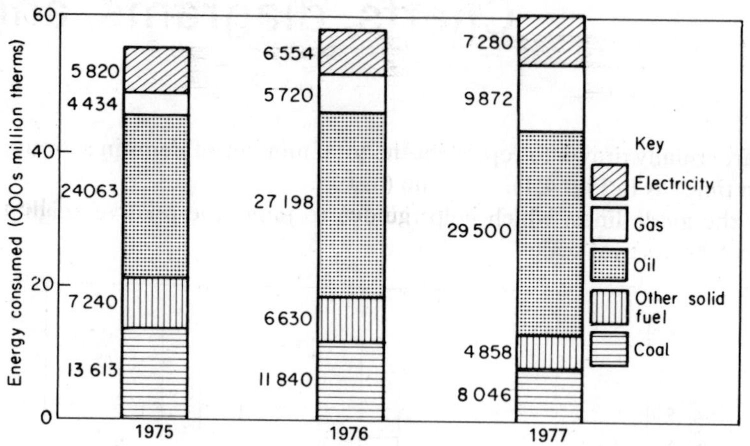

Fig. 4.3 UK Energy consumed. 1975, 1976, 1977 (figures in millions of therms)

Descriptions of the items involved may be written on, or beside, the bars, as may the actual or percentage amounts. Colouring or shading may also be used, but it is preferable to show the actual scale used, in all cases.

In all cases, the *length* of the bar is proportional to the size of the item it represents, while the *width* of all bars in a diagram remains the same. Where axes of measurement are used, these should always begin at zero. A special application of a bar chart is the *histogram* (see Chapter 5).

Circular or 'pie' diagram

Like the component bar diagram, the 'pie' diagram can be used to represent the parts of a whole group. The different values of each item are drawn in proportion as the slices of the pie.

The pie diagram may be constructed on a percentage basis, or the actual figures may be used.

We have a percentage pie. Since there are 360° in a circle, and this represents the total of the items (100 per cent), it follows that 1 per cent = 3·6°. The circle is marked out according to the percentages of the parts.

Pie diagrams may also be used to compare values in different years.

	Percentage
Wages	$33\frac{1}{3}$
Expenses	$12\frac{1}{2}$
Materials	25
Tax	$16\frac{2}{3}$
Profit	$12\frac{1}{2}$
TOTAL	100

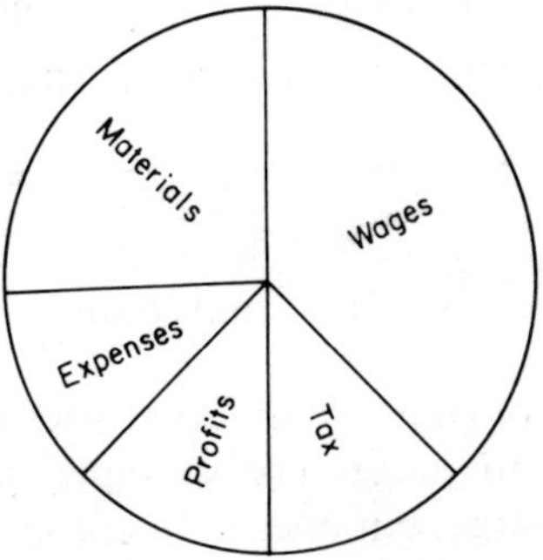

Fig. 4.4 Percentage outgoings in each £1 sales income

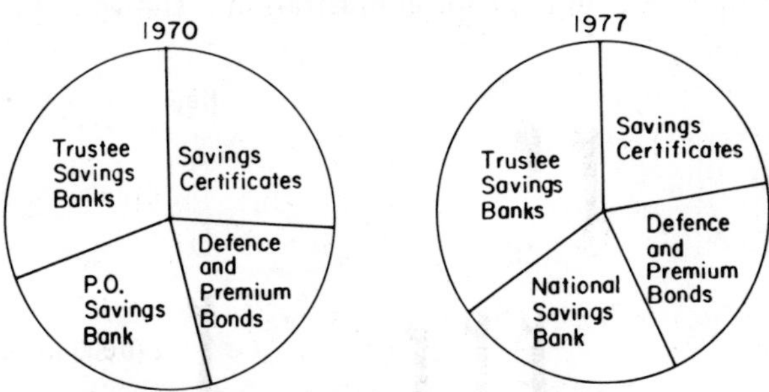

Fig. 4.5 Pie diagrams of National Savings, 1970 and 1977

In Fig. 4.5 we have a comparison of National Savings in 1970 and 1977. In addition to working out the angles for the slices in each pie, we must make the 1977 pie proportionately larger. This is done as follows:

(*a*) The respective totals (in £ million) are (1970) £7 786 and (1977) £9 171. Therefore, the areas of the circles must be in this proportion, i.e., as 1 is to 1·18.

(*b*) Since the area depends on the square of the radius (area of a circle is πr^2) we must first find the square roots of 1 and 1·18. These are 1 and 1·09 respectively. We therefore draw circles with radii of (say) 2 cm and 2·18 cm.

(*c*) We now split each pie according to the subdivisions. We give the figures below as an illustration.

	£m
Savings Certificates	2 032 = 94·0°
Defence and Premium Bonds	1 610 = 74·4°
P.O. Savings	1 779 = 82·3°
Trustee Savings Banks	2 365 = 109·3°
TOTAL	7 786 = 360°

The whole circle (360°) is represented by 7 786. By simple proportion, 2 032 is

$$\frac{360 \times 2\,032}{7\,786} = 94{\cdot}0°$$

Similarly, 1 610 is $\frac{360 \times 1\,610}{7\,786} = 74{\cdot}4°$, and so on.

In general, comparison of circles of different sizes is best avoided, because the real variation is difficult to judge. For example, a circle which is twice the diameter is four times as large, but does not look so.

Pictograms Sometimes these are known as picturegrams. An almost limitless variety of picture symbols may be used to represent values. As in the case of bar diagrams or pie diagrams, the picture symbols may show values at one point in time, or variation over time. A simple pictorial illustration is shown in Fig. 4.6.

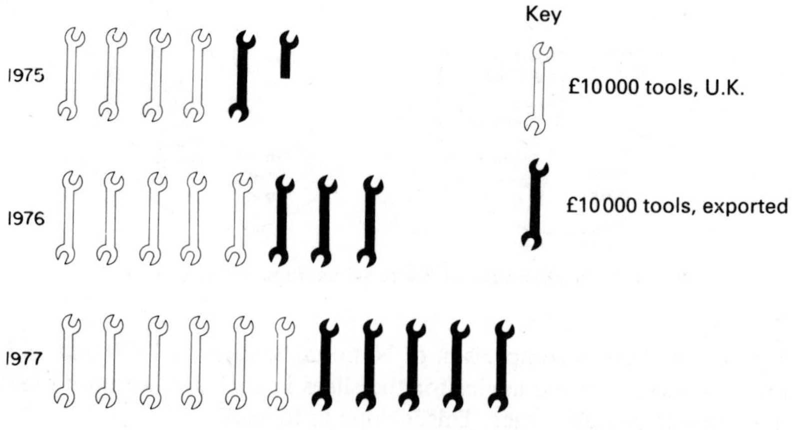

Fig. 4.6 Sales of tools

Each symbol represents a certain amount, e.g., £10 000 of tools is represented by a single spanner. Home sales and exports are distinguished by shading.

A defect of pictograms is their lack of precision, e.g., the sales can only be shown in units of £10 000. Occasionally, one sees a portion of a symbol drawn, as in 1975, but there are obvious limits to this device. If one seeks greater precision by letting each symbol represent a smaller amount, the number of symbols needed becomes excessive, and the eye is unable to take them all in.

Cartograms

A striking way of presenting geographical data by diagrams is the cartogram, as shown in Fig. 4.7.

This form of diagram demands, perhaps, more preparation, because a map has to be drawn and divided into the desired regions. Shading or hatching may be used, through frequently symbols can be placed according to the location of the item illustrated.

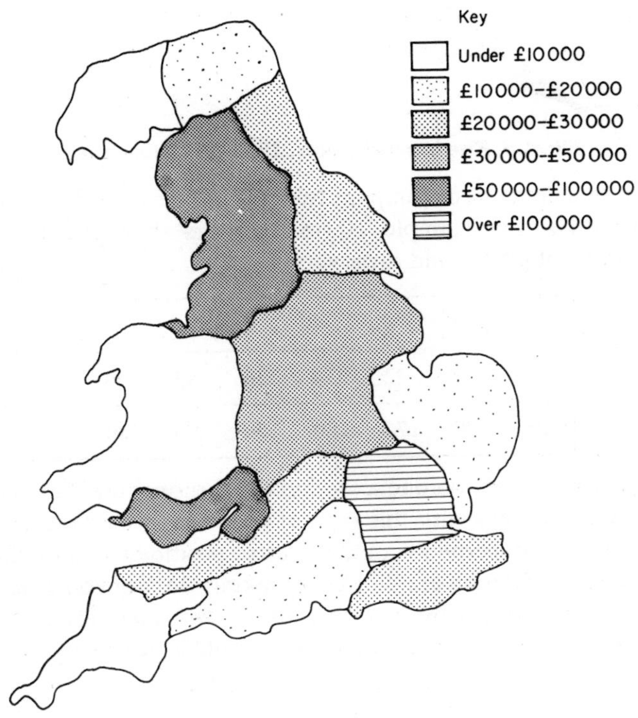

Fig. 4.7 Distribution of sales XYZ Ltd, 1977

In presenting this kind of geographical diagram, it is helpful to provide a key, as in the cartogram given.

Period change charts

This diagram shows the simple percentage change in a series between two fixed points in time. It can be seen that the 'base date' (earlier date) is regarded as zero on the vertical (percentage) axis. Straight lines are drawn radiating from the origin to points which fix the percentages changes (+ and −) and the end date (time on the horizontal axis).

Neither grids nor guide lines are used, because they might falsely show points of increase or decrease *within* the two dates. Axes should always be marked, but only the vertical axis need be calibrated, because the dates of the period are given by (*a*) the origin, and (*b*) the end of the change lines.

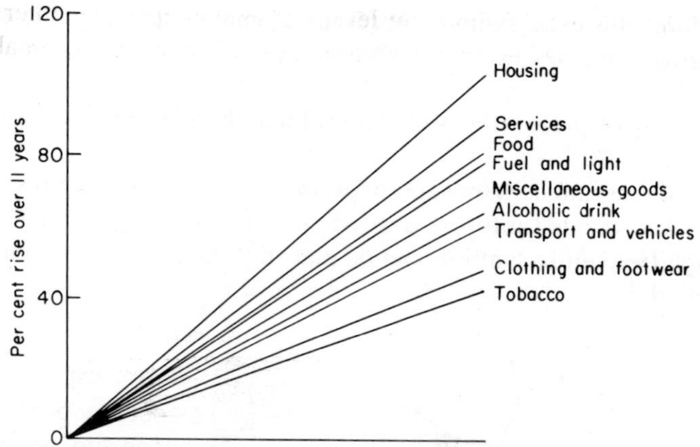

Fig. 4.8 Rise in retail prices, 1967–1977 (inclusive)

Scatter diagrams

Frequently we may wish to compare two sets of figures and to show how they vary with each other. For example, 10 small grocers' shops recorded the following weekly figures of profits and turnovers:

Shop	*1*	*2*	*3*	*4*	*5*	*6*	*7*	*8*	*9*	*10*
Profit (£)	25	29	32	34	38	42	54	59	63	74
Turnover (£)	125	170	174	180	190	215	260	300	320	400

We mark scales of profit on one axis, and the turnover on the other.

Note It is not necessary with this type of diagram to start the scales at zero, because we are only concerned with the *relative* positions of the points.

The points on our diagram are plotted by taking the profit and the turnover of shop No. 1, and marking it by reference to the two axes. Proceed to plot the remaining points until a series of points is built up as in the following diagram:

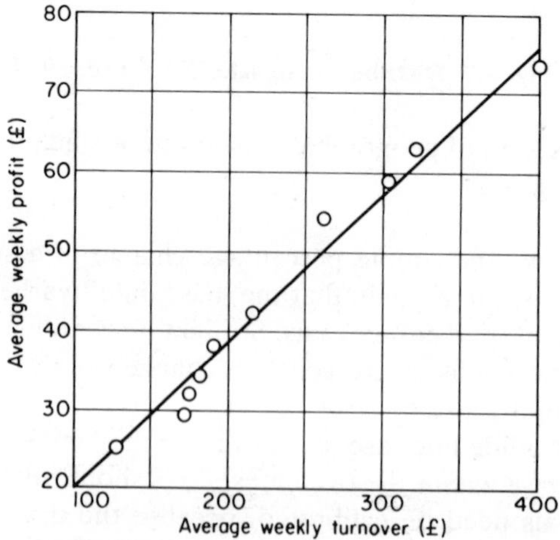

Fig. 4.9 Profit and turnover of ten grocers shops, 1977

The resulting cluster of points will show the relation (or, more properly, the correlation) of profits to turnover in these shops.

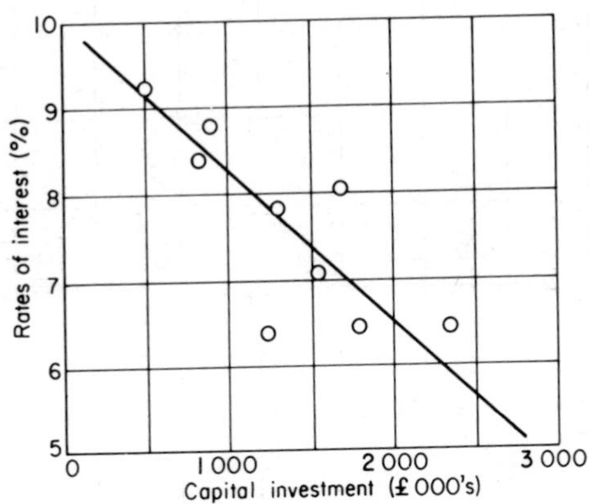

Fig. 4.10

If the points tend to lie along a line (as in Fig. 4.9), there is said to be a *strong linear correlation*. Also, as it appears in the diagram that profits increase as turnover increases, this is called a *strong positive correlation*.

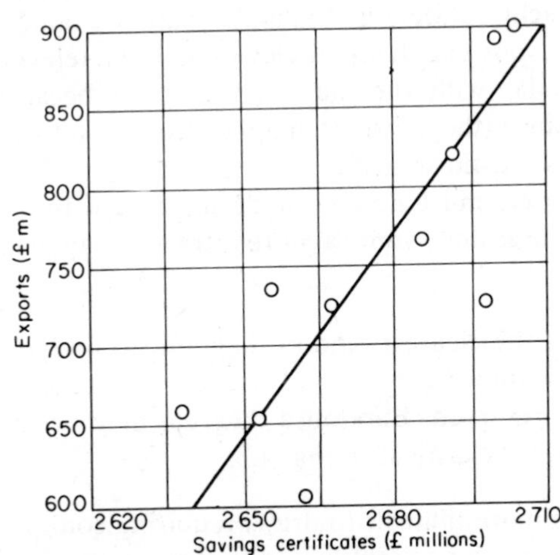

Fig. 4.11

In many cases we may have *negative correlation* where, as one item increases, the other decreases (see Fig. 4.10). Finally, we may have *weak correlation* (Fig. 4.11), or *no apparent correlation* at all (Fig. 4.12).

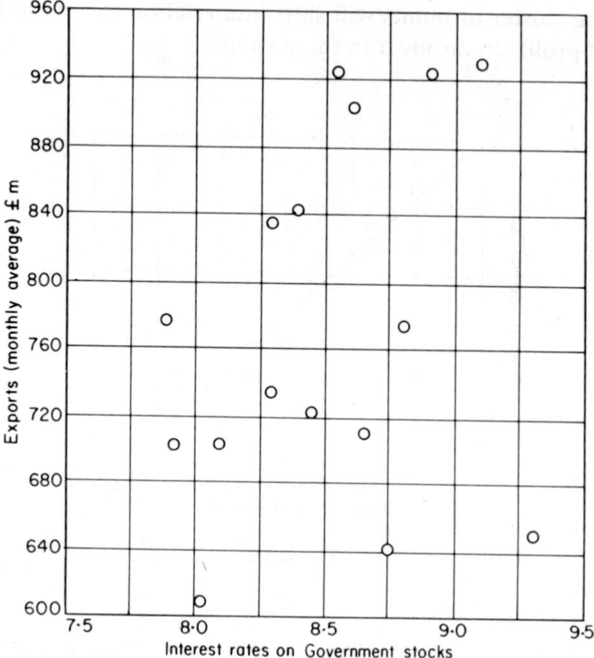

Fig. 4.12

Use and interpretation

The methods described in this chapter are extremely popular ways of presenting statistics without technical details. Examples may be found every day in newspapers, magazines, posters, bank reviews, and on television. Good, simple examples are popular with the man in the street because they are readily understood at a glance (they also often appeal to the statistician because he can express some of his artistic ability!).

Simplicity, however, must not be made an excuse for inaccuracy, and the desire to make pictures and symbols more attractive can lead to error as well as confusion.

Bar diagrams

Bar diagrams are the clearest kind of diagrams to understand, as well as the easiest to draw. It is difficult to mislead the reader if accuracy in the width and heights of bars is preserved. Bars on a diagram may be drawn touching each other or spaced out for clarity as in Fig. 4.3.

Pie diagrams

Pie diagrams are more difficult to draw, requiring compasses and protractor. They do not give the reader a very clear idea of the proportions involved because the eye can measure lengths of bar much more easily and accurately than slices of pie. Again, to compare two or more pies of different sizes in difficult. For example, the reader might imagine that the sizes of the pies are proportional to their diameters, whereas it is the *areas* of the circles (squares of the radii) which are really important—but which are difficult to compare.

Pictograms

Pictograms can be misleading, especially if drawn in a haphazard manner.

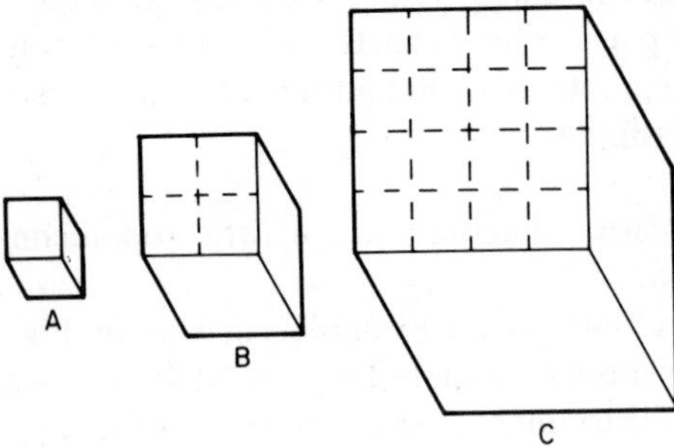

Fig. 4.13

Imagine that the cubes, A, B, and C represent crates of exports. Suppose that we wished to show that in three years exports had doubled by the second year, and doubled again by the third year. That is, the size of exports (cube C) in the third year is four times the size of exports (cube A) in the first year.

Obviously, the symbols drawn above are wrong. Although the *length of a side* of the cube A has been increased four times in cube C, the *volume* of cube C is far larger than it should be.

The proper ratio of the exports should be 1:2:4, but it is, in fact, $1^3:2^3:4^3 = 1:8:64$, if we judge by the symbols!

Of course, the same kind of error could be made in *two-dimensional* symbols. What would be the size of error if A, B, and C where *squares* instead of cubes?

The lesson here is that you should use only one symbol for each unit represented, and multiply the symbols as you represent multiples of the unit.

Cartograms

Cartograms are clear, attractive, easy to understand and free from misleading details, provided that a simple and accurate key is given.

Period change charts

Period change charts are often used as additional illustrations, or in cases where the absolute figures are quoted in the text of an article. This is perfectly valid. The danger is that the casual reader might interpret such charts too literally. They give no indication of the changes within the two dates where such changes may have varied greatly in positive and negative directions. The charts might mislead in that no indication of the size of items at the base date is given. Thus if the table below was drawn on a period change chart, the change line for imports would be higher on the chart and steeper than that for national income, even though the latter's absolute increase is more than double the former's.

Item	*1963*	*1972*	*Absolute increase*	*Percentage increase*
National Income (£m)	27 191	52 404	25 213	93
Imports (£m)	4 984	11 172	6 188	124

Percentage changes in small items often appear huge when small absolute changes have taken place. These charts are best used when the items shown are of the same group (e.g., items within a total), and when the absolute sizes of the items are not too dissimilar.

Scatter diagrams

Though useful, scatter diagrams are a little too technical for the average reader to understand.

The point here is that, in an example such as in Fig. 4.9, the profit and turnover figures are simply compared, i.e., related. The worst mistake in interpreting this diagram is to imagine that one series of figures *causes* the other. A shop could have a low turnover with a high profit, or vice versa. In our example, a high profit happens to go with a large turnover. But good salesmanship might be the cause of a high turnover, and a good position in the centre of town might be the cause of high profits. One could hardly say that a good position in the centre of town causes good salesmanship. Thus, the two series of figures illustrated on the scatter diagram might have completely different causes to account for each.

It is natural to suppose that a scatter diagram shows how one series influences another, but here lies the gravest error. If one series might influence another (see Fig. 4.10, *Interest rate and capital investment*), we may show it on a scatter diagram, but we must explain the connection in a way other than by graphs.

Statisticians often amuse themselves by finding examples of nonsense correlation, i.e., where the apparent cause of the relationship is not a true one. For example, there is a high degree of positive correlation between the number of television licences and the number of admissions to mental hospitals. Can we draw the conclusion that watching television drives people insane? We may be sorely tempted! The more likely explanation is that they are both related to some common factor, e.g., the increase in the size of the population, or the increasing industrialization of society.

Note In all the examples of scatter diagrams which have been given, the number of pairs of items has been small—in most cases only 10. This is for purposes of illustration, and is also a common practice in examination questions, but whenever a real scatter diagram is constructed, the number of items should be considerably larger so that at least a hundred points appear on the diagram. This is because we are taking a sample, and if it is to reflect the behaviour of the whole group of items, then the sample should be fairly large.

5

Graphs

Method

The word 'graph' could well be associated in the student's mind with the word 'graphic', which means 'vivid', or 'springing to life'. This is exactly the kind of function which the graph should perform for the table from which it is drawn, because most people can grasp pictures more readily than figures.

This is not to say that graphs should be sensational. Graphs, 'line charts', as they are often called, are really a diagrammatic type of representation, though one usually thinks of a graph as having extra technical features (i.e., statistical information) which would be out of place in popular diagram or symbol presentation. This may be a good place to say that the most accurate information which can come into the statistician's hands is the primary data, e.g., completed questionnaires and interviewers' answer sheets. From that point onwards, the data is subject to human errors of miscalculation and to the classification process (e.g., putting into class frequencies) in which some precision must be lost. After this 'boiling down' process it is then probably reshaped for the tabulation stage. It comes finally to the point where it is put into graphical terms and, as we shall see, it is further slightly distorted. It is up to the statistician to make the inevitable distortions at every stage as small as possible. It is certainly up to him to prevent and expose the tortured and dishonest examples of graphical work to be found in 'Use and interpretation' (pages 52–55).

Graphs generally

The graph is drawn on a grid (squared paper) to a certain scale. The basis of this grid is shown in Fig. 5.1.

This grid shows the four quadrants with zero, the origin, at the centre. In a graph, lines or curves are drawn on the grid to illustrate the relationship between two variables. As variables may be negative as well as positive, this is provided for by carrying the axes on to the left of zero on the horizontal axis, and below zero on the vertical axis. In practice, the student will not often meet with negative values and therefore there is usually no need to draw the negative arms of the axes.

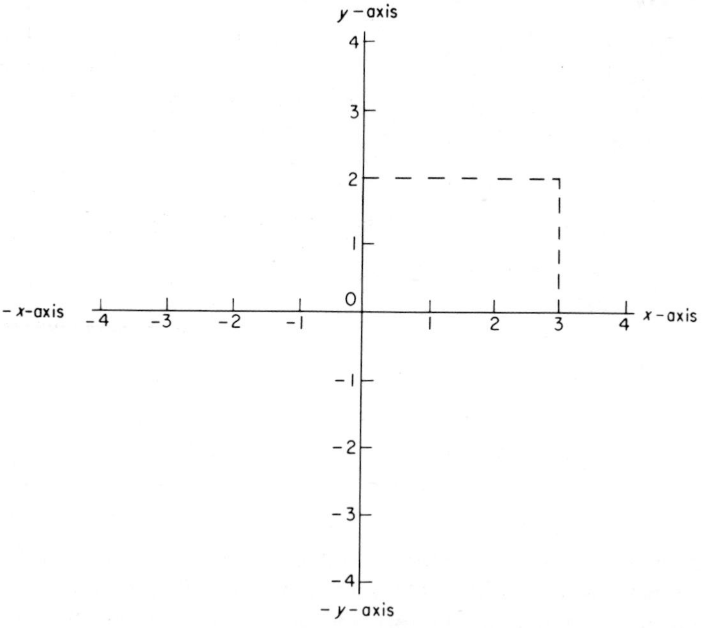

Fig. 5.1

(All graphs in this book are reproduced without grids in the interest of printing clarity.)

DEPENDENT AND INDEPENDENT VARIABLES

The horizontal axis, known as the x-axis, is scaled in units of the independent variable. In a frequency distribution, the scale can be taken as the limits of the class intervals. In the graph of a time series, the independent variable on the x-axis is 'time'.

The vertical axis, known as the y-axis, is scaled in units of the dependent variable. In a frequency distribution, the scale can be chosen according to the range of the class frequencies. In the graph of a time series, the dependent variable on the y-axis is the value of the series at the regular intervals of time.

The independent variable is the one which is chosen to be stated in class intervals, and the class frequency is, therefore, the dependent variable. There is no certain way of choosing, say, the independent variable in most exercises concerning frequency distributions. For example, if we were to relate the two variables of output and cost in a firm, it might be impossible to decide which is dependent on which. Is the cost dependent on the output, or is the output dependent on the cost? From different points of view, each is true. There is no doubt, however, that the student will be able to recognize the independent variable (and hence, the dependent variable) in his work, because these have usually been decided upon in the problems which will be presented to him.

PLOTTING THE CURVE

The curve joins the points of relationship of the two variables on the graph. (The word 'curve' is commonly used, even when a straight line is actually drawn in the graph.) The position of any point on the curve is decided by reference to the axes; e.g., in the basic grid (shown above) a point has been plotted at:

$$+3(\text{on } x\text{-axis}) \text{ and } +2(\text{on } y\text{-axis}).$$

These are the 'bearings' or 'co-ordinates' of that point. The point of intersection is marked with + or, better still, by a ring. Either is better than × which does not reflect the vertical and horizontal nature of the axes. A set of points is thus built up, one for each pair of facts, and these are joined to form the curve.

DISCRETE AND CONTINUOUS VARIABLES

The curve may be a freehand smooth curve, or simply a joining of straight lines from point to point. Certain considerations govern which one is used, however.

If the dependent variable to be illustrated is discrete then, strictly speaking, the set of points should be joined by straight lines. If continuous, then the points should be joined by a smooth curve (i.e., one that is not sharply angled between one point and the next).

In practice, however, a certain latitude is sometimes allowed; e.g., a time series of National Income figures should not be plotted as a discrete series, although money is, strictly, a discrete variable. The steps between one point and the next, even if they represented £1 million, would appear as a smooth curve when the total National Income stood at its present figure of thousands of millions. On the other hand, yearly sales figures of a firm should be joined by straight lines, even though the totals involved might still be very large, compared with the units involved. This is because we have no information of what is happening between one point and the next. There might actually be a drop in sales for certain months, and a continuous curve would suggest that there is a steady rise (or fall) in the figures, through time.

Finally, if more than one curve is drawn on a graph it is usual to distinguish the curves by labelling them separately and clearly, or by drawing the curves in different colours, or by drawing them in different ways e.g.,

A broken line
A dot-dash line
An unbroken line
A dotted line
A hatched line
A ring line

A key must be inserted on the graph unless the curves are separately labelled.

The histogram

This must not be confused with the historigram (graph of a time series—see Chapter 10). Students can avoid this confusion if they remember that *history* relates to *time*.

Let us suppose we are given the following frequency distirbution in a table:

Weekly earnings (£)	*No. of workers* (*000's*)
20–29·99	52
30-39·99	256
40–49·99	170
50–59·99	68
60–69·99	30
70 and over	24
TOTAL	600

Table 5.1 Weekly earnings in an industrial region

To draw this as a histogram, the horizontal axis is scaled in class intervals and the vertical axis in 'No. of workers'. On each class interval is erected a rectangle the height of which is determined by the number of workers in the class in relation to the vertical scale. The last class in the frequency distribution is an example of an open-ended class. The usual method of treating such a class is to assume that it is of the same size as the classes immediately preceding it, i.e., in this case—70–79·99—unless there is good reason to suppose otherwise.

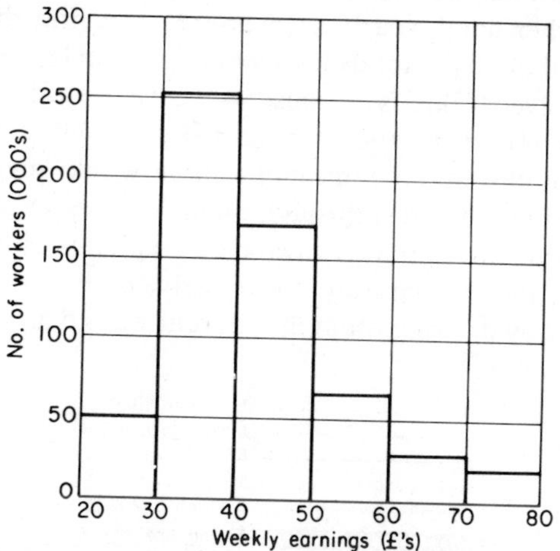

Fig. 5.2 Weekly earnings in an industrial region

The total area of the histogram represents the total of the frequencies (600). The *area* of each rectangle represents the number of items falling into that particular class. This does not mean that the area *equals* the frequency, because we have scaled down the height and the width, according to our choice of units for the two axes. Nevertheless, the relative areas of the various rectangles are

always strictly *proportional* to the class frequencies, whatever scale is chosen for the diagram. As all the class intervals in the distribution are equal, this is the same thing as saying that the height of each rectangle represents the number of items falling into each class in this particular case.

Quite often, in statistics, the rule that all class intervals should be equal is broken. In our example, the frequency distribution might have been written as follows:

Weekly earnings (£)	*No. of workers* (*000's*)
20–24·99	12
25–29·99	40
30–39·99	256
40–49·99	170
50–59·99	68
60 and over	54
TOTAL	600

Table 5.2 Weekly earnings in an industrial region

Here we see that the first two intervals are of £5 each, the last one (closed at 79) is £20, and the remainder are £10, as before.

The histogram may easily be adapted to deal with such unequal intervals. The width of each rectangle is determined by the class interval, but the heights must be adjusted to preserve the area relationships.

First, a 'standard' width of bar must be selected. This should be the class interval which occurs most often in the table. (The reason for this is to reduce the number of adjustments needed.) In the example this is the £10 group. Next, each frequency is divided by the actual class interval and multiplied by the standard. The resultant figures are the frequencies to be plotted, i.e., the heights of the various rectangles:

$(a)\ \frac{12\times 10}{5}=24$ $(b)\ \frac{40\times 10}{5}=80$

$(c)\ \frac{256\times 10}{10}=256$ $(d)\ \frac{170\times 10}{10}=170$

$(e)\ \frac{68\times 10}{10}=68$ $(f)\ \frac{54\times 10}{20}=27$

Hence, the first two bars are made twice as high (to compensate for the narrower width), the last bar is only half as high (because it is twice as wide as the rest), and the remaining bars are unaltered. In practice, no calculations would be needed for the groups of standard size.

A histogram would appear as follows:

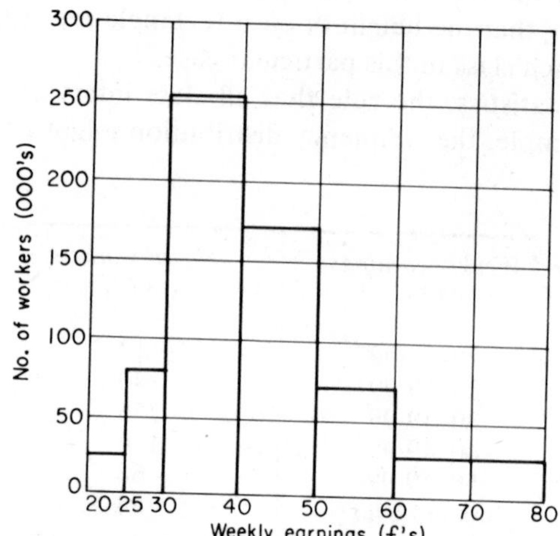

Fig. 5.3 Distribution of weekly earnings in an industrial region

Unequal groups are often found in published statistics under the following circumstances:

(*a*) When the original data falls naturally into certain groupings. For example, in an age distribution of factory workers, the first group would be '16 and under 21' since this would include the apprentices and so on. Thereafter, '21 and under 30', '30 and under 40', and so on, until we get '50 and under 65', and finally '65 and over', to include those of pensionable age.

(*b*) When the items within a group are not spread evenly throughout it. This is the case in the example given. The first class interval of £10 has only 12 workers under £25, while there are 40 workers earning over £25. Splitting this group into two £25 groups reveals that the upper portion is heavily weighted with items.

(*c*) When certain classes contain few or no items, it is better to combine them, in order to get a larger frequency.

The frequency polygon

This can be constructed from the histogram by joining the midpoints of the top of each rectangle. This is done by straight lines. The ends of the diagram (i.e., the two last points) may be left, or alternatively they can be joined to the base line at the centres of the adjoining class intervals. For example, the 80–90 group has no items. The centre-point of the (imaginary) rectangle is therefore on the base line. The following diagram shows both methods, but in practice one or the other should be used.

If the question merely calls for a frequency polygon, there is no need to draw the histogram at all. We merely locate each point by reference to the given frequency (on the vertical scale), and the midpoint of the class interval (on the horizontal scale).

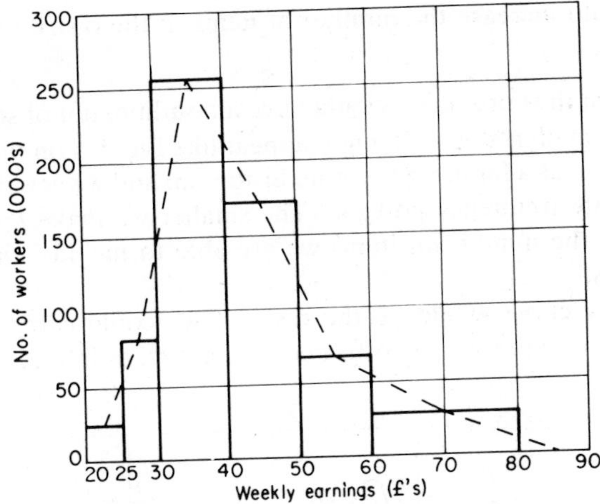

Fig. 5.4 Weekly earnings in an industrial region

The frequency curve

Neither the histogram nor the frequency polygon gives a very accurate picture of a frequency distribution. This histogram suggests that frequencies are the same throughout the class interval—when they probably are not. The frequency polygon suggests that sharp, angular differences occur between the mid-points of the class intervals—when this also is probably untrue. However, they may give us a fair *idea* of the distribution, and, so long as only this is required, they will be useful.

A more accurate picture of the distribution would emerge if we could make two adjustments:

(*a*) If we could draw a rectangle (say, in the histogram) for each individual item in the distribution or, at least, subdivide the class intervals, so as to make a greater number of smaller class intervals.

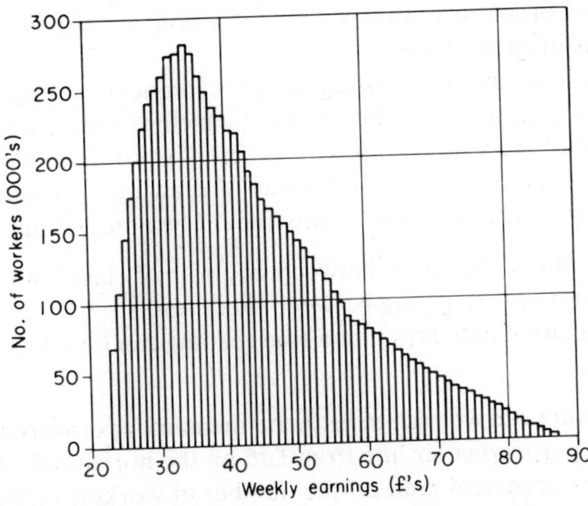

Fig. 5.5 Weekly earnings in an industrial region

(*b*) If we could increase the number of items in the distribution (if this were possible).

The histogram thus produced would have an outline, not of solid 'blocks', but one with much smaller 'steps'. It might appear like Fig. 5.5 on the previous page.

This would give us a far more accurate histogram and we could derive from it a far more accurate frequency polygon. The smaller we make the class intervals and the greater the number of items we are able to include, the smoother the outline becomes.

The frequency curve would be the result if we could carry this process far enough to be able to draw a smooth, freehand curve, as in Fig. 5.6.

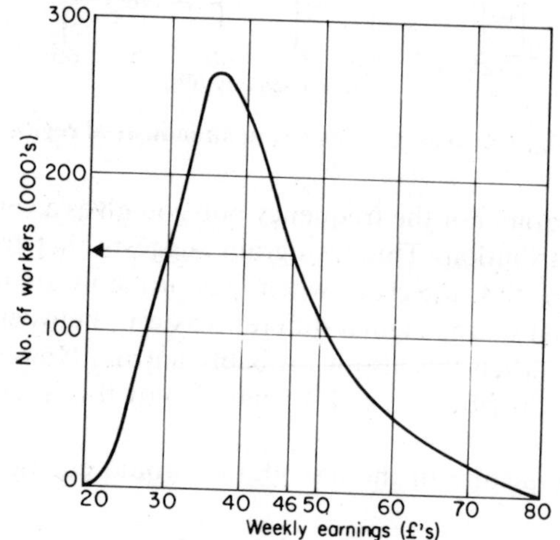

Fig. 5.6 Frequency curve from Table 5.1

It is usually considered not possible to draw such a curve unless there are at least 1 000 items in the distribution. This is because we need about 100 groups or rectangles, in order to ensure small steps, and we also need a reasonable number of items in each group.

It is permissible to smooth a histogram or a frequency polygon if we believe, for example, that a *sample* distribution from which we constructed our diagrams is representative of the whole population, were it possible to tabulate the latter.

The frequency curve is a convenient way of drawing distributions in order to make comparisons easier, but two points should be noted about this curve:

(*a*) The area under the curve between any pair of class limits represents the number of items occurring between those limits.
(*b*) To draw a curve indicates that a true reading can be taken at any point on the curve.

For example, suppose we wish to estimate the number of workers earning, say, £46. We draw a perpendicular line from £46 on the horizontal axis, to the point where it cuts the curve, and read off the number of workers on the vertical scale (see Fig. 5.6).

The cumulative frequency curve

To plot this curve, the frequencies are added cumulatively, i.e., in successive additions, as in the table below:

Weekly earnings (£)	*No. of workers* (000's)	'Cum' *less* (000's)	'Cum' *more* (000's)
20–29·99	52	52	600
30–39·99	256	308	548
40–49·99	170	478	292
50–59·99	68	546	122
60–69·99	30	576	54
70 and over	24	600	24
TOTAL	600		

Table 5.3

The 'cum' less column shows, at any stage, the total number of workers earning *less* than the upper limit of that particular class interval. For example, 478(000) workers earn less than £49·99 (or £50).

The 'cum' more column shows at any stage the total number of workers earning *more* than the lower limit of the particular class interval. For example, 54(000) workers are to be found above the £60 point.

The two cumulative frequency curves are drawn on the graphs below:

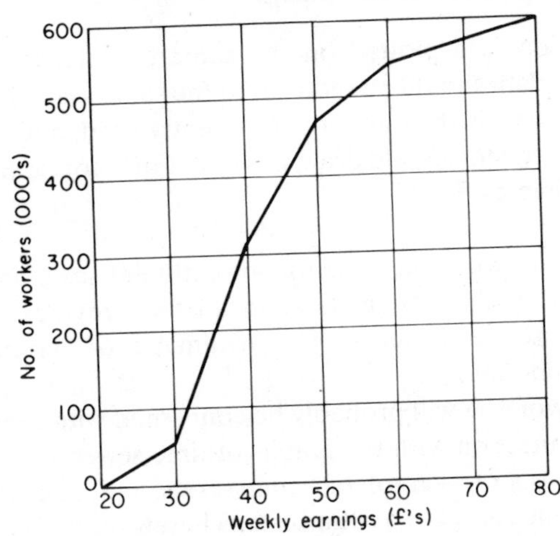

Fig. 5.7 Cumulative 'less than' frequency curve of weekly earnings

The student should note most carefully that, in plotting the frequencies, the point must be placed at the *end* of the group interval for 'less than' curves, and at the *beginning* of the interval for 'more than' curves. This is because we have not reached our total of, say, 308 until we have counted all the workers in the first two classes, i.e., until we reach a wage of 39·99 (or £40).

Straight lines are conventionally used to join the points in these graphs because the distribution of items is assumed to be even. These curves are often known as 'ogives', a term used in architecture to describe a similarly outlined S shape.

In the construction of these curves, no difficulty is caused by unequal classes; we merely join the unequally spaced points.

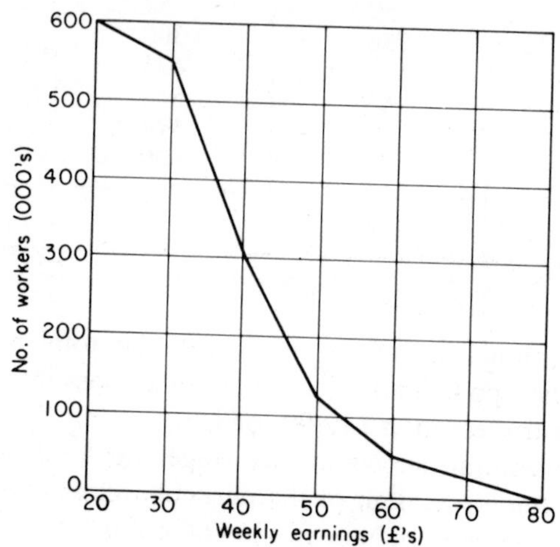

Fig. 5.8 Cumulative 'more than' frequency curve of weekly earnings

If two distributions are plotted on the same cumulative graph in order to compare them, the data should be reduced to the same scale, i.e., to percentages.

The 'less than' curve is the one most frequently used, and, if asked simply to draw an ogive, the student should draw this one. Further features of these graphs are discussed in Chapter 8.

The ratio curve

Such curves are drawn on a ratio (or logarithmic) scale graph and they are used to show *relative* changes in data. In all the previous chapters we were concerned with absolute (often called arithmetic or natural) changes, i.e., changes of actual amount.

In the student's work he will probably be concerned with examples of the ratio curve mostly in connection with the graphs of time series.

The graph below is a ratio graph of a time series, and, as can be seen, only one axis (the y-axis) is measured in a ratio scale. Therefore, this graph is known as a *semi-logarithmic graph.* It is not usual for the student at this level to meet examples of a full logarithmic graph, i.e., where *both* axes are scaled logarithmically.

The most important point in a ratio curve is not its position on the graph, but the *degree of slope* of the curve itself. Whereas the absolute curve measures the magnitude at any point, the ratio curve measures, at any point, the *percentage change from the last point.* Therefore any two equal distances measured on the logarithm axis will show equal percentage changes.

Suppose that, during a five-year period, a firm's sales were as follows:

Year	*1973*	*1974*	*1975*	*1976*	*1977*
Sales (£00's)	2 000	4 000	6 000	8 000	10 000

Table 5.4

On the absolute graph and the ratio graph these would appear thus:

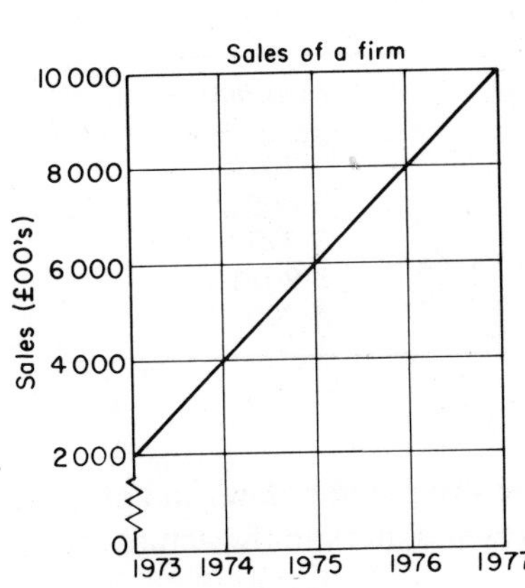

Fig. 5.9 Absolute graph

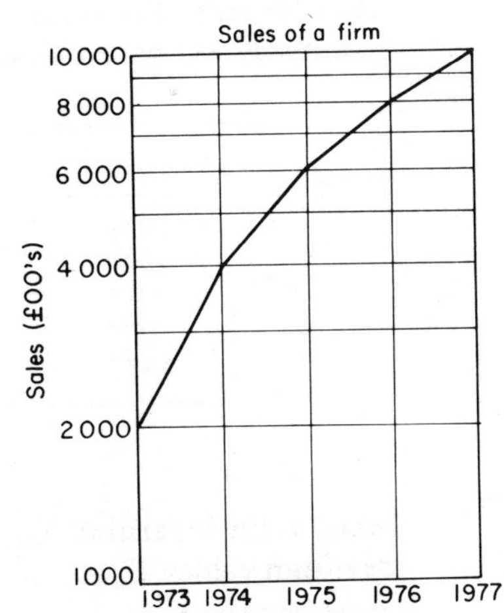

Fig. 5.10 Ratio graph

On the absolute graph, the distance from 2 000 to 4 000 is, of course, exactly the same as the distance from 4 000 to 6 000; but on the ratio graph, the distance from 4 000 to 6 000 is much smaller than the distance from 2 000 to 4 000. This is because the ratio graph measures the percentage change on the last figure, i.e.,

2 000 to 4 000 = an increase of 100 per cent;
whereas 4 000 to 6 000 = an increase of 50 per cent.

Therefore, in the case of the absolute graph, the simple magnitude of the series appears as a straight line. On the ratio graph, *using the same figures*, the curve shows a falling percentage increase of each year on the year before. To put the matter another way, the distance on the y-axis, on the ratio graph, from 2 000 to 4 000, is exactly the same as the distance from 4 000 to 8 000 because, although the absolute increases are 2 000 and 4 000 respectively, the percentage increases are exactly the same, i.e., 100 per cent.

There are two points to notice about the ratio graph:

(*a*) There is no zero base line on the graph (because the logarithm of 0 is minus infinity, which is impossible to show). Similarly, negative values cannot be plotted.

(*b*) The time axis (x-axis) is scaled in ordinary absolute measure.

TWO METHODS OF DRAWING A RATIO GRAPH

(*a*) As illustrated above. Obtain semi-logarithmic graph paper. Mark off the time axis with an absolute scale. Mark off the axis of the variable according to the range of the actual variable. Plot the actual figures of the variable and join the points.

(*b*) Usually you will have no semi-logarithmic graph paper to work with, and in this case you must proceed as follows:

Find the logarithms of the values you wish to plot. Using graph paper with ordinary absolute scale grid, mark off the time axis with an absolute scale. Measure the scale of the y-axis using an appropriate range of the logarithms you have found:

Year	*Actual value*	*Logarithm*
1973	2 000	3·3010
1974	4 000	3·6021
1975	6 000	3·7782
1976	8 000	3·9031
1977	10 000	4·0000

Table 5.5

Pencil in the logarithm figures (shown on left of graph below) and plot the logarithm values. Erase the pencilled figures and mark in the actual values on the y-axis.

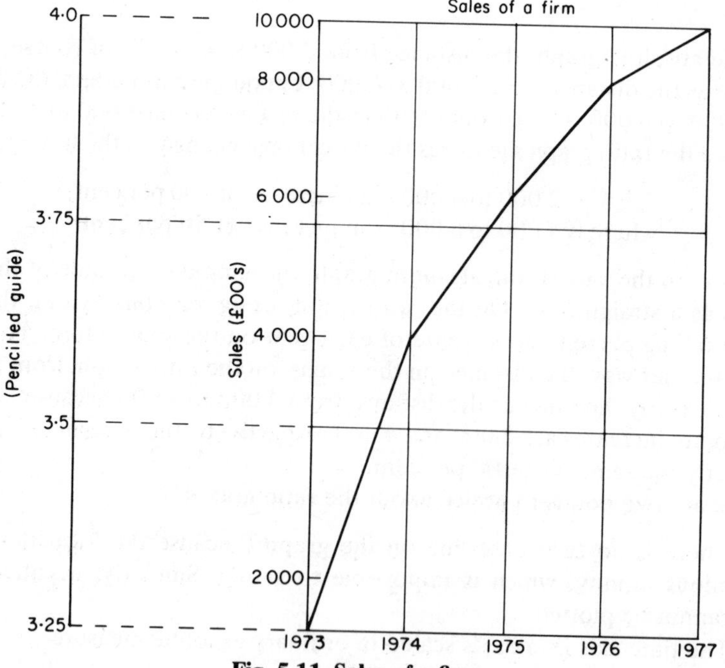

Fig. 5.11 Sales of a firm

A final example of a ratio scale graph is given below. Two curves have been plotted from the following data relating to a firm (see overleaf for graph):

Year	*No. of operatives employed*	*Bank loans (£)*
1970	734	650
1971	622	1 100
1972	510	2 500
1973	827	11 000
1974	1 050	9 050
1975	1 804	5 000
1976	2 113	5 000
1977	3 241	6 000

Table 5.6

This is an example showing how two series of completely different types, i.e., one in a monetary unit, the other in human units, and of quite differing magnitudes, may be plotted on the same graph with the same scale. This would be difficult on an absolute graph, because two different scales would be required; the curves would be more widely separated (thus making comparison difficult); and there would be no common basis for comparison (here there is the basis of the rate of change of each series—*rate of change* being the common factor).

The two ratio curves in the example have been plotted on three-cycle semi-logarithm graph paper. That is to say, there are three blocks or 'cycles' on the logarithmic axis scaled to measure the series. Because the total range of all the actual values, on both tables, was 510 to 11 000, it was decided to use all three cycles—the lower cycle being measured in hundreds (100 to 1 000), the middle cycle being measured in thousands (1 000 to 10 000), and the upper cycle measured in ten thousands (10 000 and upwards). The three cycles, measured in this way, were quite sufficient to include all the actual values. In a similar manner, the student must adapt the ratio grid to the figures he is called on to deal with.

For example, the first cycle may be in units, the next in tens, and the third in hundreds. The essential point is that the scale of each cycle must be 10 times that of the previous one.

Note Each cycle or block is subdivided into nine main sections (not ten, as in ordinary graph paper).

Time series

The analysis of a time series, with graphical examples, is dealt with in Chapter 10. It is sufficient to say here that if we wish to compare two or more curves on one time series graph we can do this in two basic ways:

(*a*) All curves which are of the *same nature and in the same units* (e.g., bank advances and bank investments) can be plotted using one axis scaled in those units. The curves will then be directly comparable.

(*b*) Two curves which are *different in nature or are in different units*, e.g., exports and savings (different nature), or unemployment and bank deposits (different nature and different units), can be plotted using the left-hand vertical axis for one type of unit, and the right-hand vertical axis for the other. In these cases, although the *rise and fall* of the curves may be compared, the curves as a whole are not directly comparable (see Fig. 5.12).

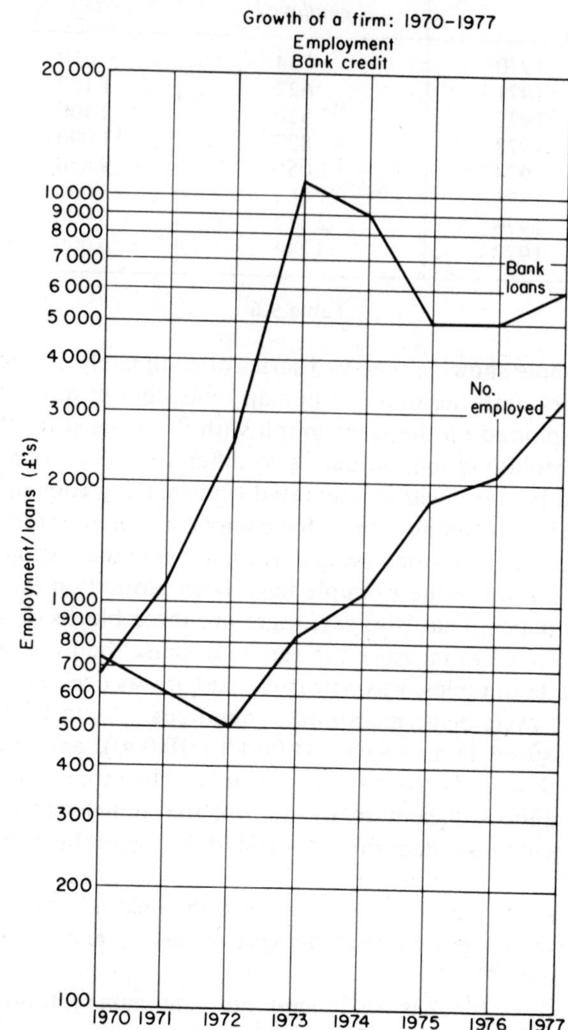

Fig. 5.12 Growth of a firm: 1970–1977. Employment, Bank credit

As has been mentioned previously, the x-axis is always chosen to show the time scale, and the y-axis to show the variable. Confusion often arises when plotting from the time axis. If the variable values are known to be mid-year, or mid-monthly figures, for instance, then the points should be plotted *between* the yearly or monthly intervals along the x-axis. In practice, say, for mid-year figures, points are usually plotted *on* the yearly limits, and a special note is included on the graph to allow the reader to make the appropriate mental correction. For example, 'Figures relate to total deposits on 30 June each year', or, 'Yearly figures of total deposits are averages of the monthly totals'.

Band curve charts

These are sometimes known as 'layer' graphs. This form of time series graph is often used where totals over a period can be broken up into constituent parts.

For example, *bank assets:* cash, bills, advances, investments.
textiles: wool, cotton, jute, man-made fibres.

A typical graph is shown in Fig. 5.13.

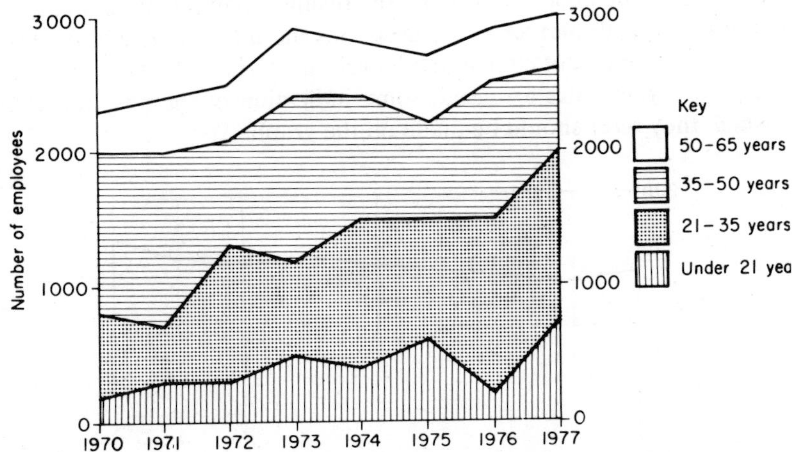

Fig. 5.13 Age distribution of employees XYZ Ltd, 1970–1977

Note The additional vertical scale at the right-hand side, and also the patterning of the bands, are to help the reader.

The series, of course, must each be sub-totals of a total group in the same units.

In this particular case, the curves were plotted directly from actual figures, but, when this is not convenient, secondary statistics can be derived, e.g., by reducing the actual values to percentages of the total (100 per cent).

Rules for graphical work

(*a*) The title must be clearly stated on the graph, and it should be written on last so as not to interfere with the curves on the graph.
(*b*) All axes should be scaled and labelled with the variable they represent, and the units of the variable should be shown where necessary.
(*c*) All lettering on graphs should follow the normal horizontal pattern except in the case of vertical axes (right and left hand) when lettering should be done as at (i) and (ii):

(i) OUTPUT or— (ii) OUTPUT and *not*— (iii) O U T P U T

(*d*) Sources and footnotes, and a key, should be provided when necessary in a clear space on the graph.

(*e*) In a natural (arithmetic or absolute) scale graph the zero line must be shown.

(*f*) The graph should not be loaded with many curves, especially if the lines of the curves tend to run closely together (in the case of histograms it is inadvisable to draw two on one graph).

(*g*) Plan the graph well, taking careful note of the range of each variable, and draw the graph to fill the available paper. Graphs which are crowded into a corner of the paper are usually the result of bad initial planning.

(*h*) If ratio (logarithmic) scales are used, this should be quite plainly shown on the graph, unless, of course, the logarithmic grid is shown.

(*i*) If percentage scales are used, some indication of the absolute values to which they refer should be made on the graph.

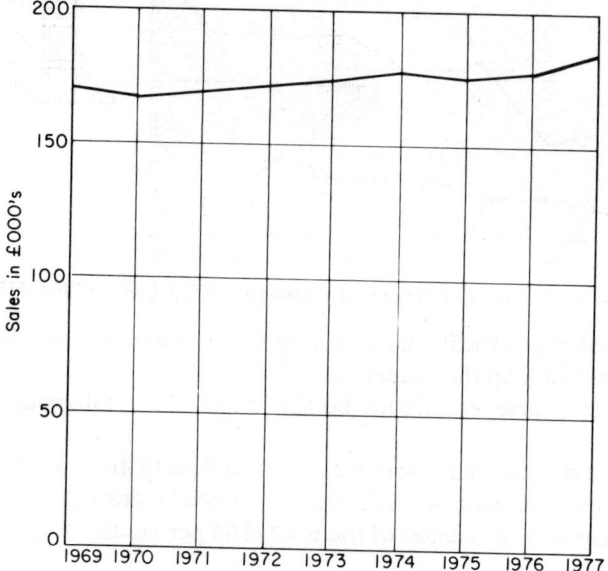

Fig. 5.14 Sales of a firm, 1969–1977

(*j*) If the application of rule (*e*) would result in much blank paper, and a compression of the vertical scale (see Fig. 5.14), this may be overcome in two ways:

(i) the vertical scale may show a 'pleated' or 'broken' portion, to indicate that some of the (empty) space has been compressed (see Fig. 5.15).

(ii) Alternatively, the vertical scale may be broken by two jagged lines running across the diagram to indicate that a portion of the (empty) space has been omitted (see Fig. 5.16).

Note In each case, a much more open vertical scale is possible which reveals any movement in the graph more clearly.

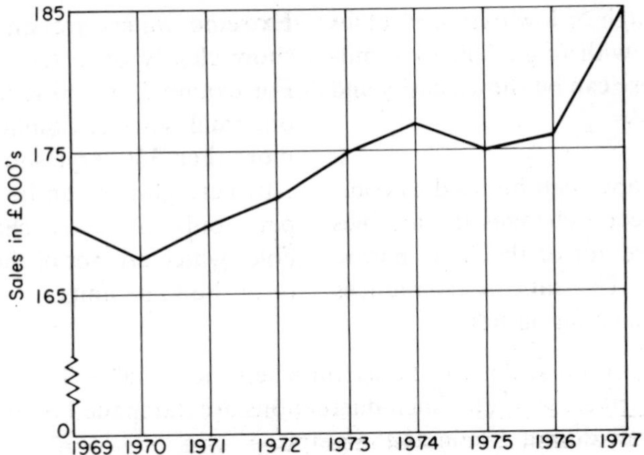

Fig. 5.15 Sales of a firm, 1969 to 1977

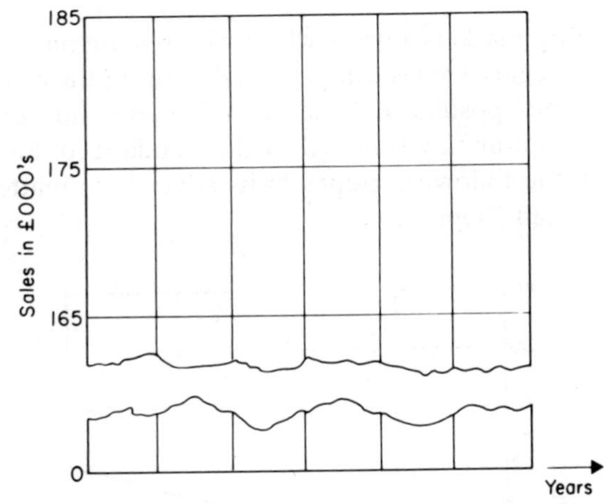

Fig. 5.16 Sales of a firm, 1969 to 1977

Use and interpretation

Comparison of ratio and absolute scales

Feature and uses:

Ratio scales	*Absolute scales*
(*a*) Show the rate of change of a variable.	Show the actual size of the change in a variable.
(*b*) No zero base line.	Zero base line included.
(*c*) Negative quantities cannot be shown.	Negative quantities can be shown.
(*d*) On the ratio axis, equal distances represent equal percentage changes.	On the absolute axis, equal distances represent equal actual values.

(*e*) Where high or low extreme values are met with (e.g., 300 to 1 million) these can be shown easily and clearly.	Extreme values are often difficult to show clearly on a fairly small graph. For example, if 300 is represented by one small square, 1 million would need more than 330 large squares.
(*f*) Ratio graphs can be used to compare directly changes in variables which are not of the same nature or units. The ratio scale reduces them to a common base.	Absolute graphs can be used to compare, only indirectly, changes in variables which are not of the same nature or of the same units.

In addition, ratio scales can be useful when the variable fluctuates violently, e.g., during strikes, war, etc. Such fluctuations are dampened by the use of ratio scales, and they do not dominate the graph.

Ratio scales are particularly appropriate for series where the current figures depend directly on past figures for their magnitude, e.g., future population and past population, birth-rate and population.

Examples of bad graphs

Suppose that a firm markets a drink which will 'release one's hidden stores of energy' and that it begins a sales campaign, advertising through various media, newspapers, magazines, posters, and television. Suppose, further, that it employs a statistician who is not unduly troubled by the standards of his profession. The firm might publish the following graphs in its advertising matter. The name of the product we will call *Zippy*.

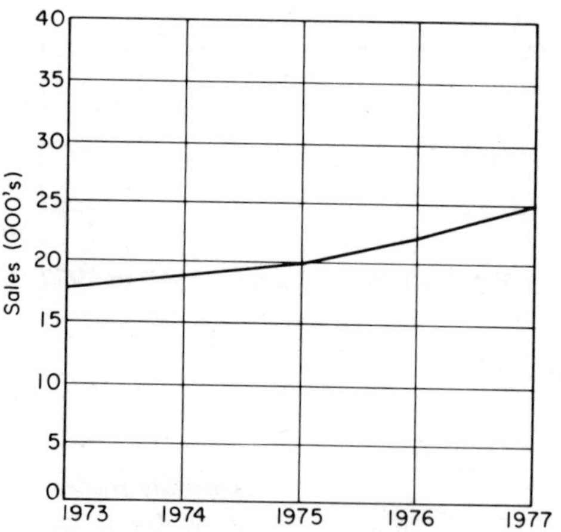

Fig. 5.17 Sales of Zippy

There appears to be nothing wrong with the graph shown in Fig. 5.17, though actually the reason for a steeper increase in sales from 1975 was possible partly because of a heavy cut in the price of *Zippy*—and were we to graph the sales curve in *value* terms (instead of units sold), the curve would be much less steep. Though the graph tells nothing of this, we cannot fairly complain.

However, it appears to the manager that the graph is not striking enough, and he suggests to the statistician that the graph might look a little better in the form of Fig. 5.18.

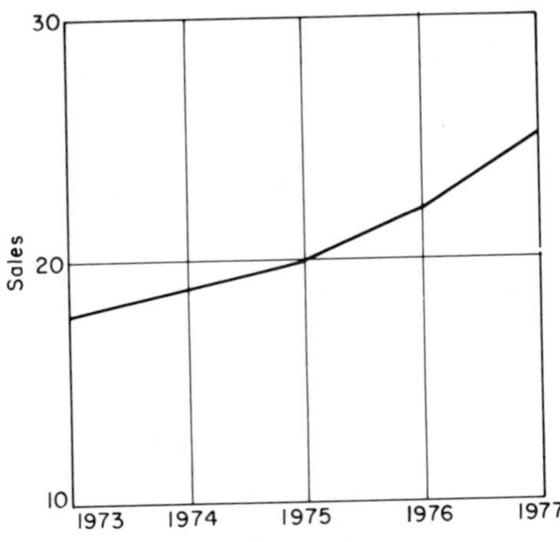

Fig. 5.18 Sales of Zippy

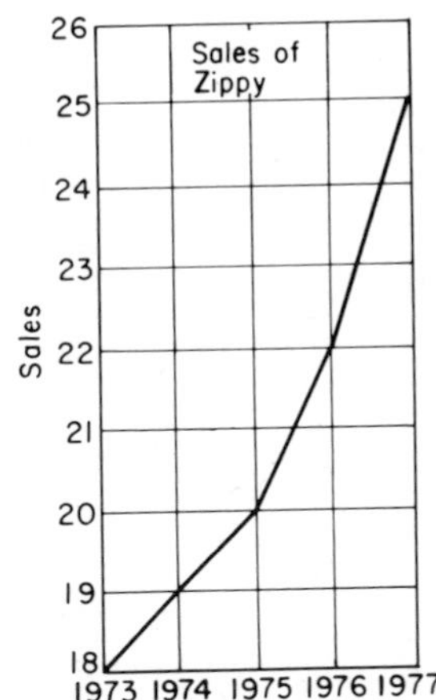

Fig. 5.19

Here we see that the extreme ends of the vertical scale have been cut off, and this gives the impression of a rather steeper rise. It is contrary to the rules of good graph-making, of course, to begin above zero, unless the axis is 'broken', and even that is not necessary here. Units have also been missed off the vertical scale.

Not content with the previous distortion, the firm produces an even more sensational graph, as shown in Fig. 5.19.

The tremendous rise in sales indicated here is achieved simply by spreading out the narrow band of sales, on the vertical axis, within which actual sales took place, and crushing together the periods on the time axis. Sales appear to have risen from almost nothing to almost the limit of possibility. The student can see that the steepness of a curve can be arranged on any graph merely by altering the scales on each axis and cutting down the frame of the graph. This graph offends the rules even more than the second graph, because there is definite intent to deceive more plainly apparent.

Having sinned twice, it seems to the firm worth little to forbear once more. So a further graph appears in the advertisements—this one calculated to have even greater emotional appeal (see Fig. 5.20).

The idea of the graph is to imply that *Zippy* will penetrate the 'tiredness barrier', which prevents 'energy release'; other drinks will not. It will be noticed that no axes are labelled either by title or unit, neither are the axes scaled. Presumably the horizontal axis is 'time', but the statistician is probably contemptuous of the kind of people who would be impressed by such a 'graph' anyhow and has not bothered to record minutes, hours, etc. The vertical axis apparently measures 'tiredness depth' in some mysterious way. As this is unmeasurable, it is pointless to include it on the graph anyway. The 'tiredness barrier' appears to be sheer nonsense.

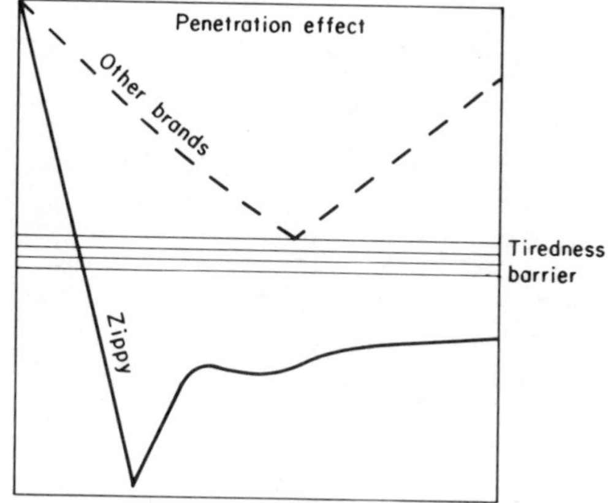

Fig. 5.20

A further way of increasing sales is, of course, to invade your competitors' market. To compare the national sales of similar beverages with *Zippy*, the firm's statistician drew the graph shown in Fig. 5.21.

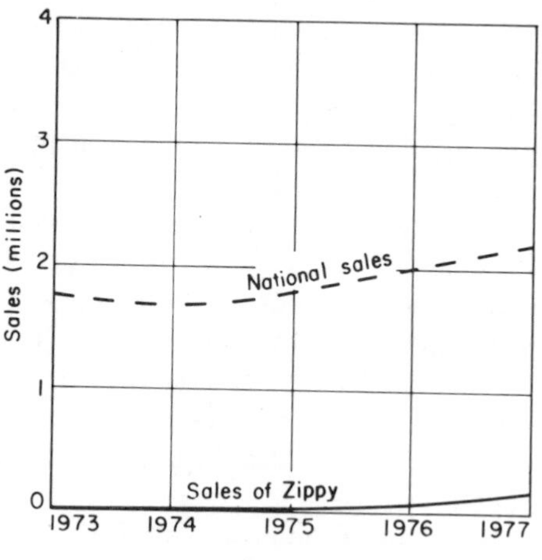

Fig. 5.21

He did not submit this to the manager for publication, however, for fear of receiving the answer that his graph lacked conviction. A few minutes more reflection turned possible defeat into victory and produced the surprising picture given in Fig. 5.22.

The effect in Fig. 5.22 is produced simply by placing two different vertical scales at each side of the graph and then manipulating them so as to produce the most favourable effect for one particular curve. The axes are scaled, but the too

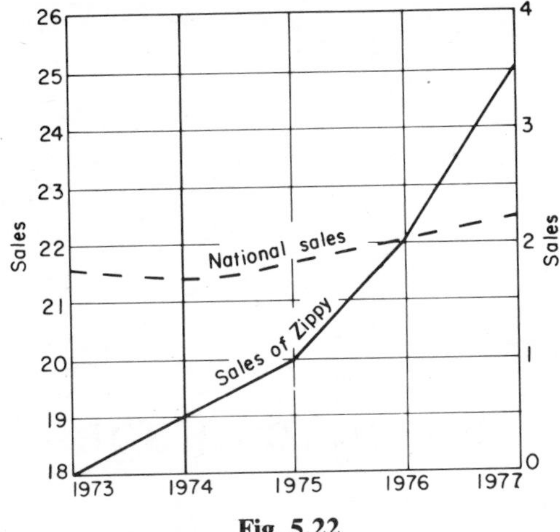

Fig. 5.22

casual reader, it is hoped, will not notice the different scales. For instance, why should only one axis begin at zero? *Note*, also, the lack of units.

It appears in Fig. 5.23 that the promoters of *Zippy* have become obsessed by delusions of future grandeur. In this graph they have actually drawn a curve between only two plotted points, and these points range over a period of eighteen years. On this pathetic basis they have projected into the future in respect of sales in a way that no honest statistician would ever dream of doing. The student will notice that the date 1984, only seven years from 1977, is marked at the same distance from 1977 as is 1959, where the difference is eighteen years!

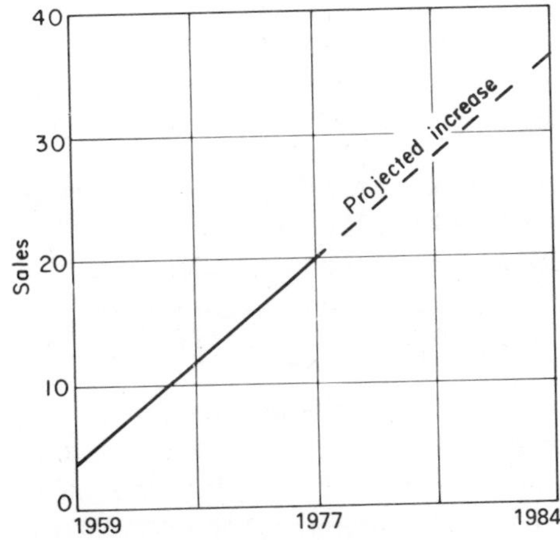

Fig. 5.23 Projected sales of Zippy

These examples do not, of course, exhaust the appetite for misrepresentation of firms like this imaginary one, and the student is urged to scan current literature for further examples. Unfortunately, he will not have far to seek.

6

Accuracy, errors, and percentages

Method

Most numbers found in published statistics are not strictly accurate (i.e., they have been 'rounded'), for reasons to be discussed later.

Rounding numbers

This is a method of expressing the approximate value of data. We are usually asked to express a number to the nearest hundred, or some similar unit, but sometimes we work to so many 'significant figures'.

An example might be the value 132 854·54 kg.

(*a*) If we wished to express this to the nearest hundred we should first determine how many hundreds are contained in the number—$1\,328\frac{54{\cdot}54}{100}$ hundredths of kg. If the remainder, or fractional part of a hundred is *exactly one half or more*, then we increase the total of whole hundreds by one. The answer in this case would be 132 900.

This rounding may be done for other units as follows:

132 854·54 kg to the nearest whole number	= 132 855
132 854·54 kg to the nearest ten	= 132 850
132 854·54 kg to the nearest hundred	= 132 900
132 854·54 kg to the nearest thousand	= 133 000
132 854·54 kg to the nearest ten thousand	= 130 000

If the method of rounding is not stated, we can determine it by the number of noughts in the estimate, for example, when there are three noughts, it is in thousands, and so on. *Note* also that 132 900, to the nearest hundred, means within the range 132 950 to 132 850. So far as we know, the true figure could lie anywhere between 50 kg either side of the approximation. We usually write this as 132 900 ± 50 kg (i.e., half the number of noughts).

Similarly, when we see at the head of a table the unit stated as '000's kg', we know that each figure in the table is subject to an error of ±500 kg.

(*b*) Another form of rounding occurs when we are asked to express a value to a certain number of significant figures.

A significant figure is usually considered to be any number from 1 to 9 (inclusive). But when zero occurs between two significant figures, then zero is regarded as a significant figure.

For example, express 34·801, 42 367, and 6 015·2 to three significant figures.

34·801 = 34·8
42 367 = 42 400
6 015·2 = 6 020

(*c*) One might be asked to find an answer 'correct to two decimal places'. In this case, the student should work out the answer to three decimal places:

474·328

and then round it to two decimal places. In other words, work out one more than is asked for, and then round to the correct number:

474·33

Degrees of accuracy

We may summarize the degrees of accuracy which one finds stated formally, for the figure 5 672·835 grams

(*a*) To the nearest hundred = 5 700 grams,
(*b*) To 3 significant figures = 5 670 grams,
(*c*) Correct to 1 decimal place = 5 672·8 grams.

Errors

POSSIBLE ERRORS

Where the actual or true value is not known, it is usual to express the degree of possible error in two more ways:

(*d*) 5 500 ± 500 grams,
(*e*) 5 600 ± 3 per cent.

These two ways show the possible error either side of the approximate, or estimated, value:

in (*d*) the possible range in which the true figure lies is 5 000 grams to 6 000 grams
in (*e*) the possible range in which the true figure lies is 5 432 grams to 5 768 grams.

ABSOLUTE ERRORS

The absolute error is the difference between the actual, or true, value and the approximate (rounded or estimated) value.

Actual value = 3 752·9 kg
Estimated value = 3 800 kg
Absolute error = +47·1 kg

When an estimate is stated as $3\,800 \pm 50$, then the 50 is the absolute error, since the true value is not known.

RELATIVE ERRORS

The relative error is found by expressing the absolute error as a percentage of the actual, or true, value. (If the actual value is not known, the absolute error is expressed as a percentage of the estimated value—the difference here will not actually be large.) For example:

$$\begin{aligned} \text{Actual value} &= 3\,752{\cdot}9 \text{ kg} \\ \text{Absolute error} &= +47{\cdot}1 \text{ kg} \\ \text{Relative error} &= \frac{+47{\cdot}1}{3\,752{\cdot}9} \times 100 = +1{\cdot}26 \text{ per cent} \end{aligned}$$

OR

$$\begin{aligned} \text{Actual value} &= 3\,752{\cdot}9 \text{ kg} \\ \text{Estimated value} &= 3\,800 \text{ kg} \\ \text{Absolute error} &= +47{\cdot}1 \\ \text{Relative error} &= \frac{+47{\cdot}1}{3\,800} \times 100 = +1{\cdot}24 \text{ per cent} \end{aligned}$$

Conversely, a relative error can easily be turned into an absolute one:

$$\begin{aligned} 3\,800 \text{ kg} \pm 3 \text{ per cent} &= 3\,800 \text{ kg} \pm \left(\frac{3}{100} \times \frac{3\,800}{1}\right) \\ &= 3\,800 \text{ kg} \pm 114 \text{ kg} \end{aligned}$$

An absolute error is always in the same unit as the figure to which it refers, but a relative error is not in any unit—it is a pure percentage—the units cancel out in the division sum.

CUMULATIVE (BIASED) ERRORS

This kind of error is produced when the errors in a table of figures are all in the same direction (see example below). This would mean, for example, that the greater the number of items in the table to be added, the larger the resulting error. (In Table 6.1, the figures in the last two columns are taken to the highest ten above the actual figures, and to the lowest ten below the actual figures.)

COMPENSATING (UNBIASED) ERRORS

These occur when the errors in a table of approximate figures tend to cancel each other out. Thus, when the figures below were rounded to the nearest ten, the total came very close to the true addition of the actual figures. In this case, when the number of items in the table to be added is greater, the compensating error tends generally to diminish.

Example:

Earnings in £'s	*True figure*	*Compensating (rounded)*	*Cumulative (highest ten)*	*Cumulative (lowest ten)*
80 and under 90	41	40	50	40
90 and under 100	62	60	70	60
100 and under 110	87	90	90	80
110 and under 120	96	100	100	90
120 and under 130	32	30	40	30
130 and under 140	39	40	40	30
TOTALS	357	360	390	330
Absolute errors		+3	+33	−27
Relative errors		+0·8%	+8·5%	−8·2%

Table 6.1 Monthly earnings of male workers

As can be seen, the compensating error, achieved by rounding, is far smaller than when the errors are cumulative.

Laws of errors

(*a*) *Addition* When approximate values are added, the total error is the sum of the separate absolute errors in the values.

300 to the nearest 10, plus 400 to the nearest 100

$$\begin{array}{r} 300 \pm 5 \\ 400 \pm 50 \\ \hline = 700 \pm 55 \end{array}$$

(*b*) *Subtraction* When approximate values are subtracted, the total error is the sum of the separate absolute errors in the values.

400 to the nearest 100, minus 300 to the nearest 10

$$\begin{array}{r} 400 \pm 50 \\ 300 \pm 5 \\ \hline = 100 \pm 55 \end{array}$$

The error here is so large as to make the estimated answer useless. This is always a danger with subtraction, and in an actual business situation, the estimates must be made as accurately as possible, even if this takes longer.

(*c*) *Multiplication* When approximate values are multiplied together, the total error is approximately the sum of the relative errors in the values.

300 to the nearest 10, times 400 to the nearest 100

$$\left(300 \pm \frac{5}{300} \times 100\right) \text{ times } \left(400 \pm \frac{50}{400} \times 100\right)$$
$$= (300 \pm 1{\cdot}67 \text{ per cent}) \text{ times } (400 \pm 12{\cdot}5 \text{ per cent})$$
$$= 120\,000 \pm 14{\cdot}17 \text{ per cent}$$

What we have done here, is to convert the absolute errors into relative errors, and then add them. A similar procedure is used in division.

(*d*) *Division* When approximate values are used in division, the total error is approximately the sum of the relative errors in the values.

400 to the nearest 100, divided by 300 to the nearest 10

$$\left(400 \pm \frac{50}{400} \times 100\right) \text{ divided by } \left(300 \pm \frac{5}{300} \times 100\right)$$
$$= (400 \pm 12{\cdot}5 \text{ per cent}) \text{ divided by } (300 \pm 1{\cdot}67 \text{ per cent})$$
$$= 1{\cdot}33 \pm 14{\cdot}17 \text{ per cent}$$

The student will find it easy to apply these rules if he remembers the following points:

(*a*) Use absolute errors for addition and subtraction. Use relative errors for multiplication and division.

(*b*) Always add errors—*never* subtract them.

Percentages

(*a*) Ratios and percentages (like the relative errors described above) tell us of the *rate* of change in given values. If we confuse them with *absolute values* we are likely to give our statistics a misleading turn and the reader a wrong impression.

Example:

In area A the number of deaths from cancer has risen by 400 per cent, while in area B, over the same period, the number of deaths from cancer has risen by only 29 per cent.

One may receive the impression that area A is somehow a much less healthy place. The true position is as follows:

	Population	*Deaths from Cancer (1)*	*Deaths from Cancer (2)*	*Absolute increase*	%
Area A	200	10	50	40	400
Area B	120 000	350	451	101	29

Table 6.2

The absolute figures of increase for area B are far greater than those of area A. Also, area A may well be a small country place with a high proportion of old people in which we would expect cancer deaths to occur with a high (and highly variable) frequency. This may have been a bad year.

Misleading figures can produce even more misleading impressions and interpretations. In this case, we must either give the reader all the relevant figures, or we must somehow scale down the exaggerated percentage (400), to take account of the very low population of area A. Every effort must be made to compare figures on the same basis.

(*b*) Another case may illustrate the misleading use of ratios and percentages. Sometimes we are asked to derive statistics (secondary statistics) from given tables of figures. For example, we may wish to calculate the percentage increases in unemployment over a number of years:

Year	*1*	*2*	*3*	*4*
Unemployment	200 000	252 000	310 000	376 000

Table 6.3

There are at least two ways in which we can calculate the percentage increase here:

Method (i)

Year 2 (increase on Year 1) = 26 per cent
Year 3 (increase on Year 2) = 23 per cent
Year 4 (increase on Year 3) = 21 per cent

Method (ii)

Year 2 (increase on Year 1) = 26 per cent
Year 3 (increase on Year 1) = 55 per cent
Year 4 (increase on Year 1) = 88 per cent

In *Method* (i), where the percentage increase seems to be falling, the percentage rise is worked out using the year immediately preceding as the base year. In *Method* (ii), the percentage increase is worked out using Year 1 as the base year for each calculation, and the rise appears to be growing rapidly!

Once again, figures must be compared on the same basis, or else the method of working must be explained to the reader.

(*c*) Some students have difficulty in averaging percentages when asked to derive statistics. The simple rule of 'weighting' (see Averages, Chapter 7), must usually be observed. In many examples, percentages are derived from different base figures, and if we wish to calculate an overall percentage from the percentage figures already worked out, we cannot simply take a straight average. An example may make this clear:

	1976	*1977*	*% Increase or decrease*
Colliery P	30 000	30 500	+1·7
Colliery Q	15 000	16 000	+6·7
Colliery R	16 000	20 000	+25·0
TOTALS	61 000	66 500	+9·0

Table 6.4 Regional coal output (kg)

In this example it would be wrong to assume that the total (or overall) percentage increase is simply

$$\frac{1{\cdot}7+6{\cdot}7+25{\cdot}0}{3}=11{\cdot}1 \text{ per cent.}$$

The correct method is to weight each individual percentage by its corresponding base year figure:

$$\frac{(30\,000\times 1{\cdot}7)+(15\,000\times 6{\cdot}7)+(16\,000\times 25{\cdot}0)}{61\,000}=9{\cdot}0 \text{ per cent.}$$

This gives the same result, of course, as the calculation of the percentage increase in the totals:

$$\frac{66\,500-61\,000}{61\,000}\times 100=9{\cdot}0 \text{ per cent.}$$

Use and interpretation

Accuracy

Strict accuracy is not to be found in any branch of applied human knowledge. Even in science, from the study of microbiology to interplanetary rocket-launching, exact measurement does not really exist.

In the social sciences, especially, we are hampered at the outset by the problem that the things we wish to measure are people, or the results of people's actions. As was suggested in Chapter 1, people and human events are much less predictable than atoms and molecules. One cannot subject people, exports, or unemployment to controlled laboratory conditions and measure them or test them for reactions. Statisticians in the business, or government fields must rely on interviewers, the postman, and on individual bodies and agencies for pieces of information collected inside or outside the country, in all sorts of conditions, and at various times. In this situation, accuracy must be very much a compromise, though we should try to make it a good compromise.

The government would never dream of publishing a statement such as 'the value of goods and services exported in 1977 was £9 740 363 217·35'. And if it did, we could be certain of one thing—the figure would be wrong! Such accuracy, especially in the matter of exports, is unbelievably precise. Not only can we disbelieve the pence, but also the figures after the first four. It is extremely doubtful whether even the first four figures are within £100 million of the true figure! Yet, this seemingly large degree of possible error is quite acceptable if we compare it with figures of thousands of millions of pounds which make up our national accounts, of which exports is a part. In this situation we are well content with a useful figure which is taken to the 'nearest million pounds'. To define the figure more precisely would cost more than such a figure would be worth, if, indeed, it were possible.

Similarly, the government found it only necessary to express the population of the UK as 55 757 thousand in 1971. This shows a greater degree of accuracy than in the previous case, and is presumably worth the far greater census expenditure entailed.

To summarize, we can say that the three limitations on accuracy are:

(*a*) the *possibility* of greater accuracy
(*b*) the *desirability* of greater accuracy
(*c*) the *cost* of greater accuracy, in time and money

Time, in the last respect, is often more valuable than money. Statistics collected probably at great cost may be useless if they are out-of-date by the time they are presented.

Many examination candidates, often in their desire to please, go beyond the requirements of the question in the matter of accuracy. This, for example, might take the form of working out more decimal places than are asked for. This is the way to lose marks. But when no particular degree of accuracy is asked for, the candidate must simply use his discretion, and work to a degree at least as accurate as the figures which make up the particular question.

Rounding

Two reasons may be given for rounding numbers:

(*a*) Most figures (see above) are approximations from the outset. Therefore, no great harm is done by rounding them, so long as we round all the figures in the same section to the same degree of accuracy.

	Wrong		Right
	361 000		361 000
	427 885		428 000
	39 000		39 000
	2 000		2 000
TOTAL	829 885	TOTAL	830 000

(*b*) The average reader (to whom we are likely to present our statistics) will be simply bemused, if not irritated, by figures running into millions which pretend to great accuracy.
£3 436m is much more readily appreciated than £3 436 428 376.

Errors

By errors in the sense of the previous section we do *not* mean mistakes in calculation or measurement. As has been said above, there are limitations to the degree of accuracy which we can achieve. Therefore, a compromise must be sought, and approximate figures agreed upon. Although one may not know the exact figures in an enquiry, one can often tell almost certainly the margin, or range, within which the correct figure lies. It is in this sense that a margin of error can be assigned to figures.

Percentages

As we suggested under *Method*, most of the percentages which the student will be asked to calculate will probably be concerned with report writing. The student is usually given a table of figures which can be compared much more easily by reducing some or all of them to percentages. As enough has already been said on percentage calculations some suggestions are offered on *report writing* in examinations.

Report writing

It is often said that there are three main rules to be observed in the writing of a report:

(*a*) Accuracy,
(*b*) Brevity,
(*c*) Clarity.

Apart from the labour of deriving additional statistics which suggest the growth and performance of the original figures, the student must break down the report into sections.

Suitable sections might be:

(*a*) A description of the changes and direction of change in the figures.
As this is not the important interpretative part of the report, it should be extremely brief and, if the student wishes, may be left out completely.
(*b*) Comments should be made on the relationship and dependence of the figures on one another. If necessary, derived statistics, tables, and charts could be used sparingly to illustrate such comments.
(*c*) This section should show why the figures have changed. Here the student's knowledge of economic or business affairs will be tested, as will his knowledge of the events of the period under discussion.
(*d*) Finally, an intelligent projection into the future, if this is possible and suitable, would not be out of place. This section should not be too long because it may be regarded as part of the previous sections.

It is often a mistake to try to sum up at the end of such a report. A conclusion of this nature may distort your previous arguments in an attempt to condense them, and at the best your conclusion may be mere repetition. Let each section stand on its own feet.

Titles and headings, references to the tables of figures, and your derived statistics, must be clear and full. A great deal depends on the student's narrative powers and on his understanding of statistics, and their everyday use. This is a searching type of question which demands more than sheer memory or the mechanical recitation of formulae.

7

Averages

Method

It is important to be able to describe a group of items so as to distinguish it from some other group which might have many similar characteristics.

If one were asked to contact Mr Jones, in a crowd of people, it would obviously help if we knew that he was the very tall man, the very fat one, or possibly the one whose left shoulder drooped. The more details given about him, the easier he would be to identify. In this chapter, we shall concern ourselves with the 'height' of Mr Jones, leaving his other features to Chapter 8.

The average value of a set of grouped or ungrouped data may be looked at in two ways. It is a method of picking out a typical or representative item from the group. It is also a measure of central tendency, i.e., a point round which the data tend to locate themselves. On a graph, it serves to fix the position of the curve, in relation to the horizontal scale.

There are several types of average which can be used to summarize a set of data. These are discussed below.

The arithmetic mean (usually referred to as A.M.).

This is the best-known type of average, and it is popularly used to summarize a batsman's or a footballer's score. It replaces a long list of runs or goals scored throughout the season.

Ungrouped data The simple arithmetic mean for ungrouped data may be expressed by this fraction:

$$\text{Arithmetic mean} = \frac{\text{total value of items}}{\text{total number of items}}$$

Thus, if during a season, a batsman scores 22, 8, 0, 14, 5, and 17 runs in 6 innings—applying the formula, we get:

$$\text{A.M.} = \frac{22+8+0+14+5+17}{6} = \frac{66}{6} = 11 \text{ runs.}$$

Note (1) The zero score must be included as an item in the denominator (6 items altogether).

Note (2) Although during his 6 innings the batsman never *actually* scored 11 runs, nevertheless, the scores above and below 11 are exactly balanced round this figure.

Grouped data Where we have grouped data to deal with, i.e., where the items are numerous and are arranged in class intervals, we must use a *weighted arithmetic mean* rather than a simple arithmetic mean.

The short table below shows the scores of 15 batsmen:

Runs scored	*No. of batsmen*
6	4
8	4
12	5
17	1
34	1
TOTAL	15

Table 7.1

The class interval here is in single runs. It is obviously incorrect simply to add the 'Runs scored' column, and divide by the total 'No. of batsmen', or even to add the 'Runs scored' column and divide by 5 (the number of class intervals). Students frequently make such careless mistakes. Each class interval must be first multiplied by its corresponding frequency (No. of batsmen) in order that due weight be given to each score.

1 *Runs scored*	*2* *No. of batsmen*	*3* *Col. 1 × Col. 2*
6	4	24
8	4	32
12	5	60
17	1	17
34	1	34
TOTALS	15	167

Table 7.2

The 'Total value of items'—167 runs—is then divided by the 'Total number of items'—15—to give the A.M. as:

$$\frac{167}{15} = 11{\cdot}13 \text{ runs.}$$

This is the correct method to use when the class interval consists of a *single figure in a discrete series.*

When we deal with grouped data where the class interval consists of values over a range (the more normal case), the method is slightly different.

Consider the table given in Chapter 5.

Weekly earnings (£)	*No. of workers* (000's)
20–29·99	52
30–39·99	256
40–49·99	170
50–59·99	68
60–69·99	30
70 and over	24
TOTAL	600

Table 7.3 Weekly earnings in an industrial region

The mid-points of the class intervals are found, and these mid-points are taken to be rough averages, representative of each class. We are making the assumption here that the number of items in each class is spread evenly round the mid-point; i.e., the average value in the first class interval is £25. This is the best we can do lacking more detailed information, in spite of the fact that our assumption may be wrong. In fact, our assumption *is* wrong! If the student will look at Table 5.2 he will see that, in this particular example, the first class interval was weighted heavily with items at its upper end. Nevertheless with only the simple table above to go on, this is the assumption we must make.

Each mid-point is multiplied or weighted by the corresponding frequency, as follows:

1 *Weekly earnings* (£)	*2* *No. of workers* (000's)	*3* *Mid-points*	*4* *Col. 2* × *Col. 3*
20–29·99	52	25	1 300
30–39·99	256	35	8 960
40–49·99	170	45	7 650
50–59·99	68	55	3 740
60–69·99	30	65	1 950
70 and over	24	75	1 800
TOTALS	600	—	25 400

Table 7.4 Weekly earnings in an industrial region

The total of col. 4 gives the Total value of items in our previous formula for the A.M. All that remains is to divide this figure by the Total number of items, i.e., the total of col. 2.

Note The figures for 'No. of workers' are in 000's, and therefore, strictly speaking, the figures in col. 4 should have been multiplied by 1 000, to give 1 300 000, 8 960 000, etc. In practice we can ignore this point, because we would merely be multiplying and dividing by 1 000.

Thus, $$£\frac{25\,400\,000}{600\,000} = £42{\cdot}33.$$

It should be realized that this answer is, at the best, only an approximation. There are several reasons for this:

(*a*) 'No. of workers' figures are presumably given to the nearest 1 000.
(*b*) Actual earnings figures may not be spread evenly over the class intervals—it would be quite remarkable if they were! Therefore, the mid-point figures may not be suitable.
(*c*) The last open-ended class is presumed to end at £80—this, in fact, may not be true.
(*d*) It is hoped that any errors made in compiling the table may be compensating—particularly in the case of the figure '600 000 workers'. It is probable that, as only six classes have been taken, there might be considerable error in this figure.

Short methods of calculating the arithmetic mean

Where the student meets with lengthy or complex frequency tables, he may adopt a short-cut by using the 'arbitrary origin', or, as it is commonly called, the 'assumed mean', or 'working mean'.

Ungrouped data In our first example in this chapter, we were given the figures for a batsman's scores as follows:

22, 8, 0, 14, 5, 17.

With such a small number of items, the A.M. is easily found by the ordinary method, but we will repeat the example to show the basic principle.

We first assume an A.M., say, 10 runs. We then take the deviations of each actual figure from the assumed mean, and give our results an appropriate + or − sign.

Runs scored	*Deviations from assumed A.M. of 10 Runs*	
	+	−
22	12	
8		2
0		10
14	4	
5		5
17	7	
TOTALS	+23	−17

Table 7.5

The balance of the + and − deviations is +6. We find the average of this total deviation by dividing it by the total number of innings (six):

$$\frac{+6}{6} = +1.$$

Finally, we add this result (or subtract if it is negative) to the assumed mean:

$$10 + 1 = 11 \text{ runs.}$$

Thus we find the same answer as before. The student must not think that, because we have 'guessed' the assumed mean, there is any guess-work or inexactness about this answer. The answer is absolutely accurate, and the 'estimated' mean of 10 was revised to the correct mean of 11 in the course of the calculation.

Grouped data We can apply the same principle to our first example in grouped data (Table 7.1), in which the A.M. score of the batsmen was calculated as 11·13 runs. Let us assume a mean of 10 runs. Our table is then set down as follows:

1 Runs scored	*2* No. of batsmen	*3* Deviation from assumed mean of 10 runs		*4* Col. 2 × Col. 3	
		+	−	+	−
6	4		4		16
8	4		2		8
12	5	2		10	
17	1	7		7	
34	1	24		24	
TOTALS	15	—	—	+41	−24

Table 7.6

The balance of the + and − weighted deviations is therefore +17. Taking the average of this deviation for the 15 batsmen, we get

$$\frac{+17}{15} = +1 \cdot 13.$$

This result is added to the assumed mean,

$$10 + 1 \cdot 13 = 11 \cdot 13,$$

which is the same answer we obtained before.

A similar short method is given below for the example in Table 7.3. The mid-points have been calculated as before, but instead of setting down 25, 35, 45, etc., we have decided to take £45 as the assumed mean (this being a convenient mid-point), and to record this in the mid-point column as 0. Because the remaining mid-points above and below £45 are all at intervals of £10, we can work in units of £10, which will reduce the deviations to single digits. For example, the mid-point of £65 is £20 more, which is 2 units of £10, or +2. Deviations below the £45 are given a minus sign.

1 *Weekly earnings* (*£*)	*2* *No. of workers* (*000's*)	*3* *Mid-points deviation from £45* *Units of £10*	*4* *Col. 2 × Col. 3 deviations*
20–29·99	52	−2	−104
30–39·99	256	−1	−256
40–49·99	170	0	0
50–59·99	68	+1	+68
60–69·99	30	+2	+60
70 and over	24	+3	+72
TOTALS	600	—	−160

Table 7.7 Weekly earnings in an industrial region

$$\text{True arithmetic mean} = £45 + £\left(-\frac{160}{600} \times 10\right) = £45 - £2{\cdot}67 = £42{\cdot}33.$$

It can be appreciated that this simplification reduces paper arithmetic to mental arithmetic, as well as cutting out one calculation (third row down) altogether. But it is essential to be careful about the correction, i.e., to balance out the plus and minus deviations, obtain the average of the result, multiply this by the class interval (£10 in our example), and either add to, or subtract from, the assumed mean. *Note* The correction $\left(-\frac{160}{600} \times 10\right)$ which we make to the assumed mean must be fully worked out before we subtract it from, or add it to, the assumed mean. For this reason the correction is put in brackets.

A point of interest in calculations using the assumed mean is that if the plus and minus deviations were to cancel out each other *exactly*, this would mean that we had chosen, by chance, the true mean as our assumed mean. This illustrates the idea of the A.M., which is a point in a distribution where plus and minus deviations of the individual items cancel each other out.

The mode

Another well-known average, the mode, is best remembered by the French phrase *à la mode*, meaning 'in the fashion'. In a distribution, the modal average is the most fashionable value among the items. 'Fashionable' is taken to mean 'most frequently occurring', so that the modal average is the value which most frequently occurs among all the items in the distribution. For example, in Table 7.6, listing runs scored by 15 batsmen, the mode is 12 runs, because 5 batsmen made this score, while the other scores were achieved by fewer batsmen in each case.

It is usual to refer to the 'modal class' where data is presented in class intervals containing a range of values. Thus, in the last example (Table 7.7), the modal class is the second—30–39·99, because 256 000 of the 600 000 items fall into this class.

On a frequency curve, the mode is easily found, because it is the highest point of the curve. This is considered in more detail in the next chapter. Unless the values of all the items in a distribution are known, it is not possible to determine the mode with precision. However, two methods may be used to find an approximate value for the mode.

GRAPHICAL METHOD

The modal value may be measured by drawing a vertical line through the highest point of the frequency curve and reading off the value on the *x*-axis. If the information is limited to a frequency distribution, then the modal value may be found by the use of a histogram. We find the modal class, i.e., the highest column of the histogram, and join the top corners of this column diagonally to the adjacent corners of the columns on either side. This is shown below. This latter method is valid only when the class intervals of the modal class and the two classes (one on each side) are equal.

ARITHMETIC METHOD

If we take the example of Weekly earnings (Table 7.7), we have already seen that the modal class is the second down—30–39·99. Obviously, the mode is somewhere within this class. A fair guess at the mode might be the mid-point of this class, i.e., £35. If we examine the distribution of all the items, however, it will be noticed that the frequencies rise sharply at the lower values and tail off more gradually at the higher values. This would suggest that the mode is *more* than £35, i.e., between £35 and £40. This conclusion is drawn because the class

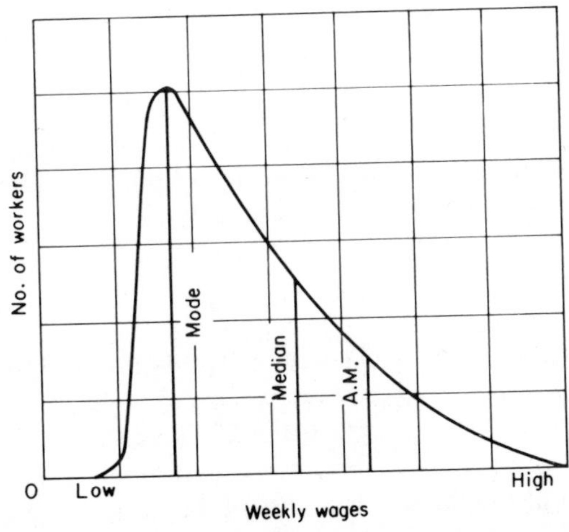

Fig. 7.1 Weekly earnings in an industrial region

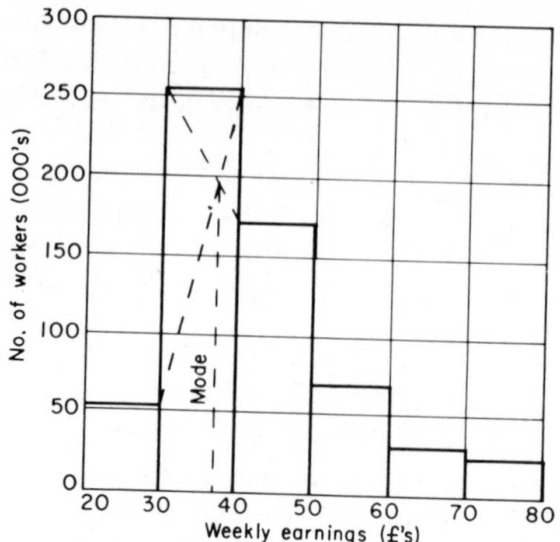

Fig. 7.2 Weekly earnings in an industrial region

interval 40–49·99 contains more items (170) than the class interval below the modal class, which contains only 52 items. The distribution is more heavily weighted or pulled to one side, in favour of the higher values within the modal class 30–39. By considering the classes on either side of the modal class, it is easy to calculate the extent of this pull.

The three classes in question are extracted from the table together with their frequencies:

Weekly earnings (£)	*No. of workers (000's)*
20–29·99	52
30–39·99	256
40–49·99	170

Table 7.8

First, we know that the mode is between £30 and £40, and nearer to £40. If we now subtract the two frequencies on either side of the modal frequency from the modal frequency itself, we shall get the results:

$$256 - 52 = 204$$
$$256 - 170 = 86.$$

The extent of the pull above £30 can now be measured as follows:

$$\text{Mode} = £30 + \frac{204}{204 + 86} \times £10 = £30 + £7{\cdot}03 = £37{\cdot}03.$$

To the lower end of the modal class (£30) we add the proportion of the class interval (£10) which has been divided in the ratio of 204 : 86—the differences in frequencies between the classes on either side of the modal class and the modal class itself.

The median

Ungrouped data or data grouped in single units The median is a third kind of average which is widely used. To find this average it is necessary to arrange all the items in a distribution in either ascending or descending order, and to pick out the middle item of the array. This is the median item, and its value is the median value. This is shown in the table below:

No. of employees	*Array of no. of employees*
516	22
22	48
343	71
197	91
71	197
1 245	343 ← Median
507	507
48	516
661	661
91	672
672	1 245

Table 7.9 Factory size by number of employees

In this array of 11 items, item number 6 is the middle item because it has an equal number of items (5) above and below it. Of course, it is perfectly possible to pick out a middle item when the total number of items is odd. When we have an even number of items there will obviously be two middle items with an equal number of items above and below them. To find the median value here we must take the arithmetic mean of these two middle items. In the example above, we can imagine another large item being added to bring the total to 12 items. The two middle items will then be 343 and 507. The arithmetic mean of these is

$$\frac{343+507}{2}=\frac{850}{2}=425.$$

It can be seen that this median value does not correspond to any actual figure in the array. Thus, in ungrouped data such as that in our table, we have the rule that, if the number of items is odd, the median value will be an *actual value*, while if the number of items is even, the median value will be an *estimated value*. A useful formula for finding the position of the median when the data is either ungrouped or simply grouped in single units (as is usually the case with discrete units) is:

$$\text{Position of median}=\frac{N+1}{2}.$$

After the position of the median has been found it is always necessary to find its value.

The table below shows a discrete series (number of rooms) in grouped form:

No. of rooms	*No. of houses in type*	*Cum 'less'*
3	38	38
4	654	692
5	311	1 003
6	42	1 045
7	12	1 057
8	2	1 059
TOTAL	1 059	

Table 7.10 Housing types in a district

In this table, a cumulative 'less than' column has been added. Applying the formula:

$$\text{Position of median} = \frac{N+1}{2}, \text{ we get } \frac{1\,059+1}{2} = \frac{1\,060}{2} = 530.$$

The 530th item in the cumulative 'less than' column obviously lies in the 4-roomed house type. Therefore the median value is 4 rooms.

Data grouped in class intervals containing a range

Where data has been classified in intervals each containing a range of values, the position of the median is found by applying the slightly different formula:

$$\text{Position of median} = \frac{N}{2}$$

To illustrate this we take again the table of weekly earnings:

Weekly earnings (£)	*No. of workers* (*000's*)	*Cum 'less'*
20–29·99	52	52
30–39·99	256	308
40–49·99	170	478
50–59·99	68	546
60–69·99	30	576
70 and over	24	600
TOTAL	600	

Table 7.11

Applying the formula $\frac{N}{2}$, we find the position of the median to be $\frac{600}{2} = 300$, from either end of the distribution. From a glance at the cumulative column it can be seen that the median will lie at the *upper end* of the class interval

'30–39·99'. Once again we must assume that items within each class are distributed evenly throughout the class. The median value is now found by interpolation, as follows:

Below the class interval '30–39·99' there are 52 items. Therefore, to find the value of the median, the 300th item, we must continue counting for a further 248 items from the bottom of class interval '30–39·99'. In fact, because there are 256 items in the latter class, we must proceed $\frac{248}{256}$ths of the way up this class. The median value will be, therefore, $£30+\frac{248}{256}\times £10=£30+£9{\cdot}69=£39{\cdot}69$.

As in the case of the mode, the value of the median may be found graphically from the cumulative frequency curve.

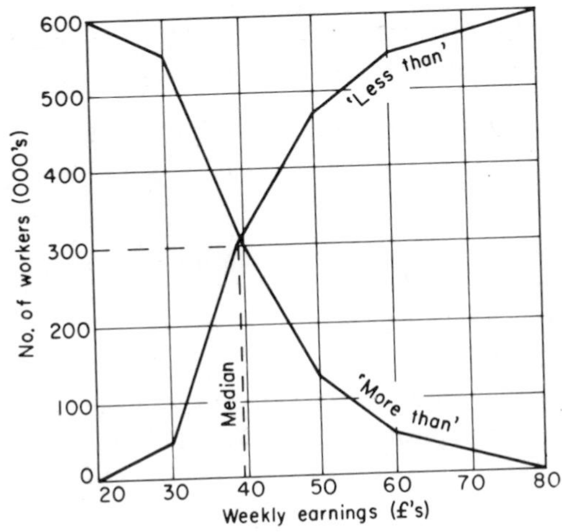

Fig. 7.3 Cumulative curves (ogives) of weekly earnings in £'s

Two ogives have been drawn. In one, the cumulative totals have been calculated in *ascending* order of the groups, by value (less than), while the other is in *descending* order (more than). For example, there are 548 workers earning more than £30, 292 earning more than £40, and so on. It is really only necessary to draw one of the curves and then draw a horizontal line from the median position (300) and drop a perpendicular to the *x*-axis to find the median value. The two curves show that the position and value of the median can be found from the point where they intersect.

The geometric mean

A fourth kind of average, which is not as frequently met with, is the *geometric mean* (G.M.). To find the geometric mean of a number of items, the values are multiplied together and the root of their number taken. If a number of items had the values: 75, 11, 17, 24, for example, the formula for the geometric mean would be $(75\times 11\times 17\times 24)^{\frac{1}{4}}$.

This can more easily be calculated by the use of logarithms.

Value of item	*Logarithm*
75	1·8751
11	1·0414
17	1·2304
24	1·3802
TOTAL	5·5271

Table 7.12

Note The student is referred to Chapter 20 for the use of logs.

We divide this logarithm by 4 (i.e., the number of items), to get the 4th root, $\frac{5\cdot5271}{4} = 1\cdot3818$. The anti-logarithm of this figure gives the answer 24·08 as the geometric mean.

The harmonic mean

This is calculated by first converting each number or value into a reciprocal (i.e., 1 divided by the number).

We next find the simple A.M. of these reciprocals, which will, in general, be fractions.

Having found this, we write down its reciprocal, which means that we reverse the numerator and denominator of the answer. This gives us the *harmonic mean* (H.M.).

Example:

Find the H.M. of the following numbers: 12; 8; 24; 6.

(*a*) The reciprocals are $\frac{1}{12}, \frac{1}{8}, \frac{1}{24}$, and $\frac{1}{6}$.

(*b*) Because there are four items, the simple A.M. is their total divided by 4:

$$\frac{1}{4}\left(\frac{1}{12}+\frac{1}{8}+\frac{1}{24}+\frac{1}{6}\right)=\frac{1}{4}\left(\frac{10}{24}\right)=\frac{10}{96}.$$

(*c*) The reciprocal of this is $\frac{96}{10} = 9\cdot6$.

The corresponding A.M. is 12·5.

Use and interpretation

The five kinds of average already described possess certain advantages and disadvantages in use. Some are more suitable than others, according to the type and kind of data to which the statistician wishes to apply them. Often the wrong kind of average is used either deliberately or carelessly.

Desirable qualities in an average

(*a*) Easy to calculate.
(*b*) Easy to understand.
(*c*) Suitable for arithmetic treatment, i.e., it should be flexible in other uses.
(*d*) It should preferably be based on the values of all the items in the distribution.
(*e*) It should be an exact value, not an estimated one.
(*f*) It should not be unduly distorted by the influence of extremely high or low values.

The arithmetic mean

The use of this particular average is so general and widespread that it is pointless to try to list its various applications. There is, indeed, a dangerous assumption on the part of the public that the word 'average' *means* what is known to the statistician as the arithmetic mean. This, of course, is wrong. Every reference to an average should say what kind of average is meant. Unfortunately, because the man in the street cannot be bothered with such technical details he often becomes the victim of trickery and deceit.

Advantages

(*a*) The calculation of the arithmetic mean is widely understood.
(*b*) The calculation is not complicated, though it may often be more lengthy than that of the other averages.
(*c*) The value of every item in the distribution is included, and although a few extremely high or low values may distort the average as a measure typical of the distribution, nevertheless, there is an arithmetical exactness about the figure which is often missing in, say, the mode or the median.

Disadvantages

(*a*) A few items of very high or low values may make the average rather unrepresentative of the whole distribution.
(*b*) The arithmetic mean cannot be measured or checked by graphical methods.
(*c*) The figure is not likely to correspond to any actual value in the distribution itself.

The mode

Sometimes one finds statements such as 'The average family in this country has 2·317 children'. To quote the arithmetic mean in such a case makes the advantage of arithmetical exactness appear rather comic. If a journalist were writing to the layman he would do better to forego the air of exactitude and give the mode. This figure would really be quite as exact and, at the same time, preserve the atmosphere of good, solid sense.

The modal average has many uses in business and government, e.g., the builder of housing estates obviously wishes to know the modal size of family in order to know the model number of rooms. The arithmetic mean is worthless to him because, although the modal average family may exist, the arithmetic mean average family certainly does not. An army tailor or bootmaker works (often with distressing effect!) to modal sizes because, not only is this average an actual value, but often it covers the actual value for the majority of the distribution. Many people complain that too rigid acceptance of modal sizes in manufacturing and production produces lack of flexibility and poor fit in many products.

Advantages

(*a*) The mode is not unbalanced (made unrepresentative) by extreme values.
(*b*) The mode is an actual value, and often represents the majority of cases.
(*c*) One need not know the values of all the items in the distribution to calculate the mode.
(*d*) It is easy to understand, and is usually readily appreciated on a graph.

Disadvantages

(*a*) Where a distribution is widely dispersed (see next chapter) over the range, and especially if the distribution has two (bimodal) or more peaks, the mode becomes less useful as an average.
(*b*) Although the mode is particularly useful as the average of a discrete series, its value may be only approximate in a continuous series.
(*c*) Because of its lack of exactness (particularly in a continuous series), the mode is unsuitable for other kinds of calculation, as is the arithmetic mean.

The median

The median is not as widely used as the two previously described averages. We use it most frequently when we require a measure of location which is not affected by high or low value items, and when we wish to measure the change in different sets of distributions which move in a similar direction in a similar manner. Thus, the median, which divides a distribution in half by number of items, is frequently used as an average in testing general abilities. Examples are intelligence, educational scores, and tests. Other uses can be found in the measurement of changes in the cost of living, when the prices of many items of general expenditure in all parts of a country are collected and reduced to a single figure.

The journalist's joke that 'Fully half the children in the country are below average intelligence', may be sensational, but it is also exact if the 'average' is the median. In the next chapter, on Dispersion, the median receives further mention because this average is particularly useful when we wish to divide up the range of values in a distribution into fractional parts, to find out the characteristics of each part.

Advantages

(*a*) Extremely high or low values do not distort it as a representative average.

(*b*) It is readily obtained, even if we do not know the values of all the items. Also it is unaffected by irregular class intervals or 'open-ended' classes, i.e., we do not have to estimate for these.

(*c*) Unless we are dealing with class intervals which each contain a range of values, the median is an actual value.

Disadvantages

(*a*) the median gives the value of only one (the middle) item, though the surrounding items may have the same value. But if the number of items is few, or if the items are spread erratically above or below it, the median may lose its value as a representative figure.

(*b*) in a continuous series, grouped in class intervals, the value of the median can only be estimated.

(*c*) the median is not suitable for arithmetic treatment in advanced work.

The geometric mean

The main uses of the geometric mean are to be found in cases where we wish to measure changes in the rate of growth, e.g., where the magnitude of one quantity depends directly on a previous magnitude. The population size at any point in time, for example, depends on the population which preceded it, because not only do births depend on the number of married couples in the previous period, but deaths will be largely dependent on the number of old people existing in the previous period. An example might be the following:

If the population in a country in 1900 was 10 million persons, and the population in 1960 was 15 million persons, estimate the probable population in 1930.

The arithmetic mean estimate would be $\frac{10+15}{2} = 12{\cdot}5$ millions.

The geometric mean estimate would be $(10\text{m} \times 15\text{m})^{\frac{1}{2}}$ which, by logarithms is:

Number	Logarithm
10m	7·0000
15m	7·1761
TOTAL	14·1761

$$\frac{14{\cdot}1761}{2} = \text{antilog } 7{\cdot}0881 = 12{\cdot}25 \text{ millions}$$

This is lower than the arithmetic mean estimate, and is more likely to be correct. The reason for this is that population tends to grow in *geometric proportion*—an ever-increasing amount—and the use of an arithmetic mean here would assume a constant amount. This is best illustrated by means of a graph showing the arithmetic and geometric curves:

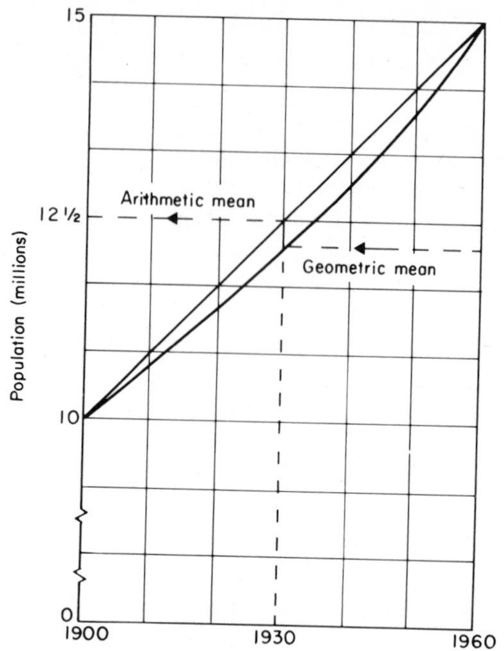

Fig. 7.4 Population growth, 1900 to 1960

In Fig. 7.4, the arithmetic (constant amount) curve is *above* the geometric (increasing amount) curve at all points between 10m and 15m. The estimated geometric mean will always be *lower* than the estimated arithmetic mean in such a case. See Chapter 5 for differences between arithmetic and geometric curves, and Chapter 17 for a comparison of arithmetic and geometric series.

Advantages

(*a*) Because the geometric mean shows the *rate of change* on a basic quantity, this average is often used to calculate index numbers (see Chapter 11), e.g., where changes in prices are calculated and averaged on a points or percentage basis of previous year.
(*b*) Every item in the distribution is included in the calculation.
(*c*) Extremely high values have not the disproportionate effect on the geometric mean as they have on the arithmetic mean (but *low* values have *more* effect on the geometric mean than on the arithmetic mean).

Disadvantages

(*a*) The geometric mean is not easily understood (why should we multiply the items and take a root of the product?), and its function as an average is not as readily apparent as in the cases of the other averages.
(*b*) It is not possible to calculate the geometric mean if the value of any item in the distribution is either zero or negative.

(*c*) The value of the geometric mean may not correspond to any actual value in the distribution.

The harmonic mean

This average is of minor importance in statistics, being restricted to the averaging of *rates* as opposed to simple values; e.g., in kilometres per hour, revolutions per second, etc.

Thus, if a car went from A to B at 30 km/h, and back again at 20 km/h, the average speed for the whole journey would be given by the H.M. of the speeds. This is 24 km/h. Most people would assume the answer to be 25 km/h, and this is because they have used the wrong kind of average, i.e., the A.M.

Students often have difficulty in deciding which of the two averages to use.

If the problem does not involve rates, speeds, etc., then the H.M. does not come into it.

Even if rates *are* involved, it does not follow that the H.M. is the correct average to use.

Taking kilometres per hour as our example, one can say that if the kilometres are constant, then the correct average is the H.M. (as above). If the time (in hours) is constant, then the correct average is the A.M.

Thus, if the motor-car in the above example had travelled, say, for one hour at 30 km/h and one hour at 20 km/h, then the average speed for the whole period of time would be 25 km/h (the simple A.M.).

Misuse of averages

Suppose, in a certain country, there is industrial conflict between workers and employers. The trade union is seeking a wage rise and the employers' federation will not agree to this demand. Both sides are seeking to impress the public with the justice of their cases.

The union emphasizes the degrading poverty of its members in relation to other workers and in the light of the rising cost of living, and it asserts: 'The average weekly wage paid this year in the industry was under £15.' .

The federation, anxious to make public the brazen manner in which they and the public are being held to ransom, states that 'The workers in the industry received last week an average weekly wage of £29·63'.

Which side is the layman to believe in the face of such staggeringly different figures? Neither? Is it a question of the reader's politics, his newspaper, or whether he is himself a worker or an employer?

If he is a statistician, the reader will realize that *both figures are likely to be right.* But certain questions will occur to the statistician.

QUESTIONS TO BE ANSWERED

We will assume that each side has made a completely accurate calculation.

(*a*) Each statement mentions an average, but does not *name* the kind of average. Can we imagine the kind of distribution of wages in the industry, i.e., the size of the frequency at each level of wages? It would probably follow a curve similar to the frequency curve illustrated overleaf.

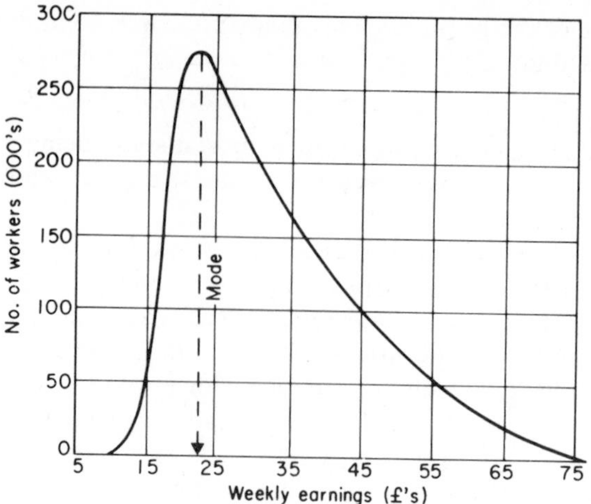

Fig. 7.5

This is much the same kind of curve as Fig. 7.1, and for much the same reasons: e.g., most workers—including women, part-time workers, and the majority of unskilled and semi-skilled workers are paid wages in the lower brackets, and the relatively fewer skilled men and supervisors receive the higher incomes. Note that the axes are scaled but we presume that the reader would not see this graph nor have information on its details.

On the curve are shown the typical positions in which the mode, median, and arithmetic mean would appear. (See Fig. 7.1.)

It is possible, therefore, for the union to understate the workers' reward by selecting the modal wage as the 'average weekly wage', this being the lowest average which offers itself. Actually, the vagueness of 'under £15' seems to suggest a modal class interval.

The employers, on the other hand, might choose the arithmetic mean in order to prove a high 'average wage'. The precision of '£29·63' suggests an arithmetic mean (an added advantage is that it has an air of accuracy which suggests careful and final deliberation).

Both the figures, therefore, are averages, but the public is not aware of the technical differences which make them non-comparable. To choose an average like this to suit your particular case might result in a difference, but probably not so large a difference as between the two quoted figures. We must look for other reasons.

(*b*) The union might have included part-time and female workers' earnings in its calculations in order to weight its average on the low side. The employers might have deliberately excluded such classes and taken full-time males only.

(*c*) The employers speak of the wage received 'last week'. This may have been a week of full work with good overtime and bonus on piecework, etc. The union speaks of the wage paid 'this year'. This may include the slack winter period when short-time piecework was the rule. Such differing bases would tend to inflate and deflate the averages respectively.

(*d*) Finally, there may be differences in the definitions of 'wage', 'industry', etc., (see Chapter 19 for a discussion of this).

Unless the union and the federation have calculated correctly, and in the same manner, the figures they arrive at will be different, and the results will be more or less worthless for purposes of comparison. Their efforts will only have been 'successful' if the public has been deluded in one way or the other.

8

Dispersion

Method

In Chapter 7 we discussed one method of describing our imaginary Mr Jones—namely, by mentioning his height. If, however, there are other individuals present of similar height, this will not serve to identify him, and we must mention some other feature which will distinguish him, such as the fact that he is fat, or that he is lop-sided. In the present chapter we consider these further points of difference, between one individual, or group, and another. In other words, we shall discuss the amount of spread and the degree of lop-sidedness, or skewness.

Kinds of curve

The average is a measure of where a centre is located in any distribution; i.e., it is a *measure of location.* Although the centres, mode, median, and mean are useful as clues to the values of central items, they do not tell us how the items are spread, or dispersed, throughout the distribution.

To get a more complete picture of a distribution than the simple average will give us, we need a *measure of dispersion.*

The five curves on the graph below are all *unimodal* (one mode), and completely *symmetrical* (one side is exactly the same, a mirror reflection, as the other). All the curves have exactly the same mean value, and, as in curves of this character, the mean, mode, and median are all equal to each other. We could tell little about the five distributions if we were told, for example, that the mean value was 16.

SKEWNESS

If some of the curves were skewed to one side, the values of the mean, mode, and median would differ from each other. The averages would take up different positions according to which side of the graph the curve was skewed. Figures 8.2 and 8.3 are two curves, skewed to the left- and right-hand sides of the graph, and the student should note the different positions taken up by the three averages in curves of this kind.

The modal position is, of course, determined by the peak of the curve; the position of the median is that it divides the area under curve (however skewed) in half; the arithmetic mean is determined arithmetically and its position cannot

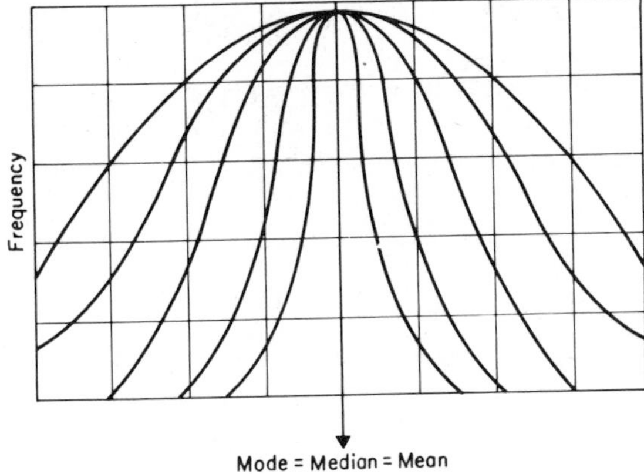

Fig. 8.1

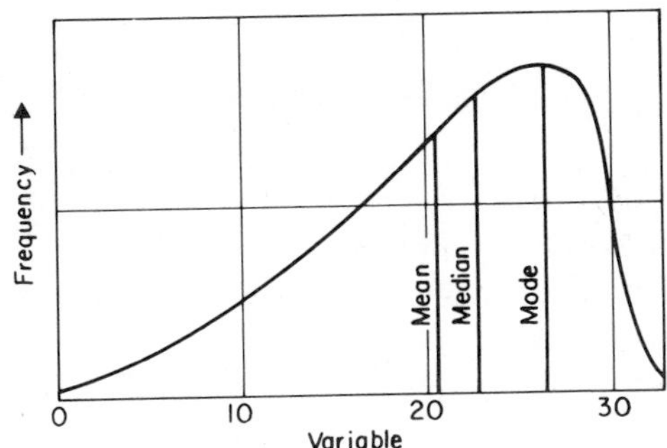

Fig. 8.2 Negatively skewed

be found merely by inspecting the curve. The more a curve is skewed away from the symmetrical, the more will the averages pull away from each other. In a skewed curve the median is always to be found between the other two averages, and, as the position of the mode is the most obvious, the student should be able to draw the approximate positions of each average on almost any curve from this simple knowledge. He might, indeed, have a vague idea of the dispersion of a

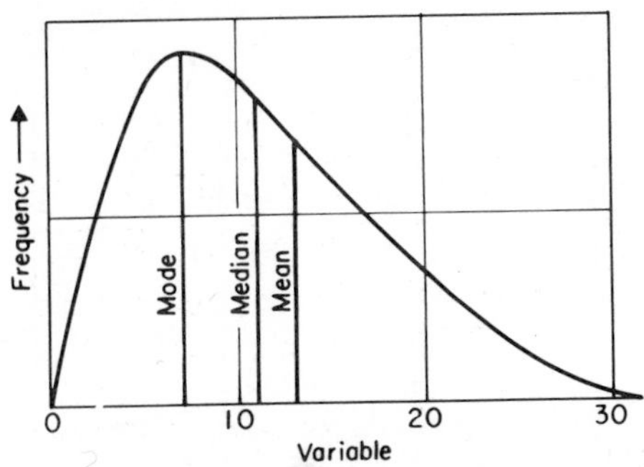

Fig. 8.3 Positively skewed

distribution if he were given the values of mode, median and mean for any distribution.

Among the infinite variety of ways in which a distribution may be skewed, certain types of distribution are well known to the statistician. Here are some of them with brief notes on the occasions on which they are found:

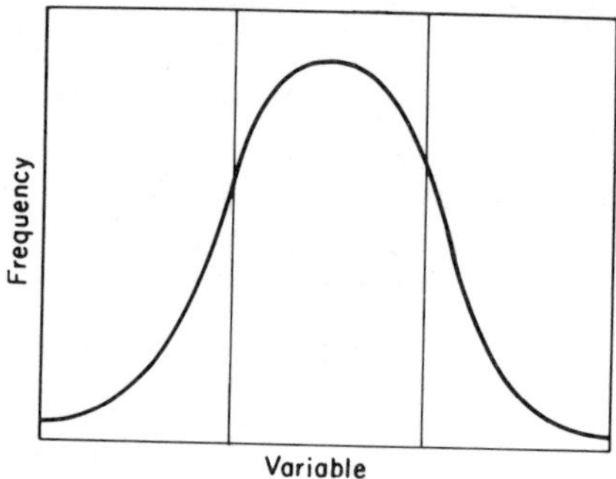

Fig. 8.4 Normal curve

The normal curve

This curve is unimodal and completely symmetrical. It is often described as having a 'cocked hat' or a 'bell' shape. The three averages are, of course, identical in this type of curve.

Typical distributions

Intelligence of population.
Height, weight, and generally in biological data.
Chiefly important in statistical sampling theory.

The J-shaped curve

This curve is extremely skewed (asymmetrical), and it can hardly be said to have a mode (this being cut at the zero line). The curve can be skewed either negatively or positively.

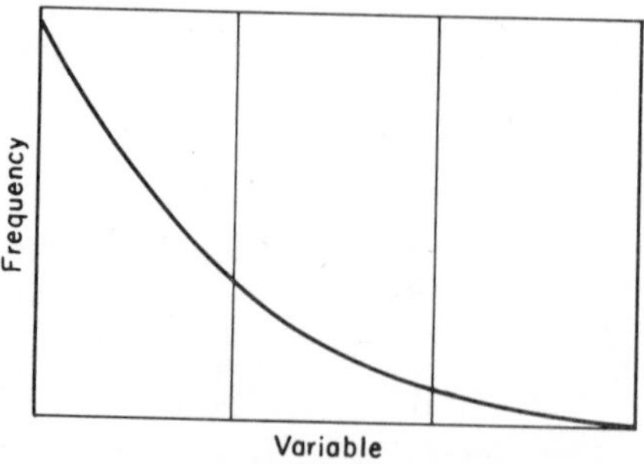

Fig. 8.5 J-shaped curve (positive)

Typical positive distributions

Income of population.
Property holding among population.
Size of community groups (towns, villages, etc.) in a country.
Size of firms.

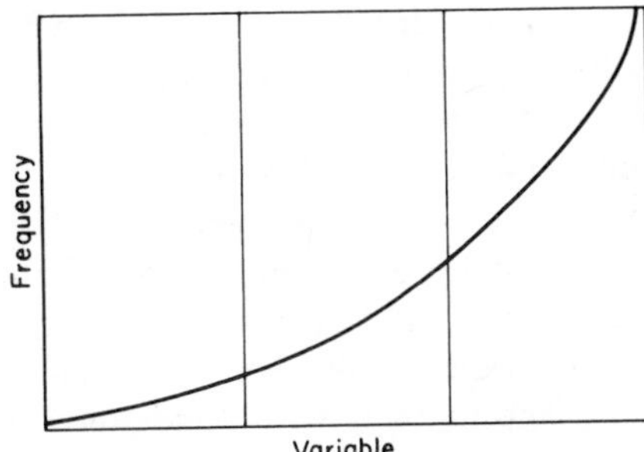

Fig. 8.6 J-shaped curve (negative)

Typical negative distributions

More rarely met with, and usually applicable to select instances, e.g., numbers of offspring of animals and insects, height of land in mountainous regions, etc.

A typical example of this type is the supply curve in economics, where the vertical scale is the price of the commodity, and the horizontal one is the quantity supplied by producers; i.e., the higher the price, the more will be produced.

The U-shaped curve

This curve is often a combination of the previous two J-shaped curves and, if the values of the variable are made very small (class intervals), it may be found to be bimodal (two modes).

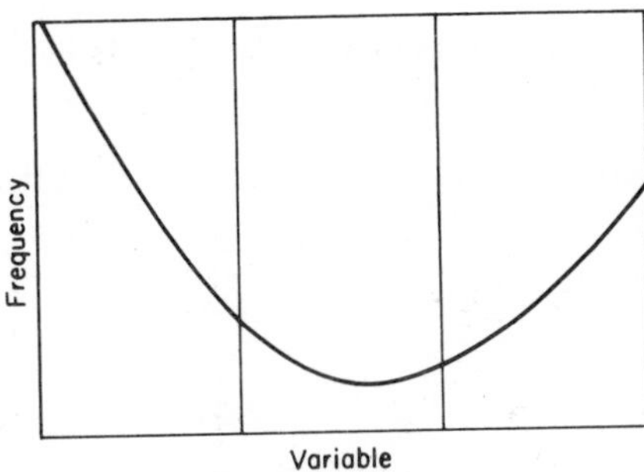

Fig. 8.7 U-shaped curve

Typical distributions

Frequency of deaths in the very young and the very old.
Degree of cloudiness in northern and southern temperate regions.

Where two different groups of items have been mixed and graphed in one curve; e.g., unskilled and skilled workers (in this case the ends of the curve might be bent over to form a bimodal curve).

The most common curves are variations or modifications of these extreme types. Many curves are combinations of one or more types of curve. An example is given below of a curve which has more than one mode and may be regarded as a combination of a U-shaped curve, or two J-shaped curves (positive and negative), and a moderately symmetrical unimodal curve.

The high infantile mortality (deaths of infants up to one year of age) and the frequent death of young children are responsible for the positively skewed, J-shaped part of the curve. The moderately symmetrical unimodal curve centred on the early 'twenties is probably the result of accidental deaths of men and women in the more active part of their lives (e.g., sporting fatalities; much greater risk of accidents to women in the home with electrical equipment, etc.; women going out to work and meeting with accidents on the street or at work, etc.). The negatively skewed curve is the mounting curve of deaths largely from the diseases of middle and old age.

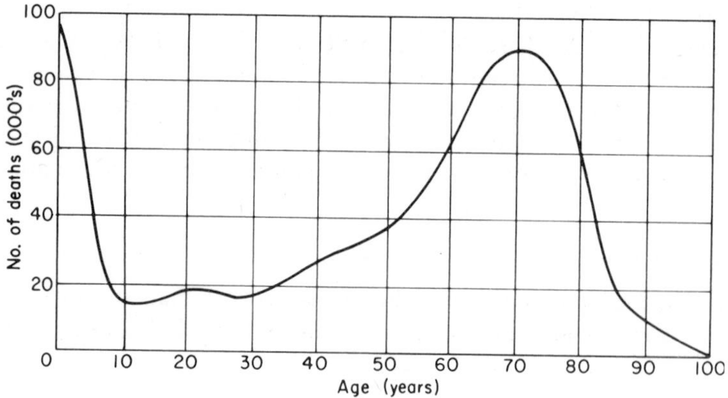

Fig. 8.8 Ages at death in a population

To summarize, so far, we have found three characteristics of any unimodal curve we care to draw:

(*a*) Location
(*b*) Dispersion
(*c*) Skewness

Three graphs, showing clearly where these differences might occur, appear on page 89.

Unless we are to quote a distribution in full, or present a graph of it, we must have some short, numerical measures of dispersion and skewness. The remainder of this 'method' section is concerned with such measures in common use.

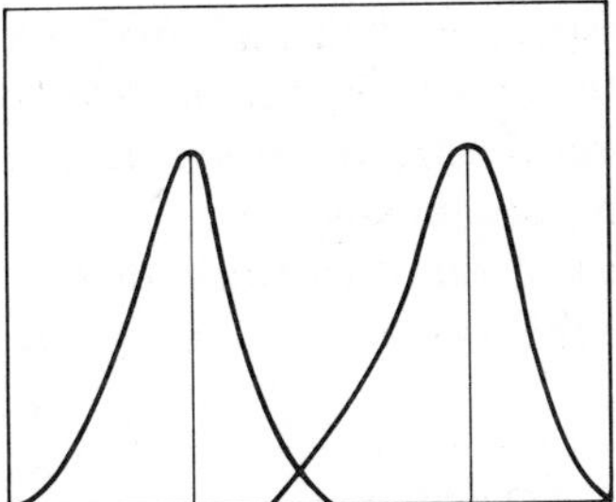

Fig. 8.9 Different location

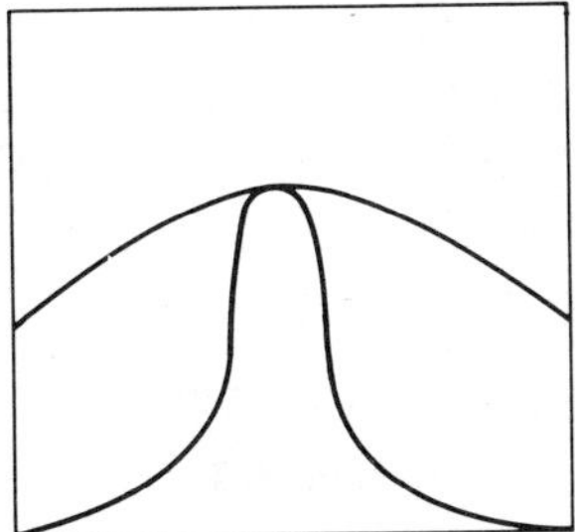

Fig. 8.10 Different dispersion

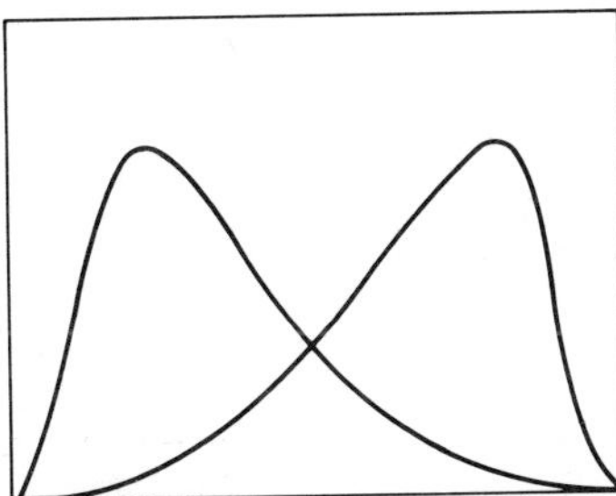

Fig. 8.11 Different skewness

The range

This is the simplest measure of dispersion and consists merely in quoting the values of the extreme items at either end of the distribution. In other words, the range is the highest and the lowest values in a distribution. It is often quoted as the actual *difference* between the two extreme values. For example, if the highest wage is £67 and the lowest is £17, then the range is £67 − £17 = £50. It has been said before that the odd, peculiarly high or low value, which is not really characteristic of the distribution but which sometimes creeps in, can distort the calculation of an otherwise worthwhile average—i.e., the arithmetic mean. Thus, in such a distribution not only the arithmetic mean but also the range will be uncharacteristic and consequently of little use. The range is the easiest measure of dispersion to understand and the easiest to obtain; it can also be the most faulty, and in any case does not tell us anything of the dispersion of values *between* the highest and the lowest.

The mean deviation

A better measure of dispersion than the range is the mean deviation which gives the average of all the deviations of items from the value of the arithmetic mean. Sometimes the average of the deviations from the median is taken, if this is more suitable for the purpose in hand.

Two examples are given of the calculation of the mean deviation from the arithmetic mean and from the median:

Value (£)	*Frequency*	*Total values* (*Products*) (£)		*Deviations from mean* (£)	*Devs* × *freq.* (£)
0	1	0		3	3
1	2	2		2	4
2	2	4	$\text{A.M.} = \dfrac{£51}{17}$	1	2
3	3	9		0	0
4	9	36	$= £3$	1	9
TOTALS	17	51		—	18

Table 8.1

$$\text{Mean deviation} = \frac{£18}{17} = £1{\cdot}06$$

Value (£)	*Frequency*	*Cum freq.*		*Deviation from median* (£)	*Devs* × *freq.* (£)
0	1	1		4	4
1	2	3	Median is	3	6
2	2	5	9th item	2	4
3	3	8	= £4	1	3
4	9	17		0	0
TOTALS	17	—		—	17

Table 8.2

$$\text{Median deviation} = \frac{£17}{17} = £1.$$

It should be noted that in this calculation the signs (+ or −) of the deviations from each average are ignored because otherwise, in the case of the first calculation, we would have got a zero, meaningless, result. In any case, the mean deviation is a measure of the extent of the *average of all deviations* and to obtain this we must treat + and − deviations on the same footing. *Note* The deviation from the arithmetic mean is never lower than the deviation from the median.

The quartile deviation

To understand this measure of dispersion, it is best to examine the divisions of the cumulative frequency curve which are usually made. It will be remembered from an earlier chapter that a distribution can be divided by the median, so that half the number of items lie above this average and half the number below it. This is shown on the cumulative frequency curve in Fig. 8.12.

The *quartiles* are also shown on the ogive. The lower quartile is a quarter of the way along the distribution arranged in ascending order, and the upper quartile is three-quarters of the way from the lower end. From the ogive the upper quartile may be estimated at £28, the lower quartile at £13, and the median value at £21.

As these three positions divide the distribution into quarters, so we can divide it into *deciles* (tenths) and *percentiles* (hundredths). Such divisions are used extensively in intelligence testing and examination marking because they provide a more detailed picture of the dispersion than do the quartiles.

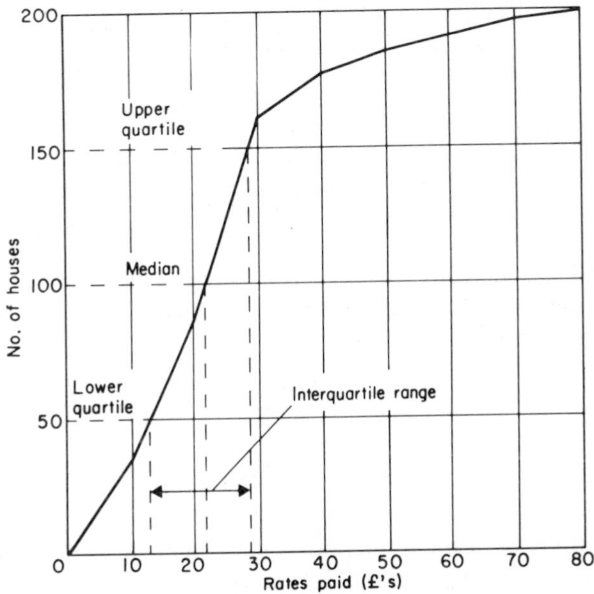

Fig. 8.12 Rates paid per quarter for 200 houses

The quartile deviation, or *semi-interquartile range*, is found by determining the *interquartile range* (upper quartile − lower quartile) and dividing this by 2. Thus, from the estimated figures in our graph:

$$\frac{£28-£13}{2} \text{ gives } £7{\cdot}50 \text{ as the quartile deviation.}$$

It should be realized that this measure of dispersion includes only that half of the distribution centred on the median, therefore it does not really cover the whole distribution. Because half the number of total items fall within the two quartiles, it follows that the smaller the quartile deviation, the more closely packed these items are, i.e., the less they are spread, or dispersed.

A defect of this measure is that the answer will be in some sort of unit—in this case £'s. Consequently, it cannot be used to compare two distributions which are expressed in different units. This is also true of the other measures we have discussed.

Quarterly rates paid (£)	*No. of houses*	*Cum freq.*
0– 9.99	35	35
10–19·99	52	87
20–29·99	76	163
30–39·99	15	178
40–49·99	9	187
50–59·99	6	193
60–69·99	4	197
70–79·99	3	200
TOTAL	200	

Table 8.3

The quartile coefficient of dispersion

To overcome this difficulty we may divide the answer by the median or, what is roughly the same thing, by half the sum of the quartiles. The whole operation may now be regarded as follows:

$$\frac{\dfrac{Q3-Q1}{2}}{\dfrac{Q3+Q1}{2}}.$$

We can multiply both the numerator and denominator by 2, which does not affect the answer, but simplifies the calculation.

This gives us:

$$\frac{Q3-Q1}{Q3+Q1} \quad \text{or} \quad \frac{\text{The difference between quartiles}}{\text{The sum of quartiles}}.$$

The units cancel out, and we get the *Quartile Coefficient of Dispersion.*

The calculation for Fig. 8.12 is:

$$\frac{£28-£13}{£28+£13}=\frac{£15}{£41}=0{\cdot}4.$$

Note The answer is always less than unity, since the sum of two numbers (denominator) is always greater than their difference.

The standard deviation

The last measure of dispersion to be discussed, and the most valuable and widely used, is the standard deviation. In the calculation of this measure of dispersion the following steps are taken:

(*a*) Find the arithmetic mean of the distribution.
(*b*) Find the deviations of the value of all items from the arithmetic mean.
(*c*) Square each deviation.
(*d*) Add the squared deviations.
(*e*) Divide the total of squared deviations by the number of items. (The result is the *variance*.)
(*f*) Find the square root of the variance. The result is the standard deviation.

A short example will serve to make this rather lengthy explanation a little clearer:

Value of item		*Deviations from A.M.*	*Square of deviations*
5		−2	4
8		+1	1
12	$\text{A.M.} = \frac{35}{5} = 7.$	+5	25
3		−4	16
7		0	0
35		—	46

Table 8.4

$$\text{Variance} = \frac{46}{5} = 9{\cdot}2$$

$$\text{Standard deviation} = \sqrt{9{\cdot}2} = 3{\cdot}03$$

In this example, *ungrouped data* have been used in a very short calculation. At this stage, the student is simply asked to note the steps (which, of course, are exactly the same for more lengthy calculations), and the fact that the deviations have been *squared*, in order to get rid of the + and − signs. The method of merely ignoring the signs, which was used in calculating the mean deviation, is really mathematically incorrect, and is one of the faults of that measure of dispersion.

For *grouped data* the calculation of the standard deviation is a little more complex. An example is given at the top of the next page.

Col. 1	*Col. 2*	*Col. 3*	*Col. 4 (2×3)*	*Col. 5*		*Col. 6 (2×5)*		*Col. 7 (6×5)*
Expenditure in £'s	*Number of households*	*Mid-points*	*Freq.× mid-points*	*Dev. of Col. 3 from arith. mean*		*Freq.× deviation*		*Freq.× devia-tion²*
				−	+	−	+	
55 and under 65	10	60	600	40		400		16 000
65 and under 75	14	70	980	30		420		12 600
75 and under 85	45	80	3 600	20		900		18 000
85 and under 95	70	90	6 300	10		700		7 000
95 and under 105	105	100	10 500	—	—	—	—	—
105 and under 115	92	110	10 120		10		920	9 200
115 and under 125	42	120	5 040		20		840	16 800
125 and under 135	22	130	2 860		30		660	19 800
TOTALS	400	—	40 000	—		2 420	2 420	99 400

Table 8.5 A household survey on food expenditure per month in 400 households

$$\text{Arithmetic mean} = £\frac{40\,000}{400} = £100.$$

$$\text{Variance} = £\frac{99\,400}{400} = £284{\cdot}5.$$

$$\text{Standard deviation} = \sqrt{248{\cdot}5} = £15{\cdot}77.$$

As in the above example, where class intervals include a range of values, the mid-point of the classes is found. Thus, up to and including the fourth column of our example, we have simply calculated the arithmetic mean as was explained in the last chapter. The standard deviation is calculated from the double-ruled line, i.e., from the last three columns only.

The 'deviations from the arithmetic mean', col. 5, are each multiplied by the corresponding frequencies to form col. 6. In the last column are the 'frequency × squared deviations', and in order to make this last calculation simpler, simply multiply col. 6 by col. 5., i.e., frequency × deviation × deviation (again) = frequency × deviation².

This is the 'long method' of calculating the standard deviation and, had the arithmetic mean run to decimal places, the calculation would have been extremely laborious. Luckily, the arithmetic mean worked out as a whole number and, because it ended in 0, this made the calculation even simpler! In fact, with a distribution of any considerable length, this 'long method' is never used for working out the standard deviation.

SHORT METHOD

In Chapter 7, we described a method of calculating the A.M. from grouped data by using an assumed mean, and correcting our answer accordingly (see Table 7.7).

We now extend this method to include the standard deviation, taking the example of the present chapter (Table 8.5).

Col. 1	*Col. 2*	*Col. 3*	*Col. 4*		*Col. 5* (2×4)		*Col. 6* (4×5)
Expenditure in £'s	*Number of households*	*Mid-points*	*Dev. from assumed A.M. of £90 units £10*		*Freq.× deviation*		*Freq.× deviation²*
			−	+	−	+	
55 and under 65	10	60	3		30		90
65 and under 75	14	70	2		28		56
75 and under 85	45	80	1		45		45
85 and under 95	70	90	0		—	—	0
95 and under 105	105	100		1		105	105
105 and under 115	92	110		2		184	368
115 and under 125	42	120		3		126	378
125 and under 135	22	130		4		88	352
TOTALS	400	—	—	—	103	503 −103 +400	1 394

Table 8.6 Expenditure on food for 400 households

$$\text{Variance} = \left[\frac{1\,394}{400} - \left(+\frac{400}{400}\right)^2\right] \text{ in units of £10}$$

$$= 3{\cdot}485 - 1^2 = 3{\cdot}485 - 1 = 2{\cdot}485 \text{ units of £10}$$

Standard deviation $= \sqrt{2{\cdot}485} = 1{\cdot}577$ units.

Since the answer is in units of £10, we now convert it to £'s.
Standard deviation $= 1{\cdot}577 \times £10 = £15{\cdot}77$, as before.

The first points to note here are that, not only are the figures much simpler, but that one column has been dropped from the table. The deviations from the assumed mean have been counted as −4, −3, −2, etc., and, as these have eventually to be squared, this cuts out unwieldy figures in the last two columns. The student must remember that, when doing this, the result is in units of 'class intervals', and that in this example the result must be *reconverted* to £'s by multiplying by £10. As we work, for simplicity, on an assumed mean (this is assumed as a convenient mid-point, usually of the largest class near the middle of the distribution), we must apply a correction when we calculate the variance. This correction is col. 5 divided by the number of items, then squared, i.e.,

$$\left(\frac{\text{Frequencies}\times\text{deviations}}{\text{No. of items}}\right)^2 = \left[\frac{(+503)+(-103)}{400}\right]^2$$

Note The student must beware of the common mistake of using the last column 'frequency × deviations²' in the correction.

The correction must be worked out (including squaring), then subtracted from the main fraction *before* the final square root is taken. In our example, the correction was unity (because, as was known previously, the true mean was actually 100, one class interval away).

Every attempt should be made to memorize and understand the columns, layout, and principles of this short method, because in most cases it is the only sensible method to use for cutting out much hard work.

The student should particularly note the following points:

(*a*) Always work in units equal to the class interval (in this case £10).

(*b*) Always choose, as the assumed mean, one of the mid-points. In theory, any one will do but, in practice, the working is simplified by picking one near the middle of the table.

(*c*) The correction is *always* subtracted from the assumed variance, whether the total of col. 5 is + or −.

(*d*) Leave the conversion into actual units until the final result is obtained, but *do not forget to do it.*

(*e*) Examination questions often call for the calculation of both A.M. and standard deviation from the same table. This method produces both answers from one set of calculations.

$$\text{The A.M.} = £90 + \left(\frac{400}{400} \times £10\right)$$

$$= £90 + £10 = £100.$$

Note For the A.M. the correction is multiplied by the class interval (units of £10) *before* it is added to (or subtracted from) the assumed mean. In the case of the A.M., rule (*c*) above does not apply. If the balancing figure of col. 6 is *negative* then the fraction is *subtracted* from the assumed mean.

Measuring skewness

To obtain a numerical measure of skewness, we rely on the fact that the greater this is, the more the averages are pulled apart. In Fig. 8.2, the three averages are:

$$\text{Mean} = 20\tfrac{1}{2} \qquad \text{Median} = 22\tfrac{1}{2} \qquad \text{Mode} = 26\tfrac{1}{2}.$$

Roughly speaking, the median is two-thirds of the distance between the mean and the mode, measuring from the mode.

For example, the difference in this case is $26\frac{1}{2} - 20\frac{1}{2} = 6$. Two-thirds of this is 4 and this, when subtracted from the modal value of $26\frac{1}{2}$, gives an estimated median value of $22\frac{1}{2}$.

We can use this information in two ways:

(*a*) Subtract the mode from the A.M. and divide the answer by the standard deviation.

(*b*) Take three times the difference between the A.M. and the median, i.e., 3(A.M. − median), and divide the result by the standard deviation.

If the distribution has *positive* skewness, the mode is smaller than the median which, in turn, is smaller than the A.M., and the answer will in each case be positive. If there is *negative* skewness, the A.M. and median are both smaller than the mode, so the result of the subtraction is negative. These measures thus indicate the *kind* of skewness as well as its extent. The reason for dividing by the standard deviation is to get rid of the units (they cancel out) so that distributions with different unit can be compared.

Use and interpretation

We have now dealt with four measures of dispersion:

(*a*) the range,
(*b*) the mean deviation,
(*c*) the quartile deviation,
(*d*) the standard deviation.

Among these measures, the standard deviation is by far the most important in use, though the desirable qualities in a measure of dispersion are not found completely in the standard deviation. Such desirable qualities are very similar to the desirable qualities for an average (see Chapter 7). They include ease of calculation and ease of understanding, stability when extreme items are involved, coverage of all the items in the distribution, and value in use and in advanced work.

The standard deviation is the most troublesome to calculate and not the easiest to comprehend—the other three are probably far superior in these respects. Both the mean deviation and the standard deviation cover all the items in the distribution, while the other two do not. The range is the worst affected by extreme items; the quartile deviation is not affected at all, and the use of the standard deviation offsets them to some degree. The superiority of the standard deviation to all the others is its flexibility in use to solve many problems in advanced statistics, and particularly its wide use in sampling theory.

A good deal has already been said about the first three measures. The range has a limited use in the field of quality control; the mean deviation is occasionally used in economics and social statistics; and the quartile deviation is used in educational statistics quite extensively. However, the standard deviation is used far more than the others put together, and the remainder of this chapter is largely devoted to describing this.

Relations between the measures

The last worked examples concerned the expenditure on food of 400 households. The standard deviation was calculated as £15·77, approximately, and the arithmetic mean as £100. The range is approximately £80 (i.e., £135 – £55). The mean deviation can be readily worked out from Table 8.5 (long method) as

$$\frac{\text{Total of frequencies} \times \text{deviations (ignoring signs)}}{\text{No. of items}}$$

$$= \frac{2\,420 \times 2\,420}{400} = \frac{4\,840}{400} = \text{£}12{\cdot}1.$$

The median and the quartile deviation are estimated from the ogive below, from which it can be seen that the median is approximately £101.

Note We should expect this to be similiar to the arithmetic mean in a fairly symmetrical distribution as is the case here.

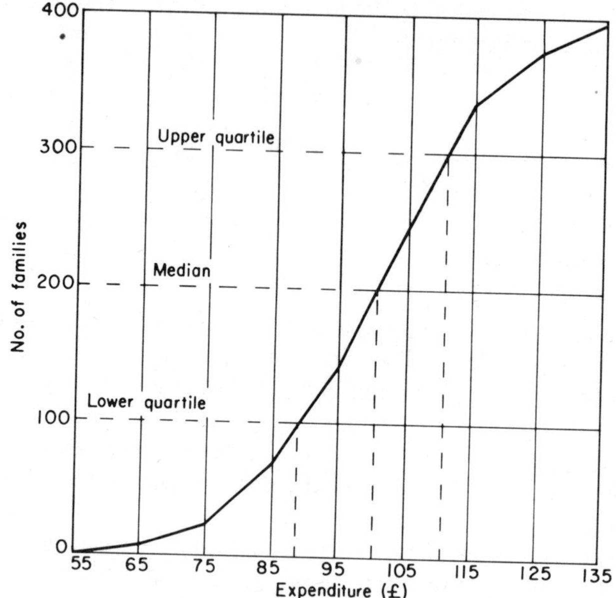

Fig. 8.13 Ogive for expenditure on food of 400 households

The quartile deviation is, of course, found by:

$$\frac{\text{Upper quartile} - \text{lower quartile}}{2} = \frac{£111 - £89}{2} = £11.$$

The mode can be estimated from the method given in Chapter 7. The modal class is obviously '95 and under 105', and as the number of frequencies (92) is larger in the class above than in the class below (70), then the mode is slightly nearer 105 than 95. Subtracting the two frequencies on either side of the modal class from the modal frequency itself we get:

$$105 - 70 = 35$$

$$\text{and } 105 - 92 = 13.$$

The extent of the pull from £95 (lower limit) is:

$$\text{Mode} = £95 + \frac{35}{35 + 13} \times £10 = £95 + £7{\cdot}3 = £102{\cdot}3.$$

A list can now be made of the averages and dispersion measures for this distribution:

Mode = £102·3
Arithmetic mean = £100
Median = £101
Range = £80
Mean deviation = £12·1
Quartile deviation = £11
Standard deviation = £16 (approx.)

For any distribution which is *symmetrical* (*or fairly symmetrical*) *and also unimodal*, certain relationships have been calculated between these measures. These may provide useful checks.

(*a*) *The values of the averages are similar.*
(As can be seen, the averages are very similar, the only slight difference being in the case of the mode (£102·3) which, in any case, is an estimated figure.)

(*b*) *The range should be approximately equal to six standard deviations.*
(Six standard deviations are 6 × £15·77 = £95, and the range is £80.)

(*c*) *The quartile deviation is approximately equal to two-thirds of the standard deviation.*
(Two-thirds of the standard deviation is $\frac{2}{3}$ × £15·77 = £10·51. The quartile deviation is £11.)

(*d*) *The mean deviation is approximately four-fifths of the standard deviation.*
(Four-fiths of the standard deviation is $\frac{4}{5}$ × £15·77 = £12·62. The mean deviation is a little lower than this—£12·1.)

From our list, then, without knowing any of the actual values of the items we can tell that the curve is:

Fairly symmetrical with only a very slight negative skewness (i.e., mode a little higher than median), and it is unimodal, centred on £100, with most of the items lying within £48 either side of this figure.

Nature and meaning of the standard deviation

It is not sufficient to know merely how to calculate the standard deviation; the student must know its meaning. This is quite simple and is shown in Fig. 8.14 on the next page.

This curve is unimodal and symmetrical about the average; in fact, it is of the 'normal curve' type described in Fig. 8.4. On either side of the mean are marked off three standard deviations—making six standard deviations for approximately the whole range of values. It has been calculated that if we mark off a frequency curve in this way, the area under the curve (which is proportional to the total number of items) will be divided into certain proportions. The percentage figures under the curve give these approximate proportions:

Within one standard deviation either side of the mean (two standard deviations in all) will lie approximately 68 per cent of the items.

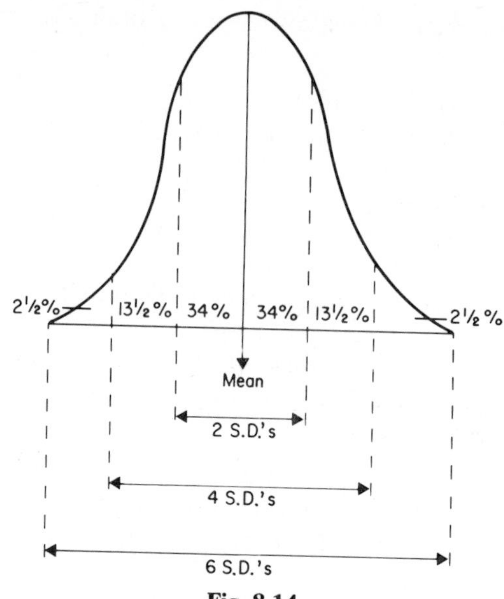

Fig. 8.14

Within two standard deviations either side of the mean (four standard deviations in all) will lie approximately 95 per cent of the items.

Within three standard deviations either side of the mean (six standard deviations in all) will lie approximately 100 per cent of the items.

The student will have realized by now that all measures of dispersion and location form a shorthand for giving us a picture of distributions quickly, rather than by building up a picture by other tedious working.

It will be remembered that we built up a picture of the curve (see description following Fig. 8.13) from the list of average and dispersion measures of 'Expenditure on food for 400 households'. Actually, there was no need to calculate all these measures, though we did this to establish the relationships. All that is necessary to get a fairly true picture of the curve is to know the mean and the standard deviation, and the number of items.

Mean = £100, Standard deviation = £16,
Number of items = 400.

With this simple information we can:

(*a*) Draw a horizontal axis and mark off £100 at the middle.
(*b*) Erect a vertical at this £100 mark and label this the mean.
(*c*) From this £100 on the horizontal axis mark off to each side three standard deviations and scale them in £'s. For example, to the right of the mean will be:

£116 = (£100 + £16)
£132 = (£100 + £16 + £16)
£148 = (£100 + £16 + £16 + £16)

and the lower values for the left-hand side.

(*d*) Calculate the number of items (from the percentages) which will make up the six divisions of the curve (standard deviations) and mark in.
(*e*) Remembering that the number of items within each section is proportional to the area of each section, it will now be possible to draw a rough curve to represent the distribution. This is done below, and the figures entered could be compared by the student with the actual figures of the distribution on page 94.

Some applications

The standard deviation may be used as a measure of dispersion in all symmetrical, unimodal and even moderately skewed distributions. Such distributions are frequently met with, and they include intelligence testing, examination marking, and many kinds of natural and biological series. In sampling theory, this measure is of great importance to the statistician, but its applications in this respect are considered in later chapters.

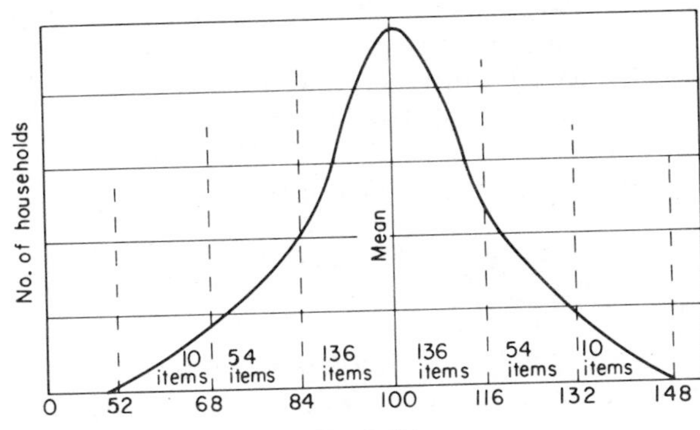

Fig. 8.15

Such a figure need not be drawn but with a little practice could be imagined or, at the most, sketched rapidly.

Coefficient of variation

Finally, the standard deviation can be used to compare the dispersion in two distributions as long as the distributions are of the same kind and are measured in the same units. For this purpose we use the *coefficient of variation.* To calculate this, we simply multiply the standard deviation by 100 to bring it to a percentage, and divide by the arithmetic mean, for each distribution.

Example:
Coal output per man over a period at two collieries was measured as follows:

Mine A A.M. 45 000 kg, S.D. 15 000 kg
Mine B A.M. 40 000 kg, S.D. 14 000 kg

applying the formula—

$$\text{Coefficient of variation} = \frac{\text{standard deviation}}{\text{arithmetic mean}} \times 100$$

we get:

$$\text{Mine A} \quad \frac{15}{45} \times 100 = 33{\cdot}33 \text{ per cent}$$

$$\text{Mine B} \quad \frac{14}{40} \times 100 = 35{\cdot}00 \text{ per cent}$$

The conclusion may be drawn that, although Mine A has a higher mean output, and although the standard deviation might suggest that the values of output were more dispersed than in Mine B, nevertheless, the dispersion, relative to the mean, is higher in Mine B, as the coefficient of variation shows.

Skewness

Taking the example of Table 8.5, we have already found the following measures:

A.M. = £100
Median = £101
Mode = £102·3 (say £102)
Standard deviation = £16 (roughly).

Using *method 1* (based on the mode) we have:

$$\frac{\text{A.M.} - \text{mode}}{\text{S.D.}} = \frac{£100 - £102}{£16} = -\frac{2}{16} = -0{\cdot}125$$

If the mode is not well defined (as often happens when the frequency curve has a plateau rather than a peak) we use *method 2* (based upon the median). We have:

$$\frac{3(\text{A.M.} - \text{median})}{\text{S.D.}} = \frac{3(£100 - £101)}{£16} = -\frac{3}{16} = -0{\cdot}188$$

Note The two methods do not necessarily give the same answer, and in any case we have approximated both the mode and the S.D.

The result indicates a moderate degree of negative skewness. A highly skewed distribution may have a value of ±1, and values up to ±3 are theoretically possible.

IMPORTANCE OF SKEWNESS

This notion is used in certain theoretical distributions (see Chapter 12 on Sampling).

It is also useful in industrial and economic statistics to know, for example, that the distribution of incomes is skewed, and to what extent. An employer would find that the age distribution of his workers was skewed, and probably their earnings under a bonus or productivity scheme. The interesting question would then arise, as to whether these two cases of skewness differed at all, in nature or extent. That is, were the older workers also the ones who earned most bonus, or was it the reverse?

9

Correlation

Method

We saw in Chapter 4 that it was possible to show the existence of correlation between two sets of data by means of a scatter diagram.

While such a device will indicate the *type* of correlation (i.e., positive or negative, linear or curvi-linear) it gives no indication of its *extent.* In this chapter we consider numerical measures of correlation.

Regression lines

When there is strong correlation in a scatter diagram, the dots tend to arrange themselves in a narrow band, which may be curved or straight.

If the band of dots is straight, the correlation is said to be *linear,* i.e., the relationship between the two variables can be represented by a straight line.

If the relationship is only approximately linear, then it is possible to construct a *line of best fit,* which runs through most of the dots, and leaves the remaining ones more or less equally disposed on either side of this line. Such a line may be fitted to a scatter diagram by inspection, and this has been done in Figs. 4·9, 4·10, and 4·11.

Three-point method for regression lines

This is the simplest method of calculating a regression line, but it does not yield an equation directly, as does the method which follows this section. The procedure is as follows:

(*a*) List the two variables in vertical columns, with one column in ascending order, and find the simple average (A.M.) of each column. The two values obtained, when plotted on our scatter diagram, will yield the *first* of our three points.

(*b*) Mark the position of the A.M. in the ranked column of figures. This will probably fall at some intermediate position between two of the original figures, since the A.M. may not be a whole number.

(*c*) For each column find the average (A.M.) of all those figures which are positioned *above* the point marked. These two values will give our *second* point.

(*d*) Do the same for all values *below* the point marked. This gives our *third* point.

(*e*) The three points calculated can now be plotted on the original diagram, and when joined will form a straight line.

Example 1:

Using the figures from Table 9.1 below, we have:

Sales of ice-cream in £00's	*Mid-day temp. (°C)*
Y	*X*
45	24
50	28
→	←
60	32
65	36
65	40
5)285	5)160
57	32

(*a*) Our first point is $Y=57$, $X=32$.

(*b*) We count the 32 in the *X* column as *below* our mark, so that we have three values in each column.

(*c*) Our second point is $Y=\frac{1}{2}(45+50)=47\frac{1}{2}$ and $X=\frac{1}{2}(24+28)=26$.

(*d*) Our third point is $Y=\frac{1}{3}(60+65+65)=63\frac{1}{3}$ and $X=\frac{1}{3}(32+36+40)=36$.

These three points, when plotted on our scatter diagram, will fall on a straight line.

Note This line will not necessarily coincide with either of those obtained from the formulae, except that the *first* point, based on the A.M.'s, will lie on all three of them.

If we wish to calculate the mathematical equation for such a line, we can approach the problem in two ways:

(*a*) We can take fixed values for the *X*'s (the variable on the horizontal scale of our graph) and find a line which minimizes the *vertical* distances between the dots and this line.

This is known as the *regression line of Y upon X*. It gives us an estimate of *Y* (the variable shown on the vertical scale) for a known value of *X*, *or*

(*b*) We take fixed values for the *Y*'s, and find a line which minimizes the *horizontal* distances between the dots and the line. This is called the *regression line of X upon Y*, and will give us an estimate of *X* from a known value of *Y*.

Actually, since the deviations may be positive or negative, with respect to the line, we use a method which minimizes the *squared deviations*.

For example, suppose we have two sets of figures, one for sales of ice-cream on certain days, and the other for the mid-day temperatures on the same days. We should expect some correlation to exist between the two, but it would not be perfect, since other factors enter into ice-cream sales, apart from temperature.

If we plot the temperatures on the horizontal scale, these would be our X's. The sales would then be our Y's.

Line 1 would give us an *estimate* of sales for a given temperature.

Line 2 would give an *estimate* of temperature from a known sales figure.

The line which one would fit by inspection would be one which is half-way between the two. This would be an over-simplification of the true position, and its position would depend upon the judgement of the individual.

The equation of a straight line

The mathematical equation for *any* straight line is:

$$Y = a + bX$$

where a and b are constants for any one line.

The value of a determines where the line will cut the Y axis on our graph, and the value of b gives the slope of the line. These values need not be whole numbers, and they can be either positive or negative.

Figures 9.1 and 9.2 show the appearance of our line for different values of a and b.

Clearly, if we know exactly where a line cuts the Y axis, and we also know its slope, then there is only one line which satisfies these requirements; i.e., we can identify *any particular* line if we know the values of a and b.

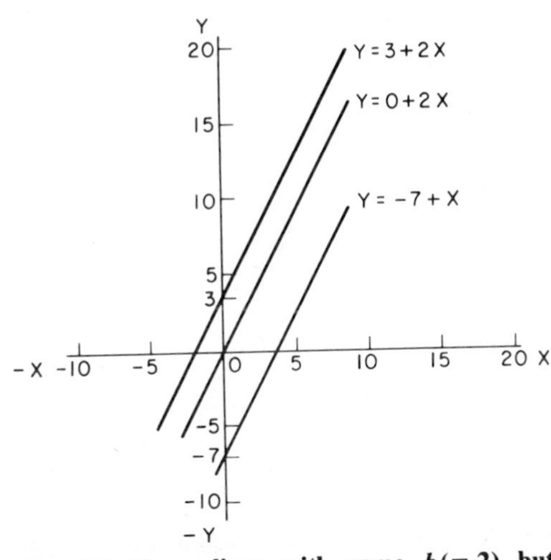

Fig. 9.1 Three lines with same $b(=2)$ but different values of a.
Note **Since the lines have the same slope ($= b$) they are all parallel**

Regression of Y upon X

To find the values of a and b in any particular case we solve the following equations:

$$\Sigma Y = na + b\Sigma X \qquad \text{(F. 9.1)}$$

$$\Sigma XY = a\Sigma X + b\Sigma X^2 \qquad \text{(F. 9.2)}$$

where n = the number of *pairs* of figures.
ΣY = the sum of the Y figures.
ΣX = the sum of the X figures.
ΣXY = the sum of the products of each X multiplied by the corresponding Y.
ΣX^2 = the sum of the squares of each individual X.

Note 1 Σ = the capital letter 'sigma' in the Greek alphabet. This is a shorthand method of writing 'the sum of . . .'.

Note 2 So far as the formulae are concerned, it does not matter which set of figures we call the X series, and which the Y series. The solutions we get, however, give the values of a and b in the equation:

$$Y = a + bX$$

i.e., the line which estimates the value of Y in any particular case.

The student should therefore make sure that he chooses for his Y series, the particular variable asked for in the question.

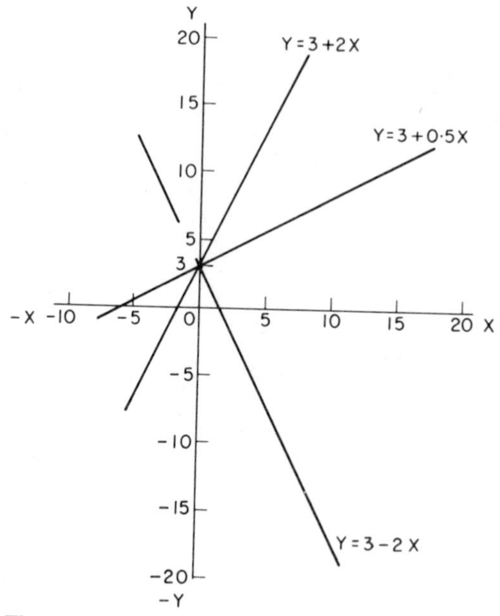

Fig. 9.2 Three lines with same *a* (= 3) but different values of *b*
***Note* Since the lines have the same *a*, they all pass through the same point ($y = 3$)**

Example 2:

The following table gives ice-cream sales (in £00's) on five days of 1977, together with the corresponding midday temperature, on the same five days. Required—to obtain the equation to the regression line of ice-cream sales on temperature.

Note 1 Since we are asked for the equation which estimates *ice-cream sales*, we make this our Y. In any event, since this is the *dependent variable*, it would represent the vertical scale on a scatter diagram (= Y axis).

Sales of ice-cream in £00's Y	*Midday temp.* (°C) X	XY	Y^2	X^2
65	40	2 600	4 225	1 600
45	24	1 080	2 025	576
65	36	2 340	4 225	1 296
50	28	1 400	2 500	784
60	32	1 920	3 600	1 024
$\Sigma Y = 285$	$\Sigma X = 160$	9 340 ($=\Sigma XY$)	16 575 ($=\Sigma Y^2$)	5 280 ($=\Sigma X^2$)

Table 9.1

Note 2 We have added a column for ΣY^2, since this is required for the next part of the exercise.

Substituting the values for ΣY, ΣX, ΣXY, and ΣX^2 in our two equations (F. 9.1, F. 9.2), and noting that $n = 5$, we have:

$$285 = 5a + 160b \qquad \text{Eq. (9.1)}$$

$$9\,340 = 160a + 5\,280b. \qquad \text{Eq. (9.2)}$$

We solve these two equations as follows:

(*a*) Multiply Eq. (9.1) by 32 (to make the a's equal to Eq. (9.2))

$$9\,120 = 160a + 5\,120b. \qquad \text{Eq. (9.3)}$$

(*b*) Subtract Eq. (9.3) from Eq. (9.2) (to eliminate a)

$$220 = 160b$$

$$\frac{220}{160} = b \qquad \text{i.e., } b = 1{\cdot}375.$$

(*c*) Substitute this value in Eq. (9.1):

$$285 = 5a + 220$$

$$285 - 220 = 5a$$

$$65 = 5a \qquad \text{i.e., } a = 13.$$

The regression line is therefore:

$$Y = 13 + 1{\cdot}375X. \qquad \text{Eq. (9.4)}$$

We can test this, as an estimate of Y, against the original data. For example, when $X = 40$, the regression equation gives:

$$Y = 13 + 55 = 68(\text{£00's}).$$

Actually, the sales on that day were 65(£00's), showing that part of the sales is due to other factors.

Regression of X upon Y

This is the line which estimates X from a known value of Y. To obtain its equation we substitute X for Y, and Y for X in the two previous formulae (F. 9.1) and (F. 9.2). That is,

$$\Sigma X = na + b\Sigma Y$$

$$\Sigma XY = a\Sigma Y + b\Sigma Y^2.$$

Substituting the values in our table, we now have:

$$160 = 5a + 285b \qquad \text{Eq. (9.5)}$$

$$9\,340 = 285a + 16\,575b. \qquad \text{Eq. (9.6)}$$

Proceeding as before:

(*a*) Multiply Eq. (9.5) by 57 (to make the *a*'s equal)

$$9\,120 = 285a + 16\,2456 \qquad \text{Eq. (9.7)}$$

(sb) Subtract Eq. (9.7) from Eq. (9.6)

$$220 = 330b$$

$$\frac{220}{330} = b \qquad \text{i.e., } b = \tfrac{2}{3}.$$

(*c*) Substitute this value in Eq. (9.5)

$$160 = 5a + 190$$

$$-30 = 5a$$

$$\frac{-30}{5} = a \qquad \text{i.e., } a = -6.$$

The equation to the regression line is:

$$X = -6 + \tfrac{2}{3}Y. \qquad \text{Eq. (9.8)}$$

As before, we can use this to estimate X, and compare it with the actual data. Taking the day when $Y = 45$(£00's) we have:

$$X = -6 + (\tfrac{2}{3} \times 45) = -6 + 30 = 24°.$$

This agrees exactly. In other words, the plot for this day will lie on the regression line.

Figure 9.3 shows the actual plots, together with the two regression lines.

Note 1 The two lines intersect at a point represented by the means of the two series

$$(Y = 57;\ X = 32).$$

(*c*) Similarly, we have the S.D. of the Y's:

$$S.D._{\cdot y} = \sqrt{\frac{331}{10} - \left(\frac{+9}{10}\right)^2} = \sqrt{33{\cdot}1 - 0{\cdot}81} = \sqrt{32{\cdot}29}$$

(*d*) The student should note most carefully that the totals of cols. 3 and 4 us the real A.M.'s of the X's and Y's. They therefore provide a ch upon the accuracy of our deviations, which should always be carried before proceeding, i.e.:

$$\text{The A.M. of the } X\text{'s is } 7 + \frac{6}{10} = 7{\cdot}6 \text{ (col. 1)}$$

$$\text{The A.M. of the } Y\text{'s is } 14 + \frac{9}{10} = 14{\cdot}9 \text{ (col. 2)}$$

(*e*) We have now corrected out two S.D.'s for the fact that we did not work from the real averages, but the total of col. 7 is also wrong, for the same reason. The correction for this will be more easily understood if we have another look at formula (9.4).

$$r = \frac{\Sigma xy}{N \times S.D._{\cdot x} \times S.D._{\cdot y}}$$

Since we already have the two S.D.'s, this leaves us with $\frac{\Sigma xy}{N}$ which is called the *co-variance*. This is the bit which needs correcting, and we do this by subtracting the product of the two correction factors already used in the S.D.'s: i.e., 6/10 and 9/10.

Hence we have:

$$\frac{-150}{10} - \left(\frac{+6}{10} \times \frac{+9}{10}\right) = -15 - 0{\cdot}54 = -15{\cdot}54$$

Note In this example, the total of col. 7 is *also negative*, so the two numbers must be added. If col. 7 had been positive, the correction factor would be taken away, and the final answer would be less.

(*f*) We can now restore the two S.D.'s, in the original formula, giving us:

$$r = \frac{-15.54}{\sqrt{8{\cdot}24} \times \sqrt{32{\cdot}29}} = -0{\cdot}9526.$$

The student would use logarithms to work this out, and may wonder how he can find the log of a minus quantity. The negative sign shows only the *direction* of the correlation, and may be ignored for purposes of working. It must, of course, be restored in the final answer.

Note 2 Although the two scales have been started from zero (to show the points of intersection with the axes), this is not necessary, unless the question calls for it. If we had started the X scale at 16, and the Y at, say, 40, we could have used a more open scale and made the difference between the two lines more pronounced.

Correlation coefficients

Although regression analysis provides a useful method for estimating one variable from another, we still lack a means for giving a numerical value to the correlation present between two sets of data. This is particularly necessary when we wish to make comparisons.

One such measure is the *Pearsonian coefficient of correlation* (sometimes called the product-moment coefficient) represented by r. This is an extension of the method employed for standard deviation.

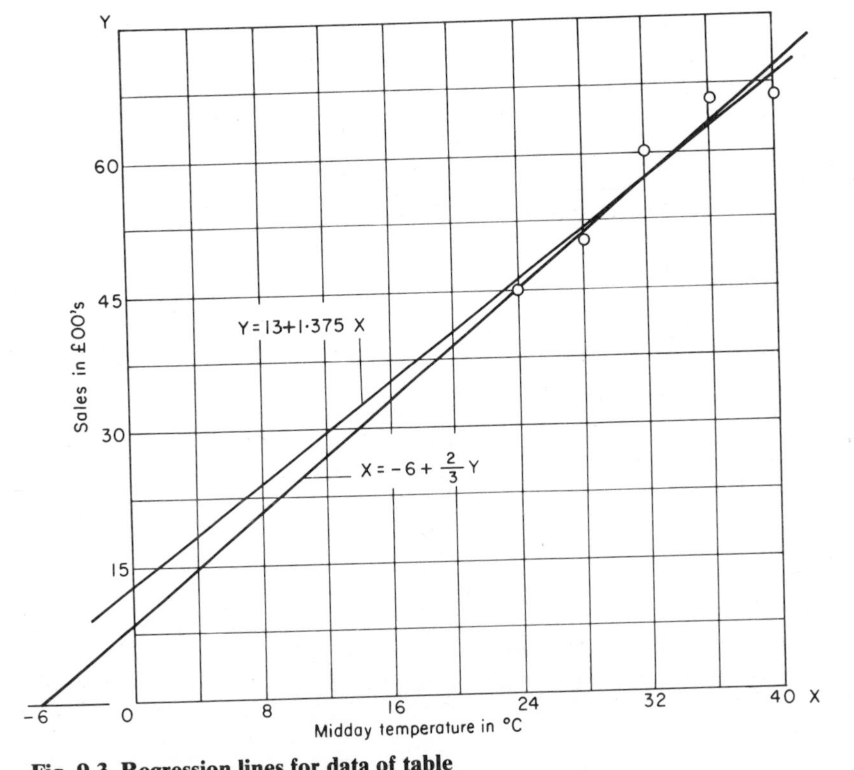

Fig. 9.3 Regression lines for data of table
Note **The regression line of X upon Y cuts the base line when $X = -6$ ($Y = 0$)**
The regression line of Y upon X cuts the vertical axis when $Y = 13$ ($X = 0$)

Application to ungrouped data

There are a variety of formulae for calculating r, each representing a different approach. The one we shall use for the moment is:

$$r = \frac{\Sigma xy}{\sqrt{\Sigma x^2 . \Sigma y^2}} \qquad \text{(F. 9.3)}$$

where X is the *deviation* of each X value from the A.M. of the X's, and y deviation of each Y value from the A.M. of the Y's. (Σ = 'the sum of . . before).

Example 3:

1	2	3	4	5	6	7	8	
Week number	*Number of machines working* X	*Output (000's)* Y	*Dev. from A.M. = 8* x	*Dev. from A.M. = 6* y	x^2	y^2	*Co. 4 × Col. 5*	
							−	+
1	7	5	−1	−1	1	1	—	1
2	10	8	+2	+2	4	4	—	4
3	6	3	−2	−3	4	9	—	6
4	8	6	0	0	0	0	—	—
5	9	8	+1	+2	1	4	—	2
	40	30	—	—	10	18	—	13
A.M. =	8	6					+13	

Table 9.2 Output and machines employed in a factory

Substituting in our formula we have:

$$\Sigma xy = 13 \quad \Sigma x^2 = 10 \quad \Sigma y^2 = 18.$$

Hence $r = \dfrac{+13}{\sqrt{10 \times 18}} = \dfrac{+13}{\sqrt{180}} = \dfrac{+13}{13{\cdot}42} = +0{\cdot}9687.$

Note The sign of the end column should always be inserted, since this indicates the *direction* of the correlation (+ or −).

The above example is a simple one, since in each case the A.M. is a whole number.

In practice, this is seldom so, but a modification of the short-cut method for S.D. will enable us to work from assumed A.M.'s.

In such cases, we use a modified formula:

$$r = \frac{\Sigma xy}{N \times S.D._x \times S.D._y} \qquad \text{(F. 9.4)}$$

where N = the number of pairs of items.

It will be remembered that the method of calculating S.D. is:

$$S.D._x = \sqrt{\frac{\Sigma x^2}{N}} \quad \text{and } S.D._y = \sqrt{\frac{\Sigma y^2}{N}}.$$

Where x and y are the deviations from the *true* A.M. in each case. Substituting

these in (F. 9.4) gives us:

$$r = \frac{\Sigma xy}{N\sqrt{\dfrac{\Sigma x^2}{N}} \times \sqrt{\dfrac{\Sigma y^2}{N}}} = \frac{\Sigma xy}{N\dfrac{\sqrt{\Sigma x^2 \times \Sigma y^2}}{N}}.$$

Cancelling out the N's gives us the previous formula (F. 9.3).

Example 4:

1	2	3	4	5	6	7	
X	Y	*Dev. from assumed A.M. = 7* (= x)	*Dev. from assumed A.M. = 14* (= y)	x^2	y^2	$(x)\times(y)$ *Col. 3 × Col. 4*	
						−	+
10	9	+3	−5	9	25	15	—
3	20	−4	+6	16	36	24	—
8	15	+1	+1	1	1	—	1
12	6	+5	−8	25	64	40	—
4	22	−3	+8	9	64	24	—
6	18	−1	+4	1	16	4	—
5	23	−2	+9	4	81	18	—
9	12	+2	−2	4	4	4	—
8	16	+1	+2	1	4	—	2
11	8	+4	−6	16	36	24	—
				86	331	153	3
76	149	+6	+9			3	
A.M. = 7·6	14·9					−150	

Table 9.3

Explanation:

(*a*) In cols. 3 and 4 we are taking the deviations from an *assumed* A.M., sin in each case the *real* A.M. is not a whole number. This is the short-c method, as previously applied to S.D. (see Chapter 8).

Note A useful tip is to take, as assumed A.M., the whole numb *immediately below* the real average (in this case, 7 and 14 respectivel This has the advantage of making the subsequent correction always po tive, thus avoiding confusion regarding signs at a later stage.

(*b*) To get the S.D. of the X's, we have:

$$S.D._x = \sqrt{\frac{86}{10} - \left(\frac{+6}{10}\right)^2} = \sqrt{8{\cdot}6 - 0{\cdot}36} = \sqrt{8{\cdot}24}.$$

There is no need to work this out, because we are not interested in answer for its own sake.

Calculation for grouped data

Example 5:

(Y) Days lost	(X) Number of workers per age group 20–30 yrs	30–40 yrs	40–50 yrs	50–60 yrs	60–	Totals
1–2	4	—	4	—	—	8
3–4	8	8	4	4	—	24
5–6	4	12	16	—	—	32
7–8	—	4	8	4	—	16
9–10	—	—	12	—	—	12
11–	—	—	—	7	1	8
TOTALS	16	24	44	15	1	100

Table 9.4 Days lost by workers according to their ages

Note 1 Where there are open-ended groups, we first close them. In general, assume that they are the same size as the rest, unless there is evidence to the contrary.

Note 2 As with all grouped distributions, we must assume that the frequencies are concentrated at the mid-points of each group.

Note 3 We use short-cut methods, i.e., work from an assumed A.M. (one of the mid-points), and state the deviations in units equal to the group interval, for each variable.

Step 1

Find the S.D. of the X series.

1	2	3	4	5		6
Age groups (yrs)	Mid-points	Dev. from A.A.M. of 45 yrs. Units of 10 yrs	Frequency	Col. 4 × Col. 3 Freq. × dev.		Col. 5 × Col. 3 Freq. × dev.^{2}
				−	+	
20–30	25	−2	16	32	—	64
30–40	35	−1	24	24	—	24
40–50	45	0	44	—	—	—
50–60	55	1	15	—	15	15
60–70	65	2	1	—	2	4
TOTALS	—	—	100	56	17	107
				−39		

Table 9.5

$$S.D._{x}=\sqrt{\frac{107}{100}-\left(\frac{-39}{100}\right)^{2}}=\sqrt{1{\cdot}07-0{\cdot}1521}=\sqrt{0{\cdot}9179}.$$

Note The answer is in class units of 10 years, and we leave it in this form, since we are not interested in the answer, as such.

Step 2

Find the S.D. of the Y series.

1	*2*	*3*	*4*	*5*		*6*
Days lost	*Mid-points*	*Dev. from A.A.M. of $5\frac{1}{2}$ Units of 2 days*	*Frequency*	*Col. 4 × Col. 3 Freq. × dev.*		*Col. 5 × Col. 3 Freq. × dev.^{2}*
				−	+	
1–2	$1\frac{1}{2}$	−2	8	16	—	32
3–4	$3\frac{1}{2}$	−1	24	24	—	24
5–6	$5\frac{1}{2}$	0	32	—	—	—
7–8	$7\frac{1}{2}$	1	16	—	16	16
9–10	$9\frac{1}{2}$	2	12	—	24	48
11–12	$11\frac{1}{2}$	3	8	—	24	72
TOTALS	—	—	100	40	64	192
				+24		

Table 9.6

$$S.D._y \sqrt{\frac{192}{100} - \left(\frac{+24}{100}\right)^2} = \sqrt{1{\cdot}92 - 0{\cdot}0576} = \sqrt{1{\cdot}8624}.$$

Again we leave the answer in class units.

Step 3

We must now find the *co-variance*, as in the previous example. In the case of a table, which is really a combination of two separate frequency distributions, the method is to multiply together the respective deviations of each distribution, and

(Y) Deviations copied from col. 3 of Table 9.6	*(X) Deviations copied from col. 3 of Table 9.5*				
	−2	*−1*	*0*	*1*	*2*
−2	4	—	4	—	—
−1	8	8	4	4	—
0	4	12	16	—	—
1	—	4	8	4	—
2	—	—	12	—	—
3	—	—	—	7	1

Table 9.7

Note 2 Although the two scales have been started from zero (to show the points of intersection with the axes), this is not necessary, unless the question calls for it. If we had started the X scale at 16, and the Y at, say, 40, we could have used a more open scale and made the difference between the two lines more pronounced.

Correlation coefficients

Although regression analysis provides a useful method for estimating one variable from another, we still lack a means for giving a numerical value to the correlation present between two sets of data. This is particularly necessary when we wish to make comparisons.

One such measure is the *Pearsonian coefficient of correlation* (sometimes called the product-moment coefficient) represented by r. This is an extension of the method employed for standard deviation.

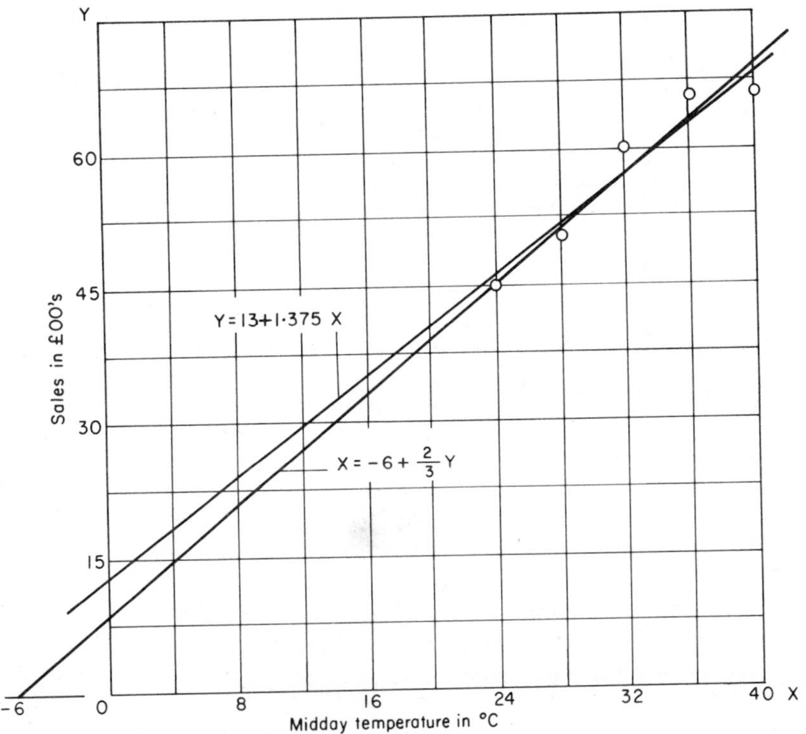

Fig. 9.3 Regression lines for data of table
Note **The regression line of X upon Y cuts the base line when $X = -6$ ($Y = 0$)**
The regression line of Y upon X cuts the vertical axis when $Y = 13$ ($X = 0$)

Application to ungrouped data

There are a variety of formulae for calculating r, each representing a different approach. The one we shall use for the moment is:

$$r = \frac{\Sigma xy}{\sqrt{\Sigma x^2 . \Sigma y^2}} \qquad \text{(F. 9.3)}$$

where x is the *deviation* of each X value from the A.M. of the X's, and y = the deviation of each Y value from the A.M. of the Y's. (Σ = 'the sum of . . .', as before).

Example 3:

1	*2*	*3*	*4*	*5*	*6*	*7*	*8*	
Week number	*Number of machines working* X	*Output (000's)* Y	*Dev. from A.M. = 8* x	*Dev. from A.M. = 6* y	x^2	y^2	*Co. 4 × Col. 5*	
							−	+
1	7	5	−1	−1	1	1	—	1
2	10	8	+2	+2	4	4	—	4
3	6	3	−2	−3	4	9	—	6
4	8	6	0	0	0	0	—	—
5	9	8	+1	+2	1	4	—	2
	40	30	—	—	10	18	—	13
A.M. =	8	6					+13	

Table 9.2 Output and machines employed in a factory

Substituting in our formula we have:

$$\Sigma xy = 13 \quad \Sigma x^2 = 10 \quad \Sigma y^2 = 18.$$

$$\text{Hence } r = \frac{+13}{\sqrt{10 \times 18}} = \frac{+13}{\sqrt{180}} = \frac{+13}{13{\cdot}42} = +0{\cdot}9687.$$

Note The sign of the end column should always be inserted, since this indicates the *direction* of the correlation (+ or −).

The above example is a simple one, since in each case the A.M. is a whole number.

In practice, this is seldom so, but a modification of the short-cut method for S.D. will enable us to work from assumed A.M.'s.

In such cases, we use a modified formula:

$$r = \frac{\Sigma xy}{N \times S.D._{\cdot x} \times S.D._{\cdot y}} \qquad \text{(F. 9.4)}$$

where N = the number of pairs of items.

It will be remembered that the method of calculating S.D. is:

$$S.D._{\cdot x} = \sqrt{\frac{\Sigma x^2}{N}} \quad \text{and } S.D._{\cdot y} = \sqrt{\frac{\Sigma y^2}{N}}.$$

Where x and y are the deviations from the *true* A.M. in each case. Substituting these in (F. 9.4) gives us:

$$r = \frac{\Sigma xy}{N\sqrt{\frac{\Sigma x^2}{N}} \times \sqrt{\frac{\Sigma y^2}{N}}} = \frac{\Sigma xy}{N\frac{\sqrt{\Sigma x^2 \times \Sigma y^2}}{N}}.$$

Cancelling out the N's gives us the previous formula (F. 9.3).

Example 4:

1	2	3	4	5	6	7	
X	Y	Dev. from assumed A.M. = 7 (= x)	Dev. from assumed A.M. = 14 (= y)	x^2	y^2	(x)×(y) Col. 3×Col. 4	
						−	+
10	9	+3	−5	9	25	15	—
3	20	−4	+6	16	36	24	—
8	15	+1	+1	1	1	—	1
12	6	+5	−8	25	64	40	—
4	22	−3	+8	9	64	24	—
6	18	−1	+4	1	16	4	—
5	23	−2	+9	4	81	18	—
9	12	+2	−2	4	4	4	—
8	16	+1	+2	1	4	—	2
11	8	+4	−6	16	36	24	—
76	149	+6	+9	86	331	153	3
A.M. = 7·6	14·9					3	
						−150	

Table 9.3

Explanation:

(*a*) In cols. 3 and 4 we are taking the deviations from an *assumed* A.M., since in each case the *real* A.M. is not a whole number. This is the short-cut method, as previously applied to S.D. (see Chapter 8).

Note A useful tip is to take, as assumed A.M., the whole number *immediately below* the real average (in this case, 7 and 14 respectively). This has the advantage of making the subsequent correction always positive, thus avoiding confusion regarding signs at a later stage.

(*b*) To get the S.D. of the X's, we have:

$$S.D._x = \sqrt{\frac{86}{10} - \left(\frac{+6}{10}\right)^2} = \sqrt{8{\cdot}6 - 0{\cdot}36} = \sqrt{8{\cdot}24}.$$

There is no need to work this out, because we are not interested in the answer for its own sake.

(*c*) Similarly, we have the S.D. of the Y's:

$$S.D._{y} = \sqrt{\frac{331}{10} - \left(\frac{+9}{10}\right)^2} = \sqrt{33{\cdot}1 - 0{\cdot}81} = \sqrt{32{\cdot}29}$$

(*d*) The student should note most carefully that the totals of cols. 3 and 4 give us the real A.M.'s of the X's and Y's. They therefore provide a check upon the accuracy of our deviations, which should always be carried out before proceeding, i.e.:

$$\text{The A.M. of the } X\text{'s is } 7 + \frac{6}{10} = 7{\cdot}6 \text{ (col. 1)}$$

$$\text{The A.M. of the } Y\text{'s is } 14 + \frac{9}{10} = 14{\cdot}9 \text{ (col. 2)}$$

(*e*) We have now corrected out two S.D.'s for the fact that we did not work from the real averages, but the total of col. 7 is also wrong, for the same reason. The correction for this will be more easily understood if we have another look at formula (9.4).

$$r = \frac{\Sigma xy}{N \times S.D._{x} \times S.D._{y}}$$

Since we already have the two S.D.'s, this leaves us with $\frac{\Sigma xy}{N}$ which is called the *co-variance*. This is the bit which needs correcting, and we do this by subtracting the product of the two correction factors already used in the S.D.'s: i.e., 6/10 and 9/10.

Hence we have:

$$\frac{-150}{10} - \left(\frac{+6}{10} \times \frac{+9}{10}\right) = -15 - 0{\cdot}54 = -15{\cdot}54$$

Note In this example, the total of col. 7 is *also negative*, so the two numbers must be added. If col. 7 had been positive, the correction factor would be taken away, and the final answer would be less.

(*f*) We can now restore the two S.D.'s, in the original formula, giving us:

$$r = \frac{-15.54}{\sqrt{8{\cdot}24} \times \sqrt{32{\cdot}29}} = -0{\cdot}9526.$$

The student would use logarithms to work this out, and may wonder how he can find the log of a minus quantity. The negative sign shows only the *direction* of the correlation, and may be ignored for purposes of working. It must, of course, be restored in the final answer.

then to multiply the product by the appropriate frequency, as shown in the original data (Table 9.4).

This is normally done in one operation, using a single table to collect the results, but in order to make clear the steps involved, we shall carry out the operation in two stages.

The figures in each rectangle are the frequencies copied from Table 9.4.

In the next table, we multiply the two deviations, and multiply the answer by the frequency in the appropriate rectangle. For example, starting in the top left-hand corner, we have $-2\times-2\times4=+16$, which we enter as shown:

					TOTALS	
					−	+
+16	—	—	—	—		16
+16	+8	—	−4	—		20
—	—	—	—	—	—	—
—	−4	—	+4	—	—	—
—	—	—	—	—	—	—
—	—	—	+21	+6		27
					—	63
					+63	

Table 9.8

Note 1 Particular care must be taken over the *sign* of the product, because some deviations are plus and some are minus.

Note 2 In the end columns, we total the figures horizontally, allowing for differences in sign, and enter the grand total at the foot.

$$\text{According to this result, the co-variance, i.e., } \left(\frac{\Sigma xy}{N}\right)=\frac{+63}{100}$$

but this figure needs correcting, since we have measured the deviations from assumed A.M.'s, instead of using the true ones.

The method of correction is exactly as in the previous example:

$$\text{Corrected co-variance}=\frac{+63}{100}-\left(\frac{-39}{100}\times\frac{+24}{100}\right)$$

i.e., we subtract the product of the two correction factors which we used in the S.D.'s—taking care over the signs.

This gives us:

$$+0{\cdot}63-(-0{\cdot}0936)=+0{\cdot}63+0{\cdot}0936=+0{\cdot}7236 \text{ (in class units).}$$

Referring to formula (F. 9.4) we have:

$$r=\frac{co\text{-}variance}{S.D._x\times S.D._y}\qquad \text{Hence } r=\frac{+0{\cdot}7236}{\sqrt{0{\cdot}9179}\times\sqrt{1{\cdot}8624}}.$$

So far, all the calculations have been in units based upon the respective class intervals. A very useful feature of the correlation coefficient is that the answer is independent of the units used—i.e., the units cancel out. Hence, no further correction is needed; the answer is a pure number and is not in any unit at all.

To show the use of logarithms in such cases, we give the working in full:

$\text{Log } 0{\cdot}7236 = \bar{1}{\cdot}8595$

$$\text{Log } 0{\cdot}9179 = \bar{1}{\cdot}9628$$
$$\text{Log } 1{\cdot}8624 = 0{\cdot}2700$$

$$\text{Add} \quad 0{\cdot}2328$$

$$\text{Square root } (\div 2) \quad 0{\cdot}1164$$

Subtract this from the numerator: $\bar{1}{\cdot}8595$

$0{\cdot}1164$

$\bar{1}{\cdot}7431$

$$\text{Anti-log } \bar{1}{\cdot}7431 = +0{\cdot}5535$$

Note The two logs are added *before* being divided by two. This saves time, since we are, in effect, finding one square root (of the product) instead of calculating each individually. The significance and meaning of this result will be discussed under 'Use and interpretation'.

Rank coefficient of correlation (Spearman coefficient)

It often happens that actual numerical values for the two variables, X and Y. are not available, or can only be obtained by the expenditure of much time and money.

In such cases, it may be possible to arrange each of the two sets of items in order of merit or importance. This is called *ranking*. For example, if we had ten apprentices and wished to examine the relationship between their command of English and their competence on the job, it would be possible for the foreman or some similar superior, to write down the names of the 10 persons, and then to allot to each individual a number, which showed his position in the ranking. The number given to any particular person is called his *rank or rating*. There would have to be two such rankings—one for English, and the other for competence—and these lists of numbers would correspond to our X's and Y's in the previous method.

It is, of course, essential to maintain the same order for the *names* of the individuals, throughout.

The rank coefficient is calculated from the following formula:

$$R = 1 - \frac{6 \times \Sigma(differences)^2}{N(N^2-1)}. \qquad \text{(F. 9.5)}$$

Where R = the rank coefficient of correlation, the differences are, for each individual item, the numerical difference between the two ranks—ignoring signs—and N is the number of items in each. Σ = 'the sum of . . .', as previously.

Example 6:

Nine apprentices are given an intelligence test, and are also ranked by their supervisor, according to their ability on the job. The results are given in Table 9.9. Find a measure of correlation between the two results.

1	*2*	*3*	*4*	*5*
Apprentice	*Rating in test*	*Rating on job*	*Difference (Cols. 2–3)*	*Diff*^{2}
A	4	5	1	1
B	2	1	1	1
C	6	6	0	0
D	8	7	1	1
E	1	4	3	9
F	9	8	1	1
G	7	9	2	4
H	5	3	2	4
I	3	2	1	1
			TOTAL	22

Table 9.9

Applying formula (F. 9.5), we have:

$$R = 1 - \frac{6 \times 22}{9(81-1)} = 1 - \frac{6 \times 22}{9 \times 80} = 1 - \frac{11}{60} = \frac{49}{60} = 0{\cdot}817.$$

Use and interpretation

Regression lines

We have seen that there are, in general, two such lines. Either one of them can be used to give an estimate of the other variable, and the greater the degree of correlation between X and Y, the closer our estimates will be to the actual values. It can be shown that the angle between the two lines diminishes as the correlation increases, and in the case of perfect correlation, this angle becomes zero—i.e., the two regression lines coincide, and become one. In such cases it does not matter whether we estimate X from Y, or vice versa.

When there is no correlation, the two lines are at right-angles to each other (the largest possible angle). One is parallel to the X axis, and the other is parallel to the Y axis.

Thus, it can be seen that there is a close connection between regression lines and correlation, and this can be expressed in mathematical terms (see correlation coefficient).

Interpolation and extrapolation

The great practical use of regression lines is the ability to predict one variable from a known value of the other one. This is valuable in two ways.

First, we may choose some *intermediate* value for our known variable (i.e., something between the two ends of the scale) and use this to get an estimate for the other variable; for example, in Table 9.1, the midday temperatures range between 24 and 40 degrees. What sales of ice-cream can we expect for, say, a temperature of 30°? We simply substitute this temperature (our X) in equation (A) and get an estimate of Y (ice-cream sales). This can be helpful in determining production schedules, stocks carried, etc., using weather forecasts, and available statistics of average temperature for the month in question. This is *interpolation*.

Second, we can project our sales, and imagine that the regression line is extended (in either direction). In other words we can choose some *external*, or extreme value for our X, which we have never met in actual practice, and use this as the basis for estimating a value of Y. This is *extrapolation*.

There would not be much point in estimating ice-cream sales for, say, a temperature of 10° below freezing, or 80° at the other end of the scale; but in research and scientific work, the ability to make such predictions is valuable. For example, a certain characteristic of a metal or alloy is known to vary with temperature. How will it stand up to extremes of temperatures such as those met with in space flight? The best estimate, short of an actual test at the desired temperature, is to extrapolate a known regression line.

The slope of a regression line, represented by the value of b in its equation, is sometimes called the *regression coefficient*. In the case of line (A) this has a value of 1·375 (in £00's). This tells us the change in our Y (in this case ice-cream sales) brought about by a change of one unit in our X (in this case 1 °C). That is, for each change (+ or −) of one degree in temperature, we should expect ice cream sales to change by £137·5.

The other line (B) will, of course, have a different slope, and consequently a different value of b.

The correlation coefficient

We have said that there is a mathematical relationship between this measure, and the regression lines. In fact, if the slopes of the two lines are represented by b_1 and b_2, then the coefficient of correlation (r) is given by:

$$r = \sqrt{b_1 \times b_2}. \qquad \text{(F. 9.6)}$$

With perfect correlation, b_1 and b_2 are the same, because the two lines coincide.

Hence

$$r = \sqrt{b \times b} = b.$$

Whenever the student is asked to draw one or more regression lines, in addition to finding their equations, this is a simple matter, if it is remembered that they are always *straight* lines, and that only two points are needed to establish a straight line.

If the equation is of the form $y = a + bx$, let $x =$ zero. This makes $y = a$—i.e., it gives the point at which the line cuts the vertical scale.

Choose as the other point a value of x which is some distance away from the first one, depending upon the magnitude of the X series, and find the corresponding value of y.

Finally, join the two points with a straight line.

Interpretation of r

It can be proved that the value of r varies between $+1$ and -1. Perfect correlation is represented by unity. (The sign indicates whether it is positive correlation or negative.) A value of 0 indicates no correlation.

Values of unity or zero are very rare in practice, and typical figures are usually of the order of 0·6 to 0·9. What does such a figure mean? The value of r is very much affected by the size of the sample (i.e., the number of items) and for small samples it should be treated with great reserve. Tables are available which show the size of sample needed for a given level of confidence in the result.

As a generalization, one can say that for small samples a value below 0·5 could have arisen by chance; i.e., it is not significant, and could disappear in further samples.

The standard error of r is discussed later, in Chapter 15.

The fact that the answer is independent of the units used is important in two ways.

First, the student need not understand what the X's and Y's mean. It would not matter if they were expressed in units he has never heard of. The calculation of r is purely mechanical.

Second, it is possible to vary the units at will to simplify the calculation. For example, if one series is in decimals, multiply it by 10 (or 100) to remove them. If one series has 0's at the end of each figure, divide them by 10 (or 100) to get rid of them. Provided all the numbers in any *one* series are treated alike, they can be multiplied or divided at will—without any further correction being necessary.

Rank correlation

This is used when actual values for X and Y are not available. It is frequently impossible to assign numerical values to a variable. For example, there is no numerical measure of shades of colour, or of character aspects such as good temper, dependability, and so on. It may be possible, however, to rank a group of individuals with regard to some quality, or to arrange various shades of colour in order of vividness. Like the Pearsonian coefficient, the value of R varies between $+1$ and -1, but the results obtained by the two methods are not necessarily comparable.

A difficulty sometimes arises when two or more items are ranked equally; i.e., given the same position number. Strictly speaking, the method of calculation does not provide for this, but when met with in an examination, there are two possible methods of dealing with it.

(*a*) If two individuals are, say, equal 6th rank, count each as 6, and the next ranking item as 8 (in other words, there is no 7).

(*b*) Alternatively, average the two (or more) items. For example, if ranked equal 6th, count one as 6th and the other as 7th. Their average rank is then

$$\frac{6+7}{2}=\frac{13}{2}=6\tfrac{1}{2}.$$

The next ranking item is 8 as in the previous method.

Needless to say, if both the X and Y series need adjustment in this way, the method used should be the same in each case, preferably method (*b*).

The ranking method can also be used for evaluating personality tests, etc. Supposing we wished to know whether a particular psychological test was useful for our purpose. We take a group of people, give them the test, and rank them according to their performance. If the test is supposed to measure ability of some kind, we then ask the supervisor, or other person who knows them, to rank the same individuals according to their actual ability on the job. We then compare the two rankings to see whether there is any correlation.

10

Time series

Method

A time series is the name given to a series of figures recorded through time. The name given to the graph on which such a series is plotted is a *historigram* (i.e., a history or record over time).

This should not be confused with the histogram, dealt with in Chapter 5.

The series may be plotted at daily, weekly, monthly, yearly, or any other intervals of time, and the horizontal axis is always chosen as the time axis.

If we were to plot the graph of a time series consisting of monthly or quarterly figures, over a large number of years, we might get somthing like Fig. 10.1.

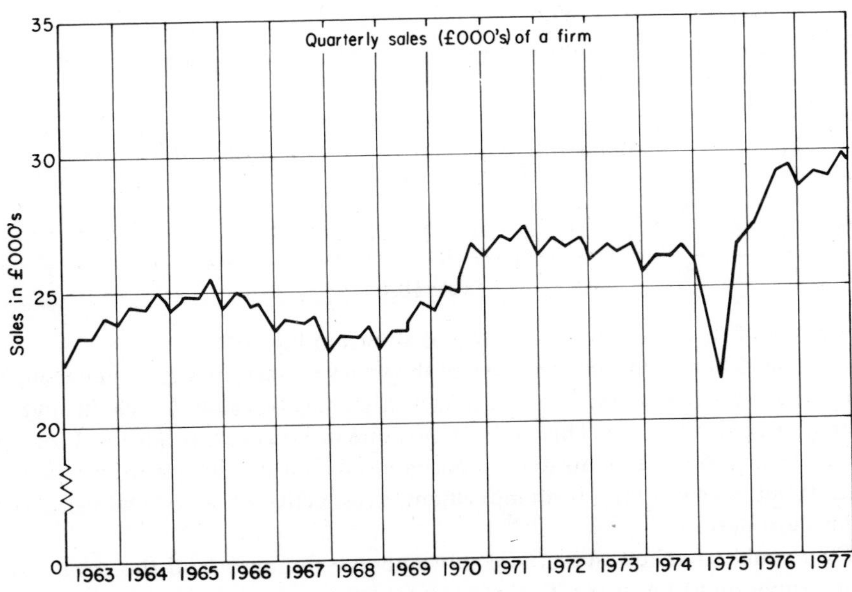

Fig. 10.1 Quarterly sales (£000's) of a firm

This actually represents a mixture of various influences, the principal ones being:

(*a*) *The long-term trend* It can be seen that the over-all picture is one of expansion, since the sales have increased from some £22 000 per quarter at the start, to a figure of roughly £30 000, at the end of the period.

(*b*) *The cyclical movement* This is the wave-like formation, generally due to the influence of booms and slumps on business activity. In the example, the period of each complete cycle, i.e., the distance in time from one peak to the next, is roughly 6 years but, in practice, this period may be anything from 5 to 14 years.

(*c*) *The seasonal variations* These are the small steps in each year, and are due to the fact that the quarterly figures follow a seasonal pattern, i.e., certain quarters are usually busy ones, while others show less active sales. This pattern will obviously vary from one industry to another.

(*d*) *The non-recurring influences* These may be good or bad, but since they do not occur with any statistical regularity, they cannot be measured or predicted.

Such an influence may be seen in 1975, where there is an unusual dip in the graph. This may have been the time when the firm's factory was destroyed by fire! Or it may have been some political event, such as a threat of war, or a financial crisis.

It is essential that we should be able to disentangle these various influences, and to measure each one separately. This procedure is known as the *analysis of a time series.*

EXAMPLE 1:

The figures given in the table below are a record of withdrawals over a period of years for a bank in an industrial area:

Year	*1969*	*1970*	*1971*	*1972*	*1973*	*1974*	*1975*	*1976*	*1977*
Withdrawals (£ten thousands)	25·8	19·2	26·0	27·1	22·8	28·7	28·5	24·5	29·6

Table 10.1

A graph of this series may be drawn as shown in Fig. 10.2.

It can be clearly seen that the curve of the series varies with occasional troughs and peaks every few years. There is, in fact, what may be called a cycle (trough to trough, or peak to peak). This cyclical movement, however, is not level for the whole of the period. It seems to be superimposed on a steady upward trend. The word 'trend' means a long-term movement, irrespective of occasional variations in the short period.

If we could somehow split these movements—the *cycle* and the *trend*—the information might be of use to the bank manager. The trend might suggest to him whether business is expanding or contracting in the long run. If the trend is

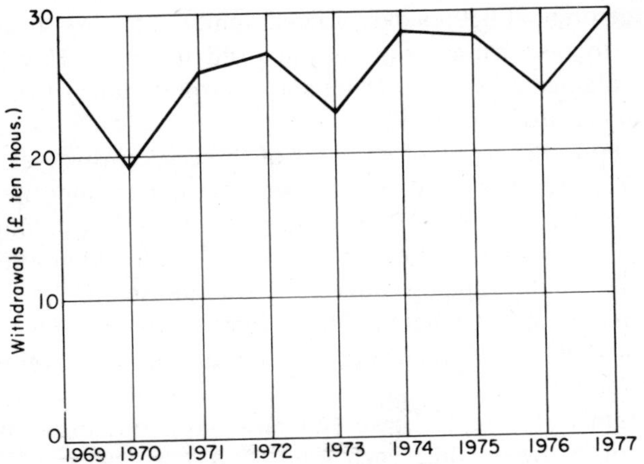

Fig. 10.2 Withdrawals from a bank in an industrial area, 1969 to 1977

upwards (as in our example), he may have to provide more staff and counter space or invest more heavily in office machinery. The cycle may suggest to him the possible interval of years during which cash is being taken out of, or left to accumulate in, his bank. This may lead him to adjust his policy in giving loans for two, three, or five-year periods.

The trend

We can separate the trend by a statistical technique known as the *moving average*. The table below shows the method:

	Trend				*Variation*
Col. 1	*Col. 2*	*Col. 3*	*Col. 4*	*Col. 5*	*Col 6*
Year	*Period of moving av.*	*With-drawals (£ten thous.)*	*Totals of 3*	*Moving av. of 3*	*Variation from the trend*
1969	1	25·8	—	—	—
1970	2	19·2	71·0	23·7	−4·5
1971	3	26·0	72·3	24·1	+1·9
1972	1	27·1	75·9	25·3	+1·8
1973	2	22·8	78·6	26·2	−3·4
1974	3	28·7	80·0	26·7	+2·0
1975	1	28·5	81·7	27·2	+1·3
1976	2	24·5	82·6	27·5	−3·0
1977	3	29·6	—	—	—

Table 10.2

In the table are columns for the years (col. 1), and for the withdrawals originally given (col. 3). To use the moving averages method, we take successive averages of the original figures over a fixed number of years. In this case it has been decided to take three years as the fixed number. (How to make this decision is explained later—see 'Use and interpretation'.) Column 2 simply shows the years renumbered in 3's.

Column 4 shows the totals of each set of three successive years, e.g., 1969, 1970, and 1971, add up to 71·0, and this figure is placed opposite the centre of these three years, i.e., opposite 1970 in col. 4. We proceed by adding the next set of three years, i.e., dropping the first year (1969) and adding the next (1972). This total is 72·3, and it is placed opposite 1971, and so on.

Column 4 is completed when we have total figures opposite all the years except the first (1969), and the last (1977), because moving averages could not be calculated for those years.

From the totals of 3 (col. 4) we can now work out the moving average, or trend, in col. 5, by dividing each total by 3, e.g., 1970 . . . 71·0 ÷ 3 = 23·7 (rounded to 1st decimal place). The name 'moving average' is a literal description of the method just used, where the *average* of a fixed block of three years is taken and *moved* over the entire period.

The moving average, or trend, is shown in the following graph, together with the graph of the original figures, given previously:

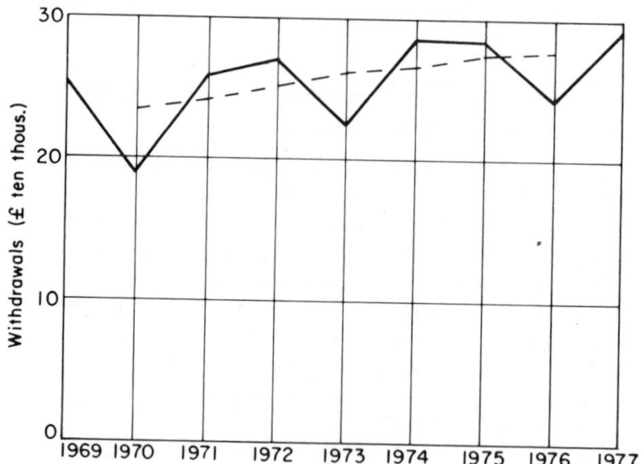

Fig. 10.3 Withdrawals from a bank in an industrial area showing 3-yearly moving average, 1969 to 1977

Note One disadvantage of the moving averages method which can be appreciated at this stage is that, because it is short at both ends, it does not cover the whole period.

The cyclical variation

To work out the second part of the problem, i.e., the cycle, we proceed as follows:

Column 6 is added to the previous table and headed 'Variation from the trend'.

This column is calculated by subtracting each trend figure (col. 5) from the corresponding figure of actual withdrawals (col. 3).

Column 3 minus column 5 = column 6

1970 $19{\cdot}2 - 23{\cdot}7 = -4{\cdot}5$
1971 $26{\cdot}0 - 24{\cdot}1 = +1{\cdot}9$

and so on.

Special attention must always be paid to the − and + signs, but we cannot go wrong if we remember that the variation figure is the variation *from* the trend. Ask yourself, 'Does the actual figure differ from the trend figure positively or negatively?' Actual figures which are *larger* than trend figures show a plus variation sign, and vice versa.

When col. 6 has been completed (once again we can have no figures for 1969 and 1977), a further step is necessary before we can finally calculate the cyclical variation.

Transfer the variation figures in col. 6 to a new table, using the 1, 2, and 3 numbers of col. 2 as your headings, thus:

	Years 1	*Years 2*	*Years 3*
	— +1·8 +1·3	−4·5 −3·4 −3·0	+1·9 +2·0 —
TOTALS	+3·1	−10·9	+3·9
Cyclical variation	+1·6	−3·6	+2·0
Adjustment	—	—	—

Table 10.3

The yearly variations are totalled in the 'totals' row, taking careful note of the addition of signs. The next row 'cyclical variation' is obtained by dividing the totals by the number of items added together in each column.

For example:

$$\text{Years 1} \quad \frac{+3{\cdot}1}{2} = +1{\cdot}6$$

$$\text{Years 2} \quad \frac{-10{\cdot}9}{3} = -3{\cdot}6$$

$$\text{Years 3} \quad \frac{+3{\cdot}9}{2} = +2{\cdot}0$$

These are our cyclical variations and they should add up to zero. It can be seen that they do, so there is no need to complete the last row 'adjustment'. Sometimes, due to the nature of the moving average method, the plus total of variations does not exactly equal the minus total of variations. The adjustment is then calculated as follows:

> If the excess is *positive*, divide it by the number of columns used and *subtract* it from each final variation.
>
> If the excess is *negative*, divide it by the number of columns used and *add* it to each final variation.

If this is done, the final variations will add up to zero.

Seasonal variation

EXAMPLE 2:

The figures given below are a record of the withdrawals from the same bank as in Example 1. This time, however, instead of covering each year from 1969 to 1977, the figures cover each quarter from the 1st quarter (January–March) in 1975, to the 2nd quarter (April–June) of 1978.

Year	*Quarters*			
	1	*2*	*3*	*4*
1975	5·2	6·8	9·1	7·4
1976	4·1	5·7	8·2	6·5
1977	5·3	6·9	9·4	8·0
1978	5·5	7·1	N.A.	N.A.

Table 10.4

The graph of the series can be drawn as shown in Fig. 10.4

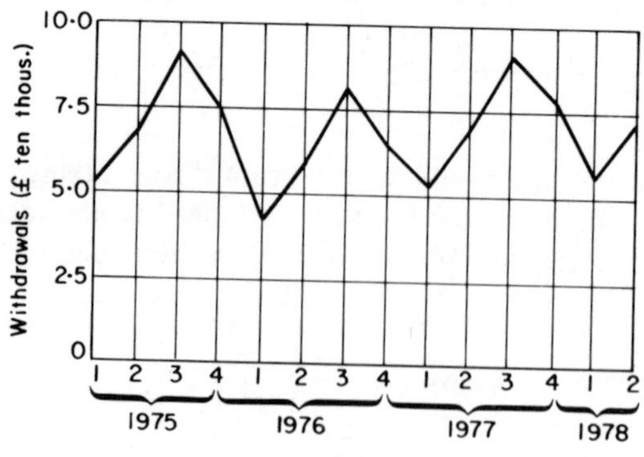

Fig. 10.4

A rising and falling pattern shows itself again in this curve, but this is no longer a cyclical variation (variation within a *number of years*). Our graph shows a *seasonal variation*, or the variation within *separate years*—'season' referring, of course, to the seasons of a year.

As the cyclical variation gave useful information, so this seasonal variation may, when we have worked it out, give the bank manager an idea of the withdrawals to be expected during the various quarters and thus, the amount of cash it is necessary to keep in his till.

(Figures for the last two quarters of 1978 were not available [N.A.].)

We proceed, as before, to separate the two associated movements in the figures. These are the trend and the seasonal variation.

Trend						*Variation*
Col. 1	*Col. 2*	*Col. 3*	*Col. 4*	*Col. 5*	*Col. 6*	*Col. 7*
Year	*Quarter*	*With-drawals*	*Totals 4-qtr*	*Centred totals*	*M.A. (÷8)*	*Variation from the trend*
1975	1	5·2	—	—	—	—
	2	6·8	28·5	—	—	—
	3	9·1	27·4	55·9	7·0	+2·1
	4	7·4	26·3	53·7	6·7	+0·7
1976	1	4·1	25·4	51·7	6·5	−2·4
	2	5·7	24·5	49·9	6·2	−0·5
	3	8·2	25·7	50·2	6·3	+1·9
	4	6·5	26·9	52·6	6·6	−0·1
1977	1	5·3	28·1	55·0	6·9	−1·6
	2	6·9	29·6	57·7	7·2	−0·3
	3	9·4	29·8	59·4	7·4	+2·0
	4	8·0	30·0	59·8	7·5	+0·5
1978	1	5·5	—	—	—	—
	2	7·1	—	—	—	—

Table 10.5

The first three columns simply show the years, quarters, and the original figures of withdrawals. As there are four quarters (or seasons) in the year, we use a moving average of four, therefore col. 4 shows the totals of blocks of four successive quarters.

Column 5 shows centred totals, i.e., successive pairs of the totals in col. 4 are added, and the results placed opposite the corresponding quarters thus:

$$28{\cdot}5 + 27{\cdot}4 = 55{\cdot}9$$

This centring is necessary whenever there is an *even* number of items in the moving average—e.g., seasonal variations (4), or even number cyclical variations (2, 4, 6, 8, etc.), in order to ensure that the moving average refers to the original figures of definite quarters of years.

Note This was not necessary in Example 1, because we took an odd number (3) of years and therefore we had a middle withdrawal figure against which to place each moving average.

In col. 6, the centred totals of col. 5 are each divided by 8 (totals of 4 × totals of 2), and the moving average or trend is obtained.

It should be noted that the first two quarters of 1975 and the first two quarters of 1978 do not yield any figures. As noted before, the trend is shortened at each end, and it should also be noted that the greater the number of items in the moving average, the more trend figures are lost at each end of the calculation.

The series can be graphed again and the trend included:

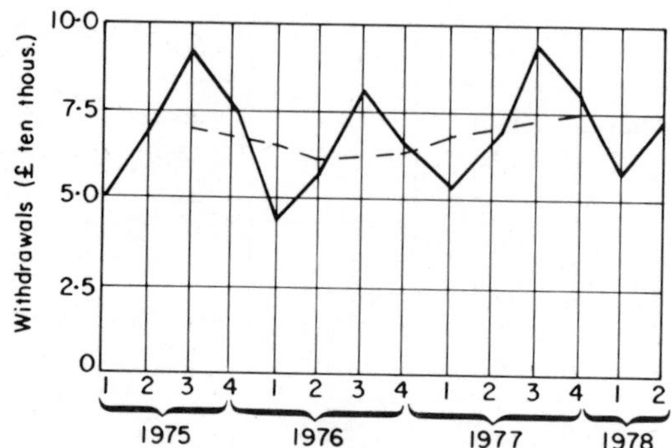

Fig. 10.5 Withdrawals from a bank showing 4-quarterly moving average, 1975 to 1978

The seasonal variation is calculated by working out col. 7 in the previous table. The trend (col. 6) is subtracted from the actual withdrawals (col. 3), and the variation (+ or −) recorded.

The variation figures are subsequently arranged (as in the case of the cyclical variation) in a table:

Year	*Quarters*			
	1	*2*	*3*	*4*
1975	—	—	+2·1	+0·7
1976	−2·4	−0·5	+1·9	−0·1
1977	−1·6	−0·3	+2·0	+0·5
1978	—	—	—	—
TOTALS	−4·0	−0·8	+6·0	+1·1
Seasonal variation	−2·0	−0·4	+2·0	+0·4

Table 10.6

It can be seen that the totals of the final figures, +'s and −'s, add up exactly to zero, so no adjustment is needed. If this total had differed significantly from zero, then an adjustment would have been made, as described in Example 1.

Note When the calculations are correct only to one decimal place (as in the examples given) it is wrong to introduce any adjustment which would involve additional decimals. The final figures cannot be any more correct than the original ones. In such cases a partial correction may be used. For example, if the total of the seasonal figures were +3·0, dividing this among the four quarters would mean a correction of $\frac{3\cdot 0}{4} = 0\cdot 75$ to be subtracted from each quarterly variation. In this case, a total correction of 2·8 could be applied. This would mean a deduction of $\frac{2\cdot 8}{4} = 0\cdot 7$ from each quarter. The totals would now add to +0·2 which is much better than before.

Least squares method

So far, in this chapter, we have described the analysis of a time series by the method of moving averages, i.e., repeatedly calculating a series of different average values as we moved along an original series, as it were, laying down a carpet of progressive snapshots. We produced a trend (as in Fig. 10.3) which was *not* a straight line. If the original figures had had a cycle which repeated itself *exactly* we should have got a straight line!

In fact it is easy to produce a straight line trend if we prefer to look at the average *overall* rate of increase (or decrease). We can do this by the method of least squares.

In Chapter 4 a line of 'best fit' was drawn on a scatter diagram (e.g., see Fig. 4.9 in Chapter 4). In Chapter 9 another method, the 'three-point method' of applying a straight regression line to two sets of data, was given. Later, in Chapter 9, we gave the formula for the equation of a straight line,

$$Y = a + bX$$

(see Fig. 9.1) whereby we could *minimize* all positive and negative deviations of the data from a straight line (which could be drawn through the data) by squaring the deviations. This is our method of least squares.

In a time series, one of the two sets of data is, of course, time itself, which increases by equal amounts (years, quarters, etc.). Therefore we can work out a straight line trend by using the above equation if we have time $= X$, and our data $= Y$, and squaring only those deviations of X (the irregular data).

Take Example 1, 'Withdrawals from a bank in an industrial area' (Table 10.1). We use the two formulae (F. 9.1) and (F. 9.2), which are repeated below:

$$\Sigma Y = na + b\Sigma X$$

$$\Sigma XY = a\Sigma X + b\Sigma X^2$$

and we now calculate the necessary figures for Example 1:

Year X	*Withdrawals* Y	X	XY	X^2
1969	25·8	0	0	0
1970	19·2	1	19·2	1
1971	26·0	2	52·0	4
1972	27·1	3	81·3	9
1973	22·8	4	91·2	16
1974	28·7	5	143·5	25
1975	28·5	6	171·0	36
1976	24·5	7	171·5	49
1977	29·6	8	236·8	64
$(n=9)$	232·2 (ΣY)	36 (ΣX)	966·5 (ΣXY)	204 (ΣX^2)

Table 10.7

Note The 'value' of the nine years themselves (1969, 1970, etc.) do not matter—only the increase of the next on the last, so, in col. 3 we write 0, 1, 2, etc., (intervals of 1 year).

Substituting, in our formulae, for ΣY, ΣX, ΣXY, and ΣX^2, we have:

$$232{\cdot}2 = 9a + 36b \qquad \text{Eq. (10.1)}$$

$$966{\cdot}5 = 36a + 204b \qquad \text{Eq. (10.2)}$$

We solve these two equations as follows:

(a) Multiply Eq. (10.1) by 4 (to make the a's equal to those in Eq. [10.2])

$$928{\cdot}8 = 36a + 144b \qquad \text{Eq. (10.3)}$$

(b) Subtract Eq. (10.3) from Eq. (10.2) (to eliminate a)

$$37{\cdot}7 = 60b$$

$$\frac{37{\cdot}7}{60} = b\text{, i.e., } b = 0{\cdot}6 \text{ (to 1 decimal place)}$$

(c) Substitute this value in Eq. (10.1):

$$232{\cdot}2 = 9a + 21{\cdot}6$$

$$232{\cdot}2 - 21{\cdot}6 = 9a$$

$$210{\cdot}6 = 9a\text{, i.e., } a = 23{\cdot}4$$

The regression line (trend) of least squares is therefore:

$$Y = 23{\cdot}4 + 0{\cdot}6X.$$

Let us now see how the trend figures obtained from this formula compare with our original series and with the trend figures (Table 10.2) we obtained from the method of moving averages:

Year	*Withdrawals*	*Moving average of 3*	*Least squares method*
Col. 1	*Col. 2*	*Col. 3*	*Col. 4*
1969	25·8	—	23·4+0·6×0=23·4
1970	19·2	23·7	23·4+0·6×1=24·0
1971	26·0	24·1	23·4+0·6×2=24·6
1972	27·1	25·3	23·4+0·6×3=25·2
1973	22·8	26·2	23·4+0·6×4=25·8
1974	28·7	26·7	23·4+0·6×5=26·4
1975	28·5	27·2	23·4+0·6×6=27·0
1976	24·5	27·5	23·4+0·6×7=27·6
1977	29·6	—	23·4+0·6×8=28·2

Table 10.8

The student will see that the two trend figures (cols. 3 and 4) are fairly close substitutes and he can guess that the more regular the cycles of the original series, the more closely they would fit with each other.

Use and interpretation

How to choose a moving average

If we were asked to find the seasonal variation and the trend, we are usually given figures of either the four quarters of the year, or figures of the 12 months of the year. It is obvious that, when 'seasonal' means 'within the year', we must use a 4-quarterly moving average in the first case, and a 12-monthly moving average in the second case.

Note Because these are even numbers, centring must be applied.

If the question concerns the cyclical variation, we may choose any number of years. The problem here is, which is the correct number?

The idea behind the separation of the trend is to eliminate the pattern of the shorter season or cycle and to obtain a smooth, long-term movement.

Consider the figures in Table 10.9 to which a 5-yearly moving average, and then a 7-yearly moving average have been applied.

Which is the correct one? Quite obviously the 7-yearly moving average. By using a 5-yearly moving average, the trend still appears (col. 4) to be rather irregular, whereas in the 7-yearly moving average (col. 6), the cyclical variation has been removed completely, and we are left with a smooth trend.

The correct method is to determine how many years lie between the troughs or the peaks (i.e., what is the cycle?), and, if the pattern is regular enough, to take this as your moving average. In the example above, it can be seen that the original figures (col. 2) are repeated exactly every 7 years. This could be seen even more clearly if we were to draw a graph of these original figures.

In Example 1 given previously, the 3-yearly moving average was obviously the best one to use, because this was the most appropriate cycle.

Col. 1	*Col. 2*	*Col. 3*	*Col. 4*	*Col. 5*	*Col. 6*
Year	*Original data*	*5-yearly moving annual total*	*5-yearly moving average*	*7-yearly moving annual total*	*7-yearly moving average*
1	22	—	—	—	—
2	22	—	—	—	—
3	20	101	20·2	—	—
4	19	97	19·4	140	20
5	18	96	19·2	140	20
6	18	98	19·6	140	20
7	21	101	20·2	140	20
8	22	103	20·6	140	20
9	22	104	20·8	140	20
10	20	101	20·2	140	20
11	19	97	19·4	140	20
12	18	96	19·2	—	—
13	18	—	—	—	—
14	—	—	—	—	—

Table 10.9

Limitations of the moving average method

As can be seen from the graphs and tables used previously in this chapter, the trend covers a shorter period than the original figures, and the greater the moving average period, the shorter will be the trend and, therefore, our calculations will be of correspondingly less use.

If calculations are to be really valuable, we should take a long series of figures when calculating the moving average (our examples were necessarily short to save elaborate calculations) and only then, if the pattern is *regular* enough, can we be sure that there are definite, *repeating* factors causing the variations.

Why do we analyse time series?

As explained earlier in the chapter, by separating the seasonal variation, cyclical variation, and the trend, we hope to learn something of the behaviour of the series with which we are dealing and probably, also, to use this knowledge as a basis for future action.

A time series can usually be split up into several associated movements. To each type of movement we can assign probable causes and possible future courses of action. The example of our bank can be used to illustrate this:

Movement	*Probable causes*	*Possible future action*
Trend (upwards)	Inflation: rise in volume of money, therefore rise (long-term) in withdrawals. Expansion of business.	Heavier capital investment in buildings, staff, and machines.
Cyclical variation	Trade Cycle—rise in withdrawals when money is in short supply and interest rates are low. Unemployment in the area.	Adjust loan policy, e.g., raise interest rates, offer services, give longer loans.
Seasonal variation	Withdrawals high just before Christmas and summer holidays.	Engage extra staff. Increase till-money.

In addition to the trend, cyclical variation, and the seasonal variation, we may also meet *special variations.* These are due to unusual happenings such as earthquakes, fire, strikes, etc.

It should be noted that, in Example 1, the cyclical variation was separated from a trend, and then in Example 2, from a *shorter* series, the seasonal variation was separated from a trend. The second trend (in Example 2) was a shorter term trend than that in Example 1, and it included the cyclical variation, as can be seen from the way that this shorter term trend dips in 1976 in the second graph (Example 2, Fig. 10.5).

Other uses of the analysis

Time series analysis is widely used in business and commerce for planning ahead in the expectation that previous performance and rhythm will be repeated to some extent. Special fields in which it is used are budgetary control, stock-holding, investment in stocks and shares and, particularly, in market research. In the latter field it can be used to try to assess what size of sales can be achieved with a given advertising budget, and how sales are increased with increases in this budget.

Extrapolation

Most of these uses involve the additional process of *extrapolation.*

For example, in our Example 1, can we tell what will be the probable amount of withdrawals in 1978?

In Table 10.2, col. 5 shows the trend which rises from 23·7 in 1970 to 27·5 in 1976. This is a rise of 3·8 over 6 years, or an average of $\frac{3\cdot8}{6} = 0\cdot6$ per year.

If we assume that the trend will continue to rise, the trend figure for 1978 would be 28·7, i.e.,

$$1976 = 27\cdot5$$
$$1977 = 27\cdot5 + 0\cdot6 = 28\cdot1$$
$$1978 = 27\cdot5 + 0\cdot6 + 0\cdot6 = 28\cdot7.$$

We know also the cyclical variation for each of the three years in any cycle (see Table 10.3), and that 1978 would fall in 'years 1' if we continued the table. As the cyclical variation for 'years 1' is +1·6, we simply add 1·6 to the estimated trend figure for 1978, thus:

Estimated trend + cyclical var. = estimated withdrawal

(28·7) + (+1·6) = 30·3.

Therefore the estimated withdrawal figure for 1978 is £303 000.

Such estimation by extrapolation, through widely practised, is not recommended. Although many economic and commercial series show a fairly regular pattern, it is often a fallacy to suppose that cycles will continue as they have in the past. There are at least two good reasons for this. First, the well-known unpredictability of scientific advance and invention, especially in the twentieth century, and, secondly, the fact that the field of government control nowadays is so widespread and deep that government interference (e.g., passing legislation, altering taxation, etc.) may suddenly upset any predictions that natural forces will continue as in the past.

Seasonal adjustment

Finally, we must mention a popular way of presenting a time series in a graph; i.e., that of presenting the 'seasonally adjusted data'. This follows very simply on what we have already learnt. To adjust a series of original figures, we calculate the seasonal variations and simply deduct these from the original figures. Thus, the seasonally adjusted figures of withdrawals in example 2 (Table 10.5, col. 3) would appear (1975 to 1976) thus:

Col. 1	*Col. 2*	*Col. 3*	*Col. 4*	*Col. 5*
Year	*Quarter*	*With-drawals*	*Seasonal variation*	*Seasonally adjusted*
1975	1	5·2	−2·0	7·2
	2	6·8	−0·4	7·2
	3	9·1	+2·0	7·1
	4	7·4	+0·4	7·0
1976	1	4·1	−2·0	6·1
	2	5·7	−0·4	6·1
	3	8·2	+2·0	6·2
	4	6·5	+0·4	6·1

Table 10.7

The seasonally adjusted data may now be graphed in the normal way from col. 5 of the table.

Comment on the least squares method

Comparison of the moving average method and the least squares method in Table 10.8 shows that the latter gives a trend which (unlike the moving average method) covers the whole of the period. Obviously we can calculate the cyclical or seasonal variations from the trend as we did in the moving average method, but, equally, extrapolation from the trend which we may perform is also open to the same dangers. Neither of the two methods is 'better' than the other. The least squares method gives a straight line and shows us an overall, single figure (b) rate of change. The longer the period of our original data, perhaps the less useful would such a single figure be, if we are dealing in terms of economic or social data which are affected by *different kinds* of influences throughout time. A straight line suggests a limited set of the same influences acting together in a single direction, which may not be the case.

11

Index numbers

Method

The chapter on time series dealt with the movement and changes in a single economic series through time. Many economic happenings are not the result of merely one changing series but of a collection or group of series. The change which affects the ordinary man and woman most is certainly the change in prices of goods and services which are consumed every day. The cost of day-to-day living includes a great variety of purchases at prices which change at different rates quite frequently.

Although we can directly measure the change in price of any one type of goods, it is more difficult to measure the average change in a special group of prices. It would be extremely useful to calculate some kind of average which would tell us by how much living costs had risen or fallen. This is the job which an index number tries to perform. *An index number is a measure, over time, designed to show average changes in the price, quantity, or value of a group of items.*

Most of us are chiefly concerned with retail prices, but index numbers are not restricted to these. Index numbers showing economic and business trends include *quantity indexes* (e.g., volume of industrial production, volume of foreign trade) and *value indexes* (e.g., retail sales, value of exports). Nor are *price indexes* confined to retail prices. They also include stock and share prices, raw material prices, wage rates (price of labour), etc.

Construction of an index number

PRICE INDEX

The first step in construction is to ask exactly what job the index will be expected to do. Let us assume that it should show the changes in price of a group of commonly bought goods and services. Obviously we require as a beginning:

(*a*) A list of commonly bought goods and services. We may specify types and varieties according to how detailed the enquiry is.
(*b*) A list of the corresponding prices of these items.

We might next ask who usually buys such goods and services. To take the individual as our 'purchasing unit' would not be satisfactory. Men, women, and children make very different purchases; therefore we would require three lists, or else have to restrict our enquiry to one of these narrow groups. It would be more useful to take the family or the household as a basic purchasing unit to include all types of purchasers.

Another question which faces us immediately is what kind of household are we dealing with—rich or poor, large or small? If we wish to cover the maximum number of people in our enquiry we should once more compromise and choose the large group of lower income households. In addition, we might choose a household of average size.

Finally, there is the time element. The index number must have a starting point. This may be an actual date (e.g., prices on 15 January 1974, for the General Index of Retail Prices), or the average over a certain period (e.g., average prices for the whole of 1970 in the case of official Index Numbers of Wholesale Prices). This starting point is known as the *Base Period* or *Base Year.*

Later comparisons are usually made on a monthly basis, i.e., the average is re-calculated month by month, so as to measure the change since the base period. Some index numbers are, however, calculated on a quarterly basis, and there is no reason why an individual firm should not calculate its own internal index numbers on a weekly basis if so desired.

Supposing that, after clearing up these problems, we now add up the prices of all items in our list and divide by the number of items in order to get an average. We should certainly get a false average. Several problems would appear:

(*a*) Does the price of 5 or 10 eggs count as one item? Should we count cheese in kg or grams, and should we measure milk in $\frac{1}{2}$ litres or litres?

(*b*) If salt at 2p per 500 grams rises by 50 per cent to 3p per 500 grams, does this count equally with a rise of 50 per cent in the price of butter (50p to 75p per kg)? Surely, the rise in the price of butter will be felt much more by the 'basic family'?

Both these problems can be solved by the simple method of weighting. In fact, most index numbers are only weighted averages, similar to those already met with in Chapter 7. If our index is truly to represent the cost to a basic family of a group of commonly bought goods and services, then the most sensible method would be to decide, say, how much per week such a family spends, and then to split this weekly budget into expenditure on the various items.

Thus, taking only three obvious items, we might get:

Item	*Units*	*No. of units bought per week*	*Price per unit (p)*	*Expenditure (price × quantity)*
Milk	Litre	12	10	120
Matches	Box	6	2	12
Coal	50 kg	2	90	180
		TOTAL EXPENDITURE		312

Table 11.1

The weight, or importance, we attach to each item in the budget will vary according to how much of the total expenditure is spent on it. The proportion of expenditure on each item is 10 : 1 : 15 (reading down the last column). These are the weights.

Price index

By the same time next year, prices will probably have changed. We will assume that they have all risen, but that the household still uses the same *quantities* of each item. Table 11.2 shows the changes, and it can be seen that the percentage rise in price has not been the same in each case:

Item	*Price in year 1 (p)*	*Price in year 2 (p)*	*Percentage change*
Milk	10	12	$\frac{12}{10}\times 100 = 120$
Matches	2	$2\frac{1}{2}$	$\frac{5}{4}\times 100 = 125$
Coal	90	99	$\frac{99}{90}\times 100 = 110$

Table 11.2

The figures in the last column are known as *price relatives* because they show, in percentage form, the new prices in year 2 relative to the old prices of year 1. For instance, if the price in year 1 is assumed to be 100, then the price in year 2 of, say, milk would be 120. We now have sufficient data to calculate the index—the percentage change in each price, and the weights of each item.

Item	*Price relative*	*Weight*	*Price relative × weight*
Milk	120	10	1 200
Matches	125	1	125
Coal	110	15	1 650
	TOTALS	26	2 975

Table 11.3

It is convenient now to work in points and we can call year 1 the base year and count it as 100. If we were to count the price relative of each item in year 1 as 100, and then multiply it by the weights, as above, we would obviously have $26\times 100 = 2\,600$. This compares with the total price relative × weight for year 2, of 2 975. Simplifying, with year 1 = 100, then year $2 = \frac{2\,975\times 100}{2\,600} = 114{\cdot}4$. We can say that the index number has increased by 14·4 points.

Note We cannot say 14·4 per cent, even though we calculated in the form of percentages. Suppose the index number rose to 120 in year 3, we should say that from year 2 to year 3 the index number rose by 5·6 points. It would be wrong to say that it had risen by 5·6 per cent, because 5·6 per cent of the previous figure of 114·4 is $\frac{5\cdot6\times114\cdot4}{100}=6\cdot4$, and, when this is added to 114·4, we get 120·8 as the index number for year 3, instead of the true figure of 120. To avoid confusion, therefore, it is far better to express the index numbers themselves in units of points, which have no connections with fractions or percentages.

This method of calculating the index seems reasonable enough. Yet objections may be raised. Some might say that the increase of 14·4 points gives a false impression, because freak weather produced abnormally low prices in year 1, and abnormally high prices in year 2. It is easy to see that if this were true, the increase in the index from year 1 to year 2 would be greatly magnified. It is argued that a year in which prices are about normal should be chosen as the base year. In this way, the abnormal, temporary price movements could easily be recognized for what they were. It is easy to see, also, that if the base year was a high price year, and this was followed by a year in which prices increased normally, the index would appear to have decreased! Why should we bother to object? The reason is that many wage and salary claims (among other things) are heavily dependent on the index as an argument in favour of higher rewards. If it is possible to calculate more than one figure for the index, wage and salary earners would naturally prefer the one which suits their case. As it is impossible to suit everyone, the selection of almost any year as a base year will cause argument in some quarters.

Summary of the steps

Purpose of the index Until this vital point is decided, planning is impossible.

Nature of the index In a retail price index, for instance, the list of items (often called a 'representative basket of goods and services') must be decided, and the corresponding prices known for each period of calculation.

Type of index The one described above is a 'weighted arithmetic mean' of prices, using price relatives.

Unit of enquiry In our example this is the household in the lower income groups. Size of household, i.e., average number of persons, may be used to define the unit even further, but in practice, with a large number of households, a random sample might be taken (see Chapter 2).

Base year This should be a normal year for the index, so far as it is possible to choose this. For example, we should not start a price index in a year of very low prices (a slump), because all future calculations will show an exaggerated rise. Also, the pattern of expenditure at such a time (the 'weights') might not be typical, because of unemployment, short-time working, etc. The index in our example is often called a 'fixed base' index, because the first year of calculation equals 100 points, and future years are calculated from this base.

Quantity index

The construction of a quantity index follows exactly the same method as the price index. Instead of using price relatives we use, of course, quantity relatives. The weights used are, once again, proportional to the expenditure on each item in year 1. The index number of quantities calculated below shows the same items as were used for the price index:

Item	*Quantity in year 1*	*Quantity in year 2*	*Quantity relatives*	*Weights*	*Quantity relative × weight*
Milk	12 litres	12 litres	$\frac{12}{12}\times 100 = 100$	10	1 000
Matches	6 boxes	3 boxes	$\frac{3}{6}\times 100 = 50$	1	50
Coal	2 (50 kg)	3 (50 kg)	$\frac{3}{2}\times 100 = 150$	15	2 250
			TOTALS	26	3 300

Table 11.4

If year 1 (the base year) = 100, then the index number for year 2 will be $\frac{3\,300}{26} = 126{\cdot}9$ points, an increase of 26·9 points.

It may be noticed that, in this example, only the quantity of coal increased, while the quantity of milk remained the same as in year 1, and the quantity of matches actually decreased. However, the final index number still shows an increase because the far heavier weight given to coal easily cancels out the fall in matches with plenty to spare, even though one has increased by 50 per cent and the other has decreased by 50 per cent. An *unweighted* arithmetic mean would (quite wrongly, of course) have shown no change in the index.

Types of index

The indexes dealt with above are often known as price, or quantity, relative indexes. Many other types of index have been invented and are used. As all are averages of one kind or another, they have the advantages and disadvantages common to averages. Just as there is no perfect average, so there is no ideal index. Some are more suitable than others for particular purposes.

The aggregative index

The aggregative method of calculation will give the same results as the 'relative' method, and it can be used to calculate a price or a quantity index.

An example of the price index is given, using the same material as above:

Item	*Price in year 1 (p)*	*Price in year 2 (p)*	*Quantity in year 1*	*Price (year 1) × quantity (year 1)*	*Price (year 2) × quantity (year 1)*
Milk	10	12	12	120	144
Matches	2	$2\frac{1}{2}$	6	12	15
Coal	90	99	2	180	198
			TOTALS	312	357

Table 11.5

If year 1 (the base year) = 100, then the index number for year 2 will be $\frac{357}{312} \times 100 = 114{\cdot}4$ points.

By this method there is no need to convert the prices into price relatives. The formula to remember is simply:

$$\frac{\text{Total (price [year 2]} \times \text{quantity [year 1])}}{\text{Total (price [year 1]} \times \text{quantity [year 1])}} \times 100$$

The quantity index can easily be calculated from the amended formula:

$$\frac{\text{Total (quantity [year 2]} \times \text{price [year 1])}}{\text{Total (quantity [year 1]} \times \text{price [year 1])}} \times 100$$

This is a slightly different approach from the price relative method, and the latter is usually preferred in practice.

The geometric index

The previous examples have all used the A.M. to average the items. In theory we could use any of the other averages (geometric mean, median, or mode), and the present method uses the geometric mean.

Weights are employed, as before, but in this case we use the *logarithms of the prices* for years 1 and 2, instead of the prices themselves. The rest of the calculation is similar to Table 11.5, except that we must subtract the final total for year 1 from that for year 2, and divide the result by the total weights. The answer is in logarithms, so we find the anti-log, and multiply the result by 100 to give the index number for year 2.

Col. 1	*Col. 2*	*Col. 3*	*Col. 4*	*Col. 5*	*Col. 6*	*Col. 7*	*Col. 8*
Item	*Price in year 1* (*p*)	*Price in year 2* (*p*)	*Quantity in year 1* (*weights*)	*Logs of year 1 prices*	*Logs of year 2 prices*	(*Year 1 logs*) × *weights* (*Col. 5*)× (*Col.* 4)	(*Year 2 logs*) × *weights* (*Col. 6*)× (*Col.* 4)
Milk	10	12	12	1·0000	1·0792	12·0000	12·9504
Matches	2	$2\frac{1}{2}$	6	0·3010	0·3979	1·8060	2·3874
Coal	90	99	2	1·9542	1·9956	3·9084	3·9912
TOTALS			20			17·7144	19·3290

Table 11.6

$$(\text{Col. } 8) - (\text{col. } 7) = 19{\cdot}3290 - 17{\cdot}7144 = 1{\cdot}6146$$

$$\text{and} \quad \frac{1{\cdot}6146}{20} = 0{\cdot}0807$$

$$\text{Anti-log } 0{\cdot}0807 = 1{\cdot}204$$

With year 1 (the base year) = 100, then the index number for year 2 will be $1{\cdot}204 \times 100 = 120{\cdot}4$ points.

The chain base

All the previous examples in this chapter have been calculated on the fixed base method, that is, by selecting a base year (100), and taking the changing prices (or quantities), as a percentage of that year. Another method is the 'chain base' method by which the changing prices (or quantities) for each year (or period) are taken as a percentage of the year immediately before. This method is suitable when weights are changing rapidly because new items are being brought into the index and old items are dropping out. Thus, over a period, if changes in weights have taken place, the chain base method would, year by year, have modified itself to take account of these. In the fixed base method, such changes in weights could not have been included in the index until they amounted to such proportions that the whole index would have to be revised to prevent its going out-of-date. Although the chain base method might be superior for some purposes in the fairly short period, there is bound to come a time when the index number of the last year of the series bears little serious relation to the first year of the series (e.g., if weights have been changing fairly frequently). In the table below years are shown in row 1, a chain-based index (calculated as stated above) is shown in row 2. In row 3 is shown the conversion of row 2 into a fixed-base index which will allow the student to compare the two indexes:

Year	*1*	*2*	*3*	*4*	*5*
Chain base	*100*	*103*	*107*	*110*	*115*
Fixed base	100 ↓ = 100	$\frac{100\times103}{100}$ ↓ = 103	$\frac{103\times107}{100}$ ↓ = 110·2	$\frac{110{\cdot}2\times110}{100}$ ↓ = 121·2	$\frac{121{\cdot}2\times115}{100}$ ↓ = 139·4

(*The pattern of calculation is shown by the guide arrows.*)

Table 11.7

The reasoning behind the above steps is as follows:

Note 1 In year 2, prices had risen by 3 per cent (103 − 100) compared with year 1. Therefore, on a fixed base, prices in year 2 would be $\frac{103}{100}$ of those in year 1 (103).

Note 2 In year 3, prices had risen by 7 per cent, compared with year 2. With a fixed base, they would rise by 7 per cent of the previous year's figure (103). That is, the new index is $\frac{107}{100}$ of 103 = 110·2 points.

Note 3 In year 4, prices had risen by 10 per cent, compared with year 3. The fixed base index is thus 10 per cent more than the previous figure of 110·2. That is, $\frac{110}{100}$ of 110·2, and so on.

Use and interpretation

As in the case of many published figures, members of the public are apt to put far too much faith in index numbers, and to use them for arguments for which they were never intended. It is perhaps too much to ask that anyone who uses the General Index of Retail Prices to support or deny a wage claim, or to criticize or praise the government, should know the faults and limitations of this index. Most people are only too willing to cling with blind faith to an official figure, especially if it tends to support their actions.

Limitations of index numbers

(*a*) Tastes and habits change in the course of time. Therefore, weightings become out-of-date, together with the index. For example, there is more money spent on leisure activities than there was 50 years ago. This problem is overcome to a certain extent in the latest Index of Retail Prices by the use of a chain base.

(*b*) Inventions may make certain products cheaper (this would, of course, be reflected in a price index), but they may create new basic forms of expenditure, such as television sets, or eliminate old basic forms of expenditure, e.g., the use of the telephone for communication, instead of costly travel. These also change weightings.

(*c*) Data used in the calculation of indexes are rarely up to date, and often incomplete (see Index of Industrial Production).

(*d*) Indexes usually cover only a part of the field of enquiry—e.g., the General Index of Retail Prices only considers the prices of some 350 items, out of thousands of possible ones. These are chosen as being typical, or representative items, but this is often a matter of opinion. From 1975 the weights have been chosen on the basis of a sample of households.

(*e*) Because no particular year can strictly be called a normal year, the index contains a further element of approximation.

(*f*) Index numbers contain an increasing degree of error, the longer they are used without revision. If they *are* revised, it is not strictly correct to compare one series with another. For example, a later index might represent a higher level of 'happiness' than an earlier one.

(*g*) Indexes calculated for the whole country can be seriously in error when they are applied to regions within the country—e.g., the high cost of housing in London makes living costs much dearer than for those in the north, yet the General Index of Retail Prices gave the weighting of $\frac{126}{1000}$ in 1973 for housing for the whole country.

(*h*) Some kinds of data are not suitable for measurement, although they could be of great importance in an index. For example, income tax, doctors' and dentists' fees, and mortgage payments are not included in the General Index of Retail Prices.

(*i*) An index is an average, with the advantages and disadvantages of an average; it tells us nothing, for example, about particular prices or groups of prices.

(*j*) Data used in the compilation of indexes are often subject to error. For example, the Index of Industrial Production is based on returns by firms; the General Index of Retail Prices is based on a sample of households. The volume indexes of exports and imports rely on traders' records.

There are many more limitations of index numbers, but perhaps enough has been said to warn the student not to take the figures too literally. No sensible person would deny, however, that properly based index numbers advance considerably our knowledge of changes in business and in society.

Misuse of indexes

Something has already been said about the choosing of a base year. The student will readily appreciate how a government may choose as a base year a past year in which prices were high in order to make present prices seem low by comparison. An opposition may do just the reverse in order to argue that a government has not kept its promise of maintaining stable prices. In a similar way, the rate at which prices have changed over a period may be the subject of much argument:

Example:

	Year 1 (*June*)	*Year 2* (*June*)	*Year 3* (*June*)
Index	140	150	180

Possible quotations in the Press (*in year 3*)

(*a*) 'Prices have risen by 40 points since Year 1'.
(*b*) 'Since Year 1 prices have risen by 29 per cent.'
(*c*) 'Up to Year 3 prices had risen by 22 per cent.'
(*d*) 'The average increase in prices since Year 1 has been 20 per cent.'
(*e*) 'The average rate of increase in prices since Year 1 has been 13·5 per cent.'

The range of increase here (13·5 to 40) would seem large enough to suit anyone, though stranger results than these could no doubt be achieved with a little judicious juggling of base years! Let us see how they were calculated:

(*a*) This is a simple, true statement, expressing the increase in points.
(*b*) This calculation is obtained by expressing the difference in points between year 3 and year 1, i.e., 40 points, as a percentage of year 1, thus

$$\frac{40}{140}\times 100 = 29 \text{ per cent, which seems reasonable enough.}$$

(*c*) This result is obtained by expressing the difference in points between year 3 and year 1, i.e., 40 points, as a percentage of year 3, thus

$$\frac{40}{180}\times 100 = 22 \text{ per cent.}$$

This is inexcusable, because one would normally take the earlier year as the base quantity, unless specially asked to do otherwise.

(*d*) This result is obtained by taking the difference between the years, 10 and 30, adding them and dividing by 2, thus $\frac{10+30}{2}=20$ points (not per cent!).

(*e*) This result is obtained by taking the differences between the years, 10 and 30, expressing them as percentages of previous years, i.e.:

$$\frac{10}{140}\times 100=7 \text{ per cent and } \frac{30}{150}\times 100=20 \text{ per cent (correct so far)}$$

and simply adding the 2 percentage changes and dividing by 2 for an average, i.e.,

$$\frac{7+20}{2}=13{\cdot}5 \text{ per cent.}$$

The correct method to obtain a *rate* of increase is to take the geometric average $\sqrt{107\times 120}=13{\cdot}3$ per cent. This means that if 140 is increased by 13·3 per cent the result will be approximately 159, and if this figure is increased again by 13·3 the result for Year 3 will be 180 (approximately, because only one decimal place of the geometric mean was calculated). Thus, only the geometric mean can be used to calculate a *rate* of increase.

Therefore, only calculations (*a*) and (*b*) are really correct. One fact is brought out in the statements—that of the need for clear thinking when one is speaking of points and percentages.

The remainder of this chapter is devoted to a brief analysis of the General Index of Retail Prices, as an example of a price index on a chain base, and the Index of Industrial Production, as an example of a quantity index on a fixed base.

The index of retail prices

PURPOSE OF THE INDEX

To measure the monthly degree of change in the retail prices of goods and services for the whole field over which households distribute their expenditure.

The index is compiled by the Department of Employment and published in the *Monthly Digest of Statistics*, the *Department of Employment Gazette*, the *Annual Abstract of Statistics*, and *Economic Trends.*

NATURE OF THE INDEX

The index is calculated from prices taken on a particular Tuesday each month for the following groups and weightings:

	Group	*Col. 1 1972 Weights*	*Col. 2 1973 Weights*
I	Food	251	248
II	Alcoholic drink	66	73
III	Tobacco	53	49
IV	Housing	121	126
V	Fuel and light	60	58
VI	Durable household goods	58	58
VII	Clothing and footwear	89	89
VIII	Transport and vehicles	139	135
IX	Miscellaneous goods	65	65
X	Services	52	53
XI	Meals bought and consumed outside the home	46	46
	TOTAL	1 000	1 000

Table 11.8

Each of the above groups contains a number of sections—e.g., 'Food' contains 32 sections. Within each section there may be various items—e.g., 'Potatoes' (section No. 25 in group 1) is divided into (*a*) old potatoes, (*b*) new potatoes (in season), (*c*) potato crisps.

The calculation of the weights is based upon the findings of the Family Expenditure Survey, which operates as follows:

The Family Expenditure Survey This was started in January 1957, the first report, covering the years 1957–8–9, being published in October 1961. It included Northern Ireland from 1958 onwards.

The survey is at present based upon a sample of between 10 000 and 11 000 addresses each year, so chosen that every private household in the country has an equal chance of selection, and that the sample is spread evenly over the year.

The method used is based upon a three-stage sampling procedure, with stratification, and all members of a household over the age of 16 are asked to co-operate by keeping detailed expenditure records for 14 consecutive days with supplementary information about regular, longer-term payments (e.g., rent, electricity, and insurance). They are also asked about their incomes. About two-thirds of the households approached agree to co-operate.

During 1972, the weights quoted in Table 11.8, col. 2 were used, and these represented the average pattern of expenditure during the three years ending June 1971, re-priced at January 1972 prices. From 1975 the weights have been based on the Family Expenditure Survey of the previous year.

Certain items of expenditure are not included in the index. They are: income tax payments, national insurance contributions, life insurance premiums and payments to pension funds, household insurance (except building insurance), trade union subscriptions, friendly societies, hospital funds, church collections, cash gifts, pools and other betting payments, doctors' and dentist's fees, mortgage payments for house purchase and for major structural alterations.

The reasons for not including these are that many of them are highly variable and often not measurable in units, and many are in the nature of investments rather than unavoidable consumer expenditure.

Published indexes of prices often give separate indexes for groups within the index. It is official policy to give index numbers rounded to the first place of decimals.

The student is advised to read, *Method of Construction and Calculation of the Index of Retail Prices*, Studies in Official Statistics, No. 6, (HMSO for the Department of Employment). A full description of the Family Expenditure Survey is provided by the technical handbook, *Family Expenditure Survey: Handbook on the Sample, Fieldwork and Coding Procedures*, (HMSO).

The index of industrial production

PURPOSE OF THE INDEX

To measure the changes over time in the volume (or quantity) of industrial production of a major part of the industry of the nation. The index acts as an economic indicator of industrial activity in the economic record of the country.

The index is compiled by the Central Statistical Office in collaboration with other government departments, and is published in the *Department of Employment Gazette*, the *Monthly Digest of Statistics*, the *Annual Abstract of Statistics*, and *Economic Trends*.

NATURE OF THE INDEX

The index covers manufacturing, mining and quarrying, building and construction, and gas, water, and electricity supply. It does not include agriculture, forestry and fishing, trade, transport, finance, and all other public and private services. In the industries included, the index covers the production of capital and consumption goods, for the home or export market, or for the armed services. The industries covered account for nearly half of the gross domestic product.

About 890 *series* of production are taken and classified as 20 *Industrial Orders* as defined by the Standard Industrial Classification. The weightings for these industries are shown in Tables 11.9 and 11.10 overleaf.

The weight given to each industry and each series is proportional to the average monthly production in 1975, i.e., 1975 = 100. The estimated production of each series is multiplied by its weight, and the various products are combined, according to their industrial groupings, and the index is calculated. This is a highly simplified account of an index which conceals many difficult problems and compromises, and the student is advised to read, *The Measurement of Changes in Production*, Studies in Official Statistics, No. 25, (HMSO for the Department of Employment). Additional notes are provided in *Statistical News*, Feb. 1977 and Nov. 1977.

The Index of Industrial Production is a typical example of a 'base-weighted' index, i.e., one which shows the relative importance of items in the base period. This is a common type, but the student should note that weights for other indexes may be calculated at some other period of time, e.g., on the current year's importance of items. Such weights have the advantage of being more

	Weight
Mining and quarrying	41
Manufacturing	
Food, drink, and tobacco	77
Coal and petroleum products	9
Chemicals and allied industries	57
Metal manufacture	47
Mechanical engineering	92
Instrument engineering	12
Electrical engineering	66
Shipbuilding and marine engineering	14
Vehicles	68
Other metal goods	46
Textiles	40
Leather, leather goods, and fur	3
Clothing and footwear	24
Bricks, pottery, glass, cement, etc.	28
Timber, furniture, etc.	25
Paper, printing, and publishing	58
Other manufacturing industries	31
Construction	182
Gas, electricity, and water	80
TOTAL	1 000·0

Table 11.9

Order	*Industry*	*Series*	*Weight*
Mining and quarrying	Coal mining	Bituminous—unscreened	1·3
		—large	5·7
		—graded	7·4
		—treated smalls	9·6
		—untreated smalls	8·7
		Anthracite	0·3
	Stone and slate quarrying and mining	Cement	2·3
	Chalk, clay, sand, and gravel extraction	Aggregate (Great Britain)	
		China clay	3·0
	Other mining and quarrying	Iron ore	0·5
		Tin ore	0·1
		Salt	1·0
		Gypsum	0·1
	Petroleum and Natural gas	Natural gas	0·3
		Crude oil	0·7
		TOTAL	41·0

Table 11.10 Example: The analysis of one industrial order

up-to-date and they are called 'current weighted'. A base weighted index is said to be of the *Laspeyre* type, whilst one with current weights is called a *Paasche* type.

An example of both Laspeyre and Paasche type indexes, using the figures of Tables 11.4 and 11.5, are given below:

Laspeyre price index:

$$\frac{\text{Total [price(year 2)} \times \text{Quantity (year 1)]}}{\text{Total [price (year 1)} \times \text{Quantity (year 1)]}} \times 100 \qquad \text{(F11.1)}$$

$$= \frac{(12\times 12)+(2\tfrac{1}{2}\times 6)+(99\times 2)}{(10\times 12)+(2\times 6)+(90\times 2)}\times 100$$

$$= \frac{357}{312}\times 100 = 114.4 \text{ points.}$$

Paasche price index:

$$\frac{\text{Total [price (year 2)} \times \text{Quantity (year 2)]}}{\text{Total [price (year 1)} \times \text{Quantity (year 2)]}} \times 100 \qquad \text{(F11.2)}$$

$$= \frac{(12\times 12)+(2\tfrac{1}{2}\times 3)+(99\times 3)}{(10\times 12)+(2\times 3)+(90\times 3)}\times 100$$

$$= \frac{448\tfrac{1}{2}}{396}\times 100 = 113.3 \text{ points.}$$

The difference between the base-weighted Laspeyre and the current-weighted Paasche can be seen in the two formulae (F11.1) and (F11.2). In a price index of the Paasche type, the *quantities* are of the current year. In a quantity index of the Paasche type, the *prices* are of the current year.

The numerical difference between the two price indexes given arises because the price rise (of all three commodities) is offset by the heavy consumption (in quantity) which we have used to multiply year 1 and year 2 prices. If price inflation exists *and* consumption (in quantity) is rising, then the Paasche index will be less than the Laspeyre index. If price inflation exists and the consumption is falling, the position will be reversed. The student may guess how the two indexes would compare if consumption remained the same in the two years!

Little precision can be attached to any index number, they are more reliable as trend indicators. The Laspeyre index is more popular than the Paasche type as the latter has to be recalculated each year and it is generally supposed that prices will alter more than quantities consumed from year to year.

12

Theory of sampling

Method

We have seen in previous chapters that we are frequently asked to make some assessment of a *group* of items, on the basis of a sample.

Types of universe

The group from which we draw our sample is called the *universe* or *population*. This is so, even if the items or members are inanimate, or purely abstract.

A *finite* universe is one with a fixed number of items, e.g., population of a city, or customers of a firm. We may not know the exact number, at any moment, but there are obviously limits.

An *infinite* universe is one with no theoretical limit to the number of items, e.g., the stars in the heavens.

Furthermore, the items may not actually exist. Such a universe is termed *hypothetical* or *theoretical*. For example, we could take a die and throw it, observing the result. We could repeat the experiment an infinite number of times (or until the die wore out!), and each result would be an item in our universe of throws. But we need not actually throw the die at all; we could consider the theoretical possibilities of such an experiment. The above example has a universe which is infinite, but hypothetical.

Universes may also differ according to whether the thing being measured is *continuous* or *discrete* (see Chapter 3 on Frequency distribution). For example, the theoretical universe of throws of a die will possess values such as a 'one', a 'two', and so on up to six (if it is the usual 6-sided type of die), but we cannot have intermediate values such as 3·14. Therefore it is *discrete*.

On the other hand, if we were measuring the heights of males in the UK, we could have individual items which varied (at least in theory) by infinitely small amounts—i.e., the distribution would be *continuous*.

Estimation

The central problem of sampling is how to estimate some statistical measure of the universe from the corresponding statistic of the sample. For example, we could calculate the A.M. of a sample and ask ourselves whether this is a good estimate of the A.M. of the universe. Equally, we could try to estimate any of its other features, such as dispersion, skewness, etc.

We use the word 'estimate' because we can never be certain that our sample will be an exact miniature copy of the universe itself. We might take a coin and toss it ten times, getting three heads. This represents a proportion of three out of ten, or 30 per cent heads. If we applied this result to the universe of tosses, we should obviously be in error, since the chances of a head, with a perfect coin, are one in two, or 50 per cent—i.e., half the universe would be heads, and half tails.

A secondary problem is to decide how much confidence we can place in our estimate. In general, we do this by specifying certain limits within which the true answer can lie, and, obviously, the wider the margin of error we allow ourselves, the greater the degree of confidence we can place in our estimate.

Taking samples

The accuracy of our estimates will depend upon:

(*a*) The method of taking the sample.
(*b*) The size of the sample.

The method usually preferred is that of random sampling (see Chapter 2), because the errors of estimation can be calculated in such cases. This is not true of the other methods mentioned.

In random sampling, each item in the universe must stand an equal chance of being selected, and the drawing of one sample or item must not affect the chances of subsequent drawings.

The first requirement can be satisfied for a finite universe in several ways.

Numbered cards or discs can represent the items, and the sample can be drawn as in a lottery. Even so, unless the items are well mixed, some of them may lie at the bottom of the pile, and have little or no chance of selection. The difficulties increase as the universe gets larger, and an alternative is to use a set of 'Random numbers' (e.g., those of L. H. C. Tippett). This consists of tables of four-figure numbers (10 400 in all) whose random quality has been confirmed by numerous experiments (see section on Use and interpretation).

Another method, where the universe consists of a card index (say of a firm's customers), is to choose a number by chance (say 17) and take every 17th card in the collection until a sample of the required size is obtained. The number must be such that all the cards are covered, preferably several times, during the selection process. If there are about 20 000 cards, and a sample of 500 is needed, we would use a number in excess of 100 (say 160). Taking every 160th card would only give some 125 items when we have run through the universe, and we would carry on to the beginning again, giving other cards a chance of selection.

If the universe is infinite (throws of dice), we simply carry out an experiment, by throwing, say, 100 times, and regard this as our sample. Because the number which turns up each time is a matter of chance, it is obvious that all the numbers have an equal possibility of selection—provided the dice are not loaded!

The importance of the second point can easily be seen, if we take a pack of cards as our universe. Suppose we are sampling for kings; there are four such cards in the pack, so the probability of drawing one is 4/52. If we are successful, there would only be three kings remaining. Our next draw has only a 3/51 chance of success, and so on. With a small universe, we can replace the item, i.e., the card before further drawings are made. With very large universes of, say, 10 000, the effect is negligible and may be ignored.

The sample should be as large as possible. We shall show, later, that the accuracy of our estimate varies inversely with the square root of the sample size, i.e., if we want to be twice as accurate (half the error) we must make the sample four times as large.

Samples of 1 000 or more are certainly large enough for most purposes, and even those of 100 are often met.

It will be assumed, in what follows, that the above-mentioned conditions are satisfied.

Sampling fluctuations

Even when samples are correctly drawn, it is found that successive samples vary, or fluctuate, and they do so according to a definite pattern. The precise form taken will depend upon the type of universe.

We saw that certain universes were discrete, as regards the quality or statistic being investigated, and we shall consider such cases first.

The thing being studied is known as an *attribute*, and every item in the universe either possesses the attribute, or does *not*. For example, in market surveys, every individual is, say, a cheese-eater, or he is not. We are not concerned here with how much cheese he eats; only with the category in which we place him. Rolling of dice, or tossing of coins, are similar cases. We either get a six, or we do not; we get a head, or we do not.

Note All possible alternative results (as with dice) are grouped together in the *not* category.

Sampling of attributes

The appearance in our sample of the attribute we are examining is termed a *success*. Thus, if we were sampling a universe of business firms to investigate bankruptcies, then a bankruptcy would be regarded as a success! The non-appearance of the attribute is termed a *failure*.

The *probability* (P) of an event is expressed by a decimal, usually stated to three places only. Thus, the probability of getting a head when tossing a coin is 1/2, or 0·5.

If the chances of a success are 1 in 10, this is stated as 0·1. Similarly, 0·025 would represent 25 chances in 1 000. The smallest possible figure is zero. This represents an absolute impossibility. Thus, the probability that the sun will rise in the west tomorrow is 0. Similarly, the largest figure is 1. This represents an absolute certainty, such as that the sun will rise tomorrow.

If we show a success by the letter p and a failure by q, then it follows that $p+q=1$, because the successes and failures taken together cover every possible eventuality. This fact is useful when we are only told *one* of the possibilities. We can find the other by subtracting from unity.

Suppose we have a universe, in which 50 per cent of the items are successes, and 50 per cent failures (say, black and white sweets). We take a large number of random samples, each of 50 sweets, and note the number of successes (say, the white ones). We should expect, in each sample, to get 25 white sweets ($\frac{1}{2}$ of 50) but, in fact, we should get a variety of results, ranging from 15 to 35 (approx.). If we noted the number of times that each result occurred, we would have a frequency distribution, and this could be plotted as a frequency polygon.

Note The diagram would not be a smooth curve, since the distribution is discrete—going up in steps of 1 success.

Table 12.1 illustrates the kind of result one would expect if 1 000 such samples were taken from our population of black and white sweets.

Number of successes	*Frequency*
14	0·8
15	2·0
16	4·3
17	8·8
18	16·0
19	27·0
20	41·9
21	59·9
22	79·0
23	96·0
24	108·0
25	112·6
26	108·0
27	96·0
28	79·0
29	59·9
30	41·9
31	27·0
32	16·0
33	8·8
34	4·3
35	2·0
36	0·8
TOTAL	1 000·0

Table 12.1 Frequency distribution of successes when $p=\frac{1}{2}$, $q=\frac{1}{2}$ for 1 000 samples of 50

The distribution is shown in Fig. 12.1, and it can be seen that it is symmetrical, and very similar to the normal curve. The A.M. and S.D. could be calculated from the frequency distribution, using the short-cut method of Chapters 7 and 8, but we have a much simpler method, based upon the fact that such a distribution is predictable from the binomial theorem, a well-known mathematical device.

Binomial distribution

If the sample size is n, and the probabilities of success and failure are p and q respectively, then:

$$A.M. = np. \qquad \text{(F. 12.1)}$$

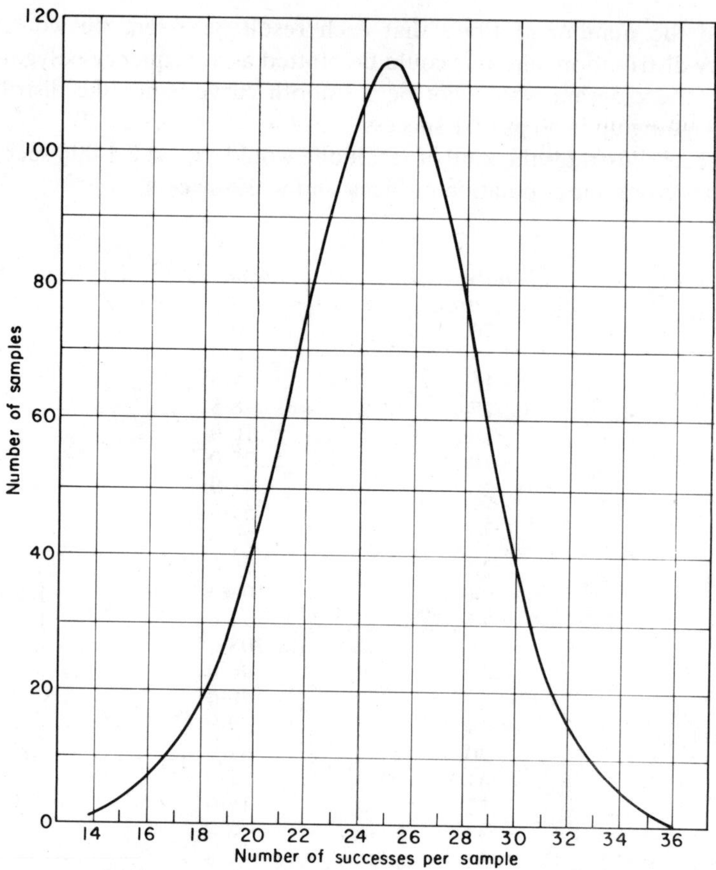

Fig. 12.1 Frequency polygon showing distribution of samples of 50 when $p=\frac{1}{2}$ and $q=\frac{1}{2}$ total samples of 1 000

This is often called the 'expected' number of successes, and is the mean value of *all* samples.

and $$S.D. = \sqrt{npq}. \qquad \text{(F. 12.2)}$$

For example, a sample of 50 items is taken from our universe of sweets, where $p=\frac{1}{2}$ and $q=\frac{1}{2}$.

Then, $A.M. = 50 \times \frac{1}{2} = 25$ white ones (or black ones, because p and q are assumed to be equal).

$$S.D. = \sqrt{50 \times \tfrac{1}{2} \times \tfrac{1}{2}} = \sqrt{12\tfrac{1}{2}} = 3{\cdot}5 \text{ approx.}$$

We saw in Chapter 8 that roughly 95 per cent of the total area of the normal curve is included within A.M. ± 2 S.D., and that 99 per cent is within A.M. ± 2·58 S.D. The range of A.M. ± 3 S.D. includes practically the whole of the distribution (99·73 per cent).

Confidence limits

These facts allow us to predict the likely behaviour of samples, with some confidence.

Hence, although sample results will fluctuate, we can be 95 per cent sure that they will lie within the range of A.M. ± 2 S.D.; or, to put it another way, the chances of a sample falling *outside* these limits are 5 in 100 (5 per cent).

This is known as the 95 per cent confidence limit, or the 5 per cent level of significance.

Similarly, A.M. ± 2·58 S.D. is the 99 per cent limit, or the 1 per cent level of significance.

The range of ± 3 S.D. will only be exceeded once in 500 times; it is the 0·2 per cent level of significance.

These limits give the probabilities of exceeding a given range in either direction (+ or −). If we only consider one of them, then they are halved—i.e., the chances of getting a sample with more than A.M. + 3 S.D. (36 white sweets in our example) are 1 in 1 000.

In the above example we can now say:

(*a*) Ninety-five per cent of our samples will lie within the range: $25 \pm (2 \times 3\frac{1}{2}) = 25 \pm 7$ white sweets.
(*b*) The chances of getting a sample with more than 36 white ones $25 \pm (3 \times 3\frac{1}{2})$ is only about 1 in 1 000—i.e., it is so unlikely as to be rejected.

Therefore, if we do get such a sample (unless there has been some change in the conditions of sampling, etc.), we can assume that our universe has changed, and now contains more than 50 per cent of white sweets. This is the basic idea of *quality control* (see Chapter 15).

We may also wish to find the probability of getting some specified number of successes. This involves the use of *factorial numbers*. Factorial 5 = $5 \times 4 \times 3 \times 2 \times 1 = 120$ and is written 5! That is, we multiply our number by all the lesser numbers down to unity. The 1 may, in practice, be omitted, since it does not affect the result.

Note Factorial 0 is treated as equal to 1, although it is difficult to visualize such an operation.

The formula we use is:

$$P_X = \frac{n!}{(X!)(n-X)!} p^X q^{n-X} \qquad \text{(F. 12.3)}$$

where n = sample size, and X = our desired number of successes. For example, in samples of 10, with our black and white sweets ($p = \frac{1}{2}$, $q = \frac{1}{2}$), what is the probability of getting a sample with 3 white ones? Since $X = 3$ and $n = 10$, we have:

$$P_3 = \frac{10!}{3!7!}(\tfrac{1}{2})^3(\tfrac{1}{2})^7.$$

Note 1 Since $X = 3$, $(n - X) = 10 - 3 = 7$. Therefore we want factorial 7.
Note 2 Since p and q are equal, we can rewrite

$$(\tfrac{1}{2})^3 \times (\tfrac{1}{2})^7 \text{ as } (\tfrac{1}{2})^{10}.$$

Note 3 We can cancel out the whole of 7! with part of the numerator, by striking out all the numbers from 7 downwards. In fact, we need not write them in.

Note 4 We then cancel out the 3! into the rest of the numerator.

Note 5 It is usual to put dots between the numbers instead of writing out a lot of multiplication signs.

Therefore we have:

$$P_3 = \frac{\overset{3.4}{10.\not{9}.\not{8}.\not{7}.\not{6}.\not{5}.\not{4}.\not{3}.\not{2}.\not{1}}}{(\not{3}.\not{2}.1)(\not{7}.\not{6}.\not{5}.\not{4}.\not{3}.\not{2}.\not{1})}(\tfrac{1}{2})^{10}$$

$$= 120(\tfrac{1}{2})^{10} = 120/1024 = 0{\cdot}1171.$$

This means that the chances are 117·1 in 1 000 trials that we should get exactly 3 white sweets, or alternatively, if we took 1 024 samples, 120 of them would have 3 successes. The student should note that a *probability* (as above) can always be converted into a *frequency* by multiplying it by the total number of samples (total frequencies).

Note Although the expected frequency (in samples of 10) is 5 white sweets, yet in roughly 12 per cent of the samples, we would actually get only 3 white ones. This illustrates the effect of sampling fluctuations. It should also be remembered that our samples here are small ones, and this makes for wider fluctuations.

EXAMPLE 1:

In a random sample of 100 people, 40 per cent of them eat cheese. What proportion of the whole population are cheese-eaters?

Here we have $p = 40/100 = 0{\cdot}4$ and $q = 0{\cdot}6$, whilst $n = 100$.

Therefore, $A.M. = np = 40$. $S.D. = \sqrt{npq} = \sqrt{100 \times 0{\cdot}4 \times 0{\cdot}6}$

$$= \sqrt{24} = 4{\cdot}899.$$

Whatever the actual proportion in the population, it should be within $3 \times 4{\cdot}899 = 14{\cdot}697$, of the expected frequency of 40 per 100.

Therefore, the true proportion is $40 \pm 14{\cdot}7$ per cent (approx.), i.e., between 54·7 and 25·3 per cent.

If we had chosen the 95 per cent level (2 S.D.), this would have given us a possible variation of $2 \times 4{\cdot}899 = 9{\cdot}798$ in each 100 (say, 9·8 per cent).

Therefore, we could be 95 per cent sure that the true proportion was $40 \pm 9{\cdot}8$ per cent.

The reader might object that a possible variation of nearly 15 per cent is too wide to be of any value. In this case, the remedy is to increase the sample size, say to 1 600. If the same result of 40 per cent were obtained, we would now have:

$$A.M. = np = 1\,600 \times 0{\cdot}4 = 640 \text{ cheese-eaters.}$$

$$S.D. = \sqrt{npq} = \sqrt{1\,600 \times 0{\cdot}4 \times 0{\cdot}6} = \sqrt{16 \times 24} = 4\sqrt{24}.$$

This is four times the orignal S.D., and equals 19·596. Taking a possible variation of 3×S.D. gives us 58·788, but this is in relation to a value of 40 per cent of our larger sample, i.e., 640.

We now have a result of 640±58·788, which in percentage form is 40±3·676 per cent (58·788 out of 1 600).

Note 1 This is only a quarter of the original variation (14·7 per cent), because our sample is 16 times bigger. That is, the error is inversely proportional to square root of sample size, and $\sqrt{16} = 4$.

Note 2 The theory assumes that p and q are the proportions in the universe itself, but if these are unknown (as in this example), no great error arises from using the sample figures, provided the sample is sufficiently large.

Note 3 When p and q are not equal, the sampling distribution becomes skewed. The greater the inequality, the greater the skewness, but increasing the sample size will offset this tendency to a great extent, and we can still use our confidence limits.

Note 4 Instead of working on the *number* of successes in our samples, we could use the *proportion*, that is, $1/n$th of the number in the sample.

The amended formulae now are:

$$A.M. = p \qquad \text{(F. 12.4)}$$

$$S.D. = \sqrt{\frac{pq}{n}}. \qquad \text{(F. 12.5)}$$

EXAMPLE 2:

A sample of 1 000 days from the weather records of a city shows that 10 per cent of them are frosty. What is the actual proportion of frosty days?

Here $p = 1/10$, $q = 9/10$, and $S.D. = \sqrt{1/10 \times 9/10 \times 1/1\,000} = \sqrt{9/100\,000} = 0{\cdot}0095 = 0{\cdot}95$ per cent.

Taking 3×S.D. gives us 2·85 per cent, and our estimate is 10 per cent±2·85 per cent.

The Poisson distribution

When p becomes very small (theoretically say, 1 in 1 000, or less), but the sample size is very large (in theory, over 1 000), we get a special case, which is best described by amended formulae.

$$A.M. = np \qquad \text{(F. 12.6)}$$

$$S.D. = \sqrt{np} \qquad \text{(F. 12.7)}$$

This type of distribution (known as the Poisson) is found where we are sampling for a comparatively rare event, e.g., the chances of having a particular type of accident, or catching some rare disease (see also Use and interpretation).

The 3×S.D. rule may still be applied, but the other limits should be used with caution because of the possible skewness of the distribution.

EXAMPLE 3:

A sample of 4 000 workers in an industry shows that 4 of them suffer from a particular industrial disease. What is the estimated proportion in the industry as a whole?

Since $n = 4\,000$, and p is $4/4\,000$, i.e., $1/1\,000$, we have $A.M. = np = 4\,000 \times 1/1\,000 = 4$. $S.D. = \sqrt{4} = 2$. $3 \times 2 = 6$. Therefore, our estimate is 0·1 per cent ± 0·15 per cent (6 in 4 000 = 0·15 per cent).

In this case, the application of the − sign gives a theoretical limit to the left of the mean of −0·05 per cent which is, of course, impossible. This is because of the skewed nature of the distribution. The practical limits of the range are therefore 0 to 0·25 per cent.

Our previous formula for estimating the probability of getting a specified number of successes also requires modification, and now becomes:

$$P_X = \frac{(m)^x}{X!} \times \frac{1}{(2{\cdot}718)^m} \qquad \text{(F. 12.8)}$$

where $m = A.M.$ (i.e., np) and 2·718 is a *constant* (like π in the formula for the area of a circle).

A practical example will make clear the use of this last formula.

EXAMPLE 4:

In a mass production process, where 0·1 per cent of the articles are defective, they are packed in boxes of 1 000.

(*a*) What proportion of the boxes would we expect to be free from defective articles?

(*b*) What proportion would contain *2 or more* defectives?

Here we have $n = 1\,000$ and $p = 0{\cdot}001$ (or $1/1\,000$).

Therefore $m\ (= np) = 1\,000 \times 1/1\,000 = 1$ defective.

(i) Applying our formula for $X = 0$, we have:

$$P_0 = \frac{(1)^0}{0!} \times \frac{1}{(2{\cdot}718)^1}.$$

Since any number to the power of 0 = 1, and remembering that 0! also equals 1, the first fraction reduces to unity, and can be ignored.

We therefore have $\frac{1}{2{\cdot}718} = 0{\cdot}3679$.

Since $P_0 = 0{\cdot}3679$, we should expect no defectives 36·79 times in 100, i.e., 37 per cent.

(ii) When $X = 1$ we have:

$$P_1 = \frac{(1)^1}{1!} \times \frac{1}{(2{\cdot}718)^1}.$$

The first fraction is again unity, and the answer is again 0·3679.

Adding the two answers together gives 0·3679 + 0·3679 = 0·7358.

This is the probability of 0 or 1 defectives.

To get the probability of two or more, we subtract our previous answer from unity.

$$1 - 0{\cdot}7358 = 0{\cdot}2642 \text{ or } 26{\cdot}42 \text{ per cent.}$$

The student should be quite sure he understands this last step, because it often arises in examinations. The explanation is as follows:

If we add together the successive probabilities of 0, 1, 2, 3—up to 1 000 defectives per box, we have got all possibilities. This is a certainty, and in our terminology is represented by unity.

If we subtract from this total, the sum of the first two probabilities (0 and 1), we are left with 2, 3, 4, ... up to 1 000, which is the same as saying 'two or more'.

Standard error

So far, we have mentioned the standard deviation of the universe, and we have also talked about the standard deviation of our samples. In order to avoid confusion, it is usual to refer to the standard deviation of our samples as the *standard error*. In other words, if we consider the distribution of Fig. 12.1, which we saw was like the normal curve, then it can be described in a similar manner, by mentioning two features; its average value (in this case 25), and its standard deviation. The latter measure we shall henceforth call the standard error (S.E. for short).

Probable error

This is the equivalent of 0·6745S.E., and is so called because, in a symmetrical distribution, a range of A.M. ± 0·6745 × S.E. includes exactly half the items, i.e., it is as likely as not that a sample value will fall inside (or outside) this range. Hence it is, in a sense, the most probable result.

Apart from examination questions (where it still persists) this measure is of little importance.

Significance

It often happens that we expect a particular frequency of successes in our sample, either on the basis of our knowledge of the universe itself, or because our universe is purely theoretical and is therefore predictable on the strength of the underlying theory.

Suppose we get an actual frequency of successes which differs appreciably from expectation. If our sampling technique is above suspicion, the question arises whether the difference can be due to sampling fluctuations, in which case it might be reduced, or even eliminated, in further samples.

If the difference is too great to be explained in this way, it is said to be *significant*, i.e., it means something. What it means will depend upon circumstances. In general, it casts doubt upon our original assumptions. Either the universe has a different proportion of our attribute than we thought, or our theory is shown to be at fault. At least it directs the attention of the investigator towards the need for further enquiry and testing.

To determine what is significant, we use one or other of our confidence limits.

EXAMPLE 5:

A die is thrown 1 024 times, and if a 4, 5, or 6 turns up, it is regarded as a success. The total number of successes recorded is 608. Is this result significant?

Since a die has 6 sides, and 3 of them count as a success, the probability of a success $(p) = 3/6 = \frac{1}{2}$. Hence, $q = \frac{1}{2}$ also.

This experiment may be regarded as a sample of 1 024 from an infinite universe, i.e., $n = 1\,024$.

Using our binomial formulae we have:

$$A.M. = np = 1\,024 \times \tfrac{1}{2} = 512$$

$$S.D. = \sqrt{npq} = \sqrt{1\,024 \times \tfrac{1}{2} \times \tfrac{1}{2}} = \sqrt{256} = 16.$$

The expected frequency of successes according to our theory (the binomial theorem) is 512. Actually, we have got 608, a difference of $608 - 512 = 96$. Since the S.E. of our sampling distribution is 16, this represents a deviation of $96/16 = 6$ S.E. from the A.M.

We have seen that the chances of exceeding 3 S.E. are roughly 1 in 1 000. In fact, a deviation of 6 S.E. would only happen 1 in 10 million times. This result is clearly significant, and suggests that our basic assumption $(p = \frac{1}{2})$ was wrong—i.e., the die was biased, or loaded.

If our result had been 550 successes, the deviation from 512 would have been $550 - 512 = 38$. This represents just over 2 S.E. Hence, we could say the result was significant *at the 5 per cent level.* In other words, when judging significance we have to choose between two alternatives:

(*a*) That a deviation is due to sampling fluctuations.
(*b*) That it is due to something else.

If the first explanation is unlikely, we plump for the second. In the latter case, if a 20 to 1 chance is regarded as unlikely (which is, to some extent, a matter of opinion) we choose the second explanation, and say that the result is significant—at that particular level.

Note Although a significant result casts doubt upon the original assumptions, the converse does not apply. In other words, if the expected frequency is based upon some theory or hypothesis, the fact that the deviation is well within 3 S.E. does not prove that the hypothesis is correct. It only shows that there is no disagreement between the two.

Sample differences

Suppose two samples give different proportions of our attribute. Can we say that they are therefore drawn from two different universes, or might it be that the difference is due to sampling fluctuations (i.e., it is not a 'real' difference) and could disappear in the case of two other samples, taken in exactly the same circumstances? If we assume that they are both from the same universe, we need to know something about the distribution of sample differences, in such cases.

Suppose a large number of such pairs of samples were taken, and the difference between each pair was noted each time. If we take the differences in the same way throughout (e.g., sample 1 − sample 2) we should find that some differences were positive, and some negative, and we would expect the *average* difference to be zero, because we are assuming the same universe throughout, and therefore there should, in theory, be no difference.

The differences could be represented by a frequency distribution, and the frequencies plotted, as in Fig. 12.1. We should get a similar type of graph, but with A.M. = 0, and a S.E. given by the formula,

$$S.E._{diff.} = \sqrt{p_0 q_0\left(\frac{1}{n_1} + \frac{1}{n_2}\right)} \qquad \text{(F. 12.9)}$$

where p_0 and q_0 are the proportions given by the two samples combined, and n_1 and n_2 are the sizes of our two samples (they need not be the same).

We can now apply our levels of significance as before. If we get a difference greater than 3 S.E. this is so unlikely as to be rejected—i.e., our hypothesis that the samples were from the same universe was wrong. The difference between the two samples is a real one (significant) and cannot be explained by sampling fluctuations.

EXAMPLE 6:

A sample of 400 people from Town A reveals that 40 per cent have blue eyes. A sample of 600 from Town B shows only 35 per cent with blue eyes. Is this difference significant?

We make an estimate of the proportion in the universe (assumed the same) by combining the two samples. This gives a more reliable result, because the sample size is thereby increased.

	Sample size	*Percentage blue-eyed*	*Number of blue-eyed*
Town A	400	40	160
Town B	600	35	210
TOTALS	1 000		370

Table 12.2

Therefore, the percentage of blue-eyed in the two together = 37, i.e. $p_0 = 37$ per cent $q_0 = 63$ per cent.

Note 1 When working in percentages $p + q = 100$ per cent (not 1).

Substituting these values in our formula, and noting that $n_1 = 400$, and $n_2 = 600$, we get:

$$S.E._{diff.} = \sqrt{37 \times 63\left(\frac{1}{400} + \frac{1}{600}\right)} = \sqrt{37 \times 63\left(\frac{3+2}{1\,200}\right)}$$

$$= \sqrt{\frac{37 \times 63 \times 5}{1\,200}} = 3{\cdot}117 \text{ per cent.}$$

Note 2 When working in percentages, the answer is a percentage. The actual difference between our two samples is 40 per cent − 35 per cent = 5 per cent. Since one S.E. = 3·117 per cent, the difference is 5/3·117 = 1·6 S.E. (approx.).

This is not even significant at the 5 per cent level, which would require a difference of 2 S.E.—i.e., the two samples could very well be drawn from the same universe.

An alternative approach is to assume that the two samples are from *different* universes, and test whether the actual difference between them is capable of disappearing in further samples. The formula for this is:

$$S.E._{diff.} = \sqrt{\frac{p_1 q_1}{n_1} + \frac{p_2 q_2}{n_2}} \qquad \text{(F. 12.10)}$$

where p_1 and p_2 are the proportions in each of the two samples, and n_1 and n_2 are their sizes.

$$S.E._{diff.} = \sqrt{\frac{40 \times 60}{400} + \frac{35 \times 65}{600}} = \sqrt{6 + 3{\cdot}79} = \sqrt{9{\cdot}97}$$

$$= 3{\cdot}129 \text{ per cent.}$$

Again, the difference of 5 per cent is under 2 S.E. and is not significant. That is, the difference might not show itself in two further samples.

Use and interpretation

Advantages of samples

(*a*) We have already seen that an accurate estimate of a universe can be made from a sample, provided it is correctly drawn. This is obviously cheaper and more time-saving than a complete investigation of every item; e.g., in social surveys and public opinion polls.

(*b*) Frequently the information is required quickly, or at regular intervals, so that it would not be possible to make a complete enumeration each time; e.g., in dealing with index numbers, which must be produced monthly; or in quality control, where tests are frequently made hourly.

(*c*) Sometimes, the information needed can only be obtained by destroying the item investigated, e.g., in quality control. A manufacturer of electric lamps needs to know the burning life of his product. He cannot burn them all until they fail, otherwise he would have no product left for sale! Destruction tests are essential for vehicle tyres and similar manufactured products, and sampling is the only way.

Error versus bias

The student should understand the important difference between sampling *error*, which is the inevitable fluctuation of samples, and *bias*, which was described in Chapter 2.

Two particular kinds of bias are likely to be the subject of examination questions.

One is known as *non-response*, and refers to the failure of certain items in the sample to respond to the enquiry. This may be deliberate, as when a postal questionnaire is not returned by the addressee, or when a person being interviewed refuses to answer. This indicates a certain attitude, and since all such people will be excluded from the final figures, the sample is no longer truly representative.

It may also be due to chance, as when an interviewer calls at an address on his sample list, and, getting no reply, calls next door instead. The original choice might be a young couple who both work, or elderly people who are deaf, or infirm. The fact that the occupants are available during the day places them in a different social group from their neighbours, and the balance of the sample is therefore upset. Sometimes, bias may be deliberately introduced for sound statistical reasons.

This occurs when the frequency of occurrence of certain items in the sample should be proportional to their *size* or *importance*, rather than to their *probability of occurrence* as in ordinary random sampling.

For example, a firm supplies products to a particular industry which includes a few very large concerns and a large number of small ones. It is desired to make a sample survey of the industry, for sales purposes. If a random sample were taken, the chances of a particular firm being included in it (i.e., its probability of occurrence) might be, say, 1 in 100. If that firm, by virtue of its size, represented 20 per cent of the industry, its importance would be 1 in 5. Consequently, a stratified sample is more useful, with a system of weights, such that the chances of inclusion of the large firms are weighted, according to their relative importance. This might be done by drawing, say, 75 per cent of the sample from such firms, or by multiplying the results from each by an appropriate weight, before totalling the sample figures.

Sample size independent of universe

We have already explained that the reliability of samples increases with their size, and this is apparent from the various formulae quoted, where the size of the sample always appears, under a square-root sign. The student might wonder why the size of the universe does not also enter into it.

One would assume that a sample of 100 out of a village with a population of 2 000 (i.e., 1 in 20 of the inhabitants) would be more reliable than one of 1 000, out of a population of 200 000 (i.e., 1 in 200). Yet none of the formulae for sampling take any note of this. The underlying assumption in sampling theory is that the universe is very large, and in general, this is true. Even if we sample from a pack of cards, the number of possible samples is infinitely large. Provided we replace each card after drawing it, we could go on indefinitely.

Random numbers

Reference has already been made to these, and several such tables are available. We now explain their use.

Suppose we want a random sample of 1 000 from the inhabitants of a town. We take any of the numbers in the table, and write them down, until we have 1 000 of them. We then consult the Rating and Valuation list at the local town hall, or the Voters' List, and take the people who correspond with the numbers. For instance, if our first number were 0672, we should take the 672nd name on the list, and so on. The reader might object that certain inhabitants (e.g., children) were not on the list, and have, therefore, no chance of being selected. If we wished to include them, we could visit the address in question, and ask all the occupants the relevant questions.

We mentioned that these numbers are limited in size (e.g., those of L. H. C. Tippett contain four-figure numbers). If the voting list contained more than 9 999 names, those at the end would have no chance of selection, because there are no corresponding numbers. We can easily overcome this difficulty by running the numbers into one another, and reading them off in groups of, say, six digits, which would cover up to 1 million of a universe.

This method is commonly employed by large firms who wish to carry out a market survey.

Sample differences

These tests of significance are very useful in order to discover whether a given universe has changed between samples. This is of major importance in quality control (see Chapter 15), but the basic principle can be used in many other business situations. We consider its use in advertising.

EXAMPLE 7:

A manufacturer of breakfast cereals takes a random sample of 1 000 households in a certain area of the country. It reveals that 10 per cent of them use his product. After an intensive advertising campaign in the area, he takes a further sample of 1 000 which reveals that 15 per cent use his product. Is the difference between the two results significant?

The manufacturer hopes that the advertising has altered the character of the universe, i.e., that the universe of the second sample is a different one from that of the first—in the sense that its liking for the product has increased. On the other hand, the difference may be simply due to sampling fluctuations.

Using formula (F.12.10), which is the easier to apply, $p_1 = 10$ per cent, $q_1 = 90$ per cent, $p_2 = 15$ per cent, $q_2 = 85$ per cent; n_1 and n_2 are both 1 000, since in this case the samples are the same size. We therefore have:

$$S.E._{diff.} = \sqrt{\frac{10\times 90}{1\ 000}+\frac{15\times 85}{1\ 000}} = \sqrt{0{\cdot}9+1{\cdot}275} = \sqrt{2{\cdot}175}$$

$$= 1{\cdot}475 \text{ per cent.}$$

The actual difference is 15 per cent − 10 per cent = 5 per cent, which is more than 3 S.E. Therefore it is most unlikely to be due to sampling fluctuations and could not disappear if further samples were taken. Therefore, it is a 'real' difference, and the result is significant.

Note 1 To find the actual difference, we merely take the smaller result from the larger. In the present case, this is sample 2 − sample 1, but since the distribution is symmetrical, we are not concerned with the *sign* of the difference (+ or −) but only with its *magnitude*.

Note 2 The two universes are almost certainly different, but as previously explained, this does not *prove* the theory that advertising is the cause. It could be some economic or social factor, but it certainly *suggests* that the advertising has paid off.

Note 3 The student should never waste time calculating the *exact* deviation in standard errors (3·389 in the above case). He need only test whether it is more than 2 S.E. (for 5 per cent level), or 3 S.E., according to the chosen level of significance.

13

Probability

Method

The meaning of probability

This concept is basic to many business problems and plays an important role in statistics, particularly in sampling theory (see Chapter 12). Probabilities may be regarded as *relative frequencies*, i.e., the proportion of the time an event takes place.

This relative frequency, considered *in the long run*, is the probability that the particular event will happen.

When we say 'the probability that the contract will be completed on time is 0·8' we mean that on the basis of past experience, 80 per cent of all similar contracts were finished on time.

The probability of getting *heads* when we toss a perfect coin is $\frac{1}{2}$. This does *not* mean that if we toss the coin 10 times we shall necessarily get 5 heads, but if we repeat the experiment a large number of times, we should expect to approach 50 per cent heads, and the greater the number of times we tossed the coin, the closer our approximation would get.

We can see from this that probability is a substitute for certainty. If a businessman could always be certain that his decisions would turn out to be correct, there would be no problem. In a world full of uncertainty, and with many alternative decisions possible, he needs to know the relative probabilities of success, so that he may choose that course of action which offers the best chance. This will not protect him from expensive mistakes but in the long run he will make fewer of them.

Rules of probability

(1) Mutually exclusive events Two or more events are said to be *mutually exclusive* if the occurrence of any one of them excludes the occurrence of *all* the others, i.e., only one can happen.

If three events, A, B, and C, are mutually exclusive, and P = probability of occurrence, then P(A or B or C) is given by the *Special rule of addition*

$$P(\text{A or B or C}) = P(\text{A}) + P(\text{B}) + P(\text{C}) \qquad \text{(F. 13.1)}$$

i.e., the answer is the sum of the individual probabilities.

EXAMPLE 1:

The probability that a firm will move its head office to Town A = 0·3, to Town B = 0·1, and to Town C = 0·4. Then the probability that it will move to *one or other* of them is

$$0{\cdot}3 + 0{\cdot}1 + 0{\cdot}4 = 0{\cdot}8.$$

(2) Independent events Two or more events are said to be *independent* if the occurrence or non-occurrence of one of them in no way affects the occurrence or non-occurrence of the others.

If A and B represent the result 'heads' in two successive tosses of a coin, then the events are independent, since the second toss cannot possibly be influenced by what happened before.

This principle is seldom grasped by gamblers, who imagine that because a coin has come up 'heads', say, five times in succession, it is more likely to come up 'tails' on the sixth trial.

On the other hand, if A stands for Mr Jones's being promoted, and B for his getting a car, these events are *not* necessarily independent.

When two events, A and B, are independent, the probability that they will *both* occur is given by the *Special rule of multiplication*

$$P(\text{A and B}) = P(\text{A}) \times P(\text{B}) \qquad \text{(F. 13.2)}$$

i.e., the answer is the product of the individual probabilities, no matter how many of them there may be.

EXAMPLE 2:

Mr Jones is up for interview for a new job. The probability that he will get it is 0·8, and the probability that it will rain on that day is 0·3.

Since the two events are clearly independent, then the probability that they will both happen is

$$(0{\cdot}8)(0{\cdot}3) = 0{\cdot}24.$$

(3) Conditional events Two or more events are said to be *conditional* when the probability that event B takes place is subject to the proviso that A has taken place, and so on. This is usually written $P_{\text{A}}(\text{B})$.

Note $P_{\text{B}}(\text{A})$ would be the other way round, the assumption being that B has first taken place.

If a firm were to spend a sum of money on more efficient machinery, it is probable that profits would increase. In this case $P_{\text{A}}(\text{B})$ would indicate the probability of increased profits, provided that the new machinery were purchased. Similarly, $P_{\text{B}}(\text{A})$ would be the probability that new machinery would be bought, provided that profits had *already* increased. This, of course, is also a possibility.

Events such as these are clearly not independent, and the inclusion of such possibilities enables us to re-state our previous rules in more general terms.

General rule of addition

$$P(\text{A or B}) = P(\text{A}) + P(\text{B}) - P(\text{A and B}). \qquad \text{(F. 13.3)}$$

The reason for subtracting $P(\text{A and B})$ is because A and B are no longer necessarily mutually exclusive, and therefore *both* events might occur.

If we used the special rule, we would be counting such cases *twice*, since they are A's and also B's. We must therefore deduct the proportion of such cases in arriving at our answer.

EXAMPLE 3:

Statistics show that, in a certain line of business, the probability of a firm failing through shortage of capital is 0·6 and the probability of failing through shortage of orders is 0·5.

If we used the special rule (F. 13.1) we should get the impossible result:

$$P(\text{A or B}) = 0{\cdot}6 + 0{\cdot}5 = 1{\cdot}1.$$

This is impossible because the largest possible answer is *unity*. As we say in Chapter 12, this represents an absolute certainty and we cannot have a stronger probability than this.

The two possibilities are not mutually exclusive; a firm could fail through *both* these causes. If the proportion of such cases were 30 per cent (0·3), then the use of (F.13.3) would give:

$$P(\text{A or B}) = 0{\cdot}6 + 0{\cdot}5 - 0{\cdot}3 = 0{\cdot}8.$$

General rule of multiplication

$$P(\text{A and B}) = P(\text{A}) \times P_{\text{A}}(\text{B}) \qquad \text{(F. 13.4)}$$

or

$$P(\text{A and B}) = P(\text{B}) \times P_{\text{B}}(\text{A})$$

depending upon the order in which the events are assumed to occur.

EXAMPLE 4:

The probability that a firm will spend an extra £10 000 on advertising is 0·6. The probability that sales will increase *provided* that the extra £10 000 is spent on advertising is 0·9.

Then the probability of *both* events happening is:

$$P(\text{A and B}) = P(\text{A}) \times P_{\text{A}}(\text{B}) = (0{\cdot}6)(0{\cdot}9) = 0{\cdot}54.$$

Conditional probability under dependence

In example 4, we assumed that the conditional probability was 0·9. If we wish to calculate such probabilities, we can use the formula:

$$P_{\text{A}}(\text{B}) = \frac{P(\text{AB})}{P(\text{A})}. \qquad \text{(F. 13.5)}$$

EXAMPLE 5

On a Board of 10 directors, 4 are rich (over £20 000 p.a.) and 6 are not; 3 of the rich and 2 of the non-rich are bankers (5 bankers in all).

Since being a banker affects the probability of being rich, the two events are dependent.

Let B = banker and A = rich, then $P(\text{AB}) = 0{\cdot}3$ and $P(\text{A}) = 0{\cdot}4$ (from the data) and

$$P_{\text{A}}(\text{B}) = \frac{0{\cdot}3}{0{\cdot}4} = 0{\cdot}75,$$

i.e., granted that he is rich, the chances are 3 out of 4 that he is a banker.

Similarly,

$$P_{\text{B}}(\text{A}) = \frac{P(\text{AB})}{P(\text{B})} = \frac{0{\cdot}3}{0{\cdot}5} = 0{\cdot}6,$$

i.e., granted that a director is a banker, the chances are 3 out of 5 that he is rich.

If we wanted the probability of getting a non-banker, granted that he is rich, then A = rich, as before, and B = non-banker.

$P(\text{AB}) = 0{\cdot}1$ (there is only 1 rich non-banker) and

$$P_{\text{A}}(\text{B}) = \frac{0{\cdot}1}{0{\cdot}4} = 0{\cdot}25.$$

Note 1 To get the probability of AB we *do not* use the formula $P(\text{AB}) = P(\text{A}) \times P(\text{B})$ since this assumes statistical independence, which is not the case.

Note 2 The probabilities 0·75 and 0·25 add up to unity. This is because *all* the rich directors are either bankers or non-bankers and the two together represent a certainty, which is a probability of 1. Knowing this, we could have deduced the last answer by subtracting the first one from unity, $(1 - 0{\cdot}75 = 0{\cdot}25)$.

Revising first estimates of probability

The ability to revise our estimates of probability as more information comes in makes our theory of great value when a businessman has to make decisions under uncertainty.

EXAMPLE 6:

A manufacturer has a chemical plant which mass-produces a compound. If the plant is properly adjusted, it will produce 90 per cent acceptable batches. If incorrectly set up, it will only produce 50 per cent acceptable. Past experience reveals that adjustments are correctly done 60 per cent of the time.

Before we inspect the first batch produced, we can only infer that the probability of a correctly adjusted plant is 0·6, based upon past experience.

Suppose we run off 4 batches, test them, and find them to be correct. What is our revised probability that the plant is correctly adjusted?

We first construct the following table:

1	*2*	*3*	*4*	*5*
Event (adjustment)	*(P) Event*	*(P) one good batch for event*	*(P) 4 good batches for event*	*Joint P of event and 4 good batches*
Correct	0·6	0·9	0·656	0·3936
Incorrect	0·4	0·5	0·0625	0·025
				0·4186

Table 13.1

Note 1 P of an incorrect adjustment is $1-0{\cdot}6$, since the two probabilities must add up to 1.

Note 2 P of 4 good batches with a correct adjustment is:

$$0{\cdot}9 \times 0{\cdot}9 \times 0{\cdot}9 \times 0{\cdot}9 = 0{\cdot}656.$$

Note 3 P of 4 good batches with an incorrect adjustment is:

$$0{\cdot}5 \times 0{\cdot}5 \times 0{\cdot}5 \times 0{\cdot}5 = 0{\cdot}0625.$$

Note 4 Column 5 is the P of the joint occurrence of columns 1 and 4. The calculation is:

Correct $\quad 0{\cdot}656 \times 0{\cdot}6 = 0{\cdot}3936$
Incorrect $\quad 0{\cdot}0625 \times 0{\cdot}4 = 0{\cdot}025$
(based upon [F. 13.4])

The revised probability is obtained from (F. 13.5).

$$\begin{array}{l}P \text{ of correct adjustment} \\ \text{(granted 4 good batches)}\end{array} = \frac{P(\text{correct adjustment with 4 good batches})}{P(\text{4 good batches})}$$

$$= \frac{0{\cdot}3936}{0{\cdot}4186} = 0{\cdot}9404,$$

i.e., 94·04 per cent sure.

We have been able to improve our original estimate of a correct adjustment (0·6) to one of 0·94, on the strength of 4 batches produced. In other words, we are now 94 per cent sure that the plant is corréctly set up.

Of course, the 4 batches might not all be acceptable. For example, we might find 3 good and 1 bad but, whatever the outcome, we can still calculate the probability of such a result, using the binomial formulae of Chapter 12, and applying the same technique.

The probability of getting 3 good batches out of 4, when the plant is correctly adjusted, is in fact 0·2916. The student might care to check this, using formula (F. 12.3) of Chapter 12. This principle, of continually revising our estimates as additional results come in, is a form of *sequential sampling*.

Use and interpretation

Students often have difficulty in deciding between mutually exclusive and independent events. They should remember that mutual exclusion occurs when there are several possible outcomes of a *single* action, such as the site for a new branch.

Independence is found when there are *several* actions which can occur *together*, such as engaging a sales manager and buying some new machinery. The difference between the *general* and the *special* rule is as follows.

ADDITION

The distinction rests upon the interpretation of 'or' in 'A or B', which may be *inclusive*, and include the possibility of *both* events. In this case, we use the *general* rule:

$$P(\text{A or B}) = P(\text{A}) + P(\text{B}) - P(\text{A and B})$$

When the events are *mutually exclusive*, then, by definition, they cannot *both* occur, so that $P(\text{A and B}) = 0$. Consequently, (F. 13.3) reduces to (F. 13.1) which is the *special* rule of addition.

MULTIPLICATION

The *general* rule is $P(\text{A and B}) = P(\text{A}) \times P_{\text{A}}(\text{B})$, but if the two events are *independent*, then $P(\text{B})$ is in no way affected by $P(\text{A})$.

In other words, $P_{\text{A}}(\text{B})$ is simply $P(\text{B})$. Consequently, (F. 13.4) reduces to (F. 13.2) which is the *special* rule of multiplication.

Frequency distributions

The probability for any particular class is obtained by dividing the number of items in that class by the total frequencies.

1	*2*	*3*
Value of articles sold (£)	*Number of days*	*Probability (P)*
100 up to 120	40	0·16
120 up to 140	64	0·256
140 up to 160	80	0·32
160 up to 200	30	0·12
200 up to 300	20	0·08
300 up to 500	16	0·064
TOTALS	250	1·000

Table 13.2 Sales analysis of a firm, 1977

To find the probability of selling £100–£120 on any particular day, we divide the frequency of occurrence (40) by the total frequencies (250). This gives $40/250 = 0{\cdot}16$, and similarly with the rest.

Note 1 The total of all the probabilities is *unity*, since the table is assumed to cover all possible sales outcomes.

Note 2 A table based upon cols. 1 and 3 is called a *probability distribution*, and would be used by the manager for the type of calculation we have been discussing earlier.

Note 3 The various rules of this chapter could be applied to these probabilities, e.g., the probability that sales on any one day would be £200 or more is $0{\cdot}08+0{\cdot}064=0{\cdot}144$.

We use here (F. 13.1) since we might sell £200–£300 *or* £300–£500, but we cannot have *both* situations on any single day. The events are mutually exclusive.

This type of calculation would be of great value to a manager in deciding the level of stock to be carried.

Probability distributions

The figures of Table 13.2 represent a continuous type of distribution, since the sales can attain any value between (say) £300 and £500. Other situations might result in a discrete type of distribution, such as Table 12.1 of Chapter 12, which gives probabilities, when we divide each frequency by 1 000. In this case, we might find (say) 20 white sweets in a sample, or possibly 21, but we could not have 20.3 white ones.

All the theoretical distributions discussed in the chapters on sampling are, in fact, probability distributions. The Binomial and Poisson types are discrete, and the normal distribution is continuous. These theoretical distributions are used in business situations whenever we have events which occur in a random manner, i.e., they depend upon a combination of causes which are governed by chance.

A Table such as 13.2 is a sample of 250 days taken from a much larger universe of thousands of days, assuming that the firm has been in existence for some years. As such, it is subject to sampling fluctuations, and the probabilities actually calculated from it would not agree exactly with the theoretical probabilities calculated on the basis of (say) a normal distribution. The manager, faced with a probability distribution based upon his own historical records would first *assume* that a particular theoretical distribution applied to his business, basing his choice upon whether the information was discrete or continuous. He would then calculate the theoretical frequencies predicted by it and compare them with the actual results.

This can be done by multiplying each probability by the total frequencies of the distribution.

For example, in Table 13.2, the probability for the first group is 0·16. Multiplying this by the total of 250 gives 40, which is the appropriate frequency.

A comparison of these theoretical frequencies with those actually extracted from his records would reveal whether his original choice of theoretical distribution was a good one, bearing in mind that, quite apart from sampling fluctuations, *no* theoretical distribution will fit exactly a particular business situation. The manager is satisfied if the 'fit' is good enough to make reasonable deductions from it.

A more exact test would be provided by χ^2 (see example 2 of Chapter 15).

Once he has established a particular pattern of events he can then use the theory to forecast the likelihood of any given result in the future.

Mathematical expectation

The probability approach to decision-making under conditions of uncertainty can be used in a variety of ways. The past behaviour of sales or production, etc., is analysed, and probabilities assigned to possible outcomes. The aim is to maximize one's expectation of profit or to minimize the possible loss.

EXAMPLE 7:

A chain store is opening a new branch. The company estimates that the probability of success in site A is 0·8, and that, if successful, the annual profit would be £50 000. If not successful, the annual loss is estimated at £8 000. On site B, the chance of success is 0·6, with a likely profit of £60 000, or a loss of £12 000. Where should the branch be located, so as to maximize the expected profit?

If no information were available about probable success, the directors would locate the branch on site B, since the difference between expected profits and losses is £48 000, but on site A it is only £42 000.

In the light of the information on probability, a table would be set up as follows.

1	*2*	*3*	*4*	*5*	*6*	*7*
Site	*P*	*Possible profit*	*Possible loss*	*(2)×(3) Product*	*(1−P)×(4) Product*	*(5)−(6) Expectation*
A	0·8	£50 000	£8 000	£40 000	£1 600	£38 400
B	0·6	£60 000	£12 000	£36 000	£4 800	£31 200

Table 13.3

Note 1 Since the branch is bound to make either a profit or a loss, the two probabilities add up to *unity*. The probability of a loss is $1-0{\cdot}8=0{\cdot}2$ for site A, and 0·4 for site B. These are the probabilities used in col. 6.

The probability of a branch 'breaking even' is simply a case of zero profit or loss. It is merely a question of definition.

Note 2 We see from col. 7 that the branch ought to be at site A, since the expectation of profit is maximized.

Note 3 If no information on probability of profit or loss were available, and the directors of the firm were *confirmed optimists*, they would choose site B, since they would look on the bright side and go for the more attractive profit.

Note 4 If they were *confirmed pessimists*, they would seek to minimize any possible loss, and would choose site A.

This example shows the importance of statistical analysis of available figures, when making decisions. Otherwise, the businessman is at the mercy of 'hunches' and mental attitudes.

Conclusion

The central problem of business nowadays is the allocation of scarce resources of capital, man-power, and production, etc., so as to maximize the possible outcome in terms of profit, or productivity.

The manager must use the tools of forecasting, and statistical inference and, by a careful analysis of existing statistical information, estimate the probabilities associated with various alternative decisions.

Only in this way can he choose that combination of possible courses of action which will be most likely to achieve his aims.

14

Sampling of variables

Method

In Chapter 12 we were only interested in whether items in a sample did, or did not, possess a certain attribute. We now consider the *extent* to which they possess it.

Some qualities do not lend themselves to this kind of study. For example, in our discussion of a universe of black and white sweets, the question does not arise; a sweet is either black or white. The question of *degree* of whiteness does not enter into it.

If, however, we consider qualities which are capable of variation, e.g., the *weight* of a box of sweets, or the *dimension* of a manufactured component, it is obvious that all the items in our universe will possess this characteristic to a greater or lesser extent. Those which do not possess it (e.g., people who do not eat cheese), may be regarded as zero cases.

In general, the values of the variable, in our universe, will be spread over a range, which in theory may be unlimited. In practice, we can usually assign limits based upon experience (e.g., the heights of human beings), or upon mathematics.

Furthermore, the individual items in our universe may vary by infinitely small amounts (even though we cannot measure them) so that the distribution becomes *continuous* instead of *discrete*.

Sampling distributions

If we take a large number of samples from such a universe, and calculate in each case some statistical measure (usually called a parameter) such as the A.M., we shall get a series of different results, and for each such measure, the results may be arranged in a frequency distribution and graphed.

The resultant graph will in each case resemble that of Fig. 14.1, and if the sample size is sufficiently large, it will no longer be a frequency polygon but a smooth curve.

This is clear when we remember that instead of having only some 20-odd values to plot, as in our previous graph, we shall now have as many values as we like, because the variation is continuous. In other words the group intervals of our frequency distribution can be made smaller and smaller, until the plots on our graph are touching one another.

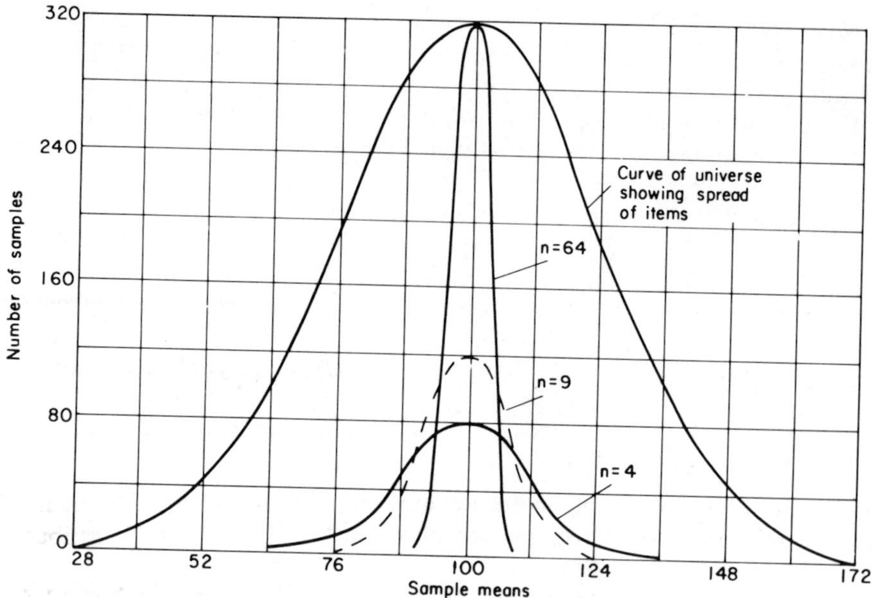

Fig. 14.1 Distribution of 1 000 sample means from a normal universe (A.M. = 100 S.D. = 24) for various sample sizes (n)

To sum up, so far, we now see that if our universe is continuous, then the sampling distribution will be continuous, provided the sample size is large enough, i.e., it will be a curve.

The normal curve

We have seen (Chapter 8) that many actual universes tend to the normal form, as regards their distribution. The curves of samples from such universes will also approximate to the normal curve. In fact, even if the parent universe departs somewhat from normality, this does not seem to affect the normality of the sample curve, provided the sample size is large.

We can therefore describe these sample curves in terms of their A.M. and standard error, and each statistical measure will have its own sampling curve, with its own standard error. For example, if we are considering the arithmetic means of samples, then the sample curve will have a central value which corresponds with the true A.M. of our universe, and the larger our sample size, the closer will be the correspondence. The S.E. of our sample curve will be given by the formula:

$$S.E._{A.M.} = \frac{S.D.}{\sqrt{n}} \qquad \text{(F. 14.1)}$$

where S.D. is the standard deviation of the universe from which the samples were drawn, and n is the sample size. If this former value is not known, we may, as before, use instead the S.D. obtained from our sample, as the best estimate available.

Note As before, the spread of our samples is inversely proportional to the square root of the sample size (n), which appears as the denominator in our formula.

In other words, we would expect our sample averages to group themselves more closely round the real average, than do the values of individual items in the universe itself.

To take an actual example, suppose we consider the heights of male adults in this country. Individual people might vary quite widely from the national average of say 1·67 m. Some might be as small as 1·30 m, while extreme cases might reach 2·15 m. But if we took samples of 100 men, it is inconceivable that any sample average would reach even 1·80 m, because some men would be below average height, while others would be above it. It is equally unlikely that any sample would have an average as low as 1·50 m. The bigger our samples, the more likely our heights will average out. Figure 14.1 illustrates the type of thing we would get.

Note The spread of our sample means is very much less when the sample size is increased. When $n = 64$ we get a very fair approximation to the A.M. of the universe, and the majority of our samples lie within ±9 units of the true A.M. of the universe.

EXAMPLE 1:

A random sample of 100 people in a certain city shows an average weekly consumption of meat of 700 g, with a S.D. of 300 g. What is our estimate of the average consumption in the city as a whole?

Using formula (F. 14.1), we have $S.D. = 300$ g, $n = 100$.

Hence, $S.E._{A.M.} = \dfrac{300 \text{ g}}{\sqrt{100}} = 30$ g.

We could be 95 per cent sure that the true A.M. consumption was within $700 \text{ g} \pm 2 \times 30 \text{ g} = 700 \pm 60$ g.

We could be 99·7 per cent sure that the answer lay within $700 \text{ g} \pm 3 \times 30 = 700 \pm 90$ g.

Were we to increase the sample size to 1 600 then the $S.E._{A.M.}$ would be $\dfrac{300 \text{ g}}{\sqrt{1\,600}} = \dfrac{300 \text{ g}}{40} = 7\frac{1}{2}$ g, and we could now be more precise about our estimate, and say that at the 95 per cent level of confidence the true answer is 700 ± 15 g.

Use of tables of normal curve

The normal curve is actually the graph of a mathematical equation. Suppose we had an equation of two variables, such as $Y = X^2 + 7$. We could substitute a series of values for X, and the equation would tell us the corresponding value of Y in each case. We could then plot each X against the corresponding Y as a point on a graph, and if we had sufficient points we could join them up in the form of a curve.

The equation for the normal curve is much more complex than the example quoted, but the result would equally be a curve, although of a different shape. It is, of course, the familiar bell-shaped curve already referred to.

Students need not concern themselves with the equation itself, because tables are available, based upon it, but they should understand the meaning and use of the tables.

In Chapter 5 we explained that in the case of a histogram the areas of the bars are proportional to the frequencies. This is equally true of our curve, and if we know what proportion of the total area of the curve is enclosed between any two perpendicular lines, we know that the same proportion of the total frequencies will be found between those two limits.

In order to standardize our table of areas, we proceed as follows:

(*a*) We assume that the total area enclosed by the curve is unity. This will enable us to specify the *probability* of getting some particular result in our sampling, since the area of the curve covers all possible sample results, and this, according to our previous notation of probabilities, is represented by unity (a certainty).

(*b*) We adopt as one of our perpendicular lines, the one which divides the curve into two equal parts. It will be remembered that the normal curve is uni-modal and symmetrical, so this line will represent the average (A.M. = median = mode) of our distribution.

(*c*) We measure our horizontal distances from this centre line, not in any specified units, but in fractions of the standard deviation of the curve. This is because the shape and area relationships of the normal curve are governed entirely by its S.D. It also has the merit of eliminating the units in any particular problem, so that our horizontal scale is not in kg or m, but in standard deviations.

(*d*) We measure plus deviations to the right, and minus ones to the left, of the centre line.

The standard tables tell us the probability than an item (or sample) will lie within some specified portion of the total area, but the information may be presented in a variety of ways. The commonest ones are as follows (see Figs. 14.2.A–C):

(A) The area enclosed between two perpendiculars at equal distances measured from the centre line; i.e., A.M. ± a specified number of S.D.'s. *Note* Sometimes only the positive half is given.

(B) The area *beyond* some specified perpendicular; i.e., the 'tail' of the curve, measured in a *positive direction* only. This tells us the probability of getting a sample in excess of some particular value, assuming it to be due to sampling fluctuations. If we wish to include negative fluctuations as well (i.e., a very small result), we simply include the other tail in addition.

(C) The whole area *to the left* of some specified vertical. This is simply the result of the unshaded area subtracted from unity.

The student should read carefully any instructions regarding the interpretation of a given table. In particular, if the largest number in it is 0·5, then it only covers *half* of the curve (see section on Use and interpretation).

The probability given in the table is always a decimal and, when multiplied by the total frequencies, gives the theoretical number of cases within the area specified. Alternatively, we may multiply our decimal by 100 and get the *percentage* of cases.

Estimates of universe from a sample

So far we have only tried to estimate the A.M. of our universe from a sample. We could equally estimate any other statistic, and formulae are given for some of the more important ones in the following sections.

Estimating S.D. of universe. The formula is:

$$S.E._{S.D.} = \frac{S}{\sqrt{2n}} \qquad \text{(F. 14.2)}$$

where S is the S.D. of our sample, and n is the sample size, as before.

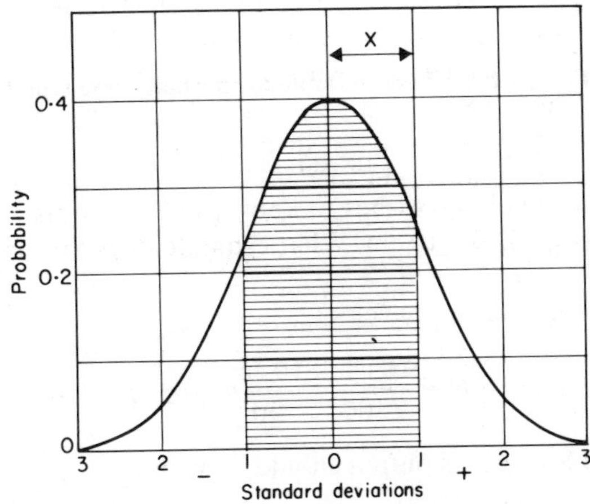

Fig. 14.2(A) Form of table for normal curve type A

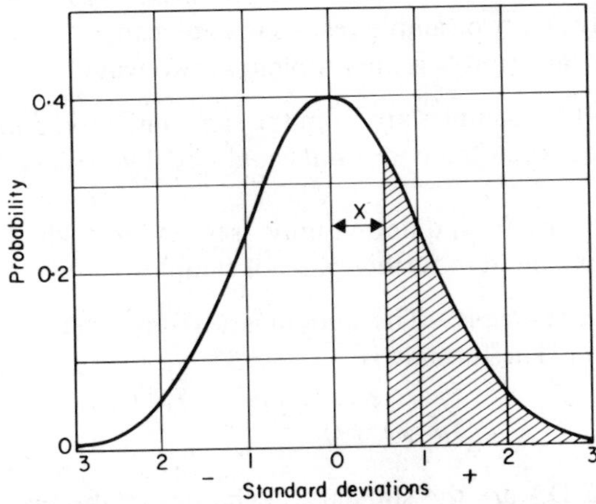

Fig. 14.2(B) Form of table for normal curve type B

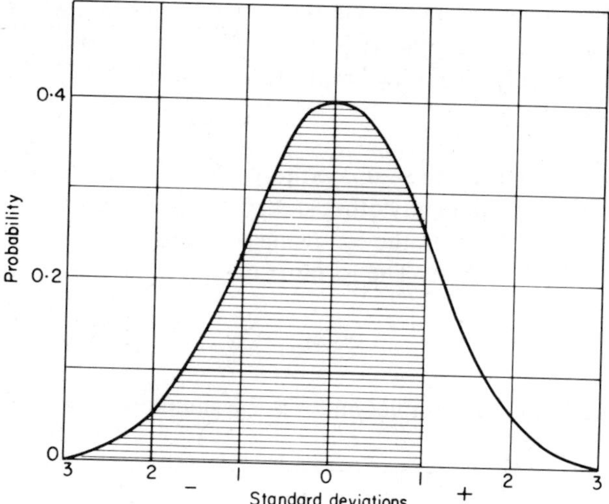

Fig. 14.2(C) Form of table for normal curve type C

EXAMPLE 2:

A manufacturer of shoelaces wishes to know the S.D. of his output. A random sample of 200 has a S.D. of 10 cm. What estimate does this provide of the true S.D.?

Using formula (F. 14.2) we have:

$$S.E. = \frac{10 \text{ cm}}{\sqrt{400}} = \frac{10 \text{ cm}}{20} = 0{\cdot}5 \text{ cm}.$$

Hence, the true S.D. of his output should lie within

$$10 \text{ cm} \pm 3 \times 0{\cdot}5 \text{ cm} = 10 \text{ cm} \pm 1{\cdot}5 \text{ cm}.$$

Sample differences

A similar problem to that of Chapter 12 now arises. How can we test whether the difference between two sample results is significant?

Here again, we can approach the problem in two ways:

(*a*) Assume that the samples are from the same universe, and test whether the difference between the two results could be due to sampling fluctuations; or

(*b*) Assume they are from different universes, and test whether the difference could be eliminated in further pairs of samples.

Differences between means The student is advised to use method (*b*), which is simpler to work out. The formula is:

$$S.E._{diff.} = \sqrt{\frac{S.D._1^2}{n_1} + \frac{S.D._2^2}{n_2}} \qquad \text{(F. 14.3)}$$

where $S.D._1$ and $S.D._2$ are the standard deviations of the two samples, and n_1 and n_2 their sizes.

EXAMPLE 3:

Two samples of electric lamps are taken from two different factories of a large organization. Sample A, of 100 lamps, has an average burning life of 1 100 hours, with a S.D. of 240 hours. Sample B, of 200 lamps, has an average burning life of 900 hours, with a S.D. of 220 hours. Is the difference between the lives of the lamps significant?

Using formula (F. 14.3), we have $n_1 = 100$, $S.D._1 = 240$ hours, $n_2 = 200$, and $S.D._2 = 220$ hours. Hence:

$$S.E._{diff.} = \sqrt{\frac{240^2}{100} + \frac{220^2}{200}} = \sqrt{576 + 242} = \sqrt{818} = 28{\cdot}6 \text{ hours.}$$

The actual difference between the two means is $1\,100 - 900 = 200$ hours.

Hence, it is well over 3 S.E. (in fact it is about 7 S.E), so that it could not possibly be eliminated by further pairs of samples. The output from the two factories is indeed different as far as average burning life is concerned.

Note We need not waste valuable time calculating the *exact* number of S.E.'s in the difference. We are concerned only with whether it exceeds our yardstick of 3 S.E., and so on, according to our chosen level of significance.

Differences between sample standard deviations A further application of the same idea is to test whether two samples, with different S.D.'s, could be from the same universe; i.e., is the difference between the two results significant?

In this case, we are only concerned with the S.D. of our samples, as related to that of the universe, and not with any other feature.

Using method (*b*), the formula is:

$$S.E._{diff.} = \sqrt{\frac{S.D._1^2}{2n_1} + \frac{S.D._2^2}{2n_2}} \qquad \text{(F. 14.4)}$$

EXAMPLE 4:

In the previous example, we proved that there was a significant difference in the A.M. life of the lamps. We now ask whether there is a significant difference between the two standard deviations.

These were 240 hours for the sample of 100, and 220 hours for the sample of 200.

We now have, using formula (F. 14.4):

$$S.E._{diff.} = \sqrt{\frac{240 \times 240}{2 \times 100} + \frac{220 \times 220}{2 \times 200}}$$

$$= \sqrt{288 + 121} = \sqrt{409} = 20{\cdot}22 \text{ hours.}$$

The actual difference between the samples is $240 - 220 = 20$ hours. This is less than one S.E. and is clearly not significant.

As a result of these two tests, we can say that the outputs of the two factories differ as regards their average burning life, but not in the variability or spread of the product.

Use and interpretation

One of the main uses of sampling techniques is in the field of quality control in industry, and we shall deal with this in detail in the next chapter.

The technique is also widely used for market research. This is a statistical investigation carried out by a manufacturer or distributor, to find out one or more of the following:

(*a*) *Who uses the product*? It may appeal to certain income groups, or people of a particular age or sex. The occupation or interests of customers may be important, and so on.

(*b*) *Why they use it* (*or do not*). This may give a line on competitors, or point to certain features as important. Sometimes the answer is surprising. Reasons given in actual surveys have included the size of the lid on the container and even the dimensions of the container itself.

(*c*) *How much people would expect to pay*. The public frequently has a built-in resistance to products outside a particular price range.

(*d*) *Buying habits*. When and where they get it; how frequently and so on. This governs:

(*e*) *Packaging*. The size and quantity packed. Style and design of package which appeals, etc.

(*f*) *Opinions about the product*. What people expect or would like; criticisms, etc.

(*g*) *Geographical differences of taste*. In the case of a firm supplying a specialized product, or appealing to a limited market, it may be possible to survey the whole of the field, but in the majority of cases a sample must be chosen. (See Chapter 2 for discussion.)

Public opinion polls are well-known applications of sampling techniques, and the student should now appreciate why different results at different times or places may have little statistical significance. This type of sample is usually a *stratified* one, so at to include a cross-section of the public.

Official samples We have already mentioned sampling in official statistics as a method of saving time and money; e.g., the 10 per cent sample in the Population Census. The Censuses of Production and Distribution also use this device, as an alternative to a full census.

The Social Survey This is a government department which undertakes surveys on behalf of other departments. These investigations are usually based upon the method of random sampling.

The normal tables The use and interpretation of these tables of probabilities often seems difficult to students, and we therefore give a series of examples covering all likely applications.

EXAMPLE 5:

A sample of 1 000 articles has an A.M. of 300 g, and a S.D. of 60 g.

1 What number of articles will lie between 270 and 330 g?

Here we are concerned with the spread on *either side* of the A.M.; i.e., A.M. $\pm$ 30 g (300 $\pm$ 30 g).

(*a*) We first reduce this to units measured in S.D.'s, i.e.,

$$\frac{30 \text{ g}}{60 \text{ g}} = 0{\cdot}5 \; S.D.$$

(*b*) We now require the shaded area of Fig. 14.2(A) where X (the distance on the horizontal scale) $= \frac{1}{2}$.

Using Table 2 (Appendix) (which is of type A but gives only *half* the area) we see that, for a distance of 0·5, the probability figure is 0·1915.

We therefore *double* this, and get 0·3830.

This is the *proportion* of the total area.

(*c*) Multiplying this by the total frequencies (1 000) gives us 383 articles.

2 What number of articles will *exceed* 390 g?

Here, the value of X (horizontal distance) is 390 g − 300 g = 90 g (ignore the sign)

Reducing this to S.D.'s we get $\frac{90 \text{ g}}{60 \text{ g}} = 1{\cdot}5 \; S.D.$

We now require the shaded area of the curve on Fig. 14.2(B).

Our table for 1·5 S.D. gives a proportion of 0·4332, but this is not the portion we want. Our table value is the area between the centre line (300 g in this example) and a vertical line at 390 g.

Remembering that the total area of our standard curve is unity, and that the right-hand portion is therefore 0·5, we subtract our tabular answer from 0·5.

We now have 0·5 − 0·4332 = 0·0668.

Multiplying this by 1 000, as before, gives us our answer, namely 66·8 (67 articles).

3 What proportion of the articles will weigh *less than* 198 g?

This is 300 − 198 = 102 g, i.e., 1·7 S.D.

This time, the distance is measured to the *left* of our centre line. The situation is similar to the shaded area of curve (Fig. 14.2(B)), except that we require the area of the *other* tail. Since the curve is symmetrical, the two tails are identical, so we can use our table directly.

For a distance of 1·7 S.D. the proportion is 0·4554. Taking this from 0·5 as before, to get the tail, we have 0·5 − 0·4554 = 0·0446.

As a *proportion* is called for, we can let this answer stand, or multipy it by 100 = 4·46 per cent.

EXAMPLE 6:

Assume a universe with a mean of 100 and a S.D. of 20.

(*a*) If the probability that a certain value of the variable will be exceeded is 10 per cent, what is the value?

We are told that the area of the tail in Fig. 14.2(B) is 0·1. Taking this from 0·5, to get the remainder of the right-hand portion, we have: 0·5 − 0·1 = 0·4.

We now find this value, as closely as possible, in our Table 2 (Appendix). The nearest value is 1·3 S.D.

Note Much more detailed tables of the normal curve are available (see references).

Since one S.D. = 20, this gives us $1\cdot3 \times 20 = 26$ (measured from the centre line = A.M. of our curve).

Hence, the value required = $100 + 26 = 126$.

(*b*) The probability that a certain *deviation from the mean* will be exceeded is 10 per cent. What is the deviation?

This type of question may be interpreted in two ways, depending upon what we mean by 'exceeded'.

(i) In the ordinary sense of the word, we mean bigger than, i.e., we need only consider the right-hand portion of the curve, and the answer is 26, as in case (a).

(ii) If we mean a deviation in *either direction* (±), then we are considering the unshaded area of Fig. 14.2(A). If this is 10 per cent (0·1), then each tail is 0·05, and taking this from half the curve (0·5) gives us: $0\cdot5 - 0\cdot05 = 0\cdot45$.

We cannot find this exact value in our table, but it is about half way between 1·6 S.D. and 1·7 S.D., i.e., 1·65 S.D.

Therefore the required deviation is: $\pm(1\cdot65 \times 20) = \pm33$.

EXAMPLE 7:

In a normal distribution, 30 per cent of the items are under 50, and 10 per cent are over 86. Find the A.M. and S.D. of the distribution.

Steps

(*a*) Since 50 per cent of the curve is to the left of the A.M., we know that the vertical at 50 must also be to the left (since only 30 per cent of the curve is to the left of this line). That is, the 30 per cent is the tail of the curve.

(*b*) The left half of the curve has an area of 0·5. The tail is 0·3 (30 per cent). Hence the area between A.M. and 50 = $(0\cdot5 - 0\cdot3) = 0\cdot2$. From our table, 0·2 represents a distance (X) of 0·5 S.D. Hence,

$$A.M. - 50 = 0\cdot5\ S.D. \qquad \text{Eq. (14.1)}$$

(*c*) By similar reasoning, the 10 per cent represents the right-hand tail of the curve (=0·1).

(*d*) Hence, the area between 86 and the A.M. is $0\cdot5 - 0\cdot1 = 0\cdot4$. From our table, 0·4 represents a distance of 1·3 S.D., and so:

$$86 - A.M. = 1\cdot3\ S.D. \qquad \text{Eq. (14.2)}$$

(*e*) We now have two equations:

$$A.M. - 50 = 0\cdot5\ S.D. \qquad \text{Eq. (14.1)}$$

$$86 - A.M. = 1\cdot3\ S.D. \qquad \text{Eq. (14.2)}$$

Adding them:

$$86-50=0{\cdot}5\ S.D.+1{\cdot}3\ S.D.\quad 36=1{\cdot}8\ S.D.\quad \frac{36}{1{\cdot}8}=1\ S.D.,\ \text{i.e.,}\ S.D.=20$$

(*f*) Substitute this value in Eq. (14.1):

$$A.M.-50=0{\cdot}5\times 20.\quad A.M.-50=10.\quad A.M.=60.$$

The distribution can now be visualized as follows:

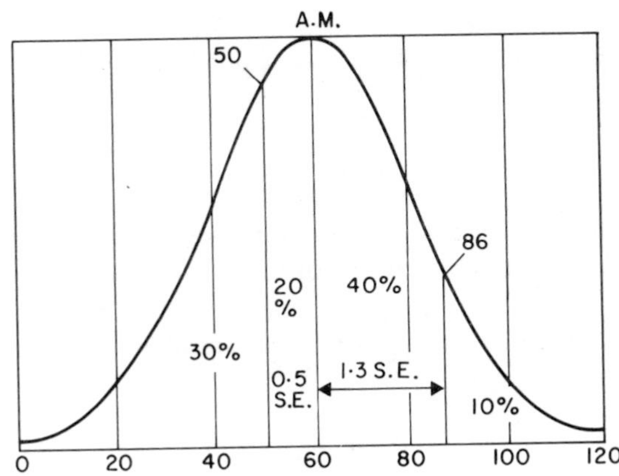

Fig. 14.3

Determination of sample size

EXAMPLE 8:

The S.D. of a universe is 60 g. What size of sample must we take to be 95 per cent sure that the sample A.M. will not differ from the A.M. of the universe by more than 10 g?

We use formula F. 14.1 for the S.E. of the A.M.

$$S.E._{A.M.}=\frac{S.D.}{\sqrt{n}}=\frac{60\ \text{g}}{\sqrt{n}}.$$

We know that the 95 per cent confidence limits are

$$A.M.\pm 1{\cdot}96\ S.E.$$

This is one of the limits which the student *must* remember.
Hence:

$$1{\cdot}96\times\frac{60\ \text{g}}{\sqrt{n}}=10\ \text{g},\quad \text{i.e.,}\ \frac{117{\cdot}6\ \text{g}}{\sqrt{n}}=10\ \text{g}$$

$$10\sqrt{n}=117{\cdot}6.\quad \sqrt{n}=11{\cdot}76.\quad n=(11{\cdot}76)^2=138\ \text{or}\ 139.$$

Note Instead of 1·96 S.E., a round figure of 2 S.E. may be used.

15

Further applications of sampling

Method

The correlation coefficient (r)

In previous chapters we discussed sampling theory in general terms. We now consider a few specialized applications of these principles.

For samples from a normal universe, the standard error of the Pearsonian coefficient of correlation is given by:

$$S.E._r = \frac{1-r^2}{\sqrt{n}} \qquad \text{(F. 15.1)}$$

where n = the sample size, as before.

For large samples (say 100 or more pairs of observations) the distribution of r approximates to the normal curve, and we can use the levels of significance previously described. Thus, a sample value which exceeds 3 S.E. is most unlikely to be due to sampling fluctuations, i.e., it is significantly different from zero, or it is 'real'.

This measure is of limited use, as will be explained in 'Use and interpretation'.

EXAMPLE 1:

A sample of 400 pairs of items gives a value of r of 0·3. Is there evidence of correlation?

Applying formula F. 15.1 we have:

$$S.E._r = \frac{1-0{\cdot}3^2}{\sqrt{400}} = \frac{1-0{\cdot}09}{20} = \frac{0{\cdot}91}{20} = 0{\cdot}046$$

We now apply what is sometimes termed the *null hypothesis*, i.e., we assume that there is zero correlation in the universe from which the sample is drawn, and that the value of 0·3 obtained is, therefore, due to sampling fluctuations.

If this is so, then the deviation from zero is

$$\frac{0{\cdot}3}{0{\cdot}046} = \text{about } 6\tfrac{1}{2}\ S.E.$$

We have already said that a deviation of more than 3 S.E. is about the highest sampling fluctuation possible. Hence, this result is too high to be explained in this way, and our null hypothesis must be rejected. In other words, the correlation is real.

Note If the same result had been obtained from a sample of 25, however, the calculation would be:

$$S.E._r = \frac{0{\cdot}91}{\sqrt{25}} = \frac{0{\cdot}91}{5} = 0{\cdot}18.$$

In this case, the deviation from zero is

$$\frac{0{\cdot}3}{0{\cdot}18} = 1{\cdot}67 S.E.$$

This is less than 2 S.E. and is not even significant at the 5 per cent level.

The student will see that little reliance can be placed upon results from small samples.

The χ^2 test of significance

In previous discussions, it has been emphasized that the sample size must be reasonably large. We next consider a test which can be applied to samples of all sizes.

Its purpose is to find whether the results obtained from a sample are likely ones, on the basis of some theory or law. The sample results will be termed *actual* ones, while the results suggested by our theory are termed *expected* ones. If the actual results are identical with those expected, there is no problem. Such correspondence does not prove the theory, as was pointed out in Chapter 12, but there is no difference to explain away.

If, however, there is a difference between fact and theory, the question arises as to whether the differences could be due to sampling fluctuations, or whether they are too large to be explained in this way, in which case they are *real* or *significant.*

In other words, we need an indication of whether the sample results fit the theory. For this reason, such tests are often called *goodness of fit* tests.

The χ^2 *test* (pronounced *kigh*-squared) is so-called because it is represented by the small Greek letter *chi.* From its wide variety of uses, we select two which commonly appear in examination questions.

EXAMPLE 2:

Application to frequency distributions Table 15.1 gives the experimental results obtained from throwing a die, together with those predicted by theory. In this instance, it is the theory of probability. Since a die has 6 sides, we should expect that the chance of getting any particular result would be 1 in 6, assuming the die to be unbiased. That is, the frequencies of occurrence of each number (1–6) should be the same, and equal to 600/6 = 100.

The value of χ^2 in any particular case is given by:

$$\chi^2 = \sum \frac{(F_A - F_E)^2}{F_E} \qquad (4.15.2)$$

where F_A = the actual frequency in each case,
F_E = the theoretical or expected frequency in each case,
and $\sum$ = 'the sum of . . .', as before.

In other words, the difference between actual and theoretical in each class or group is squared, and the result divided by the expected frequency for that group. These individual results are then totalled for all the groups.

1	*2*	*3*	*4*	*5*
Score	*Actual frequency*	*Expected frequency*	$F_A - F_E$	$\frac{(F_A - F_E)^2}{F_E}$
1	80	100	−20	4
2	90	100	−10	1
3	100	100	0	0
4	105	100	5	0·25
5	110	100	10	1
6	115	100	15	2·25
Totals	600	600	0	8·5

Table 15.1 Calculation of χ^2 for 600 throws of a die

Note 1 The total of col. 4 gives a check upon the accuracy of the differences, since these should always total zero.

Note 2 Because the differences are squared, the result of col. 5 is always positive. In the case where, for each class, there is complete agreement between fact and theory, all the differences will be zero, and the value of χ^2 is zero.

Note 3 The total of col. 5 gives the value of χ^2 which, in this case, =8.5.

Interpretation of the result

We have seen that, where the actual and expected frequencies coincide, the value of χ^2 will be zero. In all other cases, it will be some positive amount, which increases with the difference between fact and theory.

We must now ask ourselves whether any particular value of χ^2 could have arisen by pure chance—i.e., could it be due to sampling fluctuations?

To answer this question, we make use of special tables, as we did in the case of the normal curve. But before we can understand these tables, we must introduce a new idea, namely:

Degrees of freedom (written D/F) The significance of any particular value of χ^2 depends upon the number of degrees of freedom used in its calculation. To understand what this means, let us refer to col. 2 of Table 15.1, i.e., the frequencies. Suppose we were to fill in this column by pure chance, by putting down any number, say, which sprang to mind. Bearing in mind that the total must be exactly 600, we have perfect freedom regarding the frequencies we insert in the first 5 lines, but the final frequency (score of 6) is then taken out of our hands, since this will have to be the number which ensures that our total is exactly 600.

In other words, we have *five degrees of freedom* in this particular table. In general, for frequency distributions of this kind, the number of degrees of freedom is *one less* than the total number of classes.

The χ^2 table gives values of χ^2 arranged in rows, and each row corresponds to a particular number of degrees of freedom. The columns of the table are each headed by a figure of *Probability* (*P*). These correspond to the previous notions of Chapter 12, i.e., $P=0{\cdot}1$ means a probability of 1 in 10, and so on (see Appendix 3). For example, referring to Table 15.1, we saw that there were 5 degrees of freedom. The χ^2 table, for 5 *D/F*, shows that, for $P=0{\cdot}1$, the value of $\chi^2=9{\cdot}24$.

This means that a value of χ^2 as big as, or bigger than, 9·24 could arise from sampling fluctuations. The calculated value for Table 15.1 was 8·5. So the deviation from theory is very likely to be due to sampling fluctuations; i.e., there is no reason to suppose that the die used was in any way biased.

EXAMPLE 3:

Application to contingency tables

Sometimes, the subject of investigation is the association, or correspondence, between two or more attributes. Information of this kind is usually arranged in a table (called a *contingency table*) as below.

	Smokers	*Non-smokers*	*Total*
Males	A 160	A 40	200
	E 120	E 80	
Females	A 440	A 360	800
	E 480	E 320	
TOTAL	600	400	1 000

Table 15.2 Sample of adults, showing smoking habits by sex

Explanation The A's (actuals) are the sample results. The marginal totals give a cross-check upon the arithmetic, and add up to the grand total of 1 000—i.e., the sample size.

The problem to be decided is whether the figures suggest any association between the two attributes of smoking (or non-smoking) and sex (male or female).

Step 1 We first put forward a theory, or hypothesis, to explain the results, and calculate the theoretical or expected frequencies (on this assumption) for each of the 4 subdivisions of the table.

In all such cases, we adopt the null hypothesis, as in example1; i.e., we assume that there is *no association* between sex and smoking. If this is so, we would expect the same proportion of males among the smokers as among the non-smokers, since according to our theory, *being* a male has no influence upon smoking. The proportion of males in the sample is 200/1 000 and applying this to the total number of smokers, gives us an *expected number* of male smokers of: $200/1\,000 \times 600 = 120$. This figure has been entered in the table to explain the next step. (It is not necessary to do this in practice.)

If 120 males are smokers, then the rest are non-smokers. We can therefore place $(200 - 120) = 80$ in the next space.

Considering next the female smokers, we see that out of a total of 600 smokers, we have 120 males. Therefore, the rest $(600 - 120) = 480$ are female smokers. This only leaves the female non-smokers, and these must amount to 320, so as to give us our total of 800 females.

We have now filled in all our expected frequencies, in such a way that the marginal totals are still in agreement.

Step 2 We must now calculate the value of χ^2, as follows:

Class	*Actual frequency*	*Expected frequency*	$A-E$	$\frac{(A-E)^2}{E}$
Male smokers	160	120	40	$13\frac{1}{3}$
Male non-smokers	40	80	−40	20
Female smokers	440	480	−40	$3\frac{1}{3}$
Female non-smokers	360	320	40	5
TOTALS	1 000	1 000	0	$41\frac{2}{3}(\chi^2)$

Table 15.3

Step 3 We next determine the number of degrees of freedom in our calculations.

In our calculation of theoretical frequencies, we found the frequency for male smokers only. The remaining frequencies followed automatically from the various marginal totals. This suggests that there is only one degree of freedom, which is the case.

In general, for a contingency table for P rows and Q columns, the number of degrees of freedom is given by:

$$D/F = (P-1)(Q-1) \qquad \text{(F. 15.3)}$$

In the present case, there are only two rows and two columns (ignoring the marginal totals).

Hence, $$D/F = (2-1)(2-1) = 1 \times 1 = 1$$

Step 4 We now consult our table of χ^2 (Appendix 3). For 1 D/F we find that $P_{0\cdot001} = 10\cdot83$; i.e., the chances of getting a value of χ^2 as great as, or greater than, 10·83, through sampling fluctuations, are only 1 in 1 000. This is very unlikely, and since we actually got a value of 41·67, such a result is virtually impossible.

Hence, we reject our hypothesis that there was no association between smoking habits and sex. The result is significant, and suggests that there *is*, in fact, such an association.

Quality control charts

This is essentially a question of testing a manufactured product for *variability*, on the basis of successive samples, taken from the production line, at regular intervals throughout the working day.

If the results are recorded on a chart, the inspector is provided with a cumulative picture of what is happening, and any tendency for the process to 'drift' can be easily seen. Furthermore, the chart provides:

(*a*) an early warning system of any source of variation,
(*b*) an aid to finding out whether a change is real, or only apparent.

The type of chart used will, to some extent, depend upon whether the aspect under control is an attribute, or a variable (see Chapters 12 and 14).

Control of attributes This method applies where it is possible to lay down certain standards, on the basis of which we can accept or reject a particular article. The rejected items are called *defectives* and the aim is to make sure that the *percentage or proportion of defectives* in the bulk of the production, remains within acceptable limits. The method used is essentially the application of sampling theory to Binomial and Poisson distributions, as previously explained. The new features are the use of charts, and the use of small samples, which are much more variable.

The expected percentage defective in the bulk production may be determined in advance, as a matter of policy, or it may be based on a series of tests. Suppose it is 5 per cent. If we take periodic samples of 20 items, we should therefore exact, on average, one defective per sample. In fact, we might get as many as six defectives per sample, owing to fluctuations of sampling. We therefore lay down two limits for the fluctuation in the number of defectives found per sample.

One is called a *warning limit* or an *inner limit*, and is such that it will be exceeded, by chance, only 25 times in a thousand. This is really the 5 per cent level of significance which was discussed in Chapter 12 but here we are only concerned with *one tail* of the sampling distribution (two-and-a-half per cent).

The other limit is called the *upper limit* or the *action limit*, and the chances of exceeding this, through sampling fluctuations, are only 1 in 1 000 (the 0·1 per cent level). If a sample result falls outside the first limit, it is an 'amber light', and further samples must be taken as soon as possible, to confirm that it was simply a chance result. If the action limit is exceeded, the production is stopped, because this result is evidence that the production process has changed significantly.

The number of defectives for our two limits could be calculated on the basis of our formulae (F. 12.1), (F. 12.2), (F. 12.3) and (F. 12.6), (F. 12.7), (F. 12.8), according to whether the Binomial or the Poisson type of distribution was considered more appropriate. In practice, however, tables are available, which enable us to turn up the result immediately. The best known are those issued by the British Standards Institution, which lays down a uniform procedure.

Figure 15.1 shows a typical quality control chart of this type, with the results of 20 tests filled in. The last sample shows clearly that something has changed, and production would be stopped.

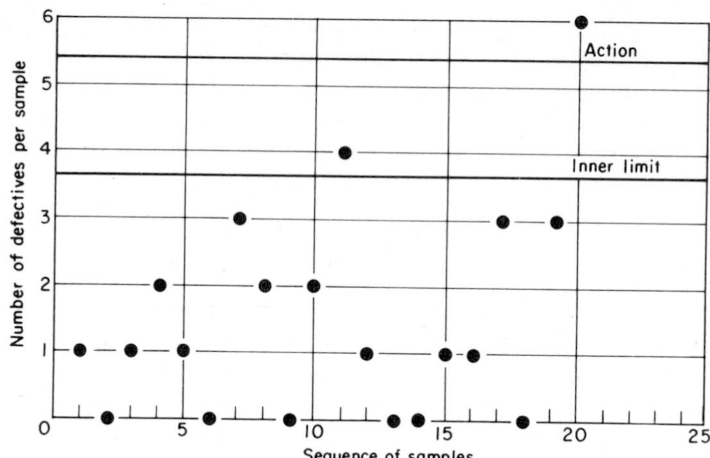

Fig. 15.1 Control chart for defectives. Samples of 20. Expected percentage is 5 (one per sample)

Control of variables This method is used when the quality under control is a continuous variable, e.g., a dimension, or a weight. Mass production, and the necessity for spare parts to be interchangeable, make it essential for all dimensions to lie within certain limits.

The two statistical measures used for such purposes are the average (usually the A.M.) and the spread or dispersion (either the range or the standard deviation). The appropriate theoretical distribution is now the normal curve, since we are concerned with a continuous variable, rather than one which is discrete.

Control chart for averages The inner control limits are fixed at A.M. $\pm$ 1·96 S.D./$\sqrt{n}$, i.e., we find the S.E. of the A.M. and take 1·96 times this figure as the 5 per cent limit of sample fluctuations.

The action limit is A.M. $\pm$ 3 S.D./$\sqrt{n}$ or 3 S.E.

Note In this case we have *two* inner and *two* outer limits, since a component which is too small in some dimension is just as much a reject as one which is too large to fit.

Process *A.M.* = 0·5 cm. *S.D.* = 0·01 cm. Samples of 16.

Inner limits $0{\cdot}5 \pm \dfrac{1{\cdot}96(0{\cdot}01)}{\sqrt{16}} = 0{\cdot}5 \pm 0{\cdot}0049.$

Outer limits $0{\cdot}5 \pm \dfrac{3(0{\cdot}01)}{\sqrt{16}} = 0{\cdot}5 \pm 0{\cdot}0075.$

Control charts for standard deviation Although the mean of a sample may be within the inner control limits, the spread of the individual items within a sample may be excessive. Some control of dispersion is therefore needed, and the best method is to use the S.D.

An estimate of the S.D. of the universe is first made, using the results from a succession of samples. The S.D.'s of individual samples, which are the values to

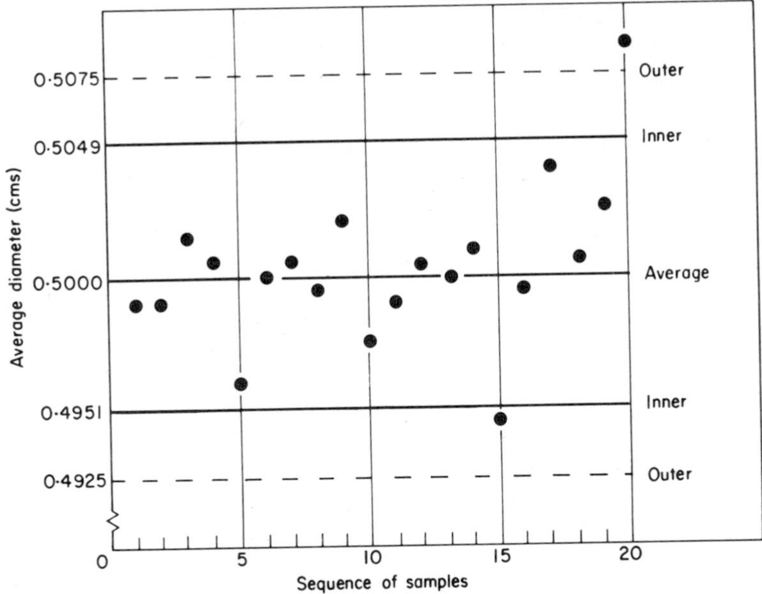

Fig. 15.2 Control chart for averages

be plotted on our chart, will fluctuate according to the normal curve, and tables are again available to give the inner and outer control limits.

As long as sample values remain within the limits, the process is under control. The moment we get a value outside the action limit, the process is stopped (see Fig. 15.3).

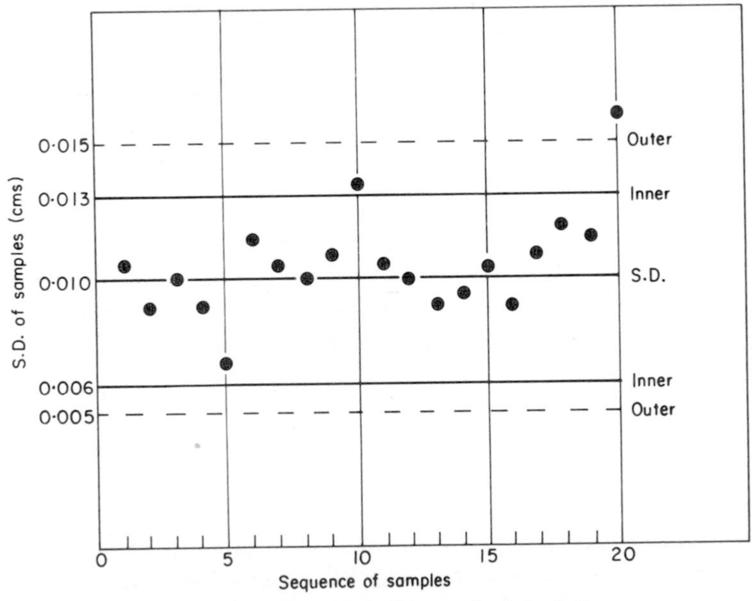

Fig. 15.3 Control chart for standard deviation

Control charts for the range An alternative method for controlling dispersion is to use the range as a measure of spread. This is more easily calculated, as the samples are taken, and is more easily understood.

The control limits for the range can be found directly from the S.D. of the universe, using suitable conversion tables, or they can be found by calculating the average range of a group of samples, and again referring to appropriate tables for the limiting values.

Fig. 15.4 is a typical chart for the range.

Process $S.D. = 0{\cdot}01$ cm. Samples of 16.

For calculation of limits we use $S.E.$ of $S.D.$ $\left(\text{i.e., } S.E._{S.D.} = \dfrac{S.D.}{\sqrt{2N}}\right)$

$$\text{Thus: Outer limit} = 0{\cdot}01 \text{ cm} \pm \frac{3(0{\cdot}01)}{\sqrt{2 \times 16}} = 0{\cdot}01 \text{ cm} \pm 0{\cdot}005 \text{ cm}$$

Note limits are not symmetrical.

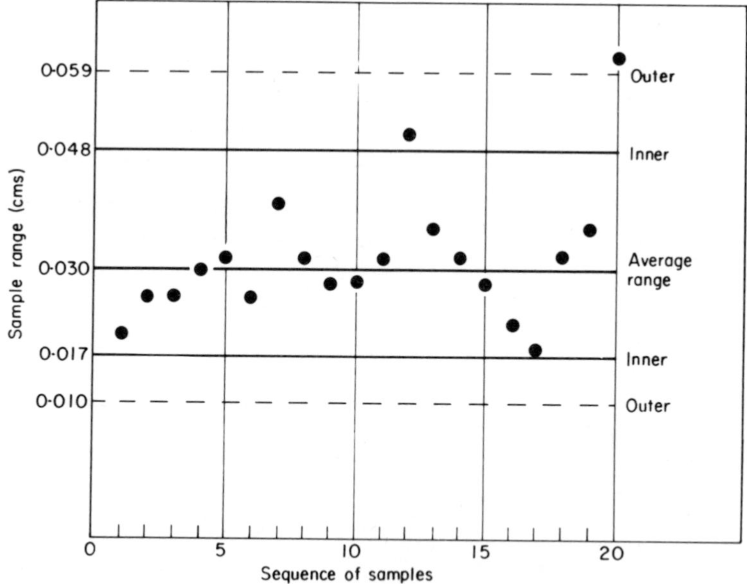

Fig. 15.4 Control chart for range of samples

Process $S.D. = 0{\cdot}01$. Process range $= 0{\cdot}03$. Samples of 10.

Use and interpretation

Standard error of *r*

We mentioned that this measure is of limited value. In addition to a large sample size (100 or more pairs), the value of r must be small—certainly less than $0{\cdot}5$.

When these two conditions are satisfied, the sampling distribution of r is roughly normal, and our various levels of significance can be used.

When r is large, the sampling distribution departs from the normal and is skewed. Hence, the above measure is not used.

There are alternative tests of significance which are used in such cases, but they are outside the scope of this book.

χ^2 Test

The student may wonder why the table of χ^2 is limited to just a few levels of probability. This is because the shape of the χ^2 curve varies according to the number of degrees of freedom (indicated in the table by ν). When $\nu = 1$, the curve is J-shaped and when $\nu = 30$, it approaches normality, but for intermediate values the curve has marked positive skewness.

Hence, for each value of ν from 1 to 30, the curve has a different shape, and to tabulate fully the various degrees of probability would require 30 separate tables on the lines of Appendix 2 of the normal curve.

To avoid such a complication, the χ^2 table gives, for each value of ν, the values of χ^2 corresponding to a few selected significance levels (values of P), which are sufficient in practice.

Strictly speaking, the idea of degrees of freedom is also applicable to standard deviation, and when calculating this measure, the divisor should be $(N-1)$—the number of degrees of freedom—and not N—the total frequencies. When the total of frequencies is a large number, the difference is of no importance, but for small samples, the divisor of $(N-1)$ is used.

Contingency tables

Students usually have no difficulty in calculating χ^2 but the interpretation of the result often troubles them. Bearing in mind that we always use the null hypothesis, i.e., that χ^2 should really be zero, it follows that if P (probability) is small, then the divergence from zero is unlikely to be due to sampling fluctuations; i.e., we must reject the hypothesis. But since this is an assumption of *no association* between the attributes, we are driven to the conclusion that *association exists*, and that the result is significant. Hence, a value of P as small as 0·05 or smaller is always significant. A very large value of P is also significant ($P = 0{\cdot}9$) since it means that there is little chance of obtaining a smaller value of χ^2. That is, the agreement between fact and theory is too good to be true.

Calculation of χ^2

This is not as difficult as it seems, since only one (any one) theoretical frequency need be found for a 2×2 table. The rest follow from the totals.

Furthermore, examination of Table 15.3 (*step 2*) shows that the differences are all the same (in this case 40). The sign is immaterial, since the results are squared.

Therefore, we need not find the remaining theoretical frequencies at all. Having obtained one difference, we use this throughout.

It is even possible to calculate χ^2 without knowing this difference, if the student cares to memorize a simple formula. Consider the general case of a 2×2 table as shown overleaf:

	A	*Not-A*	*Totals*
B	a	b	c
Not-B	d	e	f
TOTALS	g	h	N

Table 15.4

It does not matter what A and (Not-A) represent, as long as every item in our sample falls into one group or the other. For example, in Table 15.2, these columns were smokers and non-smokers. Provided there are only two columns, everything is one or the other. Similarly, provided there are only two rows, everything is B or (not-B). In Table 15.2, there were males and non-males (i.e., females).

The letters in the spaces represent the actual frequencies given in the question. The value of χ^2 is now given by:

$$\chi^2 = \frac{N(ae-bd)^2}{c.f.g.h}. \qquad \text{(F. 15.4)}$$

Cross-multiply the frequencies, and take the smaller product from the larger (the reason for this follows later). Square the difference and multiply the result by the total frequencies (sample size). Divide the answer by all the marginal totals multiplied together.

EXAMPLE 4:

Taking the actual frequencies of Table 15.2 we have:

	A	*Not-A*	*Totals*
B	160	40	200
Not-B	440	360	800
TOTALS	600	400	1 000

Table 15.5

$$\chi^2 = \frac{1\,000 \times [(360 \times 160) - (40 \times 440)]^2}{200 \times 800 \times 600 \times 400}$$

$$= \frac{1\,000 \times [57\,600 - 17\,600]^2}{200 \times 800 \times 600 \times 400}$$

$$= \frac{1\,000 \times [40\,000]^2}{200 \times 800 \times 600 \times 400} = \frac{1\,000 \times 40\,000 \times 40\,000}{200 \times 800 \times 600 \times 400}$$

$$= \frac{1\,000 \times 16}{2 \times 8 \times 6 \times 4} = \frac{1\,000}{24} = 41{\cdot}67 \text{ as before.}$$

P×Q contingency

When the number of rows or columns exceeds 2 (e.g., a 3×2), the formula cannot be used and the theoretical frequencies for each space in the table must be found as follows, using the null hypothesis, as on page 189.

EXAMPLE 5:

Factory	*Quality grade of output*			
	1	*2*	*3*	*Totals*
A	A 50	A 15	A 30	95
	E 44·3	E 15·8	E 34·9	
B	A 20	A 10	A 25	55
	E 25·7	E 9·2	E 20·1	
TOTALS	70	25	55	150

Table 15.6

Assuming the raw material quality is identical, is there a significant difference in quality of production between the two factories? As in Table 15.2, the A's are *actual* results, and the E's are those *expected* on the basis of our theory.

Step 1 Since there are only 2 D/F [(2−1)(3−1)] we need only calculate two of the theoretical frequencies (see example 3, above).

Step 2 Taking space A.1, we multiply the marginal totals and divide by the sample size, i.e.,

$$\frac{95\times 70}{150}=44{\cdot}3.$$

For space A.2, we have

$$\frac{95\times 25}{150}=15{\cdot}8.$$

The rest of the spaces can then be filled in from the marginal totals.

Step 3 We then calculate each portion of χ^2 as in Table 15.3 giving us a total χ^2 of 3·9 (approx.).

Step 4 We consult our table of χ^2 as before. For 2 D/F we find that $P_{0\cdot5}=1{\cdot}39$ and $P_{0\cdot1}$ is 4·61. We have *not* reached the 5 per cent level of significance ($\chi^2=5{\cdot}99$) which is the minimum.

Hence we conclude the differences are due to sampling fluctuations.

Yates's correction

The χ^2 distribution is a continuous one, like the normal curve, whereas the frequencies in a table such as 15·5 are discrete quantities. This is likely to introduce an error when the total (N) is small. A closer result is obtained in such cases by making a correction to the individual frequencies of the table. This consists of subtracting $\frac{1}{2}$ from those actual frequencies which exceed the corresponding expected frequency, and adding $\frac{1}{2}$ to those which fall short. The calculation then proceeds as before.

When using formula (F. 15.4) this becomes

$$\chi^2 = \frac{N(ae - bd - \frac{1}{2}N)^2}{c.f.g.h.} \qquad \text{(F. 15.5).}$$

Note 1 Take the smaller product from the larger in the numerator, so that the correction gives a smaller answer.

Note 2 This correction is only needed for 1 D/F and for sample sizes under 100.

Quality control

A simpler method of setting up control charts is to use a single control limit, based upon a probability of 0·005, i.e., the chances of a sample result falling outside it, due to sampling fluctuations, are 1 in 200.

This method is mainly intended for sampling of attributes, where we are only concerned with the percentage or proportion of defectives.

It may be adapted for the control of variables, e.g., dimensions, where it is possible to test the product by using gauges. Two of these are used, one providing a maximum permitted dimension, and the other being set for the minimum dimension. All products which pass through the first are acceptable, in the sense that excessive dimensions are rejected. Those which *do not* pass through the second are equally acceptable, since they are above the minimum. Those which pass through it are rejected.

These devices are known as 'go' and 'no-go' gauges, and by their use the excessively variable items are rejects, so that the method of percentage rejects may still be used.

Interested students are referred to the British Standards Institution publication B.S. 1313: 1947 for details.

16

Further graphical applications

Method

In Chapters 4 and 5, we studied the basic principles of pictorial and graphical representation. We now consider some specialized applications of these ideas, which are popular in examinations.

Simple bar charts

There are two common applications of this device.

1 The Gantt chart Alternative titles are *machine loading chart* or *progress chart.*

This consists of two horizontal bar charts for each period of time (usually a day or a week). One, which is simply a heavy line, indicates the *planned* production or running time, and alongside this a bar chart of the *actual* figures is drawn. Any discrepancy reveals a loss of production and is investigated. The chart may also show a *cumulative* comparison for the week as a whole.

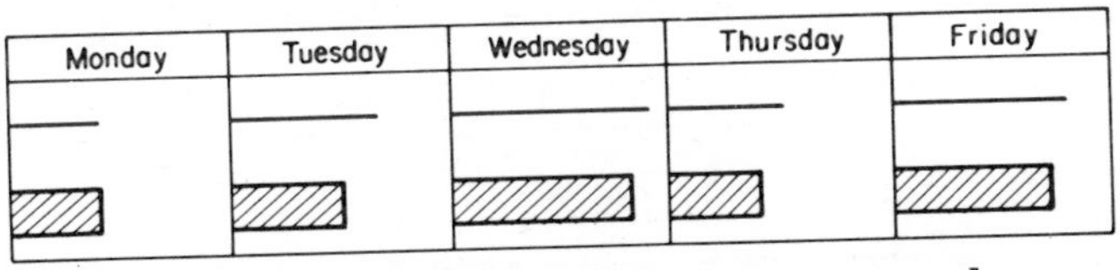

Fig. 16.1 Gantt chart showing production record

Figure 16.1 shows the sort of result which may be obtained. The horizontal scale may be in percentage form, in which case the planned production for Monday was 40 per cent of capacity. This is shown as a thin line. The actual production fell short of target on every day except Monday, and the reasons for this would be investigated.

In Fig. 16.2, we have cumulative figures for a week, subdivided for each machine. Here again the horizontal scale could be running hours, or percentage of possible time. This type is useful for allocating rush orders which might come in. For example, there is ample surplus capacity on machines 2 and 4 which could be utilized. The code letters show the reason for the failure to achieve the planned running time.

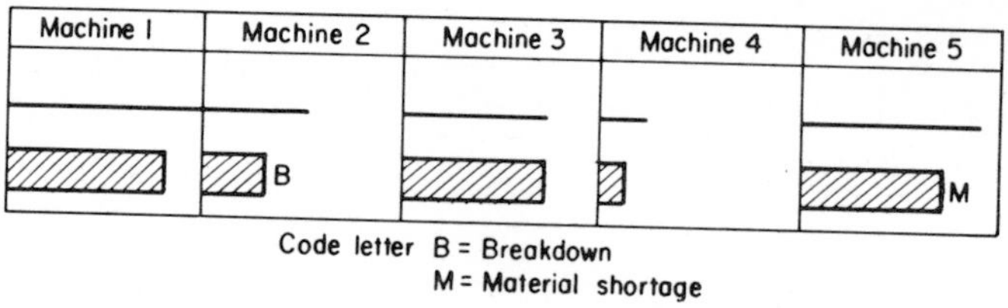

Machine 1 Machine 2 Machine 3 Machine 4 Machine 5

B M

Code letter B = Breakdown
M = Material shortage

Fig. 16.2 Cumulative weekly total of machine loading

2 The population pyramid This is illustrated in Fig. 16.3. It consists of a series of horizontal bars (one for each age-group), the length of each one being proportional to the number of people in that age-group. There are really two separate diagrams, one for males and one for females, which are placed together for easy comparison. If the number of births remained fairly constant over a long period (say $2\frac{1}{2}$ millions for each sex), one would expect each successive bar to be shorter than the one below it, since there would be a progressive reduction in numbers due to death; i.e., some of the $2\frac{1}{2}$ million would never reach the second bar (5–10 years). In this sense, one could say that the complete diagram, for both sexes, should resemble a stepped pyramid.

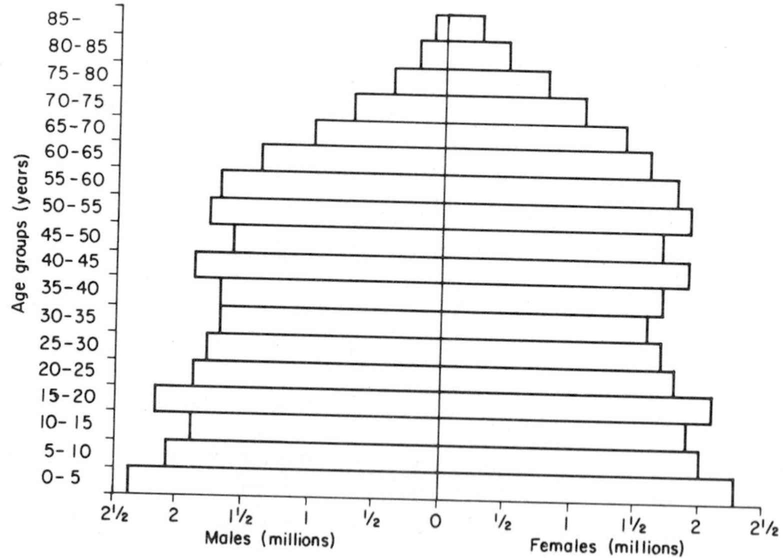

Fig. 16.3 Population pyramid showing age distribution of UK population, June 1972

Cumulative curves

The two best known applications are:

1 The Lorenz curve This is a graph to show the interrelation of two cumulative percentages. That is, it involves a comparison of two variables, which are usually presented in the form of frequency distributions.

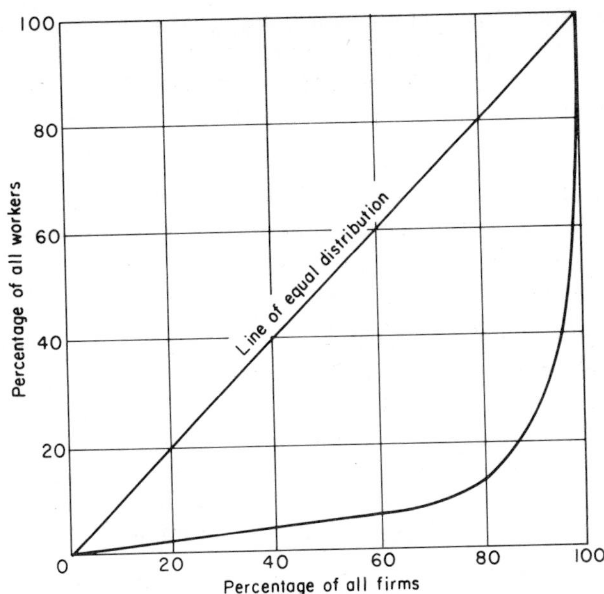

Fig. 16.4 Lorenz curve showing distribution of workers in industry, 1977

EXAMPLE 1:

1	*2*	*3*	*4*		*5*	
Number of workers	*Number of firms (000's)*	*Number of workers (0000's)*	*Percentages*		*Cumulative percentages*	
			Number of firms	*Number of workers*	*Number of firms*	*Number of workers*
Up to 10	150	75	73	9	73	9
11–24	15	26	7	3	80	12
25–49	15	51	7	6	87	18
50–99	12	81	6	9	93	27
100–249	9	135	4	16	97	43
250–499	3	114	2	14	99	57
500–999	2	105	0·5	12	99·5	69
1 000–	1	261	0·5	31	100	100
TOTALS	207	848	100·0	100		

Table 16.1 Distribution of workers in manufacturing industry by size of firm, 1977

The two frequency distributions are given in cols. 1–3. In col. 4, we express the frequencies as percentages of their respective totals. It is permissible to round-off the individual percentages, so as to make them total exactly 100 per cent in each case.

In col. 5, a cumulative total is found for each of the percentage columns.

The information is then plotted on a graph, in which each axis is of equal length and is scaled in percentages (see Fig. 16.4).

The line of equal distribution (sometimes called the 45° line) is then drawn in, by joining the origin to the intersection of the 100 per cent lines.

2 The Z chart (*or Zee chart*) This is a particular type of time chart or historigram. The intervals of time may be days, weeks, or months, and the total extent of the chart is usually one year, although it is permissible to show several years' results on one diagram, for purposes of comparison.

It is really a combination of three separate diagrams:

(*a*) A graph of the individual figures
(*b*) A cumulative total, or ogive, of the figures for the year (or each individual year)
(*c*) A moving annual total, starting with the annual total of the previous year, and adjusting this figure for each period, as the individual figures are available. The M.A.T. is the same idea as the trend figure (see Chapter 10), except that we do not divide by the number of items to obtain a moving average.

The scale used for (*b*) and (*c*) is usually smaller than that used for (*a*) since the magnitude of the figures being plotted is different, and it is better to adopt a more open scale for the original data so as to bring out more clearly the individual movements.

The scales to use will depend upon the intervals of time. For monthly figures, the scale for (*b*) and (*c*) could be 5 times that of the actual data, while for weekly figures it might be 20 times.

The chart resembles the letter Z, and hence its name.

EXAMPLE 2:

Details	*Jan.*	*Feb.*	*Mar.*	*Apr.*	*May*	*June*	*July*	*Aug.*	*Sept.*	*Oct.*	*Nov.*	*Dec.*
Sales 1975	28	24	20	18	22	23	20	19	24	28	30	32
Cumulative sales	28	52	72	90	112	135	155	174	198	226	256	288
M.A.T.	—	—	—	—	—	—	—	—	—	—	—	288
Sales 1976	22	28	30	22	26	28	30	26	30	24	32	38
Cumulative sales	22	50	80	102	128	156	186	212	242	266	298	336
M.A.T.	282	286	296	300	304	309	319	326	332	328	330	336

Table 16.2 Sales figures of a firm, 1975 and 1976 (£000's)

Note 1 The total sales for 1975 (January–December) are 288 (£000's). The M.A.T. from February 1975 to January 1976 (12 months) is £288 − January 1975 + January 1976 = £288 − 28 + 22 = £282. Subsequent totals are obtained by discarding the 1975 figure and adding the corresponding 1976 figure.

Hence, for February, we have £282 − £24 + £28 = £286: for March, £286 − £20 + £30 = £296, and so on.

Note 2 There is a check on the arithmetic in the December column, since the cumulative sales for 1976 should equal the M.A.T. for December of that year.

The graph of the three series is shown in Fig. 16.5.

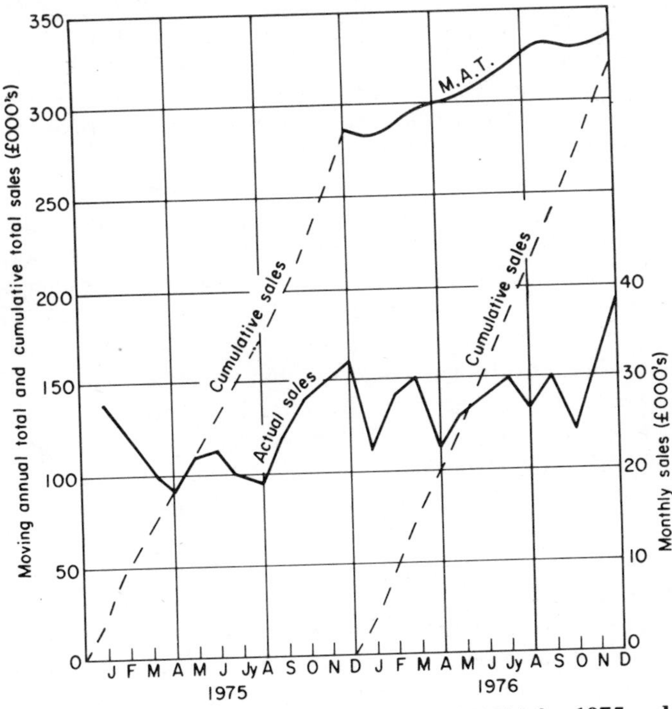

Fig. 16.5 Z chart showing sales of a firm (£000's) for 1975 and 1976

Use and interpretation

The Gantt chart

This is mainly used for the control of machines and of production processes. Ideally, there would be one chart per machine or process, and each chart would run for a week, the bars or blocks being drawn in each day, at the end of the run.

Apart from their value in indicating discrepancies between plan and performance, they have many other uses. They give a pictorial survey of the whole range of manufacture, and the extent to which there is spare capacity. If they are filed away over a period, they also provide a source of reference on comparative reliability of different types of machine, and on the efficiency of material flow and production planning.

The population pyramid

This gives an indication of the age distribution of the population at any particular time, and is valuable for the planning of social and economic projects.

Reference to Fig. 16.3 indicates clearly the so-called *population bulge* where certain bars are actually larger than those beneath them, and which is often referred to in the press. In fact, there are two bulges—one around 40–50, which forecasts an increasing proportion of pensioners in the near future, and the other in the 20–25 group.

This effect is brought about whenever there is a 'population explosion'—i.e., a significant increase in the birth rate over a few years.

The bulge rises up the pyramid and, in time, works its way out at the top.

Actually, the term 'pyramid' is seldom correct for a typical population structure, because females survive longer than males, and consequently the two halves of the pyramid are rarely symmetrical.

The Lorenz curve

This was originally suggested as a method of measuring distribution of wealth, but it gives a useful picture of divergence from the average. The more the curve departs from the line of equal distribution, the greater the concentration of divergent items at that point. For example, Fig. 16.4 reveals that some 90 per cent of the firms (i.e., the small ones) employ collectively only 20 per cent of the labour force. Alternatively, one could say that 80 per cent of the workers are employed by only 10 per cent of the firms (the big ones). Were the distribution uniform, one would expect, say, half the number of firms to employ half the labour force. The curve is, perhaps, less useful than a coefficient of dispersion, since it does not provide a numerical measure of the divergence.

The Z chart

If applied to sales, as is usually the case, the Z chart shows at a glance how sales are progressing month by month and reveals any seasonal fluctuations. The cumulative curve shows how the performance to date compares with the target figure, and with the corresponding point of time in previous years. The M.A.T. gives an annual indication, with seasonal fluctuations removed, and is a picture of the trend.

Applying this analysis to Fig. 16.5 we can see, from actual sales, that March and April are poor months, while November and December seem to be above average. The cumulative total for 1976 was ahead of the previous year from March onwards, and the overall trend is, on balance, upwards.

17

Financial mathematics

Method

In this book, as far as we have dealt with the firm, we have been concerned mainly with statistical techniques of internal control and presentation. We must now look at some techniques which may help us in setting up a business or a project, e.g., discovering statistics which will help us to decide *whether* to invest.

This branch of calculation is known as 'investment appraisal.' It is a well known tool of the cost accountant and it should be familiar to the economist who studies marginal costing. The techniques involved are simple and are well within the grasp of the statistician who may know little about accountancy or economics. The student will be thankful to learn that very little extra technical knowledge is required for the understanding of these techniques.

Arithmetic progressions

An arithmetic progression is a series of numbers where the difference between the numbers is the same.

EXAMPLE 1:

$$3, 7, 11, 15, 19 \text{ (the difference is 4)}$$

$$\text{or, } 4\tfrac{1}{2}, 3, 1\tfrac{1}{2}, 0, -1\tfrac{1}{2}, -3 \text{ (the difference is } -1\tfrac{1}{2}\text{).}$$

The difference, as you can see, can be added or subtracted. The series of numbers can be expressed in whole numbers, fractions, decimals, etc.

In calculations of the simple interest on a sum of money invested we can use the arithmetic progression.

EXAMPLE 2:

If £100 is invested for four years at a simple interest rate of 5 per cent p.a., at the end of four years, the total amount accumulated would be:

$$£100+£5+£5+£5+£5=£120,$$

i.e., the total amount would have grown, in an arithmetic progression, thus,

$$£100, £105, £110, £115, £120.$$

If we call the total amount accumulated A, and the original investment P, and r the rate of interest, then,

$$P, (P+Pr), (P+2Pr), (P+3Pr), (P+4Pr)$$

is the arithmetic progression.

The formula of the last term of this (when t is time in years) is:

$$A = P(1+tr), \text{ or } (P+tPr). \qquad \text{(F. 17.1)}$$

Thus, in example 2:

$$A = £100\left(1+4\times\frac{5}{100}\right) = £120.$$

Note 1 r is expressed as a fraction of 100, and t can be calculated as a fraction if the time involves half or quarter years, months, weeks, or even days.

Note 2 The student is invited to compare formula (F. 17.1) with the equation for a straight line ($Y = a + bX$) given in Chapter 9.

If we wished to work a problem in 'reverse' and wanted to find out how much we would have to invest (P) at simple interest (r) to provide ourselves with a certain target amount (A) at the end of a specified period (t years) the formula is simply:

$$P = \frac{A}{(1+rt)}. \qquad \text{(F. 17.2)}$$

In example 2, $P = \dfrac{£120}{\left(1+\dfrac{5}{100}\times 4\right)} = £100.$

The term 'P' is usually called the 'present value' of A at a simple interest rate (r) in t years from now.

Geometric progressions

A geometric progression is a series of numbers where the difference between the numbers is found by *multiplying* the preceding number by a fixed amount (often called the 'common ratio').

EXAMPLE 3:

4, 8, 16, 32, 64 (each number is multiplied by 2 to get the following number).

or: 160, 40, 10, $2\frac{1}{2}$, $\frac{5}{8}$ (each number is multiplied by $\frac{1}{4}$).

Geometric progressions can increase or decrease (as can arithmetic progressions) but they do so in *more* than a constant amount. (At this stage, the student might refer back to pages 79 to 80 where arithmetic and geometric series were used).

The geometric progression is used in calculations of compound interest. It is often the case, where a sum of money has been invested, for the interest payment (say, in a bank or building society account) to be re-invested, rather than to be withdrawn and spent. If this is so, then, in our previous example, we would begin with $P = £100$ in the first year, and then, at the beginning of the second year we would be investing a different $P(=£105)$ and so on, an increased 'P' at the beginning of each year. Thus, our geometric series would be:

$$P,\ P(1+r),\ P(1+r)(1+r),\ P(1+r)(1+r)(1+r), \text{ etc.}$$
$$(£100),\ (£105),\ (£110{\cdot}25),\ (£115{\cdot}7625), \text{ etc.}$$

or: $P,\ P(1+r),\ P(1+r)^2,\ P(1+r)^3,\ P(1+r)^4$, etc.
the 'common ratio' is $(1+r)$.

The formula we obtain from the last term is:

$$A = P(1+r)^t \text{ (i.e., to the 'power' of } t\text{).} \qquad \text{(F. 17.3)}$$

Thus, in example 2:

$$A = £100\left(1+\frac{5}{100}\right)^4 = £100(1{\cdot}05)^4.$$

using logarithms this gives:

$$\log 100 + 4 \log (1{\cdot}05)$$
$$\text{Therefore } A = £121{\cdot}60.$$

Comparing this with the return on a simple (arithmetic) interest we would clearly expect more if we reinvested our interest than if we did not. The extra return is $£121{\cdot}60 - £120 = £1{\cdot}60$.

The formula for compound interest can also be used for asking, what is the size of the sum which we would have to invest (P) at compound interest (r) to get a target amount (A) at the end of a certain period (t years)? The formula for this reverse process is:

$$P = \frac{A}{(1+r)^t}. \qquad \text{(F.17.4)}$$

In our example, $P = \dfrac{121{\cdot}60}{\left(1+\dfrac{5}{100}\right)^4} = £100.$

Once again, 'P' is known as the 'present value' and the method of obtaining P (by our formula) is known as 'discounting' the amount A.

Investment appraisal

When a businessman wishes to invest in a new project or a new product he will want to know how much he can expect in returns and, therefore, in profits. The issue is not always as simple as this. Usually, when a businessman has spare funds for investment he will have more than one idea for a variety of new products, or new projects, and he has to choose which will be the most profitable. It is difficult to look into the future (as was explained in Chapter 10—Time series) but there are different techniques for doing so, some of which are better than others.

These techniques fall into two classifications:

(*a*) *Conventional methods*
- (i) *Pay-back* method
- (ii) *Average rate of return* (or *accounting return based on initial investment*) method

and,

(*b*) *Discounting methods*
- (iii) *Net present value* method
- (iv) *Internal rate of return* method

These are the four methods we shall describe here, though there are variations on these. In using these methods we shall use the concepts of the progression of arithmetic and geometric series. We shall use one example to show the different methods.

(*a*) *Conventional methods*

(i) *Pay-back method*

This method is the most commonly used in investment appraisal. It is simple and crude, and it is defined as the time it takes for an investment to generate sufficient returns to pay back the original investment in full.

EXAMPLE 4:

Supposing a firm has a choice of 5 projects, each with a different initial cash investment, and each project investment is calculated to bring a certain flow of cash by every year end, as follows:

		Projects				
	End of year	*A*	*B*	*C*	*D*	*E*
Initial cash investment	*0*	*110 000*	*100 000*	*210 000*	*180 000*	*50 000*
Cash inflows	1	0	20 000	70 000	0	20 000
	2	20 000	20 000	70 000	0	20 000
	3	20 000	20 000	70 000	0	20 000
	4	20 000	20 000	70 000	0	20 000
	5	20 000	20 000	70 000	0	20 000
	6	20 000	20 000		0	
	7	20 000	20 000		0	
	8	20 000	20 000		0	
	9	20 000	20 000		0	
	10	20 000	20 000		900 000	
	11	20 000				
	12	20 000				
	13	20 000				
	14	20 000				
	15	20 000				

Table 17.1

The method is simply to add the cash inflows to find out which sum would pay back the initial cash investment.

Note In project D, we do not receive *any* cash inflow until the end of year 10! The answers can be put down thus:

	Pay-back periods				
Project	A	B	C	D	E
Years	6·5	5·0	3·0	10·0	2·5

Clearly, the best project *on this method* is Project E which takes the *shortest* time (2.5 years) to repay the initial cash investment.

(ii) *Average rate of return method* (ARR)

This method simply averages the annual cash inflow, less a deduction for depreciation, over the initial cash investment, or, if investments are made over a number of years in a project, over the average investment.

$$\frac{\text{Average annual cash inflow} - \text{average annual depreciation}}{\text{Initial cash investment}} \qquad \text{(F. 17.5)}$$

For project A, this would be (as a percentage):

$$100 \times \frac{\dfrac{£280\,000}{15} - \dfrac{£110\,000}{15}}{£110\,000} = 10{\cdot}30 \text{ per cent.}$$

The student can easily work out the complete list as follows:

	Average rates of return				
Project	A	B	C	D	E
Percentage	10·30	10·00	13·33	40·00	20·00

Obviously, project D gives the *greatest* ARR, and is therefore to be preferred *on this method.*

(*b*) *Discounting methods*

For these two methods we use what we have already learned of the progression of series. If you were offered, say, £100 now, or £100 in three years time, which would you take? Only a foolish person would turn down £100 now. The reason is quite obvious. You could, at simple interest, increase your £100 to £115 in three years time by investment, or at compound interest, to £115·7625, as we found earlier. (Also, in a time of inflation, £100 in three years time would be worth less anyhow!).

As we saw before, the present value of a future amount depends on two things:

(*a*) the number of years it takes to receive it, and
(*b*) the rate of interest at which the original investment is made. (See F. 17.4).

The diagram below shows, in graphical form, how the time and the interest rate affect the present value of £1:

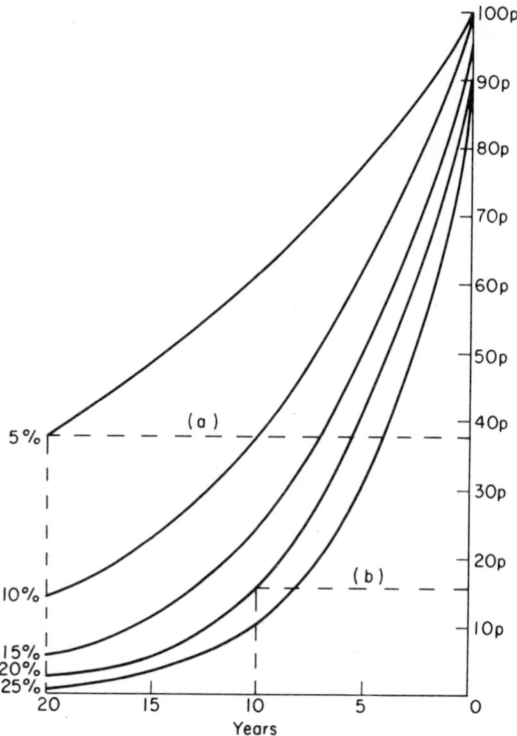

Fig. 17.1 Present value of £1

Reading from the graph we can learn, for example, that the present value of £1 to be received (a) in 20 years time at 5 per cent is about 38p, or (b) in 10 years time at 20 per cent is about 16p. We can use this discounting technique to improve on the conventional methods just described, to give a more accurate appraisal of investment decisions.

Note The *curves* of the geometric progressions on the graph if these were arithmetic progressions (simple interest) would form a series of *straight* lines. The student is invited to calculate from formula (F. 17.2) (100p = A) what P would be (a) in 20 years time at 5 per cent and (b) in 10 years time at 20 per cent and to draw the straight lines on Fig. 17.1.

(iii) *Net present value of method* (NPV)

In this method the cash inflows of the 5 projects set out in Table 17.1 are discounted to their present value, i.e., in year 0 (the time of the initial cash investment), and the total discounted cash flows are subtracted from the value of the initial cash investment. The formula is:

$$\Sigma(\text{Annual cash inflow} \times \text{discount factor}) - \text{initial cash investment} \qquad \text{(F. 17.6)}$$

There are two pieces of information we require before we can calculate this. First, we have to know the rate of interest which we must use. This is usually fixed at a rate which would give shareholders in the firm a rate at least equal to what they could expect from alternative investment opportunities outside the company. In our example we are going to fix this at 16 per cent. Second, we need a table which will give us 'discount factors' calculated for various interest rates for varying periods of years, so that we can discount the cash inflows to their present values. These are given in Appendix 4.

Note The student is invited to check the measurements on Fig. 17.1 by the 'Present value factors'.

Hence: 20 per cent for 10 years = 0·1615 (16p approx.)
5 per cent for 20 years = 0·3769 ($37\frac{1}{2}$p approx.).

Let us start with Project C. The initial cash investment is £210 000 and the cash inflows are £70 000 for each of the first 5 years. We look at Appendix 4, 'Present value factors', the column headed 16 per cent to find the discount factors we must use to multiply, year by year, the 5 cash inflows of £70 000 by, thus:

Year 1	£70 000 × 0·8621 = £60 347
Year 2	£70 000 × 0·7432 = £52 024
Year 3	£70 000 × 0·6407 = £44 849
Year 4	£70 000 × 0·5523 = £38 661
Year 5	£70 000 × 0·4761 = £33 327
TOTAL	£229 208

Table 17.2

These are then totalled. The initial cash investment is then subtracted from this total.

Note The initial cash investment may be *larger* than the total of the discounted cash inflows, in which case, the result will be *negative.*

£229 208 − £210 000 = £19 208.

This result means that the firm could borrow, for example, £229208 for project C, use £210 000 to begin the project (i.e., by investing it in the project) distribute £19 208 to its shareholders, and, by the end of the project (end of year 5) the loan would have been paid off. The project is acceptable as it allows *some* profit (£19 208) to the shareholders—but is it to be preferred to the other four projects? We must work out, in the same manner, the other four projects. This would clearly be laborious work. Fortunately, we have another table to help us in Appendix 5—the table headed 'Cumulative present value factors'.

If we look at this table, under the column headed 16 per cent, and along row Year 5, we shall find the figure 3·274. As the cash inflows for each year in project C are the same (£70 000) we can simply multiply £70 000 by 3·274. This gives us £229 180.

Note This figure is a little lower than the figure obtained previously (£229 208) but this is merely because the 'cumulative' table's figures were 'rounded off'. (If you want to prove this add up the first 5 years figures under 16 per cent in the table headed 'Present value factors').

In the following table, the calculations for all 5 projects have been made, using the 'Cumulative table':

Project A	(£20 000 × 5·575 − 0·862) − £110 000	= −£15 740
Project B	(£20 000 × 4·833) − £100 000	= −£3 340
Project C	(£70 000 × 3·274) − £210 000	= +£19 180
Project D	(£900 000 × 0·227) − £180 000	= +£24 300
Project E	(£20 000 × 3·274) − £50 000	= +£15 480

Table 17.3

Clearly project D has the highest profit (+£24 300) and is therefore to be preferred. (*Note*. Obviously projects with negative profits are not worth considering).

There are some points which the student should note about these calculations:

(*a*) All the cash inflows in our example are assumed to be received at the end of year 1. The cash outflow (i.e., the initial capital investment) occurs at the beginning of year 1, i.e., at the 'end of year 0'. The discount factor for the initial cash investment is therefore 1 000 (because the present value of £1 in year 0 is £1).

(*b*) In project D, as only one cash inflow is received (i.e., in year 10) the present value factor of 16 per cent for year 10 is used, and we cannot use the 'cumulative' table because there are no years previous to year 10 to take into account.

(*c*) In project A, if we use the cumulative table for £20 000, at 16 per cent, for 15 years (5·575) we must subtract the present value factor for year 1 (0·862) because no cash inflow was received for that year.

(iv) *Internal rate of return method* (IRR)

This method of discounting is really more common with businessmen than the NPV method. Calculation in this method can be stated as follows: that rate of interest which, when used to discount the cash flows of a proposed investment, reduces the present value of the project to zero. (It is sometimes known as the *discounted yield* method). In this method we do not require to assume our interest rate of 16 per cent.

We can therefore put the IRR formula in the form of an equation:

$$\text{Annual cash inflow} \times \text{discount factor} = \text{Initial cash investment}$$

(i.e., making the terms 'equal' is the same thing as cancelling out one side in terms of the other).

If we rearrange this formula slightly to get:

$$\frac{\text{Initial cash investment}}{\text{Annual cash inflow}} = \text{discount factor}. \qquad \text{(F. 17.7)}$$

we can substitute our known quantities in the left hand side and find the discount factor. Then, proceeding along the *row* of our cumulative table for the number of years for which cash has been flowing in we can find the discount factor we have calculated and proceed to the top of that particular column to find the interest rate.

EXAMPLE 5:

For project A substitution would give us:

$$\frac{£110\,000}{£20\,000} = 5{\cdot}5 \text{ (discount factor).}$$

Looking up 5·5 in the cumulative table for the number of years £20 000 has been flowing in (i.e., 15 years − 1 year = 14 years) we find the figure *nearest* to 5·5 to be 5·577 (i.e. 6·462 (15 yr. row) *minus* 0·885 (1 yr. row). The interest rate at the head of this particular column is 13 per cent. This is the internal rate of return for this project which will reduce the initial cash investment (approx.) to zero. The student will probably realise that this method is the reverse process of the NPV method.

The table of IRR calculations for all the projects is given below:

Project A	$\frac{£110\,000}{£20\,000} = 5{\cdot}5$ (for 14 years)	IRR = 13 per cent approx.
Project B	$\frac{£100\,000}{£20\,000} = 5{\cdot}0$ (for 10 years)	IRR = 15 per cent approx.
Project C	$\frac{£210\,000}{£70\,000} = 3{\cdot}0$ (for 5 years)	IRR = 20 per cent approx.
Project D	$\frac{£180\,000}{£900\,000} = 0{\cdot}2$ (for the 10th year on the present value table)	IRR = 17 per cent approx.
Project E	$\frac{£50\,000}{£20\,000} = 2{\cdot}5$ (for 5 years)	IRR = 29 per cent approx.

Note Obviously project A requires the lowest rate of return to make any profit, therefore this will be the favoured project *on this method*.

Use and interpretation

Arithmetic progressions The main use of the arithmetic progression is in the calculation of simple interest in business transactions. Its use is limited however, and the student should assume, unless 'simple interest' is stated in the calculation, that the compound interest calculation is required. The reason for this is that it is more realistic to assume that interest will be reinvested in an efficiently run business or fund.

Geometric progressions Geometric progressions are used in the calculation of compound interest in many business affairs. These range from the calculation of interest on bills of exchange, securities and annuity funds, tax arrears, bank and building society interest, etc. These will probably be familiar to the student and therefore we shall give only one example of the application of series, i.e., depreciation.

It should be clear to the student by now that compound interest produces a higher rate of growth in the total amount for the same interest rate on the same principal. Furthermore, the produce of compound interest will become proportionately greater if:

(*a*) the length of time money is invested increases, and
(*b*) the more frequently the interest is reinvested, i.e., if we reinvest (recalculate) the interest, say, monthly instead of yearly, or weekly instead of monthly.

Depreciation This is the gradual reduction in the value of capital assets in a firm (e.g., plant, machinery, vehicles, etc.) and it depends on the passage of time, the rate at which assets become obsolete, and the wear and tear to which they are subjected. Accountants place different emphases on these three factors and this gives rise to a variety of methods. We shall deal only with three of these methods:

1 The Straight Line method

This is a simple averaging method which allocates an equal cost of an asset to each period (e.g., year) during which it is used.

For example: Cost of machine = £1 000

Period of use = 20 years

$$\text{Annual depreciation} = \frac{£1\,000}{20} = £50$$

Accountants who use this method assume that the machine gives equal value in *use* every year of its life. The method gives an *arithmetic* series of 'written off' values.

2 The reducing balance method

In this method, the asset is 'written down' to its economic *value* at the end of each successive year of its life (i.e., it is assessed at its market value—which, when it is no longer useable as a machine, may be its scrap value).

For example: Cost of machine = £1 000

Period of use = 20 years

1st year of depreciation = £1 000 − £80 = £920

2nd year of depreciation = £920 − £90 = £830

etc.,

The method *could* give a *geometric* rate of 'written down' values e.g., the reduction of each successive year's *reduced value* by a fixed percentage or fraction.

Note These are only two of the simpler methods of assessing depreciation. The student should bear in mind that in today's changing world, a machine could become obsolete whilst it is still relatively new, therefore its value may suddenly drop sharply. On the other hand, if the inflation rate is very high, a machine could actually be worth *more* when it is older than a new one of the same type.

3 Sinking fund method

(*a*) If a firm wishes to build reserves (i.e., savings) to invest in plant or machinery in the future, it may, like a private individual, save a regular sum each year. Naturally it would 'invest' it in a safe security while the fund builds up, and in its accounts the money would be entered in a special 'reserve' or sinking fund account. Say, £100 was saved each year for four years at five per cent, then, using formula (F. 17.3), each £100 would build up like this:

$$£100 \text{ (invested at beginning of year 1)} = £100\left(1+\frac{5}{100}\right)^4 = £121{\cdot}6$$

$$£100 \text{ (invested at beginning of year 2)} = £100\left(1+\frac{5}{100}\right)^3 = £115{\cdot}8$$

$$£100 \text{ (invested at beginning of year 3)} = £100\left(1+\frac{5}{100}\right)^2 = £110{\cdot}5$$

$$£100 \text{ (invested at beginning of year 4)} = £100\left(1+\frac{5}{100}\right)^1 = £105$$

Therefore, at the beginning of year 5 we should have the *addition* of these 4 separate 'streams' of investments, i.e., £452·9. Therefore, our sinking fund would have produced £452·9.

(*b*) A more useful kind of sinking fund is one where we wish to produce a *certain* figure, e.g., to replace plant which costs a given amount of money, or to provide a depreciation fund. Here we have a *target* to aim for in a *given* number of years. How much must we invest annually?

Say we wish to produce £1 000 (using the same rate of interest [five per cent]) at the end of 4 years instead of our £452·9. Then, as our unknown *annual* investment sums would grow at the same rate over the same period of time, their growth would be proportional to £100:£452·9, i.e., x (our unknown annual investment):£1 000.

We can say $\frac{100}{452{\cdot}9}=\frac{x}{1\,000}$. In other words, x will be equal to $\frac{1}{4{\cdot}529}\times$ £1 000 = £220·9.

Therefore, our contribution to the sinking fund, in order to raise £1 000 at five per cent in 4 years time, would have to be £220·9 per year. This is an example of a sinking (or depreciation) fund which uses a discounting method.

Note 1 The student may compare formula (F. 17.3) with the calculation in section (a), and formula (F. 17.4) with the calculation in section (b). He will find that the figures have been discounted on precisely the same basis, but simply in reverse order.

Note 2 The above example is a simple one as we wish only to illustrate the concept. The labour of calculation in more complex examples is greatly lightened by the use of a book of tables such as, Yeats, A., White, J., and Skipworth, G., *Financial Tables* (S. Thorne) 1978, which contains a large variety of tables to calculate sinking funds, compound interest, annuities, etc.

Investment appraisal

The methods described above are ones which do not look at production costs per unit in the manner of the average and marginal costs of the economist. What we are concerned with are simply cash inflows (+*ve*) and cash outflows (−*ve*). If we wished to make a table of these, a very simplified one might look something like this:

Cash Outflows (−ve)	*Cash Inflows (+ve)*
Building and land costs	Sales receipts
Machinery costs	Government investment grants
Raw material costs	Tax allowances
Corporation tax	Scrap value of assets
Labour costs	

Note 1 That *depreciation* does not involve any actual cash flowing in any direction, therefore if we have recorded the initial investment as a negative cash flow, and the money we have received for the scrap value (or residual value) as a positive cash flow, then we have *assumed* depreciation by the difference between these figures.

Note 2 In our example, of comparing Projects A to E, we described a simple example, uncomplicated by tax and government grants, etc., but clearly, in a 'real life' problem, these would be entered by an accountant—and appropriately discounted to the time they were paid or received.

Note 3 We could have a situation where we are comparing projects which all have common costs, e.g., if all projects have the *same amounts* of common costs (e.g., all would use the same building then we could ignore these.)

Our simple example has, however, given the basis of the techniques used, and the student will have observed that the four methods used gave three different results.

Method	*Preferred project*
1 Pay-back	E
2 Average rate of return	D
3 Net present value	D
4 Internal rate of return	A

In order to understand this apparently puzzling result, let us look at some of the advantages and disadvantages of each method in turn:

1 Pay-back method

Advantages

(*a*) easy to understand
(*b*) simple to operate
(*c*) most useful in industries in which rapid technological change takes place since it gives preference to projects which have the shortest pay-back period.
(*d*) useful to businesses which need to have a high liquidity (i.e., have a high need for ready cash or assets which they can quickly turn into ready cash) for frequent re-investment or for crises.

Disadvantages

(*a*) The 'discounting' factor is ignored, i.e., the factor that money received now is worth more than money received later.
Note Some accountants *do* use discounting factors in the pay-back method. If they do, it makes the pay-back period longer, of course.
(*b*) It fails to take note of long-term profitability, i.e., it misses completely the earnings (cash inflows) arising *after* the end of the pay-back period (some highly profitable investments do *not* always pay high returns in the early years).

2 Average rate of return method

Advantages

(*a*) easy to understand
(*b*) simple to operate
(*c*) Unlike the pay-back method, this method does attempt to measure *profitability*.

Disadvantages

(*a*) The 'discounting' factor is ignored.
(*b*) As arithmetic mean averaging is used, no weight is given for fluctuations (e.g., long-term build-up to late high profits).

3 Net present value method

Advantages

(*a*) The 'discounting' factor is recognised as part of the calculation.
(*b*) Can be adjusted to take care of investment grants, taxes, inflation, different degrees of risk.
(*c*) Depreciation is automatically allowed for.

Disadvantages

(*a*) Appears to be more complicated than the two conventional methods, but is really quite easy to understand, and the labour of calculation is greatly eased by the use of prepared tables.
(*b*) It is difficult to set discount rates for risk. It is even more difficult to set different discount rates for different projects with different degrees of risk.

4 Internal rate of return method

Advantages

This method has, generally, the advantages of the NPV method.

Disadvantages

(*a*) Rather more complex to understand and calculate.
(*b*) When cash flows are irregular, requires extended calculation.

Conclusion

All appraisal methods suffer from man's inability to predict the future, e.g., forecasting cash inflows. The discounting methods are obviously superior to conventional methods, particularly as they assess money's worth on a more scientific and reasonable basis. There are many other problems which weaken some of these methods, e.g., assessing the degree of risk, defining exactly what is the cost of capital, etc.

In our example, different results for different methods were obtained. To interpret these surprising results, the student must note four points:

(*a*) To say that project X is 'preferred' does not mean that *all* the others are rejected. It is, for example, possible that a firm in our example, may have enough money to invest in *all* the projects, except perhaps, in projects A and B (which none of the other methods puts first).
(*b*) It is best to rely on discounting methods, except where high liquidity in a fast changing industry is desired.
(*c*) The job of the statistician and the accountant is to provide data (with all their faults and reservations) for decision-makers to act on, and to explain, if necessary, the bases on which different kinds of measures are compiled.
(*d*) Finally, the student must realise that many investments are made not on the quantitative results of statistical or accounting measurements. Many investments are often made *despite* an *adverse* report from a quantitative appraisal. They may be made on environmental grounds, for industrial relations reasons, on grounds of legality, social responsibility, or effect on public relations, quite apart from businessmen's 'hunches'.

18

Vital statistics

Method

The early importance of vital statistics has already been noted in Chapter 1; indeed, they are the basic statistics of life in an economy, e.g., births, marriages, and deaths. Many techniques already described in this book are commonly used by the demographer—the name given to the specialist in this branch of statistics. Sources for these figures are included in Chapter 19.

The student will hardly need to be reminded how 'vital' this group of statistics is to the politician, the sociologist, or the economist, and of how essential such information is as a tool for planning. He must be warned, however, that demography is an extremely sophisticated study and that an understanding of the basic methods used, and even the additional mathematical training essential to the actuary in life assurance, does not qualify one as more than an amateur in this field.

Briefly, we can say that living populations in any country depend on births, deaths, immigration, and emigration. These four factors depend further on other factors. For example, the birth rate depends on the sex ratio, the proportion of women aged between 15 and 45 years (the normal child-bearing period), the expected size of family, the rate of illegitimate births, etc. In addition, the death rate may also affect the birth rate; for example, if a war reduces the number of adult males in a country. Similarly, immigration and emigration may affect the birth rate according to the age and sex of the kind of people who enter and leave a country. Other sets of factors may affect the death rate and the emigration/immigration rates. The student might also think of social, political, and economic factors which might affect these rates. Do rising wages affect the desire for more children? Does membership of the Common Market lead to greater migration? Does a 'permissive' society lead to a larger illegitimacy rate?

In line with the pattern of this book, we now examine some of the methods of statistics which are used in the field of vital statistics to analyse changes in basic population factors.

Population

Chapter 1 stressed the importance of exact definition. The term 'population' is defined in a variety of ways in official statistics, the principal ones being:

De facto or home population This means everyone in this country at the time. Therefore, it includes seamen in British ports, foreign and colonial forces here, and so on.

Total population This is the Home population plus HM Forces overseas, less foreign forces in the United Kingdom.

Crude birth and death rates

These are simply the total (live) births or deaths during 12 months per 1 000 of the population (Home).

We can express them as follows:

$$\text{Crude birth rate} = \frac{\text{total live births} \times 1\ 000}{\text{total population}}$$

$$\text{Crude death rate} = \frac{\text{total deaths} \times 1\ 000}{\text{total population}}.$$

Similarly we can use simple rates or ratios to express other vital relationships, and these are often given as percentages, or per 1 000 of the appropriate population.

Sex ratio

$$\text{Sex ratio} = \frac{\text{total number of females} \times 100}{\text{total number of males}}.$$

Marriage rate

This can be expressed in a variety of ways:

Persons married per 1 000 population (all ages)
Males married per 1 000 unmarried females (15+)
Females married per 1 000 unmarried females (15+) and so on.

Illegitimacy rate

Here again, we find rates for:

Illegitimate births (live) per 1 000 unmarried women (15–44)
Illegitimate births (live) per 1 000 live births

Infantile mortality rate

$$\text{Infantile mortality rate} = \frac{\text{total deaths of babies up to 1 year old} \times 1\ 000}{\text{total live births}}.$$

Age specific rates

These are rates (births or deaths) for a specified age or age group (usually 5 years) as opposed to crude rates which are based on totals (i.e., all ages).

The rates given above are, however, too simple to give more than a general indication of the forces which affect population in a country. It would be misleading, for example, to compare on a time series basis, England in 1820 with England in 1978 in the matter of the crude death rate. Social and economic factors apart, the age structures of the two populations were different and a 'young' population would, by itself, tend to produce a lower death rate than the 'ageing' population of today. Similar considerations would apply to the birth rate.

When we come to compare different regions or towns within a country, and also when we seek to compare different countries, the results we would get might be totally misleading. Havarest, a seaside retirement town, and Youthville, a bustling new industrial town, might produce (*a*) a high death rate and a low birth rate, and (*b*) a low death rate and a high birth rate. How would Havarest and Youthville compare in their illegitimacy rates and in their sex ratios? It would be foolish to conclude that Havarest was less healthy than Youthville on the evidence of their crude birth and death rates.

In other words, any crude rate is the weighted arithmetic mean of a series of age specific rates, the weights being the actual numbers of people in each age group at the time. These weights will obviously differ for particular areas, or for the same area at different times.

Standardized birth and death rates

The main purpose of statistics is *comparison*, and we can only compare like with like. This means that the weights used in our calculations must be identical, so that any differences in age/sex structure are removed.

The tables below give hypothetical details for our two towns of Havarest and Youthville. (*Note* Column 8 always contains arbitrary 'model' rates chosen by the statistician himself.)

1	*2*	*3*	*4*	*5*	*6*	*7*	*8*	*9*	*10*
Age group	*Havarest*			*Youthville*			*Standard population (000's)*	*Number of expected deaths in standard population if subject to mortality of columns 4 and 7*	
	Popu-lation (000's)	*Number of deaths*	*Death rate per 1 000*	*Popu-lation (000's)*	*Number of deaths*	*Death rate per 1 000*		*Havarest (4)×(8)*	*Youthville (7)×(8)*
0–10	10	30	3	20	100	5	17	51	85
10–20	10	10	1	18	54	3	13	13	39
20–40	20	40	2	40	120	3	30	60	90
40–60	30	420	14	15	225	15	27	378	405
60–80	25	875	35	6	240	40	12	420	480
80–100	5	650	130	1	150	150	1	130	150
TOTALS	100	2 025		100	889		100	1 052	1 249

Table 18.1

Note 1 The age specific death rates are given in cols. 4 and 7.

Note 2 The crude death rates are 20·25 per 1 000 for Havarest, and 8·89 for Youthville,

That is,

$$\frac{\text{total column 3}}{\text{total column 2}} \quad \text{and} \quad \frac{\text{total column 6}}{\text{total column 5}}.$$

From these it would appear that Havarest is a more unhealthy place.

Note 3 The standardized death rates are given by:

$$\frac{\text{total column 9}}{\text{total column 8}} \quad \text{and} \quad \frac{\text{total column 10}}{\text{total column 8}}.$$

It is clear from these that Havarest (10·52 per 1 000) is actually healthier than Youthville (12·49 per 1 000), the difference in the crude rates being due to the more youthful population of Youthville.

Life tables

The data collected during the Census of Population forms the basis for certain detailed studies by the Registrar General, one of which is the *life table*. These tables are produced in detail every 10 years, but *abridged* tables are prepared between censuses and appear in the *Annual Abstract of Statistics*, as well as the publications of the Office of Population Censuses.

The life table provides two basic facts. First, it traces the mortality experience of a theoretical population from birth to death.

This is done by stating (*a*) the probability that a person aged *X* will die within 1 year, and (*b*) the number who would survive to an exact age *X*, out of the original 100 000 (or 10 000) if they were subject, throughout their lives, to the death probabilities of (*a*).

Age, X (years)	*Males*		*Females*	
	No. surviving to age X out of 10 000 born	*Average future lifetime for a person aged X (years)*	*No. surviving to age X out of 10 000 born*	*Average future lifetime for a person aged X (years)*
0	10 000	68·5	10 000	74·7
10	9 735	60·4	9 795	66·5
30	9 580	41·2	9 719	46·7
50	9 057	22·8	9 353	28·0
70	5 561	9·4	7 341	12·3
80	2 340	5·4	4 495	6·8

Table 18.2 Extract from life table

Table 18.2 is an extract from an abridged table. This is based on a theoretical population of 10 000, but the *full* tables work on a total of 100 000.

From this we see that, from a hypothetical 10 000 males born, 9 735 will survive to their tenth birthday (97·35 per cent) and 5 561 will survive to their 70th birthday.

This assumes that the hypothetical population is subjected to the same mortality experience throughout as the *actual* population upon which the table is based.

In the second place, it is possible to calculate a further set of data, called the *expectation of life*. This is the average future duration of life, for a person of specified age, if subjected to the death rates of the table.

For example, quoting from the same table, a male person aged 10 years has an average expectation of a further 60·4 years, and a person aged 70 has an expectation of a further 9·4 years.

It is important to realize that expectation of life always refers to some specified starting age.

The reader will note, from Table 18.2, that a male aged 0 has an average life span of 68·5 years. It might seem from this that men reaching 50 years have only 18·5 years to live, on average. It can be seen from the table that they can expect a further 22·8 years. The explanation lies in the fact that a newly born baby has to face all the health hazards of a lifetime, and many will fall by the wayside. A man aged 50 has already survived the risks of childhood and adolescence, and such persons have fewer remaining hurdles to surmount.

A simple example will make this clear. Suppose our population to consist of only 5 men, who die at ages of 50, 55, 59, 67 and 84. Their average life span from birth is $\frac{1}{5}(50+55+59+67+84)=63$ years. This is their expectation of life.

Starting from age 60, we only consider those who are still alive, i.e., those who die at 67 and 84, and these live for a further 7 and 24 years respectively, i.e., an average of 15·5 years beyond 60. The expectation of life at age 60 is thus 15·5 years. In a full life table, the survivors are given for each sex, separately, and for each year of life, from birth to 105. The expectation of life is also given for each single year of age.

Reproduction rates

A problem of major importance is to forecast future population trends; birth rates by themselves are a poor indication. The key factor is clearly the number of married women in the population who are between 15 and 44 (the reproductive years). The number of live births in a year, per 1 000 such women, is the legitimate *fertility rate* but this will vary according to the age composition of the women, since their fertility varies according to their position in the age group 15–44.

The procedure adopted, in a simplified form, is to take (say) 1 000 women and assume that they pass through the various age groups of the reproductive years. In so doing, they are assumed to be subject to current fertility rates, and will therefore produce a certain number of *female* babies for each age group (col. 2 of Table 18.3).

1	*2*	*3*	*4*
Age group	*No. of female babies born to 1 000 women in each age group*	*No. of survivors per 1 000 female babies*	*No. of female babies reproduced by 1 000 female babies*
15–19	100	950	95
20–24	200	900	180
25–29	250	800	200
30–34	250	700	175
35–39	150	600	90
40–44	50	500	25
	1 000		765

Table 18.3 Gross and net reproduction rates

The total number of babies so produced, per 1 000 women, is the *gross reproduction rate* of 1·000, i.e., col. 2, divided by 1 000.

Note This calculation assumes that all the 1 000 women will survive to age 44, and that all the female babies they produce will themselves survive to reach child-bearing age, and thereafter until age 44. This, of course, is not so.

Column 3 of the table shows the number of survivors (to various age limits) of 1 000 female babies.

Column 4 shows the number of female babies left behind by the original 1 000 females, allowing for deaths on the way; e.g., out of 1 000 female babies, 900 survive to age 20–24. As 1 000 females pass through this group, they bear 200 female babies (col. 2). *Hence* 900 women will bear $\frac{900}{1\,000} \times 200 = 180$ female babies (col. 4), and so on.

The total of col. 4, divided by 1 000, gives the *net reproduction rate* of 0·765. See Use and interpretation for an explanation.

Area comparability factors

Comparisons of death or birth rates between different regions are often misleading, as we have seen, because of the different age/sex structures.

The construction of standardized rates, previously illustrated for deaths, is one method of overcoming this difficulty, but it assumes that we know the number of deaths in each region, classified by age. For many regional populations, this information is not always available and it is not possible to calculate local age specific rates which can be applied to a standard population, as in Table 18.1. However, the age specific rates (births or deaths) for England and Wales as a whole are known, and can be applied to local populations. The rates employed are usually those of the latest available census.

As applied to deaths, the procedure is as follows:

(*a*) Take the numbers per age group in the region and multiply by the standard death rate for England and Wales (for that particular age group).

(*b*) Divide the total products by the total population (total weights). This gives the *expected* death rate per 1 000 for the region.

(*c*) The standard death rate of England and Wales is next found. (That is, the products of the age specific rates and the actual numbers in each group of the standard population are totalled and divided by the total standard population.) This is given at the foot of col. 4, Table 18.4.

(*d*) The standard death rate divided by the expected death rate gives the *Area comparability factor.*

This is a standardizing factor, which, when multiplied by the crude death rates for each region, will give a standardized rate for that region.

Any two such rates for different regions or areas can then be compared, as they are based upon the same age structure.

Table 18.4 illustrates this method for our mythical towns of Havarest and Youthville.

1	2	3	4	5	6
Age group	*Population (000's)*		*Standard death rates per 1 000 for England and Wales (approximate)*	*Expected deaths on basis of death rates*	
	Havarest	*Youthville*		*Havarest* (4)×(2)	*Youthville* (4)×(3)
0–10	10	20	3·4	34	68
10–20	10	18	1·0	10	18
20–40	20	40	2·3	46	92
40–60	30	15	14·9	447	223·5
60–80	25	6	39·2	980	235·2
80–100	5	1	137·0	685	137·0
TOTALS	100	100	12·6	2 202	773·7

Table 18.4

Note 1 The expected death rates per 1 000 are

$$\text{Havarest} = \frac{2\,202}{100} = 22{\cdot}02$$

$$\text{Youthville} = \frac{773{\cdot}7}{100} = 7{\cdot}74.$$

Note 2 The standard death rate for England and Wales is 12·6 per 1 000. (See step (*c*) above for the dérivation of this figure.)

Note 3 The area comparability factors (A.C.F.'s) are:

$$\text{Havarest} = \frac{12{\cdot}6}{22{\cdot}02} \simeq 0{\cdot}57$$

$$\text{Youthville} = \frac{12{\cdot}6}{7{\cdot}74} \simeq 1{\cdot}63.$$

Note 4 The A.C.F. is a *standardizing* factor, which, when multiplied by the crude death rates for each town, yields the standardized rates for the two towns. These are:

$$\text{Havarest} = 0{\cdot}57 \times 20{\cdot}25 \text{ (Table 18.1)} = 11{\cdot}54$$

$$\text{Youthville} = 1{\cdot}63 \times 8{\cdot}89 = 14{\cdot}5.$$

Standardized mortality ratios

These are published in the Census reports on occupational mortality, and are intended to summarize the mortality experience of each occupational group. They express the number of deaths in the year for men of a particular occupation (aged 20–64) as a percentage of those *expected* in that year, had the sex/age mortality of a *standard period* been operating on the sex/age *population* of the occupation and year in question.

Table 18.5 illustrates the method of calculation in a hypothetical example:

1	*2*	*3*	*4*	*5*	*6*
Age groups	*Male population in the occupation 1977 (000's)*	*Actual death rate per 1 000 in 1977*	*Standard death rate per 1 000 in 1977 census*	*Products*	
				Actual deaths (2)×(3)	*Expected deaths (2)×(4)*
20–24	5	2·0	1·0	10·0	5·0
25–29	8	1·0	1·0	8·0	8·0
30–34	15	2·0	2·0	30·0	30·0
35–39	15	2·5	2·4	37·5	36·0
40–44	20	3·0	2·5	60·0	50·0
45–49	20	6·0	7·0	120·0	140·0
50–54	10	8·0	7·0	80·0	70·0
55–59	5	22·0	20·0	110·0	100·0
60–64	2	25·0	22·0	50·0	44·0
TOTALS	100			505·5	483·0

Table 18.5

Note 1 The expected number of deaths, on the basis of the standard period is 483. Column 4 is the age specific death rate for all males in England and Wales, regardless of occupation.

Note 2 The actual number of deaths, during the year, is 505·5.

Note 3 The S.M.R. would be

$$\frac{505 \cdot 5}{483} \times 100 = 104 \cdot 7 \text{ per cent.}$$

See next section for further details.

Use and interpretation

Crude birth and death rates

These are useful, but only approximate measures which determine whether or not a population will increase or decrease in the long run. For a short-period comparison of fertility and mortality experience in *one particular area*, these rates may be useful, since changes in the age and sex structure of a region are usually slow to emerge.

Standardized rates

As previously explained, crude rates can be regarded as weighted arithmetic means, the weights being the actual numbers of people in each age group at the time.

Standardized rates use the same weights for each calculation, so that any differences in age structure between one region and another are eliminated.

They are all assumed to have the same *standard* age structure, and for purposes of pure comparison it does not matter which particular standard, or set of weights, is employed. For comparisons over a long period, however, it is desirable that this standard population should be typical of the age and sex structure of the present-day population. If the standard population were abnormally old or young, as with Havarest or Youthville, the resultant rates could be misleading.

Life tables

Readers will notice from Table 18.2 the significant difference between males and females at all ages. The expectation of life from birth is over 6 years longer for females, and although this difference tends to diminish throughout life, it is always present, being 1·4 years for persons aged 80. The same influence can be seen in the numbers surviving to any specified age. Out of our original 10 000 births, only 2 340 males remain at age 80, but there are 4 495 females.

The implications of this factor can be important for manufacturers of consumer goods, who will find it more beneficial to cater for women than for men, particularly in the older age groups. Social services, old people's homes, etc., can also be geared to this lack of balance between the sexes.

Life tables are one of the devices used by the Registrar General to estimate the size of the future population, and particularly its age structure. The present tendency is for the proportion of older people of both sexes to increase, and this has important economic implications in the field of taxation, pensions, etc. Life assurance companies base their premiums on the data of these tables, and the calculation of annuity rates also depends upon them. An account of methods and results for the mid-1976 based projections appear in, *Population Projections*, PP2, No. 8, *1976–2016,* (HMSO 1978).

Reproduction rates

The gross rate is based upon impractical assumptions and is of little real value.

A net rate of *unity* implies that the current female population is replacing itself exactly. If it remains below unity, then at some future date a fall in the population will follow unless immigration or some similar factor makes up the deficit.

In effect, the net rate defines the trend of numbers per generation that would ultimately result from the indefinite continuation of the age-specific fertility and mortality rates from which it was calculated. It is only one way of allowing for the disturbing effects of an abnormal age distribution, and other abnormalities may also affect the number of births.

Recent experience has shown that the age specific fertility rates of a particular year, or series of years, may be affected by factors such as the proportion who have *recently* married, and by fluctuations in the rate at which married couples build up their families. For example, a family may decide upon three children but may not space them out evenly throughout the reproductive years.

For many years ahead, the population will consist mainly of survivors of those already alive. As far as these people are concerned, the trend implied by current reproductivity is quite irrelevant.

Area comparability factors

The purpose of this measure is to adjust the various local crude death rates to allow for differences in the age structure.

The death rates obtained from cols. 5 and 6 of Table 18.4 are sometimes called the *index* rates. These are 22·02 for Havarest, and 7·74 for Youthville. They measure the relatively favourable age distribution of an area, as regards mortality, compared with a national standard (12·6 in the table). The figure of 7·74 for Youthville, for example, means that its age distribution is more favourable than that of England and Wales (12·6). Other things being equal, it ought, therefore, to have a lower death rate.

When this index is divided into the standard rate, the resulting *factor* will be greater than unity (1·63). When this, in turn, is multiplied by the crude rate for the same region (8·89) the effect will be to increase the crude rate. The reverse will apply for Havarest. In other words, the A.C.F. is to be compared with a figure of *unity* for the whole of England and Wales.

Areas with a factor greater than unity have more favourable age distributions, and the A.C.F. corrects for this. Similarly, of course, for areas with an A.C.F. of less than 1.

A useful measure or *ratio* is the local adjusted death rate divided by the national (standard) rate. This gives a figure of

$$\frac{11{\cdot}54}{12{\cdot}6} = 0{\cdot}92 \text{ for Havarest}$$

and

$$\frac{14{\cdot}5}{12{\cdot}6} = 1{\cdot}15 \text{ for Youthville.}$$

These ratios can be compared directly, both with each other and with any other area in that particular year. The ratio for England and Wales is *unity*.

Hence, we can conclude that Havarest is better than the national average, from the point of view of health, as well as being better than Youthville.

Standardized mortality ratios

These facilitate comparisons between the mortality of a particular occupation, and that of England and Wales as a whole.

From Table 18·5, this ratio is 104·7 per cent, indicating that this particular occupation is less healthy than the male population as a whole. A figure of less than 100 per cent indicates a *more* healthy occupation.

These ratios are calculated for 'all causes' of death, and also for specified causes, such as cancer, tuberculosis, and various types of accident. The mortality rates for each disease are analysed by social class, by sex, and by marital condition. The S.M.R. is also used to compare regional differences as regards mortality.

Final note

The use and analysis of vital statistics is a major tool of government and business. Population structure and trends form the basis of planning in Social Services, Education, Housing, Transport, and so on. Taxation policy and pensions are also governed by these factors.

In the business field, such information is of great importance. The large-scale chain stores and supermarkets must know whether a particular area will justify a new branch. This does not depend solely on population size, since the area might be changing. The age and sex distribution, birth and death rates, and the rate of change in such measures are all relevant. Youthville will support different types of shop from Havarest.

The manufacturer is equally concerned with trends in birth rates, age and sex structure, etc. How will the influx of immigrants, with possibly different birth and death rates, affect national trends?

A high birth rate is good for baby foods and clothes, prams, and toys. An ageing population needs more of the things used by older people. Pensioners have less to spend, and spend it differently.

19

Sources of statistics

The description of sources in this chapter is divided into two parts: (*a*) External statistics, and (*b*) Internal statistics, i.e., statistics which are external and internal to the business unit.

External statistics

Statistics in this section are described under six headings:

(*a*) Population
(*b*) Labour
(*c*) Production
(*d*) Prices
(*e*) Trade
(*f*) National Income.

Information and sources Tables of the principal publications which deal with the statistics under each heading are given below:

POPULATION

Information	*Publication—occurrence*	*Source*
Reports of the Census of Population (except 1941)	Census Reports (periodic)	Offices of the Registrars-General
Part 1 Deaths, death rates, causes of death *Part 2* Number in population, marriage and fertility rate. Number of electors (parliamentary and municipal) *Part 3* Tables, analysis and historical survey	Annual Statistical Review of England and Wales	Offices of Population Censuses and Surveys
Number in population, births marriages, deaths, including figures of sickness and industrial diseases.	Population trends (monthly)	OPCS
Births, deaths and infectious diseases in large centres	Monitor Series (monthly)	OPCS

LABOUR

Information	*Publication/occurrence*	*Source*
Total employees by sex and age, totals employed in various industries and by region	Annuals Report of the Department of Employment	Department of Employment
Minimum or standard rates of wages and weekly hours of work. Summaries of collective agreements and statutory wage regulation orders	Report on time rates of wages and hours of work (annual)	Department of Employment
Industrial accidents, causes, nature, site of accidents, fatalities	Annual Report of Chief Inspector of Factories	Department of Employment
Monthly summary of employment, unemployment, unfilled vacancies, overtime and short-time working, rates of wages, stoppages of work. Special articles each month	Department of Employment *Gazette* (monthly)	Department of Employment
Industrial diseases, poisoning, gassing, dust, fumes, radiation	Annual Report of Chief Inspector of Factories	Department of Employment
Trade union statistics	Department of Employment *Gazette* (monthly)	Department of Employment

PRODUCTION

Index of Industrial Production	Trade and Industry (weekly)	Central Statistical Office
Reports on the Census of Production (1970, 1971, 1972, and 1973 are the full Censuses)	Business Monitor (quarterly)	Business Statistics Office
Iron and steel employment, output at home and abroad. Import/export, fuel consumption, capacity, and types of products by the industry	Iron and Steel Industry (annual and monthly)	British Steel Corporation
Output, stocks, employment, number of mines, types of product, investment	Report and Accounts (annual)	National Coal Board
Output, employment, capacity, investment	Report and Accounts (annual)	Electricity Council
Output, employment, generating capacity, investment	Report and Accounts (annual)	Central Electricity Generating Board
Output, employment, capacity, investment	Report and Accounts (annual)	British Gas Corporation

Note Also censuses of production for Northern Ireland.
Also *Annual Report and Accounts for Northern Ireland, North of Scotland and South of Scotland.*
Also the *Digest of UK Energy Statistics*, which gives the main statistics on coal, electricity, and gas. (Department of Energy.)

PRICES

Information	*Publication/occurrence*	*Source*
Retail Price Index	Department of Employment *Gazette* (monthly)	Department of Employment
Wholesale, import, and export prices	*Trade and Industry* (weekly)	Department of Industry
Wholesale Price Index	*Trade and Industry* (weekly)	Department of Industry
Prices of agricultural supplies and products, month by month	*Agricultural Statistics England and Wales* (Annual)	Ministry of Agriculture, Fisheries and Food
Indexes of share prices of groups of shares, e.g., capital and consumer goods, commodities, securities and stocks, and financial institutions	F.T.-Actuaries Share Indexes (daily)	*Financial Times* newspaper and the Institute of Actuaries in London and the Faculty of Actuaries in Edinburgh

TRADE

Information	*Publication/occurrence*	*Source*
Reports on the Census of Distribution (full censuses 1957, 1961, 1966 and 1971)	Census Report (periodic)	Department of Industry
Monthly sales and stocks or retail establishments; hire-purchase and other instalment credit	*Trade and Industry* (weekly)	Department of Industry
Quantities and values of commodities of export trade (4 vols.)	Annual Statement of the Trade of the UK with Commonwealth and Foreign Countries	H.M. Customs and Excise
Quantities and values of commodities in monthly figures of export trade	Oversease Trade Statistics (monthly)	Department of Industry
Export and Import Price Indexes	*Trade and Industry* (weekly)	Department of Industry
Export and Import Volume Indexes	*Trade and Industry* (weekly)	Department of Industry

NATIONAL INCOME

Information	*Publication/occurrence*	*Source*
National Income and Expenditure (government and national accounts)	Preliminary Estimates (White Paper [annual])	Central Statistical Office
Gross National Income, Expenditure and Product. Consumers' expenditure, personal incomes, company incomes, central and local government budgets, capital investment	National Income and Expenditure (Blue Book) [annual])	Central Statistical Office

The tables given above form a small part only of the mass of statistics published publicly and privately. Nevertheless, they afford a good selection of the main statistics that the student is likely to need. The first published source has been used in every case through, of course, the whole of these statistics are repeated in simplified form in many later publications: e.g., nearly all these figures appear somewhere in *The Annual Abstract of Statistics*. The student should not neglect the monthly and quarterly issues of the *Business Monitor* series.

It is of vital importance that the student should make *personal contact* with several publications which contain these statistics. This is the only part of the course which this book cannot really provide. The following list is a minimum requirement for the student's reading if he is to make any real acquaintance with the official sources of statistics.

Publications

The Annual Abstract of Statistics
(Compiled by the Central Statistical Office.)

Most of the statistics tabled above are to be found in this main reference book and, in most cases, comparative figures for earlier years are included. In addition to statistics mentioned above, the student should refer to the following, under each heading:

Population Emigration and immigration, aliens (naturalization and registration).

Labour Size of firms, civil service, and armed forces staff and strength.

Production Figures of a wide variety of industrial materials; e.g., oils, chemicals, timber, textiles, minerals, etc.
Figures of building and construction.
Figures of manufactured goods.

Prices Shipping freight rates.
Agricultural and livestock prices.

Trade Road, rail, air, and sea transport, postal, telegraph, and telephone services.
Banking and insurance statistics.

In particular, the notes and definitions contained in the book should be read and understood.

The Monthly Digest of Statistics
(Compiled by the Central Statistical Office.)

This is a monthly, abbreviated version of the *Annual Abstract*. The student should look, as in the case of the *Annual Abstract*, at the various series under the six principal headings given above.

Special note should be made of the January Supplement which contains many useful definitions.

Financial Statistics
(Compiled by the Central Statistical Office in collaboration with other government departments and the Bank of England. Published monthly.)

An important publication dealing with the key financial and monetary statistics of the United Kingdom.

The contents of this publication include financial statistics of the Exchequer and Central Government, local authority borrowings and public corporation accounts, banking statistics of the commercial joint-stock banks and the Bank of England. A wide range of financial statistics includes many dealing with discount houses, trustee savings banks, hire purchase finance companies, unit trusts, insurance, building societies, etc.

Also included are the income, finance, and profits of companies, capital issues, and hire purchase credits granted. Many interest rates, security prices, and yields, and local authority and building society mortgage rates are to be found in this publication.

A section dealing with overseas finance includes gold and foreign currency reserves, the balance of payments, and foreign exchange rates.

A valuable end section deals with 'Notes and Definitions' at some length.

Economic Trends
(Compiled by the Central Statistical Office. Published monthly.)

Contains statistics and graphical illustrations on production, manufacturing, building and construction orders, labour, external trade, investment, finance, etc., prices, wages, and earnings, overseas finance, and distribution. Each month's issue features one or two special articles on some leading topic of economic interest.

An *Economic Report* is issued in March as a supplement to *Economic Trends*, and this surveys in narrative form the economic events of the past year in respect of the six headings in this chapter. A statistical appendix is also given.

Statistical News
(Compiled by the Central Statistical Office. Published quarterly.)

A comprehensive account of current developments in British official statistics and how they are compiled. This valuable publication contains many informative articles, and a cumulative index is provided.

Regional Statistics
(Compiled by the Central Statistical Office. Published annually.)

This publication deals with the breakdown of national statistics into their regional variations (these regions are the same as the Economic Planning Regions). It contains tables, sources, and definitions on a broad range of economic, social and demographic topics.

Guide to Official Statistics
(Compiled by the Central Statistical Office. Published occasionally.)

The first issue of this *Guide* was in 1976, the second issue in 1978.

This is an extremely important book and should be consulted by every student of statistics. It is really a bibliography of statistical sources, official and non-official, in the UK. All the important statistical series are covered and the

Guide refers readers to the regular publications and also to special reports, articles, etc., with significant statistical content published over the last 10 years.

Department of Employment Gazette
(Compiled by the Department of Employment. Published monthly.)

The contents of each issue include:

(*a*) A summary of the monthly statistics relating to labour: employment, unemployment, unfilled vacancies, overtime and short-time working, rates of wages, retail prices, and stoppages of work.
(*b*) Special articles related to the labour field.
(*c*) Arbitration awards, notices, orders, statutory instruments, etc., published within the previous month.

The student should proceed carefully when reading this important publication. He should, for example, try to define clearly and to his own satisfaction such topics as average wage rates, average weekly earnings, hourly earnings, and rates. Careful definition is also advisable when dealing with unemployment, because certain groups are not included in the count. (A similar position applies to stoppages of work. These figures exclude stoppages involving fewer than 10 workers, and those which lasted less than one day (except where working days lost exceeded 100).)

Trade and Industry
(Compiled by the Department of Industry. Published weekly.)

Production, prices, and trade are the main topics of this publication. More detailed figures on the whole field of industrial materials and commodities are available in this *Journal* than in other official publications. A summary of the principal statistics given in this publication is shown below:

Census of production, sales and work done, stocks, and 'work in progress'. Index of industrial production.

Industrial materials, textiles, leather, timber, wood-pulp and paper making, fertilizers and chemicals, dyestuffs, paints, etc., soap, detergents, polishes, plastics, rubber.

Manufactured goods, hosiery, knitwear, gloves, footwear, furniture, floor coverings, household equipment, sports and games equipment.

Distribution, retail and service establishments (number of establishments, turnover, number employed, volume and value indexes of sales).

External trade, value of imports and exports, indexes of value and volume, value of exports and imports by class of goods, by source and destination, volume of principal exports and imports.

Tariff, customs, import, and other regulations in overseas countries.

Prices, index numbers of wholesale prices of inputs and outputs of industry, commodities produced in the UK, index numbers of wholesale prices, annual average wholesale prices of selected commodities.

Passenger movement in and out of UK, arrivals by sea and air by nationality, emigrants and immigrants by sea between UK and non-European countries.

Hire-purchase, outstanding debt, volume of business, etc.

Cinemas, admissions and distribution of takings, regional analysis by size in Great Britain, films registered in Great Britain.

Blue Book on National Income and Expenditure
(Compiled by the Central Statistical Office. Published annually.)

This is the main source book on national income and expenditure. A brief analysis of the contents are given below:

Gross National Product
Gross National Income
Gross National Expenditure.

These three calculations are simply three different ways of looking at the money value of goods and services resulting from economic activity within the nation for one year.

For each calculation under these three headings the figures are analysed. For example, under *National Income* are such entries as:

Income from self-employment
Income from employment
Trading profits of companies
Surpluses and profits of public corporations and enterprises
Rents
Income from abroad.

Under *National Expenditure* are such entries as:
Consumers' expenditure
Public authorities' expenditure
Expenditure on capital goods (capital formation)
Imports—exports.

Under *National Product*, are such entries as:
Agriculture, forestry, and fishing
Insurance, banking, and finance
Transport and communication
Public administration and defence.

These lists are by no means complete, and the student is advised to consult the actual tables of recent date to examine the complete lists, to note the figures for recent dates of the main items, and to make himself familiar with the main definitions.

Many other tables are given in the book, and these are largely derived from the main tables above. For the most part, they are more highly detailed analyses of the sections and items above.

For example:

Breakdown of the capital and current expenditures of central and local authorities.

Distribution in class intervals of personal incomes before and after tax.

Gross capital formation at home, analysis by sector, industry, and type of asset; also on investment in stocks, and 'work in progress' by sector and industry.

The *Blue Book* contains comparative figures in most of its tables for the previous years.

The *Blue Book* is published in August, but a most important companion booklet is the *Economic Report*, published in April. The latter publication reviews the whole economy in its most important respects, and estimates the probable trends in the various sectors for the coming year, as well as setting out the economic changes which the government hopes will occur. A detailed description of the sources, methods, and definitions is given in, *National Accounts Statistics*: *Sources and Methods*, HMSO 1968) and this is brought up to date annually in the *Blue Books*.

Note on the standard industrial classification

It was emphasized in Chapter 1 that statistics are comparable only when they are collected on a similar basis. This implies that the terms and definitions used are standardized.

Published statistics are collected from a wide variety of sources, and are issued by many different government departments. The Standard Industrial Classification (SIC) was drawn up to ensure that the various government statistics should be capable of comparison.

The classification is based on industries, not occupations, and the unit is the *establishment*, i.e., the whole of the premises. Thus, a tobacco factory might include such activities as selling, packing, transport, and a canteen, as well as manufacturing. All these would be classed under the one heading.

The 1968 classification first divides the whole economic activity into 27 divisions or *orders*—each numbered in roman numerals. Thus, order V is chemicals and allied industries; order XV is clothing and footwear, and so on.

Each order (with two exceptions) is then sub-divided into a number of *Minimum List Headings*, using arabic numerals, representing branches or subsidiaries of the main industry; e.g., in order II (Mining and Quarrying), there are five of these. 101 is coal mining; 102 is stone and slate; 103 is chalk, clay, sand, and gravel; 104 is petroleum and natural gas; 109 is other mining and quarrying.

Note The gap between 104 and 109 is deliberate. The numbers omitted will allow for any additional classification which may be necessary, as new developments emerge. These gaps in the numbering occur throughout the table.

There are 181 Minimum List Headings at the moment, but their numbers range from 001 to 906.

In some cases, optional subdivision of the headings is allowed for, where a more detailed classification is needed. For example, 102, already referred to, may be subdivided into 102·1 (stone quarrying and mining), and 102·2 (slate quarrying and mining).

For each heading and sub-heading, there is an exact and detailed definition of the activities which are included. These are so worded that all forms of industrial activity must fall within one or other of these categories.

The value of the SIC to the compilers of official statistics is obvious. It ensures the standardization of terms and definitions, so that all government departments are working on a comparable basis. The SIC numbers are quoted, when relevant, in Published Statistics, as a guide to their use and interpretation.

For example, in the *Monthly Digest of Statistics*, the figures for employment of workers by industry are given in a series of tables. Each column is headed by the appropriate Minimum List Heading, and users can, therefore, turn this up, to see exactly what is included.

Taking the employment figures for 'Bread and Flour Confectionery', we find the appropriate number is 212, and referring to this in the SIC we read:

'Making bread, cakes, pastries, pies (other than meat pies), puddings (other than meat or canned puddings). Production at bake-houses attached to bakers' shops is classified in heading 820.'

Economic Progress Reports

They are prepared by the Information Division of the Treasury, in consultation with other government departments, and are published monthly.

They give valuable reports and statistics on current progress of the economy, often illustrated by bar charts, graphs, and so on.

Midland Bank Review

A quarterly magazine published by the Midland Bank, and containing articles on a variety of current topics. A 'graphical survey' is contained in the centre pages, and this deals with many economic series. Summaries of recent happenings under the title 'Government and Business' appear in each issue.

National Westminster Bank Quarterly Review

A quarterly magazine, published by the National Westminster Bank, which contains several articles, one usually dealing with the agricultural scene, and current notes of topical interest.

Lloyds Bank Review

A monthly magazine, published by Lloyds Bank, which contains several articles in each issue on important economic topics. The review has a 'Statistical Section' which consists of several pages in chart and diagram form mainly dealing with financial statistics.

Barclays Review

A quarterly magazine, published by Barclays Bank, and containing several articles usually biased towards the overseas economic scene. This is an excellent publication for the statistician, because it has a 'Statistical Section' containing many tables on many economic topics divided into 'Manpower, Production, Trade, Prices and Wages, Banking and Finance, Overseas Statistics'. Accompanying the review is usually to be found an extremely handsome coloured insert with several unusual kinds of diagram and symbol illustrations.

International Review

A quarterly review devoted to information on trade and economic conditions in many overseas countries where this bank operates. The review is published by Barclays Bank. The review contains narrative reports country by country with detailed statistical tables at the end.

Three Banks Review

A quarterly magazine published by the Royal Bank of Scotland, Williams and Glyn's Bank Ltd. The review contains articles only, and these are on economic topics usually including one of interest to economic historians.

Journal of the Institute of Bankers

A bi-monthly journal published by the Institute of Bankers, and of special interest to people in this field. A special section is devoted to the needs and interests of young bankers with a section on bankers' examinations. The journal contains articles and reviews of the economic scene.

This list of free publications certainly does not complete the range available to the student. Many of the larger firms issue house magazines and other helpful literature on request. The student of economic and business statistics cannot fairly complain that the necessary material is beyond his reach either in terms of cost or availability.

Finally, here are three other publications which the student should take note of, besides the 'city columns' of at least one better class newspaper:

The Financial Times (daily)

This is the specialist economist's and businessman's newspaper, and it contains much statistical information in varied forms—Charts, diagrams, graphs, and tables. It is the leading newspaper for day-to-day economic and business articles and special occasional articles. It is the leading source for stock and share prices and statistics, and it contains the valuable 'F.T.-Actuaries' share indexes.

The Economist (weekly)

This is the specialist weekly for the economist and businessman. It contains economic and business articles which give information about a large number of countries. Many statistical items are obviously found throughout its pages, but it also has a special statistical section on 'Money and Exchanges' and 'Stock Prices and Yields'.

The Banker (monthly)

This magazine is not restricted to the banker in its articles, nor is it restricted to this country. A special section entitled 'Financial Statistics' appears in each issue, and this consists of tables on banking, government, and external monetary statistics. In most tables, comparative figures for earlier years are given.

Internal Statistics

The statistician in business

Figures, tables, and graphs cost money to produce, and the statistician will be tested, like any other factor in production, according to the usefulness of the results he produces. His function is to be an aid to efficient management. His job is to present management with clear and concise summaries of the firm's business activities which will serve as a basis for policy, decision, and action. His main work will be to supply figures, tables, diagrams, charts, and graphs in the form of periodic returns or as business reports. On occasions he may be called upon to design, to management requirements, forms and questionnaires which will bring in the kind of figures he can use.

Different sizes of firm will need their own special degrees of statistical work. Smaller firms will often manage with very few statistics. One can hardly imagine a sweets and tobacco retailer with much statistical work on his hands, whereas the National Coal Board, without several specialist statistical departments, is unthinkable.

Different kinds of firm will be interested in different kinds of figures. The statistics in a travel agency will bear more heavily on the advertising and marketing side than those of a firm manufacturing steel girders. Statistics of stock turnover will be more apparent in egg production than in shipbuilding. Average costs of labour and labour turnover statistics will figure more prominently on the books of a market gardener than in the records of an atomic power station.

Useful statistical data

A business unit of medium size will be interested in three main kinds of statistics:

(*a*) *External—general* These statistics will relate to the movements and change in national economic series. All businessmen will be interested in changes in interest rates, hire-purchase debt, stock and share prices, regional unemployment, etc.

(*b*) *External—particular* These are the statistics of his own industry. If, for example, the businessman was a shipbuilder, his interest in particular statistics might include:

(i) *Freight rates*—a guide to the general profitability of passenger and freight ships.
(ii) *Merchant shipping output*—a guide to the prosperity of the industry.
(iii) *Export trade (by country and commodity)*—a guide to the kind of cargo ship to build and the most profitable runs.
(iv) *Passenger movements*—see (i).

All these statistics, together with many more, could be gathered from the publications mentioned in this chapter.

(*c*) *Internal statistics* These are statistics within the firm which can be compiled under the businessman's own control.

It is possible to describe the mechanism of any firm under three general headings. The table below shows these three headings with the kind of statistics which might be found under each heading:

Production	*Marketing*	*Administration*
Quality control Labour turnover Progress charts Stocks and inventories Wage rates Accident rates Sickness rates Absenteeism rates Unit costs Output charts Purchasing costs of raw materials Stock turnover	Market research Sales graphs Advertising Orders received and fulfilled Selling prices Expenses of salesmen Distribution, methods and costs Export licences	Internal audit Borrowings and loans Bad debts Management ratios Overhead expenses Personnel and welfare Training system Government requirements (payroll tax, industrial training board, income tax, census reports)

Kinds of statistical data

Note Some of these statistics may need further explanation.

For example, most rates can be derived as percentages of a ratio; thus, 'accident rate' could be the result of the formula:

$$\frac{\textit{Number of accidents in a period}}{\textit{Average number of workers in period}} \times 100.$$

The management ratios referred to above are also simple rates. As in the case of accident rates, they are simple figures for quick reference but are none the less important to management's overall picture. Some of the more important ratios might be:

$$\frac{\textit{Current assets to date}}{\textit{Current liabilities to date}} \times 100$$

and

$$\frac{\textit{Sales during period (value)}}{\textit{Average fixed assets in period, etc.}} \times 100.$$

Many other management ratios may be calculated, but their formulation is the job of the cost accountant rather than the statistician.

The title 'overhead expenses' includes most expenses (other than fixed plant) which do not vary with output, e.g., fuel, light, rates, water, stationery, secretarial work.

Kinds of statistical methods

AVERAGES

Averages are the most widely used methods in a business unit. Examples are many, but the arithmetic mean will be used for most data; e.g., in rates of wages, overtime, earnings, accident, sickness, absenteeism, costs per unit of product, labour turnover for male, female, and trainee labour in the separate grades of skill. The mode is also useful where modal sizes and types are common in stocks and inventories, stock turnover, and sales of standard sizes and models.

GRAPHS

Graphs are particularly useful in marketing and production. An obvious example is sales. Many graphs will be linked with times series analysis in order to determine seasonal trends and cycles. Other examples are output, purchases and costs of raw materials, order books, progress charts, unit costs and selling prices, stock graphs, bad debts, and borrowing and loans. Certain special graphs will be used in quality control, and semi-logarithmic graphs may be used to compare series of different kinds, e.g., orders received and advertising budget.

TABULATION

This technique is, of course, the basis of graphs, and will be used where the latter are required. Tables may be used alternatively with graphs, and they usually find a prominent place in the business reports and returns which the statistician submits to management.

TIME SERIES

As noted above, this is an important part of the information a businessman requires in order to compare present performance with the past, and also to check on seasonal movements—e.g., when to buy, when prices are lowest, when to sell, when prices are highest, and how to invest on the expectation of future performance by the extrapolation method.

QUESTIONNAIRES AND PERSONAL INTERVIEWS

In a larger firm these methods may find a place when the statistician requires information from the public about its reaction to the product, and from the worker regarding his reaction to the firm. Thus, the possible fields might be market research, and personnel and welfare.

DIAGRAMS AND SYMBOLS

Once again the statistician might use these methods in respect of the public and the worker. Help with advertising presentation may be required by the advertising copywriters' department. Production posters, target incentive displays, and information sheets may be required on the factory floor.

SAMPLING

The student can grasp some idea of the method from Chapters 2, 12 and 14. This should be sufficient for him to realize that the sampling method will be used frequently in checking work where total checks would take too long or be wasteful. The sample check of the internal audit is a good example of such use. Sampling is the basis of quality control where continuous checks must be made on a standard machine product to ensure that batches are made to specification sizes within certain tolerance margins. If the firm is large enough to conduct market research surveys, it is possible that sampling techniques will be used here as well.

Conclusions

As was noted previously, there is great variation in the possible work of a statistician in business. This is partly due to the differing sizes of firm, partly to the different requirements of each kind of firm, and partly to the fact that no standard method of statistical working exists in every firm. The student will no doubt be aware of the similar discrepancy between book-keeping theory and actual practice. Even less uniformity among firms exists in statistics than in book-keeping. Because of this, we have not entered into the details of statistical practice in business. Each firm evolves its own particular methods, and the wide variations would form no general rules for the student at this stage of his work.

20

Aids and hints

Method

Logarithms It is not intended to describe here the theory of logarithms, but simply to describe how students can use the tables provided at the back of this book, confidently and accurately.

TO FIND THE LOGARITHM OF A NUMBER

The logarithm of a number consists of two parts:

(*a*) the *characteristic*—which may be positive or negative
(*b*) the *mantissa*—which is always positive.

THE CHARACTERISTIC

The logarithm of 3 785·0 is 3·5781, and the latter is divided into the two parts thus:

characteristic		mantissa
3	·	5781
	↑ decimal point	

Because 3 785·0 is entirely a whole number, the characteristic is positive, and its value is found by taking *one less* than the number of digits to the left of the decimal place: 3 785·0 contains four digits to the left, therefore the characteristic is $4-1=3$.

In the number 0·01567, the characteristic will be negative because the number does not contain a whole number. The value of the characteristic is found in this case by taking *one more* than the number of zeros *immediately* following the decimal point: $1+1=2$. This is written $\bar{2}$ (pronounced 'bar two').

The actual logarithm of 0·01567 is:

characteristic		mantissa
$\bar{2}$	·	1950
	↑ decimal point	

THE MANTISSA

This part of the logarithm occurring after the decimal point is always positive. In our first example 3 785, it was found by turning to the tables of logarithms at the end of this book.

The first two digits (37) were taken, as well as the next digit (8). The logarithm to which they both refer is found by fixing on 37 in the extreme left-hand column, and 8 across in the top row (first group, 0–9). The bearings give the logarithm 0·5775. As for the remaining 5 in the original number—this is dealt with by taking 37 again in the extreme left-hand column and 5 in the top row (second group, 1–9). These give a figure of 6, which is added to 0·5775.

We now have:

characteristic		mantissa
3	·	5775 +
	|	6
3	·	5781

↑ decimal point

Example 1:

Find the logarithm of 57·01

The characteristic is 1

57 in the left-hand column, and 0 in the top row (0–9) give 0·7559

57 in the left hand column, and 1 in the top row (1–9) give 1

Therefore, the logarithm is 1·7560.

Example 2:

Find the logarithm of 2·5230

The characteristic in this case is 0, because one less than the number of digits to the left of the decimal point is 0 (i.e., $1-1=0$)

25 in the left-hand column and 2 in the top row give 0·4014

25 in the left-hand column and 3 in the top row give 5

Therefore, the logarithm is 0·4019.

TO FIND A NUMBER FROM A LOGARITHM

This reverse process is similar to the previous section.

For example, from the logarithm 2·0678 take the mantissa only. Fix on the first two digits (0·06) in the extreme left-hand column of the antilogarithm table, and on 7 in the top row (0–9). These bearings give 1167. Now 0·06 in the extreme left-hand column again, and 8 in the top row (1–9) give 2. Added together, they make 1169. As the characteristic is 2, this makes the number (see previously) 116·9.

Example:

Find the number of the logarithm $\bar{3}$·3751

0·37 in the left-hand column, and 5 in the top row (0–9) give 2371

0·37 in the left-hand column, and 1 in the top row (1–9) give 1
Added together, they make 2372
As the characteristic was $\bar{3}$, this will make the number 0·002372.

Calculations by logarithms

Logarithms are used mainly for easy multiplication and division.

Multiplication

Find the logarithms of the numbers to be multiplied. Add the logarithms. Find the antilogarithm of the addition.

For example, *multiply 47·3 by 0·9271*

number	logarithm
47·3	1·6749 +
0·9271	$\bar{1}$·9671
	1·6420

The antilogarithm of 1·6420 gives the answer 43·85.

Note The rules for the *addition of positive and negative* characteristics are as follows:

If the signs are the same, add the characteristics under the common sign: $2+3=5$ and $\bar{3}+\bar{1}=\bar{4}$.

If the signs are unlike, subtract the smaller characteristic from the greater, and place the result under the sign of the greater: $4+\bar{2}=2$ and $\bar{5}+3=\bar{2}$.

Note In the case above, we had 1 to carry from the addition of the mantissa, i.e., $2+\bar{1}=1$.

Division

Find the logarithms of the numbers involved. Subtract the logarithm of the denominator from the logarithm of the numerator. Find the antilogarithm of the result.

Divide 68·47 by 33·25

number	logarithm
68·47	1·8355
33·25	1·5217
	0·3138

The antilogarithm of 0·3138 gives the answer 2·06.

Note The rule for the *subtraction of positive and negative* characteristics is as follows:

Change the sign of the characteristic to be subtracted and proceed as for addition.

$3-\bar{4}$
$=3$ and 4 (change the sign of the 4)
$=7$ (proceed as for addition—see earlier)

$4-3$
$=4$ and $\bar{3}$ (change the sign of the 3)
$=1$ (proceed as in addition, i.e., for unlike signs subtract smaller from greater and place under sign of greater).

Square roots

Method 1 (by logarithms)

To find a square root, find the logarithm of the number and divde by 2.

Find the square root of 32·63

Logarithm of 32·63 = 1·5136

Divided by 2 = 0·7568

Antilogarithm of 0·7568 gives answer 5·712.

Note If the characteristic is *negative* proceed as follows:

Find the square root of 0·00256

Logarithm of 0·00256 = $\bar{3}\cdot4082$

We must now convert $\bar{3}$ to a more convenient number to divide by 2; for example, to $\bar{4}$ by subtracting 1. Then, to balance again, we must add back the 1, thus:

$\bar{3}\cdot4082 = \bar{4} + 1\cdot4082$

Dividing $\bar{4} + 1\cdot4082$ by 2 gives $\bar{2} + 0\cdot7041$

Antilogarithm of $\bar{2}\cdot7041$ gives the answer 0·05059.

Method 2 (ordinary method)

Find the square root of 473·6

```
        √4/73·60/00(21·76
          4
      41/  73
           41
     427/  3260
           2989
    4346/     27100
              26076
              -----
              1024 remainder
```

The breakdown of the stages is as follows:

(*a*) From the decimal point mark off, to the right and to the left, pairs of digits (04/73/·/60/00)

(*b*) Find the square root of the first pair (04 – square root = 2).

Note In order to work out square root calculations by this method, it is necessary to remember the square roots of whole numbers up to 100—i.e., 1, 4, 9, 16, 25, 36, 49, 64, 81.

(*c*) Place this square root figure in the answer space, then *square* it and subtract it from the first pair (see working)

(*d*) Bring down the next pair (73)

(*e*) *Double* the answer and place it on the left (4)

(*f*) *Now find a digit which, when multiplied by 40-plus-that-digit,* will divide into the pair 73 (the digit here is 1, i.e., 41 × 1 = 41, as 42 × 2 = 84 would have been too large)

(*g*) Place the digit 1 in the answer space and also after the 4 on the left

(*h*) Subtract the 41 from 73

(*i*) Bring down the next pair (60)

(*j*) As we have now calculated up to the decimal point, we must place a decimal point in the answer
(*k*) Repeat as above (*b*) to (*i*).
That is, double the answer obtained so far, and put it on the left (42). 420-plus-a-digit, when multiplied by that digit will divide into 3 260.

For example, 427 × 7 = 2989 (428 × 8 = 3424 is too large).

Continue to bring down pairs of 00's unitl the answer you obtain is as accurate as you require in respect of decimal places.

Examples:

The two examples worked out previously by the use of logarithms are repeated below using the ordinary method:

```
             √32·63(  5·712
                25
        107/763
              749
      1141/ 1400
            1141
    11422/  25900
            22844
            -----
             3056 remainder
```

```
         √0·00/25/60/00(   0·05059
              25
        100/0060
            0000
       1005/ 6000
             5025
     10109/   97500
              90981
              -----
               6519 remainder
```

Use and interpretation

Too often students forget or half-remember their logarithms and square root calculations. These are, however, an important part of elementary statistics for the reasons given below. Therefore (in spite of the seeming length of the explanations given above!), students are urged to learn the methods which take little memory power and are simple to use when electronic calculators are not available.

Quite obviously, these aids will be a quick and efficient help in nearly all multiplication and division, as well as square root calculations. In statistics they have further uses:

(*a*) Logarithms are essential in marking out ratio scales (logarithmic scales) on graphs (see Chapter 5).

(*b*) Logarithms and/or square root calculations are essential for working out the standard deviation (see Chapter 8).

(*c*) Logarithms are essential for working out the geometric mean (see Chapter 7).

The tables at the end of this book are four-figure logarithm and anti-logarithm tables. More accurate tables (i.e., where the mantissa can be calculated to more than four figures) are available, but such tables are usually unnecessary at an elementary level.

Hints to examination candidates

GENERAL HINTS

The most essential part of a student's study is the making of a plan of work for out-of-college hours. Usually this will be done for him within college hours.

There is a good deal of silliness and striking of attitudes among many students who appear to be ashamed to be caught studying outside college hours. This infantile attitude is hardly worthy of the average teacher's hard work. The student who has made little effort to organize his working and leisure time is usually the one who is constantly looking for the 'magic key' which will suddenly make the subject clear and easy. He is the student who is forever darting from book to book and reaching only Chapter 2 in each book.

As certain chapters of this book will show, there are easy ways and short cuts, and it is right that the student should know of these and be able to avoid the often meaningless grind which passed for education in his parents' day. But, as the student graduates from school to college, he is inevitably faced with more advanced and specialized work. In some subjects there is absolutely no substitute for hard work and in statistics, certainly, it is not sufficient to rely on the memorizing of formulae and methods. *What is needed in this subject is practice.* Even if the work content of our course is reduced by the help of good teachers and good textbooks, there is an inevitable percentage of work (and in statistics, as we have just indicated, this percentage is high) which cannot be reduced. To help the student to realize just how much work is expected from him we have included questions from typical examination papers on almost every chapter in this book, and this book is suitable for a one-year course.

We are great believers in telling students exactly what faces them for at least a year ahead, if only because the more intelligent students realize that a good deal of the responsibility for success rests on their shoulders, and that all educational courses are basically do-it-yourself courses. This book provides, for students in business education, a full syllabus (see Contents), typical examination papers, sets of logarithm and other tables, chapters in the techniques of statistics, notes on their use and interpretation, and suggested working in examples. In this last section is advice on how to plan the final battle.

A plan is essential. If the student's fancy lies that way, he can regard the preparation and the final examination in the light of a military campaign. The most important result of a plan is that it imposes self-discipline on a student. Self-discipline inevitably leads to self-confidence and to the disappearance of tiresome and weakening feelings of lack of preparation and panic at the last moment.

The plan falls into two parts:

PREPARATION

This should start at the beginning of the course and continue up to and beyond the revision period. It should include the following points:

(*a*) Practice makes perfect is the golden rule in statistics. It is no good reading through a textbook pretending to study statistics. Eighty per cent of study in this subject is the working out of examples and thinking about your results. It is a good guide to say that, if you are *reading rather than writing* in this subject, you are doing very little good.

(*b*) The student should not seek to economize on writing materials or on textbooks. Such economy may turn out to be the most costly bit of saving that the student is ever likely to perform in his whole lifetime.

(*c*) Always confirm and check your understanding of a lesson in class with the textbook you are using.

(*d*) Try to maintain a good attendance and a good homework average as part of the self-discipline.

(*e*) Get to know the order and content of your syllabus even if this is not given to you. The first sign of an intelligent student is one who *wants* to know where he is going.

(*f*) Plan from the start a definite programme and the time you will devote to each subject in your course. A good ratio (and not an excessive one) is two hours' private study for each hour of lesson.

GENERAL HINTS ON THE EXAMINATION

The last act of your master-plan takes place when you enter the examination room. From one point of view there is little you can do once this stage has been reached. Yet various devices are possible.

(*a*) Be sure of the place and the time of the examination. This is an obvious point but overlooking it results every year in small but select bands of students roaming our larger cities in June and July frantically trying to join imaginary meetings in unknown places.

(*b*) Beware of overeating just before the examination. It is physiological fact that a heavy meal will adversely affect the quality of work, and alertness will be lower for some hours after.

(*c*) Check, well beforehand, on the time allowed for the paper, the choice of questions allowed, the number to be attempted, and, if possible, how many marks are awarded per question.

(*d*) If possible, take into the examination room a reliable watch. Do not rely upon the invigilator calling out, or chalking up, the time. Some don't!

(*e*) You should make a strict allotment (by previous calculation) of the time you intend to devote to answering and checking each of your answers.

Stick to this. Don't be one of those people who have not enough time left to start the last question!

(*f*) When checking your work, always look to see if your answers agree with commonsense. Many fantastic answers, resulting from simple slips or carelessness, can quickly be put right:

For example, arithmetic mean wage of shop assistants = £1 320·53 per week.

(*g*) Beware of leaving the examination room before finishing time. Time, in an examination, is the *only* thing that is really rationed to the candidate; therefore it is really the only thing that is valuable to you at this stage. How you spend it during that short space may affect your future career.

(*h*) Don't join that pathetic group which hangs around the examination room door frantically swotting up five minutes before the examination begins. This is insulting to yourself and to the ones who have taught you. Remember, from now on it is the examiner you are trying to impress, not your friends.

(*i*) Remember that examiners are human. Try to convey to them your sense of purpose, the work you have done over the past year, your interest in the subject which *they* have been studying for most of their lives. Try to do this in the least irritating and most attractive way you can manage. Examiners are basically on your side and are always on the lookout for flashes of understanding and signs of intelligent working.

Particular hints on the examination

We have given above some general hints which could apply to examinations in almost any subject.

Here are hints gathered from a survey of past reports given by examiners on the papers submitted in statistics at this level:

(*a*) *Reading the question*

The most common sin of all examination candidates is failure to read the question carefully. A candidate often ignores the carefully prepared question set by the examiner and answers one of his own devising. This is a waste of time and effort. No examiner is prepared to extend the bounds of his original question to accommodate another that you have seen fit to answer. Unfortunately, many students do not wholly believe this fact. In addition, reports complain that students often give longer answers than are required. This is also a misuse of time because, after a certain point on any question (if it is answered well, of course), any extra marks are just not worth trying to collect.

(*b*) *Calculations and scrap work*

Hand in all calculations which you have done on scrap paper with your name clearly shown on each piece. Do not work out calculations and simply hand in the answer. If this is wrong, you cannot be awarded any marks, but if it is accompanied by your rough working you may collect many marks for the *method* you have used as well as the *correct part* of your answer. Many students think, wrongly, that all or even most of the marks are awarded only if the final answer is correct.

(c) *Narrative work in questions*

The first rule here is *never write out the question.* You have it beside you on the printed page, so don't waste time duplicating it. Simply indicate the question on your paper by its number.

Try to avoid spelling mistakes. This is a sign of carelessness or of immaturity. Again, this seems an obvious piece of advice. Yet, inability to spell, especially the technical words of your subject, is laughable, or at the worst simply distasteful.

Try to write clearly. Inability to express one's thoughts clearly is the bane of examiners and often the misguided hope of students! The latter often suppose that if lack of thought is wrapped up in a flannel of words the examiner (always ready to give the student the benefit of the doubt!) will consider the passage sympathetically—and some good may come out of it. Students do not realize that examiners have forgotten more examination tricks than the student has yet learned. Knowledge is useless unless you can communicate it directly and clearly. Examiners are ruthless with 'flannel', and they cannot ask you to 'just run over what you meant in the last part of question 4'—even if they wanted to, and even if you could. From the time your script is collected, it stands on its own merit, yet students perpetually think that the bulkier their script is, the more it is probably worth—presumably on the grounds that there is no smoke without fire!

(d) *Graphical work*

Every year there are complaints from examiners about the lack of neatness, the omission of titles, headings, labels, and units on the axes of graphs. Other complaints mention the crowding of graphs into a corner of the paper, and the drawing of too many curves on one graph.

(e) *Sources of statistics*

It is generally admitted that this is a serious weakness in most papers in statistics at this level. The remedy is simply to get hold of the appropriate periodicals and publications. *Only* in this way can you fully appreciate their contents and remember them. Don't merely rely on the parrot memory of lists of sources and details. Make out your own lists. Compile them personally from the publications which you have actually seen.

(f) *Most frequent errors*

(i) Candidates do not know how to treat unequal class intervals when drawing the histogram.

(ii) Candidates cannot explain the difference between natural and ratio scales, nor do they know the use of each.

(iii) Candidates frequently omit (or forget) to weight averages where necessary.

(iv) Candidates omit to centre the trend when working out the moving average of an even number of items.
(v) Candidates cannot explain why we calculate a seasonal variation, and many do not know the method of calculating it.
(vi) Candidates are weak on tabulation (especially the preparation of blank tables) which demands an orderly and systematic approach.
(vii) Candidates do not know that to plot the cumulative frequency curve they must use the maximum value of the class interval, not the mid-value.
(viii) Candidates do not know what the median is, nor how to calculate it properly, nor often, even how to spell it.
(ix) Candidates tend to skimp the discussion and comments on their results when asked to explain what their statistical calculations mean.

Conclusion

To end this chapter, and this book, we would like to say that many students every year *do* manage to pass examinations in statistics! We have probably emphasized the errors and have not said anything about the huge amount of good and accurate work submitted each year.

Finally, we have given no practice questions on logarithms or square roots at the end of this book, because the student or the teacher can obviously think of suitable examples here and, of course, no examination in statistics has questions specifically on these topics.

Typical examination questions

Chapter 2

1 Compare the advantages and disadvantages of the postal questionnaire and the personal interview as methods of obtaining primary data relating to economic matters.

2 A detergent manufacturer wishes to obtain information on a sample basis about the use of his product in a large town. Draft a short questionnaire with instructions for its completion to be sent by post to a group of families in the town. How might the families be selected for inclusion in such a survey? As this is an important enquiry the expenditure involved is not a major consideration.

3 Discuss the most important points in planning an efficient questionnaire. What also are the advantages and disadvantages of a postal enquiry and a personal interview? What can be gained by means of a Pilot Survey?

4 Of what value are the results of the Censuses of Population
(*a*) to a businessman,
(*b*) to a government body concerned with long-term planning?
Illustrate your answer with reference to the 1971 Census of Population of Great Britain.

5 (*a*) Compare and contrast the Census and the Sample methods of collection of statistical data.
(*b*) Explain three different methods of sampling and compare their usefulness in particular situations.

Chapter 3

1 (*a*) Tabulate the following information.

The number of stoppages of work due to industrial disputes in the UK beginning in July was 145. In addition, 35 stoppages which began before July were still in progress at the beginning of the month. The number of workers involved during July at the establishments where the 180 stoppages occurred is estimated as 36 500. This total includes 8 400 workers involved from the previous month. Of the 28 100 workers involved, 23 500 were involved directly and

4 600 indirectly. The aggregate of 177 000 working-days lost during July included 94 000 from the previous month.

(*b*) Write a brief report on the industrial disputes in July.

2 (*a*) Classify the following into continuous and discrete variables:

(i) The barometric heights at Kew over a period.
(ii) Number of persons visiting the local cinema per day for a month.
(iii) The tension in an elastic string when stretched beyond its natural length.
(iv) The number of goals scored per match by the school football team in a season.
(v) The number of boys per family in a given district.

(*b*) Design with careful attention to form and detail, and showing all sub-totals, a blank table in which could be shown a school's results in the General Certificate of Education for last year analysed into Ordinary and Advanced Level students, and the ages of students in years. The results can be 0 to 5 or more passes at Ordinary Level, and 0 to 3 or more passes at Advanced Level. The youngest candidates are 14 years old and a few of the oldest candidates are over 19 years old.

3 Construct a blank table to show absenteeism among the employees of an industrial establishment according to the length of absence (viz., 'under three days', 'three days and under one week', 'one week and under two weeks', 'two weeks and over'), classifying the absentees by sex, by civil condition (i.e., 'single' or 'married'), and by age ('under 18 years', '18 years and under 50 years', and '50 years and over').

(*Note* The table should be designed to apply to *one* month only. Totals and sub-totals may be included.)

4 You are asked to make a report on the length of service and efficiency of a set of typewriters. Draw up a tabulated statement giving the following information:

Age of machine—under 1 year, 1 year and under 2 years, etc.
Type of machine—Remington, Underwood, etc.
Condition of machine—serviceable, slight repairs, etc.

Chapter 4

1 The following figures relate to the sales and profits of a well-known multiple store:

Year of review	*Sales*		*Profits*	
	£ million	*Per cent increase on previous year*	*£ million*	*Per cent increase on previous year*
First	107	14·0	11·2	13·0
Second	118	10·5	12·4	10·7
Third	125	6·0	14·7	18·6
Fourth	130	4·0	16·2	10·2
Fifth	134	3·0	17·1	5·5

Draw a suitable graph or diagram to bring out the relationship between sales and profits.

2 (*a*) State the advantages and the disadvantages of diagrammatic presentation of statistical information.

(*b*) Describe the type of graph or diagram suitable for presenting the following information:

(i) the sales in *four* areas, of *three* products, for the last *two* years.

(ii) the total expenditure of a bus company during a given year, showing the proportions due to wages, fuel, maintenance, tyres, and depreciation.

(iii) broadcast receiving licences on 30 June, over the last ten years and divided into sound and television.

3 (*a*) List the advantages and disadvantages of presenting information by means of bar charts and pie charts.

(*b*) The following is a list of the subjects taught in a school and the time devoted to each subject per week. Present the information in the form of a pie chart of 2 inches radius.

Subject	*Time (hours)*
English	3
French	3
Mathematics	4
Physics	$2\frac{1}{2}$
Chemistry	$2\frac{1}{2}$

4 The following figures relate to the net profit and advertising expenditure of your Company.

Year ending	*Net profit (£'000's)*	*Advertising expenditure (£'000's)*
1973	6	0·8
1974	8	1·7
1975	10	1·9
1976	12	2·6
1977	14	2·8

By means of a scatter chart estimate for 1978 the net profit you expect from advertising expenditure of £3 200.

5 Construct suitable diagrams to represent the data given below. A different form of representation should be used for each part.

(i) The following table shows the numbers, in thousands, of votes cast for Conservative, Labour, Liberal and Independent candidates in two areas, A and B, at a General Election.

	Number of votes (thousands)			
	Conservative	*Labour*	*Liberal*	*Independent*
Area A	121	112	15	8
Area B	148	204	32	16

How would your representation have differed if, for each political party, the percentage of the total vote cast in each area had been given instead of the number of votes?

(ii) The following table shows the consumption, in million metric tons of coal equivalent, of solid and liquid fuel in Western Europe during the years 1973 to 1977.

	Consumption (10^6 metric tons of coal equivalent)				
	1973	1974	1975	1976	1977
Solid Fuel	557	539	515	485	459
Liquid Fuel	364	416	466	521	552

Chapter 5

1 The final grades in mathematics of 80 students are recorded in the following table:

68	84	75	82	68	90	62	88	76	93
73	79	88	73	60	93	71	59	85	75
61	65	75	87	74	62	95	78	63	72
66	78	82	75	94	77	69	74	68	60
96	78	89	61	75	95	60	79	83	71
79	62	67	97	78	85	76	65	71	75
65	80	73	57	88	78	62	76	53	74
86	67	73	81	72	63	76	75	85	77

Construct a frequency distribution from the above data (showing your working); comment on your choice of class intervals and plot a histogram and a frequency polygon.

2 Six-inch concrete cubes are tested to destruction by the impact of a compressive load given in tons. Arrange the results of these tests in order and condense into classes as a grouped frequency distribution. Choose groups 8–12, 12–16, etc., and draw the frequency polygon. After calculation of the cumulative totals draw a cumulative frequency curve and comment upon the usefulness of this type of graph. What percentage of the cubes disintegrate before a compressive load of 30 tons is reached?

Results of experiments in Tons

9·3	25·1	32·8	21·1	34·1	29·3	29·4	27·8	30·1	15·8
29·1	27·9	17·1	25·9	31·6	26·8	30·9	27·8	17·3	23·1
34·8	17·9	38·7	17·8	23·8	13·2	29·6	35·6	31·8	35·8
21·8	26·9	25·3	22·3	25·8	30·7	22·4	26·8	30·2	26·4
32·1	30·9	17·8	10·9	21·4	25·5	26·4	31·9	37·8	23·9
23·4	27·1	22·8	27·2	23·8	18·9	13·8	21·8	27	21·6
31·6	19·6	33·4	18·3	34	22·8	14·4	19·2	22·8	33·6
15·6	22·9	19·7	26·1	22·7	29·9	27·4	25·9	39·4	27·6
27	19·9	25·4	21·7	15·5					

3 Students admitted to courses for a First Degree:

Age of admission (years)	*Males*	*Females*
$17\frac{1}{2}$—	15	27
18 —	67	73
$18\frac{1}{2}$—	67	56
19 —	41	49
$19\frac{1}{2}$—	22	20
20 —	11	8
21 —	5	5
22 —	12	2

Combine the data into one distribution irrespective of sex. Illustrate this distribution with a cumulative frequency graph.

Find the minimum proportion of students who will attain the age of 22 years before graduation, assuming that no student will graduate in less than $2\frac{3}{4}$ years from admission.

4 The following table shows the distribution of marks gained by students in the same statistics examination. The paper, however, were marked by different examiners. If they pass the same proportion of candidates, estimate by means of cumulative percentage frequency curves (on the same axes) the pass mark for examiner A if the pass mark for examiner B is 55. Assume that the average ability and the scatter of ability of the two groups are approximately the same and that each student has done better work than those given fewer marks.

Marks	*Examiner A*	*Examiner B*
0–10	1	0
11–20	4	2
21–30	12	16
31–40	47	55
41–50	64	62
51–60	42	66
61–70	18	59
71–80	8	28
81–90	2	8
91–100	2	4

5 From the following table, which shows the number of workmen employed by 72 firms, construct:

(i) a frequency distribution table
(ii) a histogram
(iii) a frequency polygon superimposed on the histogram.

16	18	20	17	18	20	17	18
18	19	21	19	21	16	21	17
17	21	18	17	21	18	18	15
18	19	16	20	17	19	18	19
21	20	21	18	16	20	17	18
16	15	18	17	18	18	16	20
20	17	19	20	21	19	19	17
18	19	16	18	16	22	15	18
19	22	15	17	20	19	20	16

6 On ordinary graph paper, construct a semi-logarithmic chart of the UK exports of electrical machinery in the three categories given. Explain how the chart you have constructed differs from an ordinary one. Show clearly the figures you obtain to plot on your graph.

Electrical industry
(*UK Exports of electrical machinery—£million*)

	Total	*Commonwealth*	*Common Market*
Year 1	276·4	163·2	26·5
Year 2	285·2	164·9	28·0
Year 3	293·5	161·7	34·9
Year 4	318·5	156·7	47·1

Chapter 6

1 (*a*) What is meant by *statistical error*?
(*b*) Approximate the figures in the table below:
(i) to the nearest £1 000,
(ii) to the nearest £100, and
(iii) to the nearest £1 000 below.

Monthly sales of a manufacturer:

	£
January	40 075
February	41 234
March	41 652
April	42 634
May	40 861
June	38 729
July	38 451
August	37 262
September	41 295
October	43 654
November	40 431
December	38 807

(iii) the mode,
of the following numbers

10, 14, 22, 16, 15, 14, 15, 13, 14, 17.

3 In a report on the amount of travelling involved in a journey to work, a comparison was made between various kinds of employment. The data below refers to works managers.

Distance (kilometres)	*Number of Persons*
under 4	30
4–8	20
8–12	8
12–20	8
20–30	14
30–60	14
60–120	6
	100

(*a*) Calculate the mean and median for this distribution.
(*b*) Which of these two measures best describes this distribution and why?

4 Obtain by calculation the arithmetic mean and median of the following distribution. Discuss the relative advantages and disadvantages of the two measures in the example.

Age of Birmingham taxi-drivers

Age in years	*Per cent of all drivers (rounded to nearest whole percentage)*
u 35	13
35 u 40	11
40 u 45	15
45 u 50	16
50 u 55	14
55 u 60	10
60 u 65	9
65 u 70	7
70 u 75	3
75 and over	2
	100

Would you have been surprised if the percentage column had not totalled to 100 per cent? Why?

5 From the following frequency distribution of the hourly earnings of the skilled employees of Electronics Ltd (Workshop I),
(*a*) calculate the mean hourly wage and the modal hourly wage, and
(*b*) explain the characteristics of the mean and mode as representative values.

Electronics Ltd (Workshop 1)

Hourly wage (p)	*Number of employees*
50–59·9	8
60–59·9	10
70–79·9	16
80–89·9	14
90–99·9	10
100–109·9	5
110–119·9	2

6

England and Wales

Age of mother (years)	*Number of live births per 1 000 women*
15–19	31
20–24	158
25–29	161
30–34	94
35–39	46
40–44	12
45–49	1
TOTAL	503

(i) Calculate, using a short-cut method, the average age of mothers giving birth to a child.

(ii) Represent the data graphically by means of a histogram and insert the mean age in your diagram.

Chapter 8

1 What is meant by a measure of dispersion?

In what ways may these measures be put to practical use?

Calculate the standard deviation for the following data relating to the standard life of a component manufactured by a firm.

Life (hours)	*No. of components percentage total*
500–520	8
520–540	14
540–560	20
560–580	26
580–600	18
600–620	12
620 and over	2
	100

2 Two members of a sales staff have the following bonus earnings in pounds sterling per month:

Member	*Jan.*	*Feb.*	*Mar.*	*Apr.*	*May*	*June*
A	12·3	12·27	12·65	12·88	12·06	12·5
B	12·3	12·19	12·38	12·46	12·08	12·3

Member	*July*	*Aug.*	*Sept.*	*Oct.*	*Nov.*	*Dec.*
A	12·69	12·92	12·28	12·55	12·82	12·08
B	12·2	12·55	12·18	12·37	12·49	12·1

Calculate the arithmetic mean and the standard deviation of each set of results and state, giving your reasons, which member, A or B, you would prefer to work for you.

3 (*a*) What basic characteristic of a frequency distribution are represented by (i) the median? (ii) the mean deviation?

(*b*) Calculate the mean deviation of the following distribution of weights.

Weight in lb.	*Number of Boxes*
10 and under 12	2
12 and under 14	9
14 and under 16	20
16 and under 18	25
18 and under 20	24
20 and under 22	15
22 and under 24	5
	100

4 The table below gives the number of earners found per family in a social survey that was carried out in a large town. Calculate the mean and standard deviation.

No. of earners in family	*No. of families*
0	117
1	1 086
2	616
3	287
4	126
5	47
6	14
7	4
8	1
TOTAL	2 298

5 An analysis of production rejects resulted in the following figures.

No. of rejects per operator	*Number of operators*
21–25	6
26–30	17
31–35	22
36–40	34
41–45	20
46–50	12
51–55	5

Calculate the standard deviation of the distribution and estimate the limits between which the number of rejects per operator will vary with 95 per cent certainty.

6 (*a*) Why is standard deviation the most useful measure of dispersion?
(*b*) Calculate the arithmetic mean and standard deviation for the information given below:

Man-hours lost through strikes	*Number of organizations*
less than 10	5
20	12
30	25
40	141
50	456
60	173
70	98
80	52
90	21
100	1
TOTAL	984

7 (*a*) Explain and illustrate graphically the relationship between the mean, median, and mode in (i) a positively skewed frequency distribution and (ii) a negatively skewed distribution.
(*b*) Calculate the coefficient of skewness for a frequency distribution with the following values: mean = 10; median = 11; standard deviation = 5. What does your answer tell you about this frequency distribution?

Chapter 9

1 *Number of calls on customers compared with number of vacuum cleaners sold*

Number of calls	40	30	27	45	22	29	36	41	32
Number sold	10	7	5	10	3	7	9	9	8

(*a*) Prepare a scatter diagram in respect of the data given above and insert a 'line of best fit'.

(*b*) What purposes do the scatter diagram and line of best fit serve when comparing two series? Explain why two lines of best fit may be drawn and indicate the circumstances in which it is appropriate to do this.

(*c*) What disadvantages affect the line of best fit when used in these circumstances? What can be done to overcome them?

(*d*) Compare and contrast the uses of the two most common measures of correlation.

2 The following data shows the present maintenance costs and age of a sample of 8 similar machines used in a factory.

Machine	A	B	C	D	E	F	G	H
Age of machine (years)	1	3	4	4	6	7	7	8
Maintenance cost (£)	£200	£550	£650	£800	£1 150	£1 100	£1 300	£1 500

(*a*) Calculate and plot the regression line of maintenance cost on machine age.

(*b*) Use the regression line to predict the expected maintenance cost for a machine aged 10 years. Comment on the accuracy of your prediction.

3 (*a*) What is meant by a coefficient of correlation? How does correlation analysis differ from regression analysis?

(*b*) The following table gives X, the number of radio sets (in thousands), and Y, the number of television sets (in thousands), sold in Camford over the last 9 months:

X	140	150	130	100	90	80	90	120	130
Y	270	350	340	240	190	170	150	180	170

Plot this data and discuss the extent of correlation between X and Y.

4

Month	*New claims for Sickness Benefit under National Insurance. Weekly averages (thousands)*	*Average temperature (°C)*
January	372	4
February	251	4
March	253	6
April	177	8
May	173	11
June	158	14

July	149	15
August	154	15
September	163	13
October	209	10
November	221	7
December	192	5

Find the regression line which would enable you to predict the number of new claims for National Insurance for a given average temperature.

5 The following data refer to travelling expenses and duration of trips for consecutive trips made by sales engineers of a large firm.

Trip number	1	2	3	4	5	6	7	8
Expenses (£)	43	24	30	26	17	29	28	29
Duration of trip (days)	9·0	3·5	6·5	4·0	2·0	5·0	3·0	3·5

(*a*) Plot these data on a suitable graph.
(*b*) Estimate the regression equation for predicting total expense from duration of trip.
(*c*) Use the regression equation to estimate the average expense for a trip of duration 5 days.

6 Three research managers each examined 9 possible projects and ranked them in the following order of importance.

Project	A	B	C	D	E	F	G	H	J
Manager 1	5	9	3	1	4	7	2	6	8
Manager 2	4	7	2	3	6	5	1	8	9
Manager 3	6	7	2	4	1	9	3	5	8

Calculate the rank correlation coefficients between the three pairs of managers and comment briefly on the results.

If you were the managing director and had to select three projects, which would you choose in the light of these assessments?

Would you still choose the same three if, in addition, it is known that manager 3 is much more experienced than the other two?

Chapter 10

1 Calculate the four quarterly moving average trend and the average seasonal variation of the following series:

Year	*Quarters*			
	1	*2*	*3*	*4*
1974	28	31	40	27
1975	32	38	49	38
1976	43	47	55	41
1977	59	54	57	54

2

Company sales (£'000)

Year	*1st quarter*	*2nd quarter*	*3rd quarter*	*4th quarter*
1973			115	105
1974	141	156	129	130
1975	148	184	140	176
1976	224	248	196	139
1977	207	240		

(*a*) Smooth the above time series by means of a moving average.
(*b*) Plot both the original series and the smoothed series on the same graph.
(*c*) Estimate the trend of figures for sales in the third and fourth quarters of 1977, and comment on the reliance which can be placed upon these estimates.

3

UK consumption of beer
Million bulk barrels per quarter

Year	*A*	*B*	*C*	*D*	*E*	*F*
Quarter						
1	5·46	5·36	5·17	5·75	6·00	6·02
2	6·56	6·32	6·52	7·03	7·56	7·44
3	7·30	6·91	7·75	7·78	8·00	8·00
4	6·14	6·16	6·62	6·68	7·05	7·15

By applying a moving average technique, calculate the centred trend for UK beer consumption. Hence, predict the consumption figure for the first quarter of year G.

For what reasons may the actual figure differ from your prediction?

4 Determine the trend of sales over the period given from the following:

Sales of XYZ Co. Ltd.
£'000

Quarters	*1*	*2*	*3*	*4*
1974	32	45	50	38
1975	34	47	51	48
1976	30	40	49	54
1977	38	48	38	44

Present the series and trend graphically.

5 The production of small cigars in the United States 1961–70 is shown in the following table.

Year	*Number of small cigars (millions)*
1961	98·2
1962	92·3
1963	80·0
1964	89·1
1965	83·5
1966	68·9
1967	69·2
1968	67·1
1969	58·3
1970	61·2

You are required to:

(*a*) graph the data shown above,

(*b*) calculate the equation of a least squares trend line fitting the data, say what the trend value is at 1961 and 1970, and explain your result,

(*c*) estimate the production of small cigars for the year 1971.

6 State what you understand by the seasonal cycle in a time series. Estimate the seasonal element in the data below and illustrate the cycle with a diagram.

		(*£ millions*)	
	Year 1	*Year 2*	*Year 3*
1st quarter	3 118	3 191	3 376
2nd quarter	3 288	3 468	3 603
3rd quarter	3 368	3 494	3 614
4th quarter	3 618	3 767	3 822

Chapter 11

1 (*a*) Describe the various methods of Index Number construction. Give their relative advantages and disadvantages.

(*b*) From the following table calculate the weight and the Index Number for the item 'Meat and bacon'.

Item	*Weight*	*Index number*
Bread, flour, biscuits and cakes	37	135
Meat and bacon		
Fish	8	129
Butter, margarine and cooking fat	12	108
Milk, cheese and eggs	40	123
Tea, coffee, cocoa, soft drinks, etc.	14	109
Sugar, preserves, confectionery	27	141
Vegetables	24	163
Fruit	15	120
Other food	12	121
TOTAL, all food	254	131·6

2 A firm wishes to follow the relative movement of the prices of various raw materials which it uses. It decides to construct a simple index number starting from January 1977 and based on average prices from 1975.

(*a*) From the following data, calculate an index for the month of January 1977.

Raw materials	*Price (£ per ton)*		*Weight*
	Average, 1975	*January 1977*	
A	16	19	5
B	24	25	1
C	13	18	3
D	8	9	6
E	12	14	4
F	4	8	3

(*b*) What are the main points the firm should bear in mind when planning the construction of this type of index number?

3

1955		*1960*		*1970*	
Rents	*No. of tenants*	*Rents*	*No. of tenants*	*Rents*	*No. of tenants*
£ p		£ p		£ p	
0·50	1 280	0·70	1 280	1·20	1 280
0·75	760	1·00	750	1·65	750
1·00	410	1·25	580	2·00	590
1·50	86	1·85	400	2·50	700
2·00	70	2·45	250	3·25	950
4·00	10	4·60	190	5·00	1 000

Calculate aggregate Laspeyres and Paasche indexes for 1960 and 1970 with 1955 = 100. Account for the differences in the answer obtained from the two indexes.

4 Calculate as an arithmetic mean, correct to the nearest whole number, a cost of living index from the following table of price relatives and weights:

	Price relatives	*Weights*
Food	122	35
Rent	101	9
Clothing	118	10
Fuel	115	7
Miscellaneous	108	39

5

	November 1974		*March 1977*	
	Average price (new pence) per lb	*Average quantity purchased per week*	*Average price (new pence) per lb*	*Average quantity purchased per week*
Rump steak	$70\frac{1}{2}$	1 lb	98	$\frac{3}{4}$ lb
Potatoes	2	2 lb	4	$2\frac{1}{2}$ lb
Tomatoes	$16\frac{1}{2}$	$\frac{1}{2}$ lb	20	$\frac{1}{2}$ lb
Cauliflower	10	$1\frac{1}{2}$ lb	15	1 lb

From the above data find the following price indexes for March 1977 with November 1974 = 100.

(i) Unweighted index.
(ii) Laspeyre index (base year weighting).
(iii) Paasche index (current year weighting).
Comment on your results.

6 (*a*) From the following details of the prices of an average family budget, calculate indexes of price changes over a three-year period.

Commodity	*Prices*				
	Weights (w_0)	*Year 0* (p_0) £	*Year 1* (p_1) £	*Year 2* (p_2) £	*Year 3* (p_3) £
A	0·4	0·12	0·13	0·17	0·17
B	0·1	0·75	0·75	0·90	1·35
C	0·3	0·80	0·90	1·00	1·25
D	0·2	1·00	1·25	1·30	1·85

(*b*) Comment on the impact of the indexes on the averages family's cost of living over this period.

Chapter 12

1 A survey obtained the following public opinion replies to the question, 'If there were a general election tomorrow, how would you vote?'

For the Government . .	480
Against the Government	560
Total replies	1 040

Three months later the replies were:

For the Government ..	440
Against the Government	640
Total replies	1 080

Do the results suggest any significant change in political opinion over the period? Would you be surprised, if six months after the second survey, the government won the General Election?

2 Among patients having a certain disease, in Hospital A 20 per cent died and in Hospital B 8 per cent died. The number of patients in the two hospitals were

	A	*B*
Men	21	57
Women	84	18

Would you conclude that the patients received better care in Hospital B than in Hospital A? What additional figures would Hospital A use to defend its record?

3 The manufacturers of brand 'X' margarine held a tasting test to determine whether people could distinguish between their product and butter. Each subject was presented with six biscuits, five of which were spread with butter and one with brand 'X' margarine, and asked to pick out the margarine.

Of 1 680 people tested, 345 picked out the margarine-spread biscuit correctly.

(*a*) What proportion of people would you expect to pick out the odd biscuit, if their choice were purely random?

(*b*) Could the results given above be purely due to chance or could some people tell brand 'X' margarine from butter?

(*c*) How does the theory of the normal curve help in assessing the results?

4 A given type of aircraft develops minor trouble in 4 per cent of flights. Another type of aircraft on the same journeys develops trouble in 19 out of 150 flights. Investigate the performance of the two types of machines and comment on any significant difference.

5 A complex television component has 1 000 joints soldered by a machine which is known to produce, on average, one defective joint in forty.

The components are examined, and faulty soldering corrected by hand. If components requiring more than 35 corrections are discarded, what proportion of the components will be thrown away?

6 In a certain region it is thought that 55 per cent of the population vote Conservative. It is decided to conduct a survey of voters by means of a simple random sample drawn from the electorate in the region. What size of sample

would have to be taken to estimate the percentage voting Conservative so as to be 95 per cent confident that the true value lies within 3 per cent of the estimate from the sample.

Explain how you could improve on the survey design so that you could obtain the same precision with a smaller sample.

Chapter 13

1 Define probability. What is the addition and multiplication theorem of probability?

A certain firm employs 200 executives, 700 supervisors and 2 500 operators. What is the probability that:

(*a*) An employee chosen at random will be an executive?
(*b*) Either a supervisor or an operative?
(*c*) If two employees are chosen at random, the first will be an executive and the second a supervisor?

2 Three letters are typed and addressed to three different people, together with the corresponding envelopes. If the letters are put in the envelopes at random, what are the chances that 0, 1, 2, or 3 letters will be in the right envelopes?

3 Define probability.

The probability that a man will be alive in 25 years is 3/5 and probability that his wife will be alive in 25 years is 2/3.

Find the probability that,

(*a*) Both will be alive.
(*b*) Only the man will be alive.
(*c*) Only the wife will be alive.
(*d*) At least one will be alive.

4 Define probability. What is mathematical expectation?

(*a*) If a man purchases a raffle ticket, he can win a first prize of £500 or a second prize of £200 with probabilities 0·001 and 0·003. What should be a fair price to pay for the ticket?
(*b*) In a business venture, a man makes a profit of £300 with probability of 0·6 or takes a loss of £100 with probability of 0·4. Determine his expectation.

5 A process produces batches of items in which the number of defectives is known to be normally distributed with mean 10 and standard deviation 2.

(*a*) Sketch the shape of this frequency distribution, indicating its basic characteristics.
(*b*) State the probability that the defectives in a given batch will be:
    (i) less than 6.
    (ii) more than 12
    (iii) between 8 and 14.

6 Experience shows that 10 per cent of persons reserving tables at a night club will not appear. The night club has 50 tables and takes 53 reservations. Find the probability that it will be able to accommodate everyone appearing.

Chapter 14

1 The following data relate to measurements of components produced by two different machines. Is there any significant difference between the output of the two machines?

Machine	*Number measured*	*Average size*	*Standard deviation*
A	1 200	31 in.	5 in.
B	1 000	30 in.	4 in.

2 The following figures relate to an experiment carried out in the brewing industry in order to test whether continuous brewing gives results comparable with those of batch brewing. Two samples were taken from each of the six brews; one was then processed by the continuous, the other by the batch method. Laboratory analysis gave the following results relating to sugar content:

Brew number	*Processed*	
	Continuously	*By batch*
1	35	30
2	38	34
3	35	45
4	34	42
5	56	35
6	26	38

State whether there is any significant difference between the results of the two methods of processing. Would the result of this calculation be different if you were told that the samples taken from Brew No. 5 were faulty and should be excluded from the experiments?

3 A manufacturer aims to make electricity bulbs with a mean working life of 1 000 hours. He draws a sample of 20 from a batch and tests it. The mean life of the sample bulbs is 990 with a standard deviation of 22 hours. Is the batch up to standard?

4 In order to find whether intensive national advertising of milk affected sales in a particular area, two systematic samples of families were taken from the milk roundsmen's books, one before and one after the campaign. With the help of means and standard deviations, determine whether the campaign was successful, ignoring all other factors influencing the pattern of milk sales.

Number of pints bought per week	*Number of families in:* *Sample 1* *Before the campaign*	*Sample 2* *After the campaign*
Up to 5	77	81
$5\frac{1}{2}$–$10\frac{1}{2}$	151	128
11–16	213	194
$16\frac{1}{2}$–$21\frac{1}{2}$	254	295
22–27	428	372
$27\frac{1}{2}$–$32\frac{1}{2}$	230	323
33–38	92	146
$38\frac{1}{2}$ and over	45	79
	1 490	1 618

5 The standard deviation of production by individual workers in a factory is known to be 1·55. The production method is changed, and a sample of 9 workers is chosen. The numbers of units produced by the sample are as follows:

39, 41, 43, 40, 42, 44, 43, 41, 40.

(*a*) Test whether the population variance has changed.
(*b*) Assuming that the population variance has changed, find the 95 per cent confidence limits of the population mean.

6 A manufacturer aims to make a machine which will have a mean operating life of 10 000 hours. He draws a sample of 20 from a batch and tests it. The mean life of the sample is 9 900 hours with a standard deviation of 220 hours. What conclusion can he draw from this sample?

Chapter 15

1 The following measurements were taken in the course of routine quality control checks at a factory. Six items were measured every hour:

Time	*Results*
10 a.m.	95, 96, 100, 103, 98, 92
11 a.m.	102, 99, 91, 100, 95, 89
12 noon	96, 101, 99, 94, 91, 103
1 p.m.	100, 90, 98, 102, 101, 95
2 p.m.	97, 88, 100, 103, 99, 101
3 p.m.	103, 101, 105, 103, 93, 98

(*a*) Draw 'mean and range' quality control charts with the following limits:

Mean chart—warning limits: 98·5 and 93·5
action limits: 100 and 92,

Range chart—warning limit: 14
action limit: 15·5.

(*b*) Enter the information for the day's production on your charts.
(*c*) How are the values for the limits obtained in practice?

2 Two groups, *A* and *B*, both consist of 100 people who have a disease. A serum is given to group *A* but not to group *B*; otherwise, the two groups are treated

identically. It is found that in groups *A* and *B*, 75 and 65 people, respectively, recover from the disease. Does this result support the hypothesis that the serum helps to cure the disease?

Table of chi-square	$p = 0{\cdot}1$	0·05	0·01
Degrees of freedom	*Chi-square greater than*		
1	2·71	3·84	6·64
2	4·60	5·99	9·21
3	6·25	7·82	11·34
4	7·78	9·49	13·28

3 The mean weight of a large loaf produced at a bakery was found in a series of quality control checks to be 30 ounces, with a standard deviation of 1 ounce.

Sample batches of four loaves were then taken from the travelling oven at two-hourly intervals and the following are the averages of the last six consecutive sample batches:

29·6, 29·4, 29·9, 30·2, 30·3, 30·1.

(*a*) Draw up a control chart for these averages and enter the figures on the chart.

(*b*) What proportion of loaves would you expect to fall below the legal minimum weight of 28 ounces?

4 Using the chi-squared (χ^2) distribution as a test of significance, test the statement that the number of defective items produced by two machines as shown in the following table, is independent of the machine on which they were made.

	Machine output		
	Defective articles	*Effective articles*	*Total*
Machine A	25	375	400
Machine B	42	558	600
	67	933	1 000

Use the 0·01 level of significance.

5 Two factories using materials purchased from the same supplier and closely controlled to an agreed specification produce output for a given period classified into three quality grades as follows:

Quality grade	*Output in tons*			
Factory	*A*	*B*	*C*	*Total*
X	42	13	33	88
Y	20	8	25	53
TOTAL	62	21	58	141

(*a*) Do these output figures show a significant difference at the 5 per cent level?
(*b*) What hypothesis have you tested?

6 (*a*) Explain carefully the reasoning underlying a χ^2 test.
(*b*) A manufacturer is considering methods of improving the marketing of his product. He decides to wrap his product in various coloured wrappings and then note the effect on sales. He uses four different colours and offers each coloured wrapping for one month. He finds that the sales are as follows:

yellow 262; pink 281; blue 240; green 212.

Examine whether there is any evidence that the colour of the wrapping affects sales.

Chapter 16

1 Describe how a Lorenz curve is compiled.
Construct a suitable table of personal incomes and personal tax from which a Lorenz curve can be compiled.
Note The figures shown in the table need not be accurate, but must clearly indicate the type of information found in such tables.

2 Describe how a Z chart of monthly sales volume for a firm is compiled and indicate how this can be used by management in forecasting sales for the next few months.

3 What is a population pyramid? Is it important?

4 The following figures come from the Report on the Census of Production:

Textile machinery and accessories

Establishments *Nos.*	*Net output* *£'000*
48	1 406
42	2 263
38	3 699
21	2 836
26	3 152
16	5 032
23	20 385
214	38 773

Analyse this table by means of a Lorenz curve and explain what this curve shows. What other information is available from the Census of Production Report?

Monthly production of the 'XL' Company, 1976/1977
('000's units)

	Jan	*Feb*	*Mar*	*April*	*May*	*June*	*July*	*Aug*	*Sept*	*Oct*	*Nov*	*Dec*
1971	400	410	360	400	420	450	430	380	410	450	460	430
1972	420	430	410	380	410	470	450	400	460	490	510	480

Calculate and plot a Z chart for the year 1977.

Chapter 17

1 Quotations have been received from three firms for the purchase of a new machine cost price £16 000, the only difference being the terms of settlement which are as follows:

(i) Firm X—£8 000 on delivery and £2 000 payable at the end of each of the following four years;

(ii) Firm Y—£4 000 at the end of each year for the next four years;

(iii) Firm Z—£5 000 payable on delivery, £3 000 at the end of the second year and third year and £5 000 at the end of the fourth year.

The average cost of capital is 10 per cent.

(*a*) Show by means of a statement using NPV (net present value method) which quotation should be accepted.

Present Value of £1 (10 per cent)

Year 1	0·909
2	0·826
3	0·751
4	0·683

(*b*) State *two* advantages of using discounted cash flow methods when assessing capital projects.

(*c*) State *two* difficulties met with in practice when applying such techniques.

2 (*a*) Explain why discounting techniques are used to assess capital projects.

(*b*) Two similar machines are available—machine *A* and machine *B*, details of which are as follows:

	Machine A £	*Machine B* £
Cost	5 000	4 500
Net cash flows:		
Year 1	2 500	1 200
2	2 400	1 500
3	1 600	2 000
4	1 000	3 500

At the end of the fourth year the scrap value of machine A is estimated to be £500 and that for machine B—£400.

Assuming the average cost is 14 per cent, prepare statements, using DCF (discounted cash flow) methods to show which machine should be purchased.

Present value of £1 (14 per cent)

Year 1	0·877
2	0·769
3	0·675
4	0·592

Note All calculations to nearest £.

3 Explain the advantages of discounting methods of project appraisal over conventional methods.

4 An expanding company, regularly examining opportunities for new investment, is considering the following two alternative projects. It is found that when the two sets of cash flow are discounted at 15 per cent per annum, they both result in a nil present value. The cash flows, after multiplying by the discount factors, are as follows:

	Project A		*Project B*	
	Cash in	*Cash out*	*Cash in*	*Cash out*
	£	£	£	£
Year 1		30 000		26 000
2	9 000		1 000	
3	7 500		3 500	
4	6 200		5 000	
5	7 300		4 250	
6			3 600	
7			3 050	
8			5 600	
	30 000	30 000	26 000	26 000

You are required to state the principles on which a choice should be made between the two projects, making assumptions where necessary to illustrate your answer.

5 You are given the following information:

Investment at end of year 0: £31·7
Life of project: 4 years
Expected cash flow: £10 a year for 4 years

Find, by use of discounted cash flow method the rate of interest which will repay the cost of the capital investment. What amount of interest will have been earned?

6 (*a*) What sum will have been earned by investing £100 for 20 years at $16\frac{1}{2}$ per cent compound interest?

(*b*) How much has to be invested at 12 per cent compound interest to produce £1 000 in 10 years time?
(*c*) Explain the difference between arithmetic and geometric series as applied to interest rates.

Chapter 18

1 What methods are used to compare the mortality rates of local authority areas? What difficulties of composition are these methods designed to overcome?

2 Write brief notes on *four* of the following terms:
(*a*) vital statistics;
(*b*) population pyramid;
(*c*) crude birth rate;
(*d*) standardized death rate;
(*e*) General Register Office.

3 From the vital statistics of a North Midlands' town, the following data was extracted:

Age-group (years)	*0 and under 10*	*10 and under 40*	*40 and under 60*	*60 and over*
Population (000's)	16	48	12	4
Deaths in 1975	212	247	291	337
Standard age distribution	150	400	300	150

(*a*) Calculate the crude and standardized death rates.
(*b*) Explain with reasons why the crude death rates are inadequate.

4 (*a*) Contrast crude and standardized death rates.
(*b*) The following table gives the relevant vital statistics for a certain town in 1976.

Age Group	*Number of deaths*	*Population (thousands)*	*Population in United Kingdom (millions)*
0 and under 15	216	8	12
15 and under 25	200	26	7
25 and under 45	288	24	14
45 and under 65	156	6	13
65 and over	105	1	6

Calculate the crude death rate for each age group and the standardized death rate for the town.

5 Outline the basis of calculation of the occupational mortality statistics published by the Registrar-General. Discuss the value of these figures to the public health statistician.

6 (*a*) What is standardized death rate?
(*b*) Given the following data, prepare a report estimating the number of extra pupil places which were required in the first year classes of state primary schools in England in each of the years 1966–8 inclusive.

Live births in England and Wales (in thousands)

	Total	*Wales alone*
1958	739	42
1959	750	42
1960	782	44
1961	803	44
1962	840	45
1963	856	47

What further data would you like to have, and how would you use it?

Chapter 19

1 Describe the nature of the statistical information concerning the United Kingdom which is published in official sources on any *four* of the following:
(*a*) Distribution of man-power
(*b*) Production of iron and steel
(*c*) Building and construction
(*d*) Retail distribution establishments
(*e*) Retail prices
(*f*) Wages and salaries.

2 Write notes on *three* of the following:
(*a*) The census of population
(*b*) Standard industrial classification
(*c*) Retail sales indexes
(*d*) The census of distribution
(*e*) Imports and exports price indexes.

3 Explain the purpose of *each* of the following, and describe in outline the method of procedure adopted in obtaining the results for *each*:
(*a*) The Census of Production.
(*b*) The Index of Industrial Production.

4 Describe the 3 main ways of measuring the Gross National Income. What does 'gross' mean in this respect?

5 What information does the government publish in relation to labour statistics? Which are the main publications which contain these figures?

6 Describe the methods used to determine the magnitude of the overseas trade of the UK. How are these figures collected and what reliability can be placed on them?

Some useful formulae

Note Unless otherwise stated, the symbols used in these formulae have the following meaning:

$\bar{X}$ is the A.M. of the individual X's (items)
$\bar{Y}$ is the A.M. of the individual Y's (items)
and so on.
x = the deviation of each item from the *true* A.M. of the X's
y = the deviation of each item from the *true* A.M. of the Y's
Σ = the total of the individual values
f = the frequencies, or weights
N = the total number of items in the group
n = the total number of items in the sample
d = deviation of each item from an *assumed* mean
A = an *assumed* mean
σ = standard deviation.

Averages

Arithmetic mean ($\bar{X}$)

Basic formula: $\bar{X} = \frac{\Sigma X}{N}$

'Short-cut' method:

$$\bar{X} = A \pm \left[\frac{\Sigma fd}{\Sigma f} \times \text{class interval}\right]$$

Geometric mean (*G.M.*)

$$\text{Simple } G.M. = \sqrt[N]{X_1 \times X_2 \times X_3 \ldots}$$

Mode (Z)

Let F_0 = frequency *before* that of the modal group
F_1 = frequency of the modal group
F_2 = frequency *after* the modal group
C = group interval of the modal group
L = lower limit of the modal group

Then $Z = L + \frac{F_1 - F_0}{2F_1 - F_0 - F_2}(C)$

Dispersion

Quartile deviation $= \frac{Q_3 - Q_1}{2}$

Quartile coefficient $= \frac{Q_3 - Q_1}{Q_3 + Q_1}$

Standard deviation

Basic formula:

$$\sigma = \sqrt{\frac{\Sigma(X - \bar{X})^2}{N}}$$

'Short-cut' method:

$$\alpha = \sqrt{\frac{\Sigma fd^2}{\Sigma f} - \left(\frac{\Sigma fd}{\Sigma f}\right)^2} \times \text{class interval}$$

Coefficient of variation $= \frac{\sigma}{\bar{X}} \times 100$

Pearsonian coefficient of skewness (S.K.)

$$S.K. = \frac{3(\bar{X} - \text{Median})}{\sigma}$$

Correlation

Pearsonian coefficient, $r = \frac{\Sigma xy}{N \sigma_x \sigma_y}$

'Short-cut' method:

$$r = \frac{\frac{\sum (d_x d_y)}{N} - \left[\frac{\sum d_x}{N} \times \frac{\sum d_y}{N}\right]}{\sqrt{\left[\frac{\sum d_x^2}{N} - \left(\frac{\sum d_x}{N}\right)^2\right]\left[\frac{\sum d_y^2}{N} - \left(\frac{\sum d_y}{N}\right)^2\right]}}$$

where N = the number of *pairs* of items.

Rank coefficient, $R = 1 - \frac{6 \sum D^2}{N(N^2 - 1)}$

where D = the difference between rankings.

Index numbers

Weighted aggregate price index

$$\text{Index} = \frac{\Sigma(p_1 \times W)}{\Sigma(p_0 \times W)} \times 100$$

Laspeyre types

$$\text{Price index} = \frac{\Sigma(p_1 \times q_0)}{\Sigma(p_0 \times q_0)} \times 100$$

$$\text{Quantity index} = \frac{\Sigma(q_1 \times p_0)}{\Sigma(q_0 \times p_0)} \times 100$$

Paasche types

$$\text{Price index} = \frac{\Sigma(q_1 \times p_1)}{\Sigma(q_1 \times p_0)} \times 100$$

$$\text{Quantity index} = \frac{\Sigma(q_1 \times p_1)}{\Sigma(q_0 \times p_1)} \times 100$$

Note p_0 and p_1 are prices in the base and current years.
q_0 and q_1 are quantities in the base and current years.

Sampling

Binomial $A.M. = np$

$$S.D. = \sqrt{npq}$$

$$P_X \text{ successes} = \frac{n!}{(X!)(n-X)!} p^X q^{(n-X)}$$

Poisson $A.M. = np(=m)$

$$S.D. = \sqrt{np} = \sqrt{m}$$

$$P_X \text{ successes} = \frac{m^X}{X!} \times \frac{1}{2{\cdot}718^m}$$

Standard errors

Proportions (Difference between 2 samples)

$$S.E._{diff.} = \sqrt{\frac{p_1q_1}{n_1} + \frac{p_2q_2}{n_2}}$$

Variables

A.M. $S.E._{A.M.} = \dfrac{\sigma}{\sqrt{n}}$

S.D. $S.E._{\sigma} = \dfrac{S}{\sqrt{2n}}$ where $S = S.D.$ of the sample.

Difference between 2 samples:

A.M.'s $S.D._{diff.} = \sqrt{\dfrac{S_1^2}{n_1} + \dfrac{S_2^2}{n_2}}$

S.D.'s $S.E._{diff.} = \sqrt{\dfrac{S_1^2}{2n_1} + \dfrac{S_2^2}{2n_2}}$

Correlation

$$S.E._r = \frac{1 - r^2}{\sqrt{n}}$$

χ^2 *(frequency distributions)*

$$\chi^2 = \sum \frac{(F_A - F_E)^2}{F_E}$$

where F_A and F_E are actual and expected frequencies.

Contingency tables (2×2)

$$\chi^2 = \frac{N(ae - bd)^2}{c.f.g.h.}$$

Yates's correction

$$\chi^2 = \frac{N(ae - bd - \frac{1}{2}N)^2}{c.f.g.h.}$$

Financial mathematics

Progressions

Sum of arithmetic series (simple interest) $A = P(1 + rt)$

Present value (simple interest) $P = \dfrac{A}{(1 + rt)}$

Sum of geometric series (compound interest) $A = P(1 + r)^t$

Present value (compound interest) $P = \dfrac{A}{(1 + r)^t}$

Appendixes

Appendix 1

LOGARITHMS

	0	1	2	3	4	5	6	7	8	9	1	2	3	4	5	6	7	8	9
10	0000	0043	0086	0128	0170						4	9	13	17	21	26	30	34	38
						0212	0253	0294	0334	0374	4	8	12	16	20	24	28	32	37
11	0414	0453	0492	0531	0569						4	8	12	15	19	23	27	31	35
						0607	0645	0682	0719	0755	4	7	11	15	19	22	26	30	33
12	0792	0828	0864	0899	0934	0969					3	7	11	14	18	21	25	28	32
							1004	1038	1072	1106	3	7	10	14	17	20	24	27	31
13	1139	1173	1206	1239	1271						3	7	10	13	16	20	23	26	30
						1303	1335	1367	1399	1430	3	7	10	12	16	19	22	25	29
14	1461	1492	1523	1553							3	6	9	12	15	18	21	24	28
					1584	1614	1644	1673	1703	1732	3	6	9	12	15	17	20	23	26
15	1761	1790	1818	1847	1875	1903					3	6	9	11	14	17	20	23	26
							1931	1959	1987	2014	3	5	8	11	14	16	19	22	25
16	2041	2068	2095	2122	2148						3	5	8	11	14	16	19	22	24
						2175	2201	2227	2253	2279	3	5	8	10	13	15	18	21	23
17	2304	2330	2355	2380	2405	2430					3	5	8	10	13	15	18	20	23
							2455	2480	2504	2529	2	5	7	10	12	15	17	19	22
18	2553	2577	2601	2625	2648						2	5	7	9	12	14	16	19	21
						2672	2695	2718	2742	2765	2	5	7	9	11	14	16	18	21
19	2788	2810	2833	2856	2878						2	4	7	9	11	13	16	18	20
						2900	2923	2945	2967	2989	2	4	6	8	11	13	15	17	19
20	3010	3032	3054	3075	3096	3118	3139	3160	3181	3201	2	4	6	8	11	13	15	17	19
21	3222	3243	3263	3284	3304	3324	3345	3365	3385	3404	2	4	6	8	10	12	14	16	18
22	3424	3444	3464	3483	3502	3522	3541	3560	3579	3598	2	4	6	8	10	12	14	15	17
23	3617	3636	3655	3674	3692	3711	3729	3747	3766	3784	2	4	6	7	9	11	13	15	17
24	3802	3820	3838	3856	3874	3892	3909	3927	3945	3962	2	4	5	7	9	11	12	14	16
25	3979	3997	4014	4031	4048	4065	4082	4099	4116	4133	2	3	5	7	9	10	12	14	15
26	4150	4166	4183	4200	4216	4232	4249	4265	4281	4298	2	3	5	7	8	10	11	13	15
27	4314	4330	4346	4362	4378	4393	4409	4425	4440	4456	2	3	5	6	8	9	11	13	14
28	4472	4487	4502	4518	4533	4548	4564	4579	4594	4609	2	3	5	6	8	9	11	12	14
29	4624	4639	4654	4669	4683	4698	4713	4728	4742	4757	1	3	4	6	7	9	10	12	13
30	4771	4786	4800	4814	4829	4843	4857	4871	4886	4900	1	3	4	6	7	9	10	11	13
31	4914	4928	4942	4955	4969	4983	4997	5011	5024	5038	1	3	4	6	7	8	10	11	12
32	5051	5065	5079	5092	5105	5119	5132	5145	5159	5172	1	3	4	5	7	8	9	11	12
33	5185	5198	5211	5224	5237	5250	5263	5276	5289	5302	1	3	4	5	6	8	9	10	12
34	5315	5328	5340	5353	5366	5378	5391	5403	5416	5428	1	3	4	5	6	8	9	10	11
35	5441	5453	5465	5478	5490	5502	5514	5527	5539	5551	1	2	4	5	6	7	9	10	11
36	5563	5575	5587	5599	5611	5623	5635	5647	5658	5670	1	2	4	5	6	7	8	10	11
37	5682	5694	5705	5717	5729	5740	5752	5763	5775	5786	1	2	3	5	6	7	8	9	10
38	5798	5809	5821	5832	5843	5855	5866	5877	5888	5899	1	2	3	5	6	7	8	9	10
39	5911	5922	5933	5944	5955	5966	5977	5988	5999	6010	1	2	3	4	5	7	8	9	10
40	6021	6031	6042	6053	6064	6075	6085	6096	6107	6117	1	2	3	4	5	6	8	9	10
41	6128	6138	6149	6160	6170	6180	6191	6201	6212	6222	1	2	3	4	5	6	7	8	9
42	6232	6243	6253	6263	6274	6284	6294	6304	6314	6325	1	2	3	4	5	6	7	8	9
43	6335	6345	6355	6365	6375	6385	6395	6405	6415	6425	1	2	3	4	5	6	7	8	9
44	6435	6444	6454	6464	6474	6484	6493	6503	6513	6522	1	2	3	4	5	6	7	8	9
45	6532	6542	6551	6561	6571	6580	6590	6599	6609	6618	1	2	3	4	5	6	7	8	9
46	6628	6637	6646	6656	6665	6675	6684	6693	6702	6712	1	2	3	4	5	6	7	7	8
47	6721	6730	6739	6749	6758	6767	6776	6785	6794	6803	1	2	3	4	5	5	6	7	8
48	6812	6821	6830	6839	6848	6857	6866	6875	6884	6893	1	2	3	4	4	5	6	7	8
49	6902	6911	6920	6928	6937	6946	6955	6964	6972	6981	1	2	3	4	4	5	6	7	8
50	6990	6998	7007	7016	7024	7033	7042	7050	7059	7067	1	2	3	3	4	5	6	7	8

The copyright of that portion of the above table which gives the logarithms of numbers from 1,000 to 2,000 is the property of Messrs Macmillan and Company, Limited, who, however, have authorized the use of the form in any reprint published for educational purposes.

LOGARITHMS

	0	1	2	3	4	5	6	7	8	9	1	2	3	4	5	6	7	8	9
51	7076	7084	7093	7101	7110	7118	7126	7135	7143	7152	1	2	3	3	4	5	6	7	8
52	7160	7168	7177	7185	7193	7202	7210	7218	7226	7235	1	2	2	3	4	5	6	7	7
53	7243	7251	7259	7267	7275	7284	7292	7300	7308	7316	1	2	2	3	4	5	6	6	7
54	7324	7332	7340	7348	7356	7364	7372	7380	7388	7396	1	2	2	3	4	5	6	6	7
55	7404	7412	7419	7427	7435	7443	7451	7459	7466	7474	1	2	2	3	4	5	5	6	7
56	7482	7490	7497	7505	7513	7520	7528	7536	7543	7551	1	2	2	3	4	5	5	6	7
57	7559	7566	7574	7582	7589	7597	7604	7612	7619	7627	1	2	2	3	4	5	5	6	7
58	7634	7642	7649	7657	7664	7672	7672	7686	7694	7701	1	1	2	3	4	4	5	6	7
59	7709	7716	7723	7731	7738	7745	7752	7760	7767	7774	1	1	2	3	4	4	5	6	7
60	7782	7789	7796	7803	7810	7818	7825	7832	7839	7846	1	1	2	3	4	4	5	6	6
61	7853	7860	7868	7875	7882	7889	7896	7903	7910	7917	1	1	2	3	4	4	5	6	6
62	7924	7931	7938	7945	7952	7959	7966	7973	7980	7987	1	1	2	3	3	4	5	6	6
63	7993	8000	8007	8014	8021	8028	8035	8041	8048	8055	1	1	2	3	3	4	5	5	6
64	8062	8069	8075	8082	8089	8096	8102	8109	8116	8122	1	1	2	3	3	4	5	5	6
65	8129	8136	8142	8149	8156	8162	8169	8176	8182	8189	1	1	2	3	3	4	5	5	6
66	8195	8202	8209	8215	8222	8228	8235	8241	8248	8254	1	1	2	3	3	4	5	5	6
67	8261	8267	8274	8280	8287	8293	8299	8306	8312	8319	1	1	2	3	3	4	5	5	6
68	8325	8331	8338	8344	8351	8357	8363	8370	8376	8382	1	1	2	3	3	4	4	5	6
69	8388	8395	8401	8407	8414	8420	8426	8432	8439	8445	1	1	2	2	3	4	4	5	6
70	8451	8457	8463	8470	8476	8482	8488	8494	8500	8506	1	1	2	2	3	4	4	5	6
71	8513	8519	8525	8531	8537	8543	8549	8555	8561	8567	1	1	2	2	3	4	4	5	5
72	8573	8579	8585	8591	8597	8603	8609	8615	8621	8627	1	1	2	2	3	4	4	5	5
73	8633	8639	8645	8651	8657	8663	8669	8675	8681	8686	1	1	2	2	3	4	4	5	5
74	8692	8698	8704	8710	8716	8722	8727	8733	8739	8745	1	1	2	2	3	4	4	5	5
75	8751	8756	8762	8768	8774	8779	8785	8791	8797	8802	1	1	2	2	3	3	4	5	5
76	8808	8814	8820	8825	8831	8837	8842	8848	8854	8859	1	1	2	2	3	3	4	5	5
77	8865	8871	8876	8882	8887	8893	8899	8904	8910	8915	1	1	2	2	3	3	4	4	5
78	8921	8927	8932	8938	8943	8949	8954	8960	8965	8971	1	1	2	2	3	3	4	4	5
79	8976	8982	8987	8993	8998	9004	9009	9015	9020	9025	1	1	2	2	3	3	4	4	5
80	9031	9036	9042	9047	9053	9058	9063	9069	9074	9079	1	1	2	2	3	3	4	4	5
81	9085	9090	9096	9101	9106	9112	9117	9122	9128	9133	1	1	2	2	3	3	4	4	5
82	9138	9143	9149	9154	9156	9165	9170	9175	9180	9186	1	1	2	2	3	3	4	4	5
83	9191	9196	9201	9206	9212	9217	9222	9227	9232	9238	1	1	2	2	3	3	4	4	5
84	9243	9248	9253	9258	9263	9269	9274	9279	9284	9289	1	1	2	2	3	3	4	4	5
85	9294	9299	9304	9309	9315	9320	9325	9330	9335	9340	1	1	2	2	3	3	4	4	5
86	9345	9350	9355	9360	9365	9370	9375	9380	9385	9380	1	1	2	2	3	3	4	4	5
87	9395	9400	9405	9410	9415	9420	9425	9430	9435	9440	0	1	1	2	2	3	3	4	4
88	9445	9450	9455	9460	9465	9469	9474	9479	9484	9489	0	1	1	2	2	3	3	4	4
89	9494	9499	9504	9509	9513	9518	9523	9528	9533	9538	0	1	1	2	2	3	3	4	4
90	9542	9547	9552	^557	9562	9566	9571	9576	9581	9586	0	1	1	2	2	3	3	4	4
91	9590	9595	9600	9605	9609	9614	9619	9624	9628	9633	0	1	1	2	2	3	3	4	4
92	9638	9643	9647	9652	9657	9661	9666	9671	9675	9680	0	1	1	2	2	3	3	4	4
93	9685	9689	9694	9699	9703	9708	9713	9717	9722	9727	0	1	1	2	2	3	3	4	4
94	9731	9736	9741	9745	9750	9754	9759	9763	9768	9773	0	1	1	2	2	3	3	4	4
95	9777	9782	9786	9791	9795	9800	9805	9809	9814	9818	0	1	1	2	2	3	3	4	4
96	9823	9827	9832	9836	9841	9845	9850	9854	9859	9863	0	1	1	2	2	3	3	4	4
97	9868	9872	9877	9881	9886	9890	9894	9899	9903	9908	0	1	1	2	2	3	3	4	4
98	9912	9917	9921	9926	9930	9934	9939	9943	9948	9952	0	1	1	2	2	3	3	4	4
99	9956	9961	9965	9969	9974	9978	9983	9987	9991	9996	0	1	1	2	2	3	3	3	4

Note These tables are so constructed that the fourth figure of a logarithm obtained by their use is never more than one unit above or below the best 4-figure approximation. For example, if the logarithm found is 0·5014 the best 4-figure approximation may be 0·5013, 0·5014, or 0·5015. Greater accuracy than this cannot be obtained by the use of a uniform table of differences of this kind.

ANTILOGARITHMS

	0	1	2	3	4	5	6	7	8	9	1	2	3	4	5	6	7	8	9
·00	1000	1002	1005	1007	1009	1012	1014	1016	1019	1021	0	0	1	1	1	1	2	2	2
·01	1023	1026	1028	1030	1033	1035	1038	1040	1042	1045	0	0	1	1	1	1	2	2	2
·02	1047	1050	1052	1054	1057	1059	1062	1064	1067	1069	0	0	1	1	1	1	2	2	2
·03	1072	1074	1076	1079	1081	1084	1086	1089	1091	1094	0	0	1	1	1	1	2	2	2
·04	1096	1099	1102	1104	1107	1109	1112	1114	1117	1119	0	1	1	1	1	2	2	2	2
·05	1122	1125	1127	1130	1132	1135	1138	1140	1143	1146	0	1	1	1	1	2	2	2	2
·06	1148	1151	1153	1156	1159	1161	1164	1167	1169	1172	0	1	1	1	1	2	2	2	2
·07	1175	1178	1180	1183	1186	1189	1191	1194	1197	1199	0	1	1	1	1	2	2	2	2
·08	1202	1205	1208	1211	1213	1216	1219	1222	1225	1227	0	1	1	1	1	2	2	2	3
·09	1230	1233	1236	1239	1242	1245	1247	1250	1253	1256	0	1	1	1	1	2	2	2	3
·10	1259	1262	1265	1268	1271	1274	1276	1279	1282	1285	0	1	1	1	1	2	2	2	3
·11	1288	1291	1294	1297	1300	1303	1306	1309	1312	1315	0	1	1	1	2	2	2	2	3
·12	1318	1321	1324	1327	1330	1334	1337	1340	1343	1346	0	1	1	1	2	2	2	2	3
·13	1349	1352	1355	1358	1361	1365	1368	1371	1374	1377	0	1	1	1	2	2	2	3	3
·14	1380	1384	1387	1390	1393	1396	1400	1403	1406	1409	0	1	1	1	2	2	2	3	3
·15	1413	1416	1419	1422	1426	1429	1432	1435	1439	1442	0	1	1	1	2	2	2	3	3
·16	1445	1449	1452	1455	1459	1462	1466	1469	1472	1476	0	1	1	1	2	2	2	3	3
·17	1479	1483	1486	1489	1493	1496	1500	1503	1507	1510	0	1	1	1	2	2	2	3	3
·18	1514	1517	1521	1524	1528	1531	1535	1538	1542	1545	0	1	1	1	2	2	2	3	3
·19	1549	1552	1556	1560	1563	1567	1570	1574	1578	1581	0	1	1	1	2	2	3	3	3
·20	1585	1589	1592	1596	1600	1603	1607	1611	1614	1618	0	1	1	1	2	2	3	3	3
·21	1622	1626	1629	1633	1637	1641	1644	1648	1652	1656	0	1	1	2	2	2	3	3	3
·22	1660	1663	1667	1671	1675	1679	1683	1687	1690	1694	0	1	1	2	2	2	3	3	3
·23	1698	1702	1706	1710	1714	1718	1722	1726	1730	1734	0	1	1	2	2	2	3	3	4
·24	1738	1742	1746	1750	1754	1758	1762	1766	1770	1774	0	1	1	2	2	2	3	3	4
·25	1778	1782	1786	1791	1795	1799	1803	1807	1811	1816	0	1	1	2	2	2	3	3	4
·26	1820	1824	1828	1832	1837	1841	1845	1849	1854	1858	0	1	1	2	2	3	3	3	4
·27	1862	1866	1871	1875	1879	1884	1888	1892	1897	1901	0	1	1	2	2	3	3	3	4
·28	1905	1910	1914	1919	1923	1928	1932	1936	1941	1945	0	1	1	2	2	3	3	4	4
·29	1950	1954	1959	1963	1968	1972	1977	1982	1986	1991	0	1	1	2	2	3	3	4	4
·30	1995	2000	2004	2009	2014	2018	2023	2028	2032	2037	0	1	1	2	2	3	3	4	4
·31	2042	2046	2051	2056	2061	2065	2070	2075	2080	2084	0	1	1	2	2	3	3	4	4
·32	2089	2094	2099	2104	2109	2113	2118	2123	2128	2133	0	1	1	2	2	3	3	4	4
·33	2138	2143	2148	2153	2158	2163	2168	2173	2178	2183	0	1	1	2	2	3	3	4	4
·34	2188	2193	2198	2203	2208	2213	2218	2223	2228	2234	1	1	2	2	3	3	4	4	5
·35	2239	2244	2249	2254	2259	2265	2270	2275	2280	2286	1	1	2	2	3	3	4	4	5
·36	2291	2296	2301	2307	2312	2317	2323	2328	2333	2339	1	1	2	2	3	3	4	4	5
·37	2344	2350	2355	2360	2366	2371	2377	2382	2388	2393	1	1	2	2	3	3	4	4	5
·38	2399	2404	2410	2415	2421	2427	2432	2438	2443	2449	1	1	2	2	3	3	4	4	5
·39	2455	2460	2466	2472	2477	2483	2489	2495	2500	2506	1	1	2	2	3	3	4	5	5
·40	2512	2518	2523	2529	2535	2541	2547	2553	2559	2564	1	1	2	2	3	4	4	5	5
·41	2570	2576	2582	2588	2594	2600	2606	2612	2618	2624	1	1	2	2	3	4	4	5	5
·42	2630	2636	2642	2649	2655	2661	2667	2673	2679	2685	1	1	2	2	3	4	4	5	6
·43	2692	2698	2704	2710	2716	2723	2729	2735	2742	2748	1	1	2	3	3	4	4	5	6
·44	2754	2761	2767	2773	2780	2786	2793	2799	2805	2812	1	1	2	3	3	4	4	5	6
·45	2818	2825	2831	2838	2844	2851	2858	2864	2871	2877	1	1	2	3	3	4	5	5	6
·46	2884	2891	2897	2904	2911	2917	2924	2931	2938	2944	1	1	2	3	3	4	5	5	6
·47	2951	2958	2965	2972	2979	2985	2992	2999	3006	3013	1	1	2	3	3	4	5	5	6
·48	3020	3027	3034	3041	3048	3055	3062	3069	3076	3083	1	1	2	3	4	4	5	6	6
·49	3090	3097	3105	3112	3119	3126	3133	3141	3148	3155	1	1	2	3	4	4	5	6	6

ANTILOGARITHMS

	0	1	2	3	4	5	6	7	8	9	1	2	3	4	5	6	7	8	9
·50	3162	3170	3177	3184	3192	3199	3206	3214	3221	3228	1	1	2	3	4	4	5	6	7
·51	3236	3243	3251	3258	3266	3273	3281	3289	3296	3304	1	2	2	3	4	5	5	6	7
·52	3311	3319	3327	3334	3342	3350	3357	3365	3373	3381	1	2	2	3	4	5	5	6	7
·53	3388	3396	3404	3412	3420	3428	3426	3443	3451	3459	1	2	2	3	4	5	6	6	7
·54	3467	3475	3483	3491	3499	3508	3516	3524	3532	3540	1	2	2	3	4	5	6	6	7
·55	3548	3556	3565	3573	3581	3589	3597	3606	3614	3622	1	2	2	3	4	5	6	7	7
·56	3631	3639	3648	3656	3664	3673	3681	3690	3698	3707	1	2	3	3	4	5	6	7	8
·57	3715	3724	3733	3741	3750	3758	3767	3776	3784	3793	1	2	3	3	4	5	6	7	8
·58	3802	3811	3819	3828	3837	3846	3855	3864	3873	3882	1	2	3	4	4	5	6	7	8
·59	3890	3899	3908	3917	3926	3936	3945	3954	3963	3972	1	2	3	4	5	5	6	7	8
·60	3981	3990	3999	4009	4018	4027	4036	4046	4055	4064	1	2	3	4	5	6	6	7	8
·61	4074	4083	4093	4102	4111	4121	4130	4140	4150	4159	1	2	3	4	5	6	7	8	9
·62	4169	4178	4188	4198	4207	4217	4227	4236	4246	4256	1	2	3	4	5	6	7	8	9
·63	4266	4276	4285	4295	4305	4315	4325	4335	4345	4355	1	2	3	4	5	6	7	8	9
·64	4365	4375	4385	4395	4406	4416	4426	4436	4446	4457	1	2	3	4	5	6	7	8	9
·65	4467	4477	4487	4498	4508	4519	4529	4539	4550	4560	1	2	3	4	5	6	7	8	9
·66	4571	4581	4592	4603	4613	4624	4634	4645	4656	4667	1	2	3	4	5	6	7	9	10
·67	4677	4688	4699	4710	4721	4732	4742	4753	4764	4775	1	2	3	4	5	7	8	9	10
·68	4786	4797	4808	4819	4831	4842	4853	4864	4875	4887	1	2	3	4	6	7	8	9	10
·69	4898	4909	4920	4932	4943	4955	4966	4977	4989	5000	1	2	3	5	6	7	8	9	10
·70	5012	5023	5035	5047	5058	5070	5082	5093	5105	5117	1	2	4	5	6	7	8	9	11
·71	5129	5140	5152	5164	5176	5188	5200	5212	5224	5236	1	2	3	5	6	7	8	10	11
·72	5248	5260	5272	5284	5297	5309	5321	5333	5346	5358	1	2	4	5	6	7	9	10	11
·73	5370	5383	5395	5408	5420	5433	5445	5458	5470	5483	1	3	4	5	6	8	9	10	11
·74	5495	5508	5521	5534	5546	5559	5572	5585	5598	5610	1	3	4	5	6	8	9	10	12
·75	5623	5636	5649	5662	5675	5689	5702	5715	5728	5741	1	3	4	5	7	8	9	10	12
·76	5754	5768	5781	5794	5808	5821	5834	5848	5861	5875	1	3	4	5	7	8	9	11	12
·77	5888	5902	5916	5929	5943	5957	5970	5984	5998	6012	1	3	4	5	7	8	10	11	12
·78	6026	6039	6053	6067	6081	6095	6109	6124	6138	6152	1	3	4	6	7	8	10	11	13
·79	6166	6180	6194	6209	6223	6237	6252	6266	6281	6295	1	3	4	6	7	9	10	11	13
·80	6310	6324	6339	6353	6368	6383	6397	6412	6427	6442	1	3	4	6	7	9	10	12	13
·81	6457	6471	6486	6501	6516	6531	6546	6561	6577	6592	2	3	5	6	8	9	11	12	14
·82	6607	6622	6637	6653	6668	6683	6699	6714	6730	6745	2	3	5	6	8	9	11	12	14
·83	6761	6776	6792	6808	6823	6839	6855	6871	6887	6902	2	3	5	6	8	9	11	13	14
·84	6918	6934	6950	6966	6982	6998	7015	7031	7047	7063	2	3	5	6	8	10	11	13	15
·85	7079	7096	7112	7129	7145	7161	7178	7194	7211	7228	2	3	5	7	8	10	12	13	15
·86	7244	7261	7278	7295	7311	7328	7345	7362	7379	7396	2	3	5	7	8	10	12	13	15
·87	7413	7430	7447	7464	7482	7499	7516	7534	7551	7568	2	3	5	7	9	10	12	14	16
·88	7586	7603	7621	7638	7656	7674	7691	7709	7727	7745	2	4	5	7	9	11	12	14	16
·89	7762	7780	7798	7816	7834	7852	7870	7889	7907	7925	2	4	5	7	9	11	13	14	16
·90	7943	7962	7980	7998	8017	8035	8054	8072	8091	8110	2	4	6	7	9	11	13	15	17
·91	8128	8147	8166	8185	8204	8222	8241	8260	8279	8299	2	4	6	8	9	11	13	15	17
·92	8318	8337	8356	8375	8395	8414	8433	8453	8472	8492	2	4	6	8	10	12	14	15	17
·93	8511	8531	8551	8570	8590	8610	8630	8650	8670	8690	2	4	6	8	10	12	14	16	18
·94	8710	8730	8750	8770	8790	8810	8831	8851	8872	8892	2	4	6	8	10	12	14	16	18
·95	8913	8933	8954	8974	8995	9016	9036	9057	9078	9099	2	4	6	8	10	12	15	17	19
·96	9120	9141	9162	9183	9204	9226	9247	9268	9290	9311	2	4	6	8	11	13	15	17	19
·97	9333	9354	9376	9397	9419	9441	9462	9484	9506	9528	2	4	7	9	11	13	15	17	20
·98	9550	9572	9594	9616	9638	9661	9683	9705	9727	9750	2	4	7	9	11	13	16	18	20
·99	9772	9795	9817	9840	9863	9886	9908	9931	9954	9977	2	5	7	9	11	14	16	18	20

Appendix 2

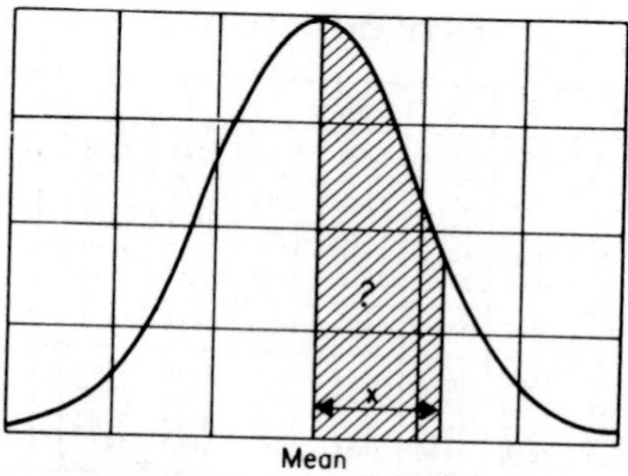

X	Area	X	Area	X	Area
0·0	0·0000	1·6	0·4452	3·0	0·4987
0·1	0·0398	1·7	0·4554	3·09	0·4990
0·2	0·0793	1·8	0·4641	3·1	0·4990
0·3	0·1179	1·9	0·4713	3·2	0·4993
0·4	0·1554	1·96	0·4750	3·3	0·4995
0·5	0·1915	2·0	0·4772	3·4	0·4997
0·6	0·2257	2·1	0·4821	3·5	0·4998
0·7	0·2580	2·2	0·4861	3·6	0·49984
0·8	0·2881	2·3	0·4893	3·7	0·49989
0·9	0·3159	2·4	0·4918	3·8	0·49993
1·0	0·3413	2·5	0·4938	3·9	0·49995
1·1	0·3643	2·58	0·4951	4·0	0·49997
1·2	0·3849	2·6	0·4953	4·1	0·4998
1·3	0·4032	2·7	0·4965	4·2	0·49999
1·4	0·4192	2·8	0·4974		
1·5	0·4332	2·9	0·4981		

Areas of normal curve

X is the distance from the mean, measured in S.D.'s, i.e., $\frac{\textit{Value-mean}}{\textit{S.D.}}$

Adapted from Table 1 of 'Biometrika Tables for Statisticians,' Vol. 1, by kind permission of the Trustees of Biometrika.

Appendix 3

v \ P	0·9	0·5	0·1	0·05	0·01	0·001	v \ P	0·9	0·5	0·1	0·05	0·01	0·001
1	0·016	0·45	2·71	3·84	6·63	10·83	**16**	9·31	15·34	23·54	26·30	32·00	39·25
2	0·21	1·39	4·61	5·99	9·21	13·82	**17**	10·09	16·34	24·77	27·59	33·41	40·79
3	0·58	2·37	6·25	7·81	11·34	16·27	**18**	10·86	17·34	25·99	28·87	34·81	42·31
4	1·06	3·36	7·78	9·49	13·28	18·47	**19**	11·65	18·34	27·20	30·14	36·19	43·82
5	1·61	4·35	9·24	11·07	15·09	20·52	**20**	12·44	19·34	28·41	31·41	37·57	45·32
6	2·20	5·35	10·64	12·59	16·81	22·46	**21**	13·24	20·34	29·62	32·67	38·93	46·80
7	2·83	6·35	12·02	14·07	18·48	24·32	**22**	14·04	21·34	30·81	33·92	40·29	48·27
8	3·49	7·34	13·36	15·51	20·09	26·13	**23**	14·85	22·34	32·01	35·17	41·64	49·73
9	4·17	8·34	14·68	16·92	21·67	27·88	**24**	15·66	23·34	33·20	36·42	42·98	51·18
10	4·87	9·34	15·99	18·31	23·21	29·59	**25**	16·47	24·34	34·38	37·65	44·31	52·62
11	5·58	10·34	17·28	19·68	24·73	31·26	**26**	17·29	25·34	35·56	38·89	45·64	54·05
12	6·30	11·34	18·55	21·03	26·22	32·91	**27**	18·11	26·34	36·74	40·11	46·96	55·48
13	7·04	12·34	19·81	22·36	27·69	34·53	**28**	18·94	27·34	37·92	41·34	48·28	56·89
14	7·79	13·34	21·06	23·68	29·14	36·12	**29**	19·77	28·34	39·09	42·56	49·59	58·30
15	8·55	14·34	22·31	25·00	30·58	37·70	**30**	20·26	29·34	40·26	43·77	50·89	59·70

Table of χ^2

v = The number of degrees of freedom
P = The probability of exceeding the tabular value of x^2 in random sampling

Abridged from Table 8 of 'Biometrika Tables for Statisticians', Vol. 1 by kind permission of the Trustees of Biometrika.

Appendix 4

PRESENT VALUE FACTORS

Years	1%	2%	3%	4%	5%	6%	7%	8%	9%	10%
1	·9901	·9804	·9709	·9615	·9524	·9434	·9346	·9259	·9174	·9091
2	·9803	·9612	·9426	·9246	·9070	·8900	·8734	·8573	·8417	·8264
3	·9706	·9423	·9151	·8890	·8638	·8396	·8163	·7938	·7722	·7513
4	·9610	·9238	·8885	·8548	·8227	·7921	·7629	·7350	·7084	·6830
5	·9515	·9057	·8626	·8219	·7835	·7473	·7130	·6806	·6499	·6209
6	·9420	·8880	·8375	·7903	·7462	·7050	·6663	·6302	·5963	·5645
7	·9327	·8706	·8131	·7599	·7107	·6651	·6227	·5835	·5470	·5132
8	·9235	·8535	·7894	·7307	·6768	·6274	·5820	·5403	·5019	·4665
9	·9143	·8368	·7664	·7026	·6446	·5919	·5439	·5002	·4604	·4241
10	·9053	·8203	·7441	·6756	·6139	·5584	·5083	·4632	·4224	·3855
11	·8963	·8043	·7224	·6496	·5847	·5268	·4751	·4289	·3875	·3805
12	·8874	·7885	·7014	·6246	·5568	·4970	·4440	·3971	·3555	·3186
13	·8787	·7730	·6810	·6006	·5303	·4688	·4150	·3677	·3262	·2897
14	·8700	·7579	·6611	·5775	·5051	·4423	·3878	·3405	·2995	·2633
15	·8613	·7430	·6419	·5553	·4810	·4173	·3624	·3152	·2745	·2394
16	·8528	·7284	·6232	·5339	·4581	·3936	·3387	·2919	·2519	·2176
17	·8444	·7142	·6050	·5134	·4363	·3714	·3166	·2703	·2311	·1978
18	·8360	·7002	·5874	·4936	·4155	·3503	·2959	·2502	·2120	·1799
19	·8277	·6864	·5703	·4746	·3957	·3305	·2765	·2317	·1945	·1635
20	·8195	·6730	·5537	·4564	·3769	·3118	·2584	·2145	·1784	·1486

Years	11%	12%	13%	14%	15%	16%	17%	18%	19%	20%
1	·9009	·8929	·8850	·8772	·8696	·8621	·8547	·8475	·8403	·8333
2	·8116	·7972	·7831	·7695	·7561	·7432	·7305	·7182	·7062	·6944
3	·7312	·7118	·6931	·6750	·6575	·6407	·6244	·6086	·5934	·5787
4	·6587	·6355	·6133	·5921	·5718	·5523	·5337	·5158	·4987	·4823
5	·5935	·5674	·5428	·5194	·4972	·4761	·4561	·4371	·4190	·4019
6	·5346	·5066	·4803	·4556	·4323	·4104	·3898	·3704	·3521	·3349
7	·4817	·4523	·4251	·3996	·3759	·3538	·3332	·3139	·2959	·2791
8	·4339	·4039	·3762	·3506	·3269	·3050	·2848	·2660	·2487	·2326
9	·3909	·3606	·3329	·3075	·2843	·2630	·2434	·2255	·2090	·1938
10	·3522	·3220	·2946	·2679	·2472	·2267	·2080	·1911	·1756	·1615
11	·3173	·2875	·2607	·2366	·2149	·1954	·1778	·1619	·1476	·1346
12	·2855	·2567	·2307	·2076	·1869	·1685	·1520	·1372	·1240	·1122
13	·2575	·2292	·2042	·1821	·1625	·1452	·1299	·1163	·1042	·0935
14	·2320	·2046	·1807	·1597	·1413	·1252	·1110	·0985	·0876	·0779
15	·2090	·1827	·1599	·1401	·1229	·1079	·0949	·0835	·0736	·0649
16	·1883	·1631	·1415	·1229	·1069	·0930	·0811	·0708	·0618	·0541
17	·1696	·1456	·1252	·1078	·0929	·0802	·0693	·0600	·0520	·0451
18	·1528	·1300	·1108	·0946	·0808	·0691	·0592	·0508	·0437	·0376
19	·1377	·1161	·0981	·0829	·0703	·0596	·0506	·0431	·0367	·0313
20	·1240	·1031	·0868	·0728	·0611	·0514	·0433	·0365	·0308	·0261

Appendix 5

CUMULATIVE PRESENT VALUE FACTORS

Years	1%	2%	3%	4%	5%	6%	7%	8%	9%	10%
1	0·990	0·980	0·971	0·962	0·952	0·943	0·935	0·926	0·917	0·909
2	1·970	1·942	1·913	1·886	1·859	1·833	1·808	1·783	1·759	1·736
3	2·941	2·884	2·829	2·775	2·723	2·673	2·624	2·577	2·531	2·487
4	3·902	3·808	3·717	3·630	3·546	3·465	3·387	3·312	3·240	3·170
5	4·853	4·713	4·580	4·452	4·329	4·212	4·100	3·993	3·890	3·791
6	5·795	5·601	5·417	5·242	5·076	4·917	4·767	4·623	4·486	4·355
7	6·728	6·472	6·230	6·002	5·786	5·582	5·389	5·206	5·033	4·868
8	7·652	7·325	7·020	6·733	6·463	6·210	5·971	5·747	5·535	5·335
9	8·566	8·162	7·786	7·435	7·108	6·802	6·515	6·247	5·995	5·759
10	9·471	8·983	8·530	8·111	7·722	7·360	7·024	6·710	6·418	6·145
11	10·368	9·787	9·253	8·760	8·306	7·887	7·499	7·139	6·805	6·495
12	11·255	10·575	9·954	9·385	8·863	8·384	7·943	7·536	7·161	6·814
13	12·134	11·348	10·635	9·986	9·394	8·853	8·358	7·904	7·487	7·103
14	13·004	12·106	11·296	10·563	9·899	9·295	8·745	8·244	7·786	7·367
15	13·865	12·849	11·938	11·118	10·380	9·712	9·108	8·559	8·061	7·606
16	14·718	13·578	12·561	11·652	10·838	10·106	9·447	8·851	8·313	7·824
17	15·562	14·292	13·166	12·166	11·274	10·477	9·763	9·122	8·544	8·022
18	16·398	14·992	13·754	12·659	11·690	10·828	10·059	9·372	8·756	8·201
19	17·226	15·678	14·324	13·134	12·085	11·158	10·336	9·604	8·950	8·365
20	18·046	16·351	14·877	13·500	12·462	11·470	10·594	9·818	9·129	8·514

Year	11%	12%	13%	14%	15%	16%	17%	18%	19%	20%
1	0·901	0·893	0·885	0·877	0·870	0·862	0·855	0·847	0·840	0·833
2	1·713	1·690	1·668	1·647	1·626	1·605	1·585	1·566	1·547	1·528
3	2·444	2·402	2·361	2·322	2·283	2·246	2·210	2·174	2·140	2·106
4	3·102	3·037	2·974	2·914	2·855	2·798	2·743	2·690	2·639	2·589
5	3·696	3·605	3·517	3·433	3·352	3·274	3·199	3·127	3·058	2·991
6	4·231	4·111	3·998	3·889	3·784	3·685	3·589	3·498	3·410	3·326
7	4·712	4·564	4·423	4·288	4·160	4·039	3·922	3·812	3·706	3·605
8	5·146	4·968	4·799	4·639	4·487	4·344	4·207	4·078	3·954	3·837
9	5·537	5·328	5·132	4·946	4·772	4·607	4·451	4·303	4·103	4·031
10	5·889	5·650	5·426	5·216	5·019	4·833	4·659	4·494	4·339	4·192
11	6·207	5·938	5·687	5·453	5·234	5·029	4·836	4·656	4·486	4·327
12	6·492	6·194	5·918	5·660	5·421	5·197	4·988	4·793	4·611	4·430
13	6·750	6·424	6·122	5·842	5·533	5·342	5·118	4·910	4·715	4·533
14	6·982	6·628	6·302	6·002	5·724	5·468	5·229	5·008	4·802	4·611
15	7·191	6·811	6·462	6·142	5·847	5·575	5·324	5·092	4·876	4·675
16	7·379	6·974	6·604	6·265	5·954	5·668	5·405	5·162	4·938	4·730
17	7·549	7·120	6·729	6·373	6·047	5·749	5·475	5·222	4·990	4·775
18	7·702	7·250	6·840	6·467	6·128	5·818	5·534	5·273	5·033	4·812
19	7·839	7·366	6·938	6·550	6·198	5·877	5·584	5·316	5·070	4·843
20	7·963	7·469	7·025	6·623	6·259	5·929	5·628	5·353	5·101	4·870

Index